CAPITAL AT WORK IN ANTWERP'S GOLDEN AGE

SEUH

STUDIES IN EUROPEAN URBAN HISTORY (1100-1800)

VOLUME 55

Capital at Work in Antwerp's Golden Age

HUGO SOLY

BREPOLS

Cover illustration: Jan van Hemessen (and/or studio of),
The Moneylenders, 1536. Monteviot House, Jedburgh, Scotland.
By kind permission of the Trustees.

D/2021/0095/324
ISBN 978-2-503-59563-4
e-ISBN 978-2-503-59564-1
DOI 10.1484/M.SEUH-EB.5.127496

ISSN 1780-3241
e-ISSN 2294-8368

Printed in the EU on acid-free paper.

For Rina, my constant source of inspiration

Contents

List of Illustrations

Plates

Maps

Tables

Figures

Acknowledgements

This book has been a long time in the making. It was started at the University of Ghent, where Wilfrid Brulez and the late Etienne ('Stef') Scholliers, each in his own way, aroused my curiosity in the mid 1960s by asking stimulating questions about the transition from medieval to early modern Europe, focusing especially on economic changes. In later years fruitful exchanges with Brulez, Scholliers, Herman van der Wee, and the late Raymond van Uytven in Belgium and with colleagues and friends in Austria, England, France, Germany, Italy, the Netherlands, and the United States led me to probe my own ideas about the rise, development, and transformations of capitalism. Studying individual money-makers in Antwerp's Golden Age seemed like the most obvious way to transpose the complex issues into concrete research. Finding and gathering adequate source material on the first half of the sixteenth century was no small task, however, as it required searches in a great many archives in Belgium and abroad. I am deeply grateful to Gustaaf Janssens and René Vermeir for their invaluable assistance in exploring archives in Simancas and Valladolid, respectively. In addition, I am thankful to Janneke van den Berg for informing me about documents preserved at the Veenendaal municipal archive. I also owe a debt of gratitude to Harald Deceulaer, who took on the onerous task of conducting an inventory of the vast and crucial fund of the Officie-Fiscaal of the Council of Brabant in the Rijksarchief Brussel. He unearthed files that shed a harsh light on commerce in sixteenth-century Antwerp, revealing that well-informed contemporaries were right in qualifying the New Exchange as a 'hellhole'. I am also greatly obliged to Jeroen Puttevils, who shared his database concerning the tax on exports from Antwerp in the mid-sixteenth century with me, significantly curtailing the time necessary for my research. Over the years, many colleagues and friends have answered specific questions on detail, supplied readings, made useful suggestions, and offered support in several different forms. In this regard, I wish to thank Heidi Deneweth, Ivan Derycke, John Everaert, Corine Kisling, Christian Laes, Jan Lucassen, Guido Marnef, Geoffrey Parker, Peter Stabel, Wim van Craenenbroeck, Viviane Vossaert, and Anne Winter. I am grateful to Iason Jongepier (University of Antwerp – Centre for Urban History) for drawing the maps in chapters 1.2 and 3.2.

Lee Mitzman took on the difficult task of translating my sometimes awkward and obscure Dutch phrases into English prose. She made valuable suggestions with regard to the translation of specialized terms. I am no less indebted to Frank Winter, who went through the penultimate version of the manuscript cover to cover, suggesting many stylistic improvements and offering important substantive critique. Also, I want to thank Marc Boone and Anne-Laure Van Bruaene, series editors of the Studies in European Urban History, who generously offered to speed up the external reviewing process. Likewise, Chris Vandenborre, Publishing Manager at Brepols, deserves credit for expediting the processing of the book.

This book would not have come about without the unconditional support of Catharina ('Rina') Lis, my lifelong companion, who has as always been a source of great inspiration. She did not search the archive sources but inundated me with difficult questions, offered relevant literature, and confronted me with alternative interpretations. In addition, she read each consecutive version of the book carefully and provided thoughtful critique. She has shared so many ideas that the book has in fact become hers as well. I therefore dedicate it to her.

Note on Currency

The monies commonly used in international commerce and finance in Antwerp during the first half of the sixteenth century were the pound Flemish, the Rhenish guilder and Spanish/Italian ducats. The value of real estate transactions in Antwerp, however, was registered in pound Brabant and from the 1520s in *Carolus florin*. These currencies are briefly presented here. All other monies are explained when first mentioned in the book.

The leading money of account in the whole of the Habsburg Netherlands was the pound Flemish of 240 groats (abbreviated as £ Fl.gr.), whereby 12 gr. equalled 1 *schelling*, which the English then called shilling. Town governments in the Duchy of Brabant, however, used the pound Brabant in bookkeeping as the current money of account, which had a permanent relation to the Flemish unit of account, viz. £1Fl.gr. = £1.5Br.gr.

During the period covered in this book the *Rheinische Gulden*, Rhenish guilder (abbreviated as Rg), was the standard currency in the Holy Roman Empire. This gold guilder had a market exchange rate of c. 42 Fl.gr. in 1490, c. 56 in 1500, c. 59 in 1521, and c. 60 in 1550.

The Spanish ducat was a gold coin issued at first in 1497. The basic denomination of account, however, was the *maravedi*, especially favoured by merchants and treasury officials. The ducat was equivalent to 375 *maravedis*. From 1537 a new gold coin, the *escudo* (of 400 *maravedis*), was minted and gradually replaced the ducat, which, however continued to be used as a unit of account. Between 1521 and 1548, the Spanish ducat was officially rated at 80 Fl.gr. (or fl.2), but the market exchange rate fluctuated between c. 76 and c. 79 Fl.gr. The same was true for the Italian ducats and florins.

In 1521, Charles V issued the *Carolus florin* (abbreviated as fl.) at the rate of 20 silver *stuivers* (in French *patards*) or 40 Flemish groats, so that £1Fl.gr. equalled fl.6. This rate remained in force from 1527 onward. The new florin – the only new gold coin to have any widespread circulation – was gradually accepted in the Habsburg Netherlands as money of account.

List of Abbreviations

ADN	Archives départementales du Nord (Lille)
AG	Archief van de griffies ('Greffes')
AGR	Archives générales du Royaume (Brussels)
AGS	Archivo General de Simancas
ANTT	Arquivo nacional da Torre do Tombo (Lisbon)
ARCHV	Archivo de la Real Chancillería de Valladolid
AV	Aveux et dénombrements
BHM	Brabants Hooggerechtshof Maastricht
BoZ	Bergen op Zoom
B-PA	Belgien-PA
CC	Chambre des Comptes
CERT	Certificatieboek
CMH	Chancellerie de Marie de Hongrie
COLL	Collectanea
CSP	Calendar of State Papers
FI	Financiële Instellingen
FU	Fonds d'Ursel
GA	Gilden & Ambachten
GAV	Gemeentearchief Veenendaal
GF	Genealogisch Fonds
GRM	Grote Raad van Mechelen
HA	Heerlijkheidsarchieven
HHS	Haus-, Hof- und Staatsarchiv (Vienna)
HUA	Het Utrechts Archief (Utrecht)
IB	Insolvente Boedelskamer
ICON	Iconografie
IISH	International Institute of Social history (Amsterdam)
LPFD	Letters and Papers, Foreign and Domestic (London)
MD	Manuscrits Divers
MPMA	Museum Plantin-Moretus, Antwerp
N	Notariaat
NA	Nationaal Archief (The Hague)
ND	Nassause Domeinraad
NEHA	Nederlands Economisch-Historisch Archief (Amsterdam)
OF	Officie Fiscaal
PEA	Papiers d'État et de l'Audience
PERG	Pergaminos

PK	Privilegekamer
PPG	Processen Procureur-generaal
PS	Processen Supplement
R	Rekenkamer (in Stadsarchief, Antwerp)
RAB	Rijksarchief Brussel (in Vorst)
RB	Raad van Brabant
RHCL	Regionaal Historisch Centrum Limburg (Maastricht)
ROPB	*Recueil des Ordonnances des Pays-Bas*
SAA	Stadsarchief, Antwerp ('Felixarchief')
SBA	Stadsbibliotheek, Antwerp
SE	Secretaría de Estado
SR	Schepenregister
T	Tresorij
V	Vierschaar
VGSV	Veenraadschap der Geldersche en Stichtse Veenen
WBA	West-Brabants Archief

Introduction

In the light of the global financial crisis of 2008-09, the recessions that followed, and on top of that the covid-19 pandemic, it has become clear that capitalism in its present form is becoming increasingly inefficient and unstable and is widely believed to be at a critical juncture. Increasing numbers of authors note that democracies are being disrupted by growing economic and social inequalities, and that capitalism is turning out to be ill-equipped to address the existential issue of the moment: climate change. The search for explanations requires analysis of the basic characteristics and specific dynamics of the economic system,[1] while stressing that it is a historical phenomenon, with a beginning and perhaps an end.[2] Economic and social historians do not avoid the challenges of their own time, as is clear from the plethora of publications on various aspects of capitalism in recent years.[3] According to some commentators, this is a 'new history' and even a (sub) discipline in its own right. These authors offer new insights, but their research is mainly concerned with the Anglo-American history of global commodity chains and the emergence of large corporations after 1750/1800, when capitalism and industrialization emerged successively and symbiotically in England and the United States. In doing so, they give extensive consideration to the increasing concentration of economic power, culminating in the monopolistic positions that the big tech companies, especially Google, Amazon, Facebook and Apple, currently hold in the information technology industry. While in some cases comparisons with other periods are made, in the 'new history' of capitalism monopolist practices in late medieval and early modern Europe are largely or even entirely disregarded. This is all the more remarkable because an extended tradition of historical and sociological research, dating back to Henri Pirenne, Max Weber, and Werner Sombart, raises important questions about the nature of the economy in pre-industrial Europe.

In any case, many historians place the origins of capitalist developments in Europe well before 1750, even though they often disagree on definitions as well as on the chronology.[4] Authors who focus on regions with early and powerful urbanization and intensive commercialization of textile production, such as Northern Italy and Flanders,

1 For an overview of different definitions and interpretations of capitalism, see Kocka (2016). Capitalism cannot exist without commodity production and commodity trade, and their existence presupposes property rights, money, and competition: Van der Linden (2016), 256-7.

2 The German sociologist Wolfgang Streeck underlines that 'it is high time [...] to think about capitalism as a historical phenomenon': Streeck (2016), 57.

3 Lipartito (2016), 112-15.

4 Different definitions of capitalism give rise to highly disparate and often incompatible explanations of Europe's pre-industrial economy. See *inter alia* Van Zanden (1993), ch. 1; Brady (1997); Duplessis (1997), 4-5, 10-12; Mielants (2007), ch. 1; Howell (2010), 8-12, 299-300; Banaji (2010), ch. 9, and (2020); Heller (2011); Anievas and Nişancioğlu (2015); Wood (2017), ch. 4; Bihr (2019). On the roles different world regions played in the making of capitalism(s), see Yazdani and Menon (2020).

are often inclined to seek the origins of capitalism in the Middle Ages.[5] According to Jacques Heers, capitalism arose in the thirteenth century and proliferated rapidly in the late Middle Ages, at least in international commerce and (especially) in finance.[6] Giorgio Cracco does not hesitate to label the powerful city-state of Venice in the thirteenth & fourteenth centuries as a 'community of capitalists' and 'a state ruled by a capitalist oligarchy', because of the substantial concentration of commercial capital that took full control of the republic.[7]

Medievalists and early modernists who define commercial or merchant capitalism as an economic system that survived more or less intact from the thirteenth or fourteenth century until about 1750, often present the rising global economy in the 'long sixteenth century' as the first major expansion of capitalism, both within and outside Europe.[8] Change in continuity remains the dominant view, however, but continuity in what respects and what type of change(s)? Philipp Rössner argues that capitalism emerged 'well' before the 1520s, and that it '[did not] change much of its shape at that time', but he emphasizes that 'capitalism's mutations and changes in drive, verve and scope, i.e. those changes in rhythm which made contemporaries aware of its potential dangers', merit additional research.[9]

A new trend was the increasing interest among theologians and legal scholars in what they qualified as 'monopolies' and the resonance of their critical reservations among broad groups of the population. For centuries the term 'monopoly' had denoted a wide variety of economic practices and market types: forestalling speculative stockpiling, one single party controlling a commodity, a market dominated by a small group of substantial sellers, agreements between merchants, producers, employers, or workers… All competition restrictions could thus be qualified as a monopoly. A fluid term, it had many connotations, but from the late fifteenth century onward it was used increasingly to deplore practices 'directed at gaining maximum control over the market'.[10] The practices of large trading companies were subject to increasing criticism. In his immensely influential treatise *De contractibus* ('On Contracts'), published in 1500, the German theologian Konrad Summenhart discussed various types of monopolies, but he targeted mainly businessmen who systematically cornered the entire supply of a specific commodity, driving up prices and precluding competition… Legal scholars, such as the German Christoph Kuppener and Filip(s) Wielant of Flanders, did likewise around this time.[11] Martin Luther's radical condemnation of the large trading companies was unsurpassed. In his sermon *Von Kauffshandlung und Wucher* ('On Commerce and Usury'), published in 1524, he wrote 'that the companies are nothing other than straight and pure monopolies […] They raise and lower prices as they please and oppress and ruin all the smaller merchants, as pike

5 For Northern Italy, see *inter alia* Renouard (1968); Goldthwaite (2009), 583-94; Pezzolo (2014). For the Low Countries, see esp. Pirenne (1914) and (1963), 132-7, 171-81; Murray (2005); Blockmans (2010), 118-24, 651-3; Van Bavel (2010).

6 Heers (2012).

7 Cracco (1967).

8 According to Wallerstein (1974), the period 1450-1600 revealed a radical transformation: the rise of the 'modern, i.e. capitalist, world-system.'

9 Rössner (2015), 11.

10 Rössner (2014), 142.

11 Höffner (1969), 85-6, 92-4; Wielant (1996), 262-5. See also Soly (2016), 197-201.

devour the little fish in the water'.[12] The socio-economic issue turned into a political and ideological factor that became impossible to ignore, and in the imperial diets between 1512 and 1530 debates were waged, specifically relating to the Fugger and the Welser firms and targeting the metal and spice trades. Nothing came of this. The large merchant houses had little support indeed, but the Emperor could simply not afford to rein them in.[13]

Clearly, research on the nature and impact of 'capitalism's mutations and changes' during early globalization requires a study of monopolies, with relations between capitalists and political rulers meriting special consideration. In Europe, after all, the rise of capitalism and state formation were closely connected. Monopolization and cartelization had already been attempted here and there in Europe in the thirteenth century, as controlling trade in important and geographically concentrated products offered exceptional opportunities for profit. According to Jakob Strieder, the early monopolies and cartels were of a fiscal nature: the objective was to safeguard state income from depreciation caused by competition.[14] Roman Piotrowski has rejected this assertion, arguing that they nearly always arose on the initiative of private entrepreneurs. While nearly all mines were owned by rulers, the standard practice was to have large firms operate them.[15] Historical research subsequent to the publication of his pioneering study demonstrates that he was right. Wealthy businessmen and especially trading companies were the driving forces behind the amber, salt, and alum monopolies in late medieval Europe.[16] Such monopolies were politically based in the sense that market forces could be constrained only with political support, but the necessary investments came from private entrepreneurs, who also made the greatest profits. There are examples of government initiatives, such as the spice monopoly of the Portuguese Crown, but even in this case private firms were the true key operators.

Until the mid-fifteenth century, trade monopolies and cartels were exceptional,[17] but from then on they became progressively more prevalent and covered a much broader range of commodities, strengthening their economic and social impact. This impact was further reinforced, as merchant capitalists extended control over industrial production in multiple ways, generally indirectly via putting-out networks but in increasing measure directly. As overseas markets opened and public authorities' need for credit grew, unprecedented opportunities arose for affluent merchants and bankers to obtain monopolist advantages. In exchange for substantial financial services, princes and other officials agreed to sign over their preferential or privileged claims to mining output to capitalists at favourable terms or to grant them exclusive rights to import or export a crucial commodity. Direct or indirect support from political rulers not only facilitated the economic initiative of capitalists but also protected them from being prosecuted for breaking the law.

Not every ruler was in a position to establish a monopoly with a major economic impact. Geopolitical factors were highly significant. The main European alum mines, for example, were located in Tolfa in the Papal State, enabling the popes to entrust production

12 Luther (1524), 187-8.
13 Mertens (1996).
14 Strieder (1925), 69-71, 162-5.
15 Piotrowski (1933), 154-75, 233.
16 Van Houtte (1939); Lopez (1971), 139-41; Hocquet (1978); Basso (2014); Venturini (2015).
17 On guilds as cartels and contemporary complaints about guild market manipulation, see Ogilvie (2019).

and distribution to large firms, which operated as monopolists. Capitalists were very well aware that some rulers could offer them economic advantages. From the late Middle Ages on, wherever they could rely on a strong State, their aim was an 'anti-market, where the great predators roam and the law of the jungle operates', as Fernand Braudel has argued. In his opinion, the market economy – the zone where strong competition prevailed, small or medium profits were made, and prices reflected supply and demand – should be distinguished from capitalism, i.e. the zone of commercial and financial concentration and a relatively high degree of monopolization, which ultimately meant 'competition without competitors'.[18] Both his definition of the market economy and his rigid distinction between market economy and capitalism are questionable from various perspectives,[19] but Braudel is right that only a monopoly in a crucial economic sector enabled capitalists to achieve massive profits over an extended period.[20] The question remains, however: which strategies did capitalists devise to become dominant market leaders in certain economic sectors? What did they have to offer political rulers able to grant monopolies? Did monopolist practices necessarily entail conflicts with other capitalists? Or were 'anti-market' rivalries avoided wherever possible, and what was decisive here? In other words: in what measure did competition figure in which economic sectors, and how did substantial businessmen deal with it? These questions have received little consideration thus far.

To shed light on the complex problem, I will focus on the activities of capitalists in the main European trade metropolis during early globalization. Antwerp's spectacular economic rise between 1490 and 1565 provides an excellent opportunity for tracing the (changing) manifestations of capitalism in relation to the process of state formation. Shortly after the turn of the century, the city took over the pivotal role of both Venice and Bruges in the European economy, and over the course of a few decades, commerce and finance experienced unequalled growth. This was the result of economic and geopolitical changes. Lisbon, Augsburg and Nuremberg profited greatly from the convergence of the rapidly expanding intercontinental trade and the revival of European transcontinental trade, but none of these cities was Antwerp's equal in terms of the commercial advantages arising from the new constellation, as Herman van der Wee has demonstrated.[21] Shifts in international trade had a significant impact, but decisions by political rulers were conducive to the rapid and irreversible shift of the commercial hub from Bruges to Antwerp. Its 'Golden Age' was both the result of Capital at work and the State at Work. The new metropolis was 'made' from the outside. It was the product of external forces.[22] In the 1480s and 90s, Maximilian of Austria ordered the foreign merchants to leave Bruges, urging them to move to Antwerp, and awarded Antwerp the staple of Italian alum – an essential mordant for fixing dyes. The commercial treaty of 1496 between King Henry VII of England and Duke Philip IV of Burgundy led the Company of Merchant Adventurers from London to offer all their cloth for sale at the fairs of Antwerp and Bergen op Zoom. The decisive measure came from King Manuel I of Portugal in 1498, when he established the staple of pepper and spices

18 Braudel (1979), II, 363-82. See also Wallerstein (1991), 355-7.
19 See *inter alia* Caillé (1986); Fabra (1986); Vries (2012); Van Bavel (2016), esp. 270-1.
20 See note 18.
21 Van der Wee (1963), II, 314-6; Van der Wee and Peeters (1970), 112-13.
22 Brulez (1975), 110-12; Braudel (1979), III, 112.

intended for Northwest and Central Europe in Antwerp. Henceforth, the Fuggers and other large South-German firms exported Central and East-European copper and silver intended for Lisbon via Antwerp.[23] Without the privileges granted by these princes, the spectacular commercial growth of Antwerp would have been inconceivable.

The growing *entrepôt* commerce in English cloth and South-German metals added a new dimension to Antwerp's economy, which featured an increasingly broad product range and experienced an influx of international merchants. No other metropolis in Europe (and the world) offered as many opportunities to make high profits and accumulate capital during the first half of the sixteenth century. 'Antwerp is the world's most grandiose marketplace', wrote a Venetian ambassador in 1551.[24] All foreign visitors expressed similar views. They were right, in the sense that Antwerp had not only become the economic capital of the Habsburg Netherlands but also the chief commercial and financial centre in Europe and the nodal point in the rapidly growing world economy.

The rapid growth of the new commercial metropolis exuded a wide appeal. The Fuggers, the Welsers, and other merchant houses from Augsburg set up trading posts. Members of large Italian firms, such as the Affaitadi, the Arnolfini, the Frescobaldi, the Grimaldi, and the Spinola family established branches, which they often ran in person.[25] The Portuguese and the 'nations' of Genoa, Florence, and Lucca were authorized by the highest authorities to open consulates. Even the Spanish merchants who had been comfortably ensconced in Bruges left for Antwerp at this point. By the middle of the century, commercial growth had created a large permanent market, and Antwerp had over 1,000 foreign merchants, financiers, and agents, as well as 400 to 500 businessmen from the Low Countries.[26]

The fascinating story of Antwerp's Golden Age, which lasted until around 1565, has been told several times. The economic ups and downs of the city have been studied in great detail.[27] Finance has been considered especially carefully.[28] International commerce has received much attention. Various groups of businessmen have been examined on the basis of their geographic origin: South Europeans, English, French, High Germans, merchants from the Low Countries.[29] Developments in commercial law[30] and the impact of institutional changes on the economy have been investigated.[31] All important aspects of the textile industry, the main source of employment and the sector for which the bulk of imports (in terms of capital value) were intended, have been examined in detail.[32] Much is therefore known about long-term trends and conjunctures, structures and institutions, associations of individuals bound together by a common purpose, and wider social forces.

The available studies, however, do not directly convey a picture of 'capital at work', and that is precisely the central theme of this book. Like Jonathan Levy, I define capital as an

---

23 Van der Wee (1963), II, 119-36.
24 'Relazione' (1840b), 202-3.
25 For short biographical sketches of some Italian merchants in Antwerp, see Denucé (1934a) and (1934b).
26 Brulez (1975), 128-9.
27 See the seminal study of Van der Wee (1963).
28 Ehrenberg (1896).
29 Goris (1925); De Smedt (1950-54); Coornaert (1961); Harreld (2004); Puttevils (2015a).
30 De Ruysscher (2009) and (2020).
31 Gelderblom (2013).
32 Thijs (1987) and (1993).

economic process, i.e. 'property capitalized – a legal asset assigned a pecuniary value *in expectation* of its capacity to yield a likely *future* pecuniary income'. The emphasis on practice means that businessmen 'must be placed front and centre, for the way they shape and act upon ideas about the future fundamentally shapes the capital proces'.[33] Capitalists have always differed from the overwhelming majority of businessmen. In late medieval and early modern Europe they were the non-specialized upper echelon of the business world. They made the highest profits, not only because they generally controlled the most lucrative market segments, but also because they managed to adapt their investments continuously to changing conditions, which required both great financial resources and/or extensive credit and high velocity of capital. Flexibility has always been key for capitalists. Diminished returns were warnings and alerts to transfer capital quickly to a more profitable sector. As Arrighi has aptly summed up: 'An agency is capitalist because its money is endowed with the *power of breeding*', regardless of the specific economic activities involved.[34]

Three capitalists will show us how maximum use was made of the new economic opportunities in Antwerp during the first half of the sixteenth century: Erasmus Schetz, Gaspar Ducci and Gilbert van Schoonbeke. All three were economically versatile, even omni-competent. Schetz was active as an international trader, banker, mine operator, brass manufacturer, and sugar refiner, and he owned vast tracts of farmland and plantations. Ducci engaged increasingly in finance but speculated on several money and exchange markets simultaneously and moreover traded internationally in woad, alum, herring, and grain. Van Schoonbeke was active in many different fields: he was a property speculator and project developer, he contracted geat public works projects, opened brick kilns and extracted peat, set up and owned a great many breweries, and he supplied the armed forces. All three moved capital between different economic sectors: between trade, finance and manufacturing (Schetz), between trade and finance (Ducci), and between the real estate market and industrial production (Van Schoonbeke). It is precisely because these men had so many different facets and so much material success that their careers reveal how much capitalists were able to achieve in this crucial period at the centre of the world economy.

Schetz, whose economic activities are examined in the first part of this book, was the most successful capitalist in Antwerp's Golden Age: upon his death in 1550, he was the wealthiest inhabitant of the city, and he was still active in business at that point. He was always a highly strategic investor. During the first phase of Antwerp's economic growth, between 1500 and 1525, trade with Portugal provided a veritable bonanza for capitalists. The spice trade, however, was dominated from the outset by major South-German and Italian trading companies. Other businessmen could succeed only if they carved out their own niche. Schetz used his virtual calamine monopoly in the Netherlands to become crucial in Portugal's brass trade with West Africa, and based on this leading position he was able to participate in the spice trade without having to deal with stiff competition. To what extent were his commercial success and his involvement in state finance interconnected? As a banker, he made loans to Charles V (who enjoyed his hospitality) and other public authorities. While he undoubtedly aimed to turn a profit, the question is whether he

---

33 Levy (2017), 487 (my italics). Anievas and Nişancioğlu (2015), 8-9, also place the emphasis on capital as a process.
34 Arrighi (1994), 8. '*The power of breeding*' is Karl Marx's expression.

regarded short-term loans to the Emperor as – or even primarily – a means to obtain or retain exclusive economic benefits? Schetz understood that engaging in industrial production was advisable and sometimes even necessary to achieve or maintain a leading position in a given market. In Aachen he organized the manufacture of brassware. In Antwerp he set up his own sugar refinery, and he signed agreements with master craftsmen to finish vast quantities of English cloth, which he exported to Leipzig. Also, he was one of the first Europeans to own a sugar cane plantation and a sugar mill in Brazil. His activities therefore raise questions on the relationship between circulation and production and on the extent to which commercial capital was conducive to industrial operations.

Ducci was also active in international trade, but he devoted his energies mainly to financial transactions. In the 1540s, when Antwerp entered its second period of economic growth, and the New Exchange became pivotal in finance in Western Europe, he benefited fully from the city's key role. Commercial growth was primarily responsible for the increasing demand for financial infrastructure and the proliferation of credit facilities, but the struggle for political and military power in Western Europe provided a major impulse for the Antwerp money market. State formation confronted princes with financial problems of unprecedented magnitude. Wars were waged on several fronts and on a far larger scale than before, forcing the three key operators in the political-military arena – Emperor Charles V, Francis I of France, and Henry VIII of England – to borrow ever larger sums.[35] In the 1540s and early 1550s Mary of Hungary, sister of the Emperor and governor of the Habsburg Netherlands, sought desperately for new sources of income. Ducci proved to be a highly resourceful merchant-banker, as is demonstrated in the second part of this book. He introduced new commercial taxes in the Habsburg Netherlands and was the first to raise large sums on the Exchange through government bonds. He convinced Charles V to grant him a monopoly on alum distribution in Northwest and Central Europe, to the astonishment and anger of major international firms and the Pope alike. At the same time, he and Anton Fugger provided huge loans to Henry VIII, and together with other capitalists he speculated on exchange rates in Antwerp and Lyon. How frequently various types of malpractice occurred on the financial markets in this period, and what their consequences were is impossible to determine, but the available source material has made it possible to focus on the most important operator in this field: Ducci. Why did the Emperor and his sister provide long-term support to a capitalist regarded by most businessmen as a dangerous and even criminal manipulator and monopolist? What does this reveal about the relationship between capitalists and political rulers?

Van Schoonbeke's career shows that other economic sectors also offered great opportunities for capital investment and capital accumulation in Antwerp in the 1540s and early 1550s. Rising demand for housing, commercial facilities, and business premises led to massive expansion of the construction industry, so that the real-estate market took on ever more importance, promoting both investments and land speculation, as well as speculative building. These aspects of Antwerp's economy merit special consideration because to date little research has been conducted on private real estate development in sixteenth-century European cities. How did Van Schoonbeke manage within just a few

35 Van der Wee (1993), 24-8, and (2000), 155-69.

years to become the greatest project developer and real estate speculator that Antwerp had ever had – and as far as can be determined ever would have? How did he operate, and how did he interact with public authorities? Based on a wealth of archival material, these questions can be answered in the third part of this book, where Van Schoonbeke's unique industrial activities are discussed as well. He set up a vertically integrated building trust, which enabled him to monopolize the largest public works in Antwerp, i.e. construction of over half the new fortifications. In addition, he concentrated local beer production in the breweries he established in a new city district and ingeniously provided with pure water. His de facto monopolization of beer production instigated a revolt that Charles V regarded as a direct threat to his authority. What was the reason for the disposition of the Emperor? Why did he grant Van Schoonbeke the *official* monopoly on beer production following the repression of the revolt?

Antwerp was immensely important to the Emperor and his representatives in the Habsburg Netherlands, for both military-strategic and financial reasons. No other European city had the same measure of support from a political-military superpower as Antwerp, provided that this served the interests of the highest authorities. Charles V and Mary of Hungary always made clear whose interests had absolute priority. In 1540 they took it upon themselves to urge the city council to replace the outdated medieval walls with a new defence system and two years later to require that this be put into effect. They were keenly aware of the growing concentration of private capital in Antwerp and wondered constantly how much they could rely on the city treasury, the Exchange, and, last but not least, individual businessmen. Both city finance and the foundations of the urban economy therefore elicited considerable interest. This is the context of the ever stronger nexus between State and big business. They were highly receptive to proposals from capitalists that might generate considerable monetary income in the near future. In exchange for such services, they were willing to grant exclusive economic advantages, even if these meant monopolizing an indispensable raw material for the textile industry (alum), massive public works, or beer production.

What was the response in the Habsburg Netherlands to the monopolies that the Emperor granted capitalists? Unlike in the German territories, where public debates dragged on for years, in the States General of the Habsburg Netherlands, which convened regularly during the rule of Charles V, the monopoly issue was never raised. Nor was it a subject of debate in the States of Brabant, where the representatives of the Antwerp city council generally took the floor. This absence from public debate did not mean, however, that monopolist practices were ignored. Scholars of law harshly condemned them. In 1531 and 1540 the Emperor even proclaimed laws against monopolies, but they were not enforced.[36] During Prince Philip's ceremonial entry into Antwerp in 1549, the Antwerp city government informed Charles V of the dangers of new techniques designed to make money quickly and about all kinds of monopolies that disrupted the market, but the Emperor ignored them.[37] Charles V and Mary of Hungary knew that monopolies might give rise to scandal, which was in fact what happened, but that did not prevent them from

36 Cowen (2007).
37 De Ruysscher (2012), 73-4, 76.

giving the capitalists concerned their protection for an extended period (Ducci) or even permanently (Schetz and Van Schoonbeke). Studying their monopolies makes it possible not only to ascertain the measure of collusion between capitalists and political rulers but also to trace and explain the reactions of other capitalists and economically active members of the social middle groups.

Did capitalists have the support of the Antwerp city council? Or were they more likely to encounter obstruction and resistance? What was the stance of the local political elite in matters of immense importance to the municipal economy? Was an economic policy in the current sense of the word pursued during the period examined? According to Oscar Gelderblom the local authorities were the main agent of economic development, modifying or manipulating institutional arrangements with the intention of bringing about well-functioning markets, driven mainly by competition with Bruges.[38] The city council did guarantee foreign merchants as much freedom to be economically active as citizens, as well as equality before the law, and was lenient toward Calvinists, among whom there were many merchants.[39] In what measure, however, was the city council commercially dynamic and proactive during the first half of the sixteenth century? Antwerp's authorities granted legal privileges to some groups of foreign merchants, known as 'nations', but that was generally the limit; only in exceptional cases did they award commercial benefits.[40] They had only limited contacts with international businessmen. Antwerp's established families were not active in commerce, finance, or industry. The local polical elite and the commercial elite existed in largely separate worlds: the 117 burgomasters, aldermen, and receivers who served between 1520 and 1555 comprised only ten *homines novi* (newcomers) who were economically active during their lifetimes, as well as four others who were probably the sons of merchants.[41] The contrast with Bruges was very pronounced, as in Bruges merchants and entrepreneurs had always been active in local government.[42] One consequence of the extremely low representation of commercial and financial stakeholders on the city council was that Antwerp's authorities were unprepared for the pivotal role that the city would have in the economy of the Habsburg Netherlands, the Empire, and Europe. Since Schetz, Ducci, and Van Schoonbeke had very different relationships with the city authorities, it is possible to explore how members of the political elite viewed various capitalist practices and developments and, more generally, to examine how they perceived the urban economy. It may be argued that they regarded Antwerp until mid-century more as a 'city with a port' than as a 'port city'.[43]

Based on detailed archival sources, I have traced the specific actions of the three capitalists in Antwerp who were most successful in obtaining monopolies in different economic fields during the first half of the sixteenth century. Schetz, Ducci, and Van

38 Gelderblom (2013). The author does not offer convincing evidence of inter-city competition. See J.L. Bolton in *Economic History Review* (2014), 1172-3, and Safley (2014).

39 The heresy laws of Charles V were undoubtedly regarded as threats to trade, but the city council initially defended local political and legal autonomy. On the Reformation in Antwerp, see the important study by Marnef (1996).

40 See the pertinent remarks of Goris (1925), 6, and Coornaert (1952), 207-8.

41 Wouters (2004), 914-15.

42 Haemers et al. (2012), 24-5; Dumolyn et al. (2018), 282-3, 309, 312, 316.

43 This changed only in the 1560s, but that period exceeds the scope of this book.

Schoonbeke were three different types of businessmen. Still, all three were active during the rise and growth of Antwerp as the 'metropolis of the west', and all three were capitalists whose spectacular success derived largely from monopolist practices. They were certainly *not* representative of most merchants, and that is precisely why I selected them. Contemporaries made it indisputably clear that these three businessmen were exceptional, from different perspectives and for different reasons, but all commentators implicitly or explicitly referred to their unique economic achievements, and they were right to do so. The exceptional careers of the three protagonists shed light on the potential of the most dynamic economic centre of Europe – and the world – during early globalization. Precisely because their economic initiatives were far more ambitious than what other businessmen in Antwerp could or would consider or achieve, their careers are ideal vantage points for observing and analysing 'capital at work'. They also provide an opportunity to examine how commercial capitalism changed and/or was transformed, and in what measure the three protagonists extended the frontiers of capitalism.

Plate 1. Portrait of Erasmus Schetz, engraved by Lambertus Suavius, 1554. Amsterdam, Rijksmuseum

PART 1

Erasmus Schetz, *c.* 1480-1550

1.1 How to Trade with Portugal

'Antwerp did not set out to capture the world - on the contrary, a world thrown off balance by the great discoveries, and tilting towards the Atlantic, clung to Antwerp, *faute de mieux*. The city did not struggle to reach the visible pinnacle of the world, but woke up one morning to find itself there.'[1] Braudel used a powerful and colourful style of expression that should not be taken too literally but in my view accurately conveys the intrinsic idea: Antwerp, like Bruges, was basically a product of outside forces, emerging as a trade metropolis from the dynamics of geopolitical balances of power and shifts in international trade.[2] Exactly how and when this happened, what constituted the decisive factors, what changes occurred over the course of the Golden Age, and with what consequences: despite the many excellent historical works on the subject, such questions continue to inspire research and debate. As a systematic discussion of these in depth would exceed the scope of this study, I will focus only on those aspects of direct importance for a clear understanding of the opportunities and challenges that capitalists in Antwerp faced.

Political and maritime dynamics transformed Antwerp from an important fair market into a permanent market, and into a true world port. Bruges paid dearly for the uprisings against Maximilian of Austria in the 1480s, as foreign merchants were ordered to leave the city.[3] Moreover, in 1491 Maximilian of Austria allocated the staple of Italian alum to Antwerp. This decision was immensely important. After all, many foreign merchants might have returned to Bruges in 1492 (as they often had in the past), had the alum staple remained there.[4] Since it was an indispensable mordant for cloth dyeing, the alum staple not only secured the supply for textile manufacturing in the Scheldt town, but also made Antwerp pivotal in international trade in raw materials for this major industry. In 1496 the *Magnus Intercursus* similarly benefited Antwerp, as the terms of this treaty allowed English merchants to sell their goods throughout the Burgundian Netherlands, except in the County of Flanders.[5] In 1498, even before Vasco da Gama returned to Lisbon, Tomé Lopes was sent by King Manuel I to Antwerp. It was the preferred venue, because most customers for such merchandise were in Northwest and Central Europe, and because this town was a hub for the precious metals needed for payments in both West Africa and India. By 1500 Antwerp had become the commercial hub, structurally changing Flemish-Portuguese

1 Braudel (1979), III, 122. English translation: Braudel (1992), III, 145.

2 See also, from a different point of view, Brulez (1975), 110-12.

3 Maréchal (1951).

4 Alum had been the principal commodity traded by the Medici firm in Bruges: Mallett (1962), 258-9; Boone (1999), 41-7.

5 De Smedt (1950), I, 100-22.

trade. Bruges had sporadically exported brass intended for West Africa, but from 1501 spice and sugar imports from Portugal/Madeira and copper and brass goods exports to Lisbon/Elmina became systematically intertwined. Together, they underpinned Antwerp's thriving international trade.[6]

The view that Antwerp's emergence as the commercial metropolis of the West was due to the fortunate combination of Portuguese pepper and spices, German copper, and English cloth,[7] might seem to be at odds with Wilfrid Brulez' reconstruction of the trade balance of the Low Countries around 1560. Products coming from or being sent to areas overseas, such as spices, sugar, carmine, and copper, by then constituted only 14.2 percent of all imported goods – a very modest share, compared with commodities such as silk, grain, wine, and wool, which accounted for 57.7 percent. Accounting for 17.5 percent of all imported goods, English cloth effectively had the significance for Antwerp's trade in mid-century that most authors have attributed to it, though it sold at lower values than Italian silk and silk wares. Based on all these figures, Brulez has concluded 'that in quantitative terms the sixteenth-century colonial expansion was merely a secondary factor in the commercial growth of the Netherlands in general and of Antwerp in particular.' While he considers that the Portuguese spice staple may have exuded a magnetic attraction in Antwerp, he emphasizes that the figures in any case indicate that the economic effects of the great discoveries and the establishment of the Iberian colonial empires should not be overestimated.[8]

However, the trade balance of the Low Countries – of which three quarters or more consisted of trade from Antwerp – had by 1560 changed entirely from what it had been during the first quarter of the century. The trade balance in the period 1500-24 is impossible to analyse in quantitative terms, but Portuguese spices and German metals, together with English cloth, were indisputably the main drivers at the time. During this accelerated rise of commercial capitalism, Portugal was pivotal. Without the spices that were distributed throughout Western and Central Europe via the Lisbon-Antwerp axis, the South-German firms would not have conveyed massive quantities of silver and copper to Antwerp (instead of Venice).[9] The relocation of Hungarian copper exports was significant: in the period 1497-1503 the Fuggers still took 32.1 percent of the total production to Venice, with Antwerp receiving 'only' 24.32 percent via Gdansk and Stettin. By 1507-09, however, the proportions had shifted to 13.3 and 49.2 percent, respectively, with the Venetian share subsequently dropping below 5 percent, while that of Antwerp increased to over 60 percent.[10] The radical shift reflected a strategic decision by Jakob Fugger, who soon understood that copper was the most suitable payment currency in India. In Cochin, the most important export harbour on the Malabar Coast, at least one third and generally half the pepper was payable in copper bars, and trade in pearls, corals, and rubies also required vast amounts of copper.[11]

The exceptional and unique interplay of political and economic dynamics during the last decade of the fifteenth century and the first quarter of the sixteenth century was

6 Merchant entrepreneurs from Cologne responded to this trend: Everaert (1991), 109.
7 Van Werveke (1944), 75; Van Houtte (1961), esp. 259-60; Van der Wee (1993), 92-7.
8 Brulez (1968), 1217-18, and (1969), 18-19.
9 See the pertinent remarks of Kellenbenz (1990), I, 9-11.
10 Van der Wee (1963), I, 523.
11 Schick (1957), 277, and Müller (1962), 120-1.

crucial. Some French historians have referred to this period as *le beau seizième siècle*, the fine sixteenth century[12]: an extended period of peace and both economic & demographic expansion that benefited various social groups, albeit not in equal measure. Between 1500 and 1525, the population of the Southern Netherlands averaged 0.7 percent growth *per annum*, an unprecedented rate of increase that was never attained again until the nineteenth century. While part of this development admittedly reflected recovery from the heavy losses in the 1470s and 80s, the first quarter of the sixteenth century remained a period of exceptionally strong demographic growth, which stimulated demand for industrial goods. At the same time, the convergence of rapidly growing intercontinental trade and the revival of transcontinental trade greatly strenghtened European commerce, initially benefiting Lisbon, Augsburg, Nuremberg, and, finally, Antwerp.

The rapid economic growth between 1490 and 1525 provided a boost to the traditional trade with the western German territories. The east-west route went from Cologne, offering access to the German hinterlands, via Düren, to Aachen, which was a *Freie Reichsstadt*, a self-governing city subject only to the authority of the Holy Roman Emperor. Around 1500 Aachen had about 15,000 inhabitants and was a commercial and industrial hub between the Rhine and the Meuse rivers. In the Late Middle Ages woollen cloth was its main export commodity, but from the second half of the fifteenth century copper processing and especially brass production took off.[13] From Aachen the east-west route continued for about 35 kilometres to Maastricht. This was a 'city ruled by two lords': the council and the judiciary were subject to the authority of both the Duke of Brabant and the Prince-Bishop of Liège. Maastricht had about 10,000 inhabitants and had its own export products but was mainly a hub for transit trade. The Meuse provided a connection to the cities of the Northern Netherlands downstream and from there to England. Upstream it connected with Liège, Namur, and Dinant. From 1492 onward, the strong industrial expansion of the politically neutral Prince-Bishopric of Liège accelerated commercial growth in Maastricht, which had close political-administrative ties with the principality.[14]

During the period from 1488 to 1513, merchants from Cologne, Aachen, and Düren – in that order – had more contracts recorded by the Antwerp aldermen than all other 'Germans' combined and three times as many as the Italians or the French. Since commercial transactions did not have to be registered, these ratios cannot be considered statistically representative, but they do indicate that the western German territories were immensely significant for Antwerp.[15] The Schetz family came originally from the Aachen-Maastricht border area, which connected the Rhineland with the cities and towns in Brabant.[16] In the 1490s Erasmus' father, Cuntz or Conra(r)d, was mint master in Maastricht to the Prince-Bishop of Liège; as a prominent civil servant, he supervised the coinage and was responsible for its value. He married Marie Kranz, the daughter of an affluent innkeeper

---

12 The phrase was coined by Le Roy Ladurie (1962), 53.

13 Bruckner (1967). See also Holbach (1994), 95-6, 356-7.

14 Steegen (2006), 39-40, 111, and (2015), 303-4, 307.

15 Doehaerd (1963), I, 31-3, 86-99. See the comment of Brulez (1973), 9-11.

16 The earliest traces of the Schetz family are from the third quarter of the fifteenth century and refer to the grandfather of Erasmus Schetz, who is said to have come from the city of Schmalkalden in southwest Thuringia: Thüringes Staatsarchiv Meiningen, GHA Sektion VII, no. 302; *Regesten* (2006), 679, no. 1480. A few decades later, however, the cities of Maastricht and Hasselt were at the centre of the family network.

from Hasselt, who was also governor of the copper mines and counsellor to the mint in Westphalia.[17] Hasselt was located in the County of Loon, subject to the authority of the Prince-Bishop of Liège. This small town benefited from the increase in transport along the east-west route. Innkeepers were pivotal in commercial transit, in part by providing secure overnight storage of goods. They possessed considerable capital. One of the Schetz-Kranz daughters (Marie) married J(oh)an (II) van Hilst, also an innkeeper, who became mayor of Hasselt; they had two sons, of whom the eldest, the merchant Adriaen, would become factor of the Schetz company in Leipzig in the mid-sixteenth century.[18]

Fortune favoured Erasmus Schetz[19] from the start. His father was an affluent and prominent man. While the school or university his son attended is unknown, Latin was taught at one or two of the chapter schools in the city where he was born, and the correspondence with Erasmus of Rotterdam demonstrates his proficiency in this language.[20] He was also fortunate in that his uncle Rutger Kranz, whose marriage to Anna Foechlin remained childless, made him heir to his entire estate in 1500, provided that he settle in Antwerp and assist him in the copper trade. It was a booming business. From the 1480s on, merchant entrepreneurs from Cologne and Nuremberg sold copper and brass goods in Antwerp, where demand for such commodities soared, as the Portuguese Crown needed them for its trade with West Africa. Ever since his youth Erasmus would therefore have understood the potential of a commodity that had become crucial in Antwerp's most spectacular period of economic growth. The dynamic youth accepted the offer from his uncle.

Rutger Kranz undoubtedly had ties with the merchant Claes van Richtergem from Aachen,[21] who had settled in Antwerp shortly after 1488 and was very active in the copper and brass trade.[22] Quite conceivably, they decided together to send Erasmus Schetz to Portugal to negotiate directly with the King and to enter contracts for the sale of brass goods and the supply of pepper. They must have been aware via the Portuguese factor in Antwerp that exchange ratios with West Africa were highly advantageous. The transactions registered in Antwerp on 25 January 1501 indicate that Schetz was efficient, quick, and focused. The merchant Peter van der Hert stated then that he owed Schetz & Co. £925 Fl. gr. – over 150 times the annual wages of a skilled worker – for one hundred bales of *greynen* and eight bales of *garbeleurs*.[23] He supplied the firm with 48 bales of *greynen*, which were delivered to the house *Almaengien* (Germany) in Antwerp, 1,200 bales of *greynen*, which were delivered to Frankfurt, and eight *timmeren* sable furs. He also delivered 39 chests of

17 d'Ursel (2004), 37-40; Correns, Rau and Van de Cruys (2014), 59.

18 In Maastricht the Schetz-Kranz couple had four more children. See d'Ursel (2004), 41-3.

19 The surname is spelled in very different ways in the archive sources: Cettes, Esquet, Esquertes, Esquetes, Kettes, Scats, Scatz, Scet(s), Scetus, Scetys, Schats, Schatz, Schet(s), Schette, Schettler, Schetz, Schetzer, Scheyts, Schütz, Skets, Sketes, Sketz, Squet(t). All personal documents are signed 'Erasmus Schetz'.

20 On this correspondence, see Bernstein (1985-6) and Godin (1987).

21 Claes van Richtergem, born around 1455, was the son of the Aachen merchant Lambrecht and Ida ('Idgen') Wolff: Wackernagel (1951), 109; Quadflieg (1962-3), 394-5. Many authors present incorrect genealogies for the Schetzes and the Van Richtergems for the fifteenth and early sixteenth centuries. Correct data based on archival sources were gathered by the late Henry L.V. De Groote in SAA, PK 3479, and were used by d'Ursel (2004), 31-49. See also Correns, Rau, and Van de Cruys (2014), 31-3.

22 SAA, SR 117, f° 228; Van Answaarden (1991), 187-91.

23 In Antwerp spices had to be cleaned of dust and impurities and were then sorted by quality before they were sold: *garbeleuren*. Geudens (1891-1904), II, 228-59.

sugar to the value of £100 Fl.gr. to Jan Bertel, factor of Erasmus.[24] *Greynen*, also known as grains of paradise, were the *Aframomum melegueta* or malagueta pepper, which was imported mainly from the West-African coast between Cape Mesurado and Cape Palmas, known as the Pepper Coast. Once the Benin coast was discovered in 1485/6, *piper Guineense* was imported from West Africa as well; it was called *pimenta de rabo* by the Portuguese and *Ashanti pepper* by other Europeans. The lion's share of both sorts of pepper was sent to Flanders, at first to Bruges but from 1501 increasingly to Antwerp.[25]

That Erasmus Schetz recorded such transactions in 1501 is highly remarkable, as this was the first year that a Portuguese ship loaded with pepper docked at Antwerp.[26] Since he had a factor carry out the transactions, he was presumably living in Lisbon at the time, where he established the contacts he needed to purchase malagueta pepper. Barely in his twenties, trading 'new' products, such as spices and sugar, venturing into substantial commercial transactions, and having his own factor were unusual. Who were his partners? Or did he trade on commission? Was Kranz involved? Van Richtergem? This is not addressed in the sources. The first known transactions by Erasmus Schetz reveal, however, that the commercial hub was shifting: trade in malagueta pepper and Madeira sugar was being transferred from Bruges to Antwerp.

In the late Middle Ages, Flanders had become Portugal's most important and most stable commercial partner. Portuguese traders exported wine, olive oil, and fruits such as figs and raisins to Bruges, where they established a 'nation' and a *feitora* (factory). Commodities from Africa and the Atlantic islands were introduced to the Flemish market in the 1460s: malagueta pepper was first recorded there in 1464/5, ivory in 1465, and Madeira sugar in 1468. Importing these commodities boosted brassware and copper exports to Lisbon.[27] The Bruges merchant Thomas Perrot understood that investing in calamine extraction, a mineral indispensable for manufacturing top-quality brass, could make trade with West Africa more profitable. Around 1470 he participated in leasing the Altenberg mine but had to withdraw from this venture a few years later, probably because the ship he sent to West Africa sank, causing him to go bankrupt.[28]

Van Richtergem and Schetz were well positioned to trade with Portugal. A crucial factor in their commercial success was the Altenberg mine, later also known as Vieille Montagne, at Kelmis (in French: La Calamine), seven or eight kilometres southwest of Aachen.[29] The mineral smithsonite or zinc spar was extracted there. This zinc carbonate – also known as calamine – was used to manufacture brass. Altenberg calamine was very pure and yielded an end product with a special hue, ranging from dark yellow to red, thereby producing brass goods distinctive from all others.[30] The Dukes of Burgundy, who were also Dukes of Limburg, had leased the Altenberg from 1469 onward to the highest

24 SAA, SR 118, f° 207, and SR 147, f°402v°-403. Also Doehaerd (1963), nos 3263 and 3267. On the highly profitable trade in furs of sables (1 *timmer* is 1,000 items), see Wijnroks (2003), 161.

25 Magalhães-Godinho (1969), 539-47.

26 Van Werveke (1944), 54.

27 Brulez (1973), 17-19; Miranda (2012), 75-7, 79.

28 Mus (1964), 93; Slootmans (1985), III, 1198-1201; *Voyage* (1992), 20-1, 118, 124.

29 As distinct from Altenberg in the Ore Mountains, in Saxony.

30 Peltzer (1908), and Irsigler (1979a), 29-30. Competition for the Altenberg calamine was so great that in 1816 the major European powers assigned a special status to the mine and the adjacent village: Neutral Moresnet, jointly

bidder, who at the same time obtained a monopoly on extracting and selling calamine in the Burgundian – later the Habsburg – Netherlands. Successive lessees entrusted technical management of the operations to Leendert van Kelmis,[31] thereby opening up new opportunities for Van Richtergem, because he married Ida/Isabella ('Beelken') van Kelmis, the daughter of Leendert, after whose death in 1491 his widow (Mechteld Cloots) continued the operation.[32] Family ties became still more important two years later, when the Altenberg was leased for a twelve-year period by Peter Wolff, a maternal uncle of Claes. This merchant entrepreneur, who served several terms as mayor of Aachen, worked with his brother Karl. Mining the Altenberg enabled them to control the calamine trade, as shown by their high revenues: they sold Rg18,000 or £4200 Fl.gr. of calamine on average *per annum*. Shortly after they started their lease, the brothers established a large plant for processing copper and manufacturing brass plates for wire-drawing in Mariaweiler at Düren, *c.* 35 kilometres east of Aachen.[33] From them, Claes van Richtergem learned the potential profit available from vertical concentration: mining calamine and trading copper, resulting in brass production. Following the death of Peter Wolff in 1507, he immediately signed a twelve-year lease of his own for the calamine quarries in Altenberg. His access to ore of exceptional quality gave him a competitive advantage in the growing trade with Lisbon, as the Portuguese trading posts along the west coast of Africa were the chief markets for brass goods manufactured in Aachen and to a lesser extent in Nuremberg and other German cities. In the period 1506-08 Van Richtergem supplied copper and brass goods valued at 1,913,250 *reais* or *c.* £1595 Fl.gr. to the factors of the *Casa real* and the *Casa da India* in Lisbon.[34]

While exporting to Lisbon was not intrinsically a problem, lucrative trade also required importing commodities. This entailed transferring all or part of the trade in malagueta pepper to Antwerp and necessitated negotiating with the highest political authorities. After all, the Portuguese Crown determined which merchants were entitled to trade African commodities and on which terms. The transactions by Schetz in 1501 indicate that he had entered into sound contracts with Manuel I. Good relations with the King of Portugal were of the utmost importance to obtain Asian spices at advantageous terms as well. The King and his advisors spared no effort to sustain a monopoly on the spice trade in Asia but at the same time tried to prevent the most powerful merchant houses from gaining complete control of distribution in Western Europe. Silver and copper were the two European products that were indispensable to the Portuguese for purchasing Indian spices,[35] and both metals were located precisely in the regions where the South-German firms had expanded their economic influence from the late fifteenth century onward. That Van Richtergem and Schetz had no ties with South-German trading firms proved to be an important advantage for Schetz during his sojourn in Lisbon, as well as afterwards.

---

administered by Belgium and Prussia. The First World War marked the end of this neutrality, and in 1920 the territory was officially annexed by Belgium: Engelen (1976) and Dröge (2016).

31 Yans (1938), 246-7, 261-70.

32 See the excellent genealogies by d'Ursel (2004), 72-80, and Correns, Rau and Van de Cruys (2014), 25-6, 28-9, 31-2.

33 Irsigler (1979b), 149-55.

34 Doehaerd (1963), nos 1780 and 1844; Pereira (1969), 130-1.

35 Between 1500 and 1520, almost the entire Central European silver production was transported to Lisbon. See the calculations and comments of Rössner (2012), 258-71, 301-6.

The King, as Wilhelm Rem later explained, 'did business with the German merchants himself, but often didn't conduct the sale the way he had promised them', meaning that he would break his word, whenever it suited him. Rem was referring to the fact that following the India expedition of 1505/6, Manuel I no longer felt committed to honour the spice contract he had signed in 1504 with Lucas Rem, a family member of Wilhelm representing the Welser-Vöhlin firm. From that point onward, the King and his representatives in Antwerp did their utmost to distribute commercial contracts for spice supplies among several firms.[36] They considered that Van Richtergem and Schetz were based in Antwerp and supplied brassware of exceptional quality, which was immensely important for trade with West Africa. Schetz's humanist interests undoubtedly facilitated his contacts with Manuel I. Years later, on 17 March 1526, he wrote to Erasmus of Rotterdam: 'In the past I had many intimate conversations with his late Majesty'.[37] The ruler indeed valued social skills, erudition, and piety, though business acumen was just as necessary, since he 'was a great merchant', as the German businessman Wilhelm Rem noted. Thanks to his good contacts with Manuel I, Schetz obtained the same commercial and legal privileges for Van Richtergem (and later for himself) as did the large trading firms from Augsburg and Nuremberg.[38]

Van Richtergem made history as a spice trader. Over half a century after his death, he was described by Lodovico Guicciardini as a *huomo di gran'faculta e di gran'qualità* ('a man of great wealth and talent'), while the Florentine recalled that he had been the very first to purchase Asian spices in Antwerp and take them to Germany, even before the Welsers, the Höchstetters, and the Imhof(f)s had done so.[39] A contract signed in Antwerp with Tomé Lopes, factor of King Manuel I of Portugal, reveals that in 1503 he did indeed purchase pepper and other spices and export them to Central Europe. Over the years he remained active in this branch, while trading Madeira sugar as well, which was also supplied via Lisbon.[40] While comprehensive figures are not available, fragmentary data indicate that he traded large amounts. In the period 1506-08 he imported 2778 *arrobas* or *c.* 35,700 kilograms of Madeira sugar. A record from 1513 shows that during the preceding years he had sold the central government 61,666 pounds or nearly 29,000 kilograms of pepper valued at *c.* £26,000 Artois. Like the Welsers, the Höchstetters, and other large trading companies, he sold spices to Antwerp brokers, but he exported mainly pepper and sugar on his own account to Germany, especially to Aachen, Cologne, and Frankfurt.[41]

Small wonder that he became wealthy. He owned several houses in Antwerp, including some prestigious buildings. In this rapidly growing city, with its burgeoning economy, these investments entailed no risk at all and moreover made credit easier to obtain. Van Richtergem was sensitive to the prestige associated with certain properties, especially the large mansion with vast gardens, annexes, and stables purchased in 1498 from the heirs

---

36 Denucé (1909); Almeida (1993), 45; Pohle (2000), 101-4, 156-65. Rem quoted by Johnson (2008), 179.

37 Erasmus, Ep. 1681: *Correspondence* (2003), 102-3.

38 ANTT, Chanc. de D. Manuel, no. 25, f° 44.

39 Guicciardini (1567a), 84 and 95. See also SBA, B11285, f°18.

40 Dias (1964), II, 289-90; Everaert (1986), 447; Vieira (1987), 56, 204.

41 ADN, B 2229; See also ANTT, CC/2/15/25, nos 18-77, and 19-4; Doehaerd (1963), nos 1313, 1445, 1780, 1844; Van der Wee (1963), II, 140; Pereira (1969), 130-1; Slootmans (1985), I, 628.

of burgomaster Hendrik van Berchem; it was valued at £560 Br.gr. or *c.* £373 Fl.gr., i.e. 63 years' wages of a skilled worker. He moved in there and had a sign affixed above the gate featuring the name he had selected: *in Aken* ('in Aachen'). A few years later he purchased the adjacent houses and grounds, so that he owned a vast area in the centre of Antwerp.[42] In 1509 he sold another complex of buildings to Jakob Fugger (the Rich) for an undisclosed amount,[43] which in no way suggests that he became dependent on the Augsburg firm, as some historians have argued.[44] The two parties did business with each other as equals, even though Fugger had far more capital.

Van Richtergem married twice. The date his first wife died is unknown, but in 1502 he remarried. His new wife, Margriete Meeus, was many years younger and came from a well-to-do Antwerp family with several highly respected members.[45] A German merchant who had lived in Antwerp less than fifteen years and yet succeeded in becoming related to local dignitaries via his second marriage: it was an impressive example of social advancement. Such connections may have led Van Richtergem to finance the construction of the chapel for the Guild of Our Lady's Praise, an exclusive fraternity dedicated to worshipping the Virgin Mary. Members held positions of honour in the illustrious procession or *ommegang* to honour Our Lady that was held every year in August on the first Sunday after Assumption Day and was described in detail by Dürer in 1520.[46] In 1505 Van Richtergem was one of the two 'officiating masters', who agreed to manage the fraternity, considered to be a great honour. He was buried in the fraternity's chapel in 1511. Beside his grave a magnificent brass chandelier was placed, with his name inscribed on its base.[47]

Shortly before or after his death, Ida (his eldest daughter) married Erasmus Schetz. She was 21 or 22, and her husband was about ten years older, a difference that was not unusual in sixteenth-century merchant circles. Had her father selected him as a future son-in-law? That is very likely. Van Richtergem greatly appreciated Schetz, as he made clear by introducing him to the Guild of Our Lady's Praise. Nor could he have one of his own children or another son-in-law continue his firm. Lambrecht, his only son, had no experience at all in business. No record exists of any commercial activity on his part, and he is referred to in later documents only as 'Lord of Rechteren' – hardly indicative of a merchant. The other two daughters (Maria and Catharina) were not yet married.[48] At any rate, the marriage contract between Erasmus and Ida was signed on 11 July 1511 and was followed by the church wedding on 27 July.

Much had to be arranged following the marriage. Van Richtergem's widow was not to cause any problems with respect to the business end of the union. Van Richtergem's

---

42 SAA, SR 112, f° 283, SR 132, f° 64 and 274. This large house was located in Spuistraat (which has since disappeared), connecting Korte Nieuwstraat with Ankerrui (now Jezuïetenrui).

43 SAA, SR 129, f° 83, and SR 135, f° 51v°.

44 See esp. Pölnitz (1949), II, 149-50, which also contains many other inaccuracies.

45 Her sister Jozijne was married to *ridder* (knight) Gillis van Berchem, who served several terms as burgomaster of Antwerp. Claus de Buekelere, a canon of the Church of Our Lady, the main church (and a cathedral from 1559) in the city of Antwerp, was an in-law.

46 Op de Beeck (1978); Dürer (1978), 11-12.

47 Guicciardini (1567b), 96.

48 Both married only in 1514/15: Catharina to Conrad (III) de/van Gavere(n), Lord of Elsloo, Diepenbeek, and Monschau (respectively located near Maastricht, Hasselt, and Aachen), and Maria to Francesco de Vaille: d'Ursel (2008), 78.

children reached an out-of-court settlement with their stepmother, who had no children of her own.[49] Erasmus Schetz was authorized by his brother-in-law and his sisters-in-law to manage the assets and liabilities of the estate. While the value of the movable goods is impossible to trace, some of the properties, which were distributed only in 1516, were worth a small fortune. Ida and Erasmus were given the 'House *of* Aachen' on Spuistraat: its name was no longer 'House *in* Aachen'. Its value was appraised at Rg5120. They also received annuities equalling Rg416, bringing the total to Rg5536 or *c.* £1292 Fl.gr., i.e. 187.5 years' wages of a skilled worker. The three other heirs received goods representing an equivalent value or were paid in cash.[50] Part of the property holdings thus had a total value of £5168 Fl.gr.

When she married, Ida had already contributed the valuable Berensberg country estate near Aachen, on the condition that her two sisters were paid an annuity of Rg1000. She also received all the jewellery that had belonged to her mother. The stipulation was that if no children were born from the marriage, all items were to be returned to the family, but that the surviving spouse would keep half the accrued value, as well as an annuity of Rg500 and all movable goods.[51] Erasmus contributed to the marriage the Orsbach 'seigniory', which had belonged to his father and had been ceded by his mother in exchange for an annuity of Rg400. In addition, Anna Foechlin, the widow of Rutger Kranz, gave the newlyweds several properties: a large house with small adjacent houses in Antwerp's Saint George Parish, a *huis van plaisantie*, i.e. a *villa rustica* or summer residence, with stables, barns, orchards, and fish ponds, along with *c.* 5.3 hectares of arable land in the same parish, and a mansion near the Saint Anthony Hospital in Lier.[52]

Erasmus benefited greatly from the marriage, not so much because of the direct financial income as because of the opportunity to continue the economic enterprises set up by Van Richtergem, associated with the Altenberg calamine operations and his trade in brass goods. Lambrecht, Maria and Catharina agreed to let their brother-in-law take over the Altenberg lease that their father had entered into in 1507 for a twelve-year period. Via Mary, moreover, he became kin to international merchants who traded with the Iberian Peninsula. In 1514 or 1515 she married Francesco de Vaille, a wealthy Spanish merchant. His father Antonio, who was from Burgos, had settled not in Bruges but in Antwerp in the late fifteenth century, reflecting the shift of the commercial hub. He traded spices and sugar with Portugal. Following the death of Antonio around 1511, his eldest son Francesco and his son-in-law Francesco de Moxica continued the firm, which in addition to its commercial activities, provided huge loans to the government.[53]

---

49 She received her dowry (which had a value of £160 Fl.gr.), all goods she had brought with her into the marriage, her share of the household effects in Antwerp and a life annuity of 100 Crowns or £20 Fl.gr. She waived all claims to other goods, whether movable items or properties. SAA, SR 141, f°141, and SR 142, f° 123v°-124. In 1512 she remarried to Johan Rotaller, receiver-general to the Duke of Saxony.

50 SAA, PK 149, f°24v°-25. Calculations based on Scholliers (1960), 87-90, and Munro (2001), 104.

51 AGR, FU, L 182. The contract stated explicitly that their mother Ida/Isabella van Kelmis, who had passed away long ago, had made a bequest to Ida with the consent of her only son Lambrecht and her two other daughters Catharina and Maria. Since in 1502 Claes van Richtergem entered into a second marriage, this time with Margriete Meeus, the provision was most likely agreed upon while arranging the inheritance.

52 AGR, FU, L 182 and R 4.

53 ADN, B 2309; Henne (1858-60), III, 12 and 287; Ehrenberg (1896), I, 356-8; Goris (1925), 374 and 399; Bataillon (1974), 53-4; Kellenbenz (1976/7), 307-9; Fagel (1996), 110-13.

Family and kinship networks were immensely important to a merchant like Schetz. In the sixteenth century this was more the rule than the exception,[54] as 'in a business world where the unknown was a credit risk and the entrepreneur's success lay so much in the hands of men beyond his immediate control, the ties of the family, of religion and of the social community which went with both, were the cement of commercial confidence and commercial organization'.[55] This is confirmed by several empirical studies. Merchants from Burgos in England and France, Italians operating in Lisbon, or Portuguese based in Antwerp: their commercial relations in the sixteenth century derived from the family unit.[56] In this period, Antwerp constituted a rapidly changing economic environment that offered opportunities but was also rife with uncertainties and risks. Ongoing immigration made for rapid and strong demographic growth. At any given point in time, newcomers accounted for over half the population. Most merchants involved in international trade were not born in the Habsburg Netherlands, and many came from remote areas. Their background was often unknown, as was their financial solvency. Nor was it possible to anticipate whether they would stay temporarily or settle permanently in the city. Organizing a business around family networks therefore offered many advantages, especially in terms of mutual trust. On the other hand, such networks could make it more difficult to mobilize financial resources, information, and expertise.[57] These potential drawbacks were of no consequence in this case, however, as Schetz had sufficient capital and was very well informed about all aspects of the Lisbon-Antwerp trade. Since trust was the most important factor, he chose his partners from the members of two related families: Jan Vleminck the Elder and Aert (Arnold) Pruynen.

Jan Vleminck the Elder came from a family originally from Aachen, Maastricht, and Limburg. There were close ties with the Van Kelmis family, who had been mining the Altenberg for many decades,[58] and with whom Van Richtergem had become related via his first marriage. Vleminck married the widow Agnes Schetz,[59] and always introduced himself as a cousin of Erasmus. When he and his wife drew up their last will and testament in February 1527, they stipulated that they were leaving most of their plentiful and valuable possessions to their son, also called Jan (the Younger), but that they wished to leave a share to two cherished relatives as well. After all, Jan Vleminck explained, 'for a very long time I have had a company' with my cousin Erasmus Schetz and my brother-in-law Arnold Pruynen 'and I am still their partner. We made our greatest fortune together, when we were young and spent our best time together'. He died a few months later.[60]

---

54 Puttevils (2015a), 83-5, notes that 19 of the 27 partnership contracts registered by notaries in Antwerp between 1526 and 1588 united merchants with no family connection, but the author rightly remarks that registration was not required, and that partner unfamiliarity could well explain why these contracts were registered by a notary.

55 Supple (1977), 410.

56 Trivellato (2009), ch. 5; Puttevils (2015), ch. 3; Ribeiro (2016), 123-9.

57 Ogilvie (2011), 332.

58 Between 1486 and 1491, the father of Jan Vleminck the Elder was married to Mechteld Cloots, widow of Leendert van Kelmis; he died in 1514.

59 Daughter of Cornelis Schetz and Margriet Vrancx. Cornelis was most likely a brother of Erasmus' father.

60 Testament edited by Meulleners (1890), 325, my translation. 'When we were young' was not strictly accurate for Schetz, who was born around 1480, but it did apply to Vleminck and Pruynen, who were about ten years younger. Correns, Rau and Van de Cruys (2014), 25-6, 39.

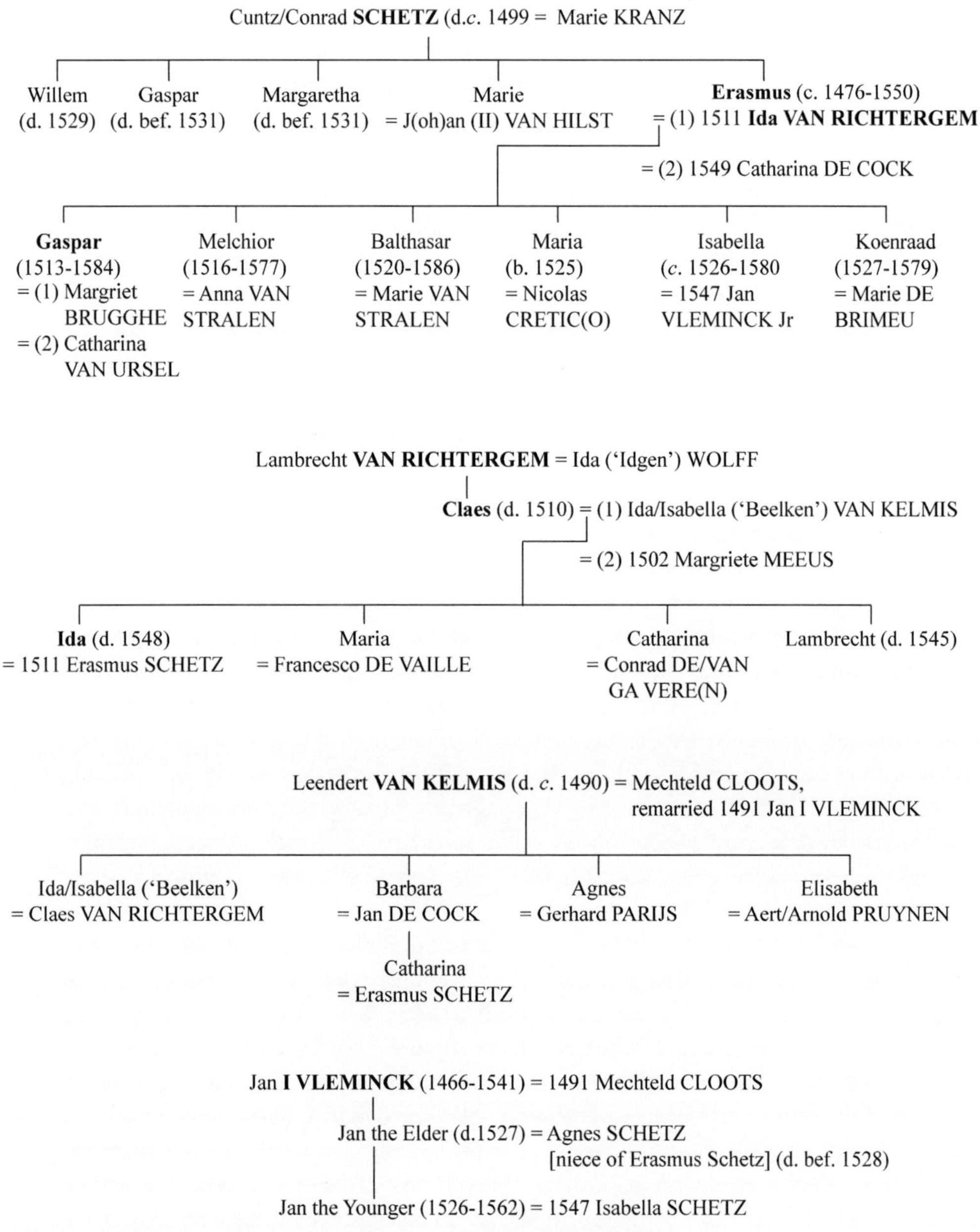

Figure 1. Family trees: Schetz, Van Richtergem, Van Kelmis, and Vleminck

The Pruynens[61] had close ties with the City of Maastricht, where several members held important office in the Late Middle Ages. Arnold wed Elisabeth van Kelmis and thus became the brother-in-law of both Claes van Richtergem and Jan Vleminck the Elder, and an uncle of Erasmus Schetz. He and his wife had four children, all of whom died in infancy. Elisabeth died in 1520. By then the couple had probably already been living in Antwerp for several years, as in 1515 Arnold's son Christoffel was born out of wedlock to Helena Dierickx of Antwerp. This child was recognized by the father in 1525 and later succeeded him in his business. Two years later Arnold married again; this time to Maria van Bombergen, daughter of the wealthy merchant Cornelis, who traded mainly with Venice, where his sons Anthonis and Daniël were active. He died in December 1536 and was buried at the Church of Our Lady in Antwerp.

Schetz, Vleminck the Elder, and Pruynen were born into and/or married into affluent families from border regions in the West of what is now Germany and the East of the Low Countries. Several members held prominent public office in the cities of Aachen, Maastricht, Hasselt, or Limburg. Fathers, fathers-in-law, brothers, and brothers-in-law had launched thriving economic activities, and many traded calamine, copper, or brass directly or indirectly. This proved to be of immense economic importance for the three partners and especially for Erasmus. The Schetz & Co. partnership was certainly active from the 1510s. Pruynen and Vleminck were in their twenties then, and Schetz was in his early thirties. After Vleminck died in 1527, Schetz and Pruynen continued the firm. When Pruynen died in 1536, Erasmus no longer saw any need to include relatives as partners and brought his eldest sons into the business. Ida van Richtergem had borne him four sons and two daughters: Gaspar in 1513, Melchior in 1516, Balthasar in 1520, Maria in 1525, Isabella around 1526, and Koenraad in 1527. When Gaspar was 23 or 24, his father started to involve him in some of his business transactions, and in the 1540s he brought his sons Melchior and Balthasar into the business as well. In 1545 their participation was formalized, and the firm continued as 'Erasmus Schetz & Sons'.

The bonds between the Van Richtergems and the Schetzes and subsequently the kinship ties between Schetz, Vleminck the Elder, and Pruynen were essential from an economic perspective, because they were conducive to establishing and running a firm with integrated commercial and industrial interests. In the 1540s (and afterwards) material motives continued to figure in the quest for suitable marriage partners, in the interests of securing the family fortune and, better still, enlarging it, which in turn contributed to the solvency of the firm. Erasmus Schetz did not, however, primarily seek partners for his children in business circles. He entrusted increasingly more transactions to Gaspar and later on to Melchior and Balthasar as well. As his eldest son continued to expand the already vast commercial and financial network and was to carry on the firm together with his brothers, Schetz did not need his sons-in-law to be economically active. He ensured simply that the marital partners were financially comfortable and, if possible, were from well-respected families, as both facets would increase public trust in the firm.[62]

---

61 The surname is spelled in many different ways in the sources: Braun, Praun, Prenn, Prewen, Proen, Pruin, Prün, Proenen, Pruinen, Prunen, Pruynen.

62 d'Ursel (2008), passim, and Correns, Rau & Van de Cruys (2014), 26, 63-6, 73.

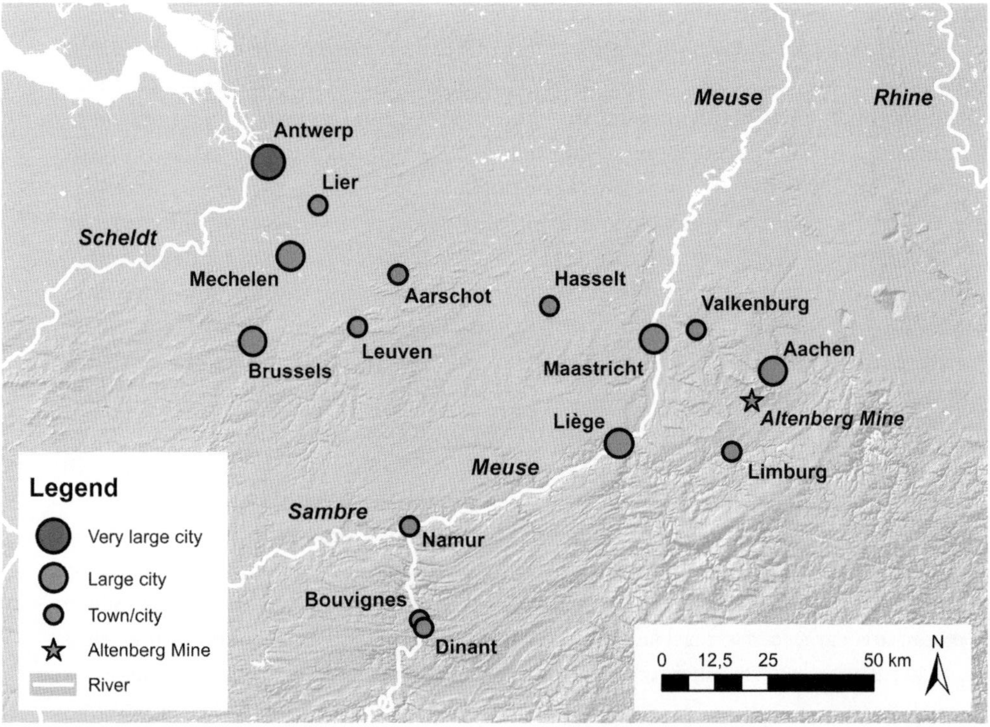

Map 1. Location of the Altenberg Mine

However important family relations and networks were, they do not intrinsically explain Schetz's tremendous and enduring success. He wanted for nothing during his childhood and was instructed in business by a wealthy uncle; in addition, he received several inheritances, and his marriage offered good economic prospects: fate favoured him, but he was certainly not the only merchant who set off to a good start in early sixteenth-century Antwerp. Although little is known about his activities in Lisbon, all indications suggest that even as a young man he had already developed a keen business acumen and very sophisticated social skills. The question remains, however, as to exactly what he did after the death of Claes van Richtergem to continue expanding Schetz & Co. for decades, placing the firm solidly in the lead in Antwerp business circles by the middle of the century.

1.2 The Calamine Monopoly and Brass Production

No other European industry between 1470 and 1540 was as tightly controlled by capitalists as mining. Extraction and processing of precious metals experienced explosive growth, as demand for silver and copper soared to unprecedented levels. Erasmus Schetz cared most of all about the growing need of the Portuguese for copper and copper alloys as a suitable currency for barter and payment in West Africa and India, but the interaction of political-military, socio-economic, and cultural domains greatly increased public and private demand for copper throughout Europe. State formation entailed changes in warfare, which led to increasing use of both bronze canon and portable firearms made of copper or copper alloy. Overseas expeditions and intensified sea trade around Europe led to the construction of more and larger ships, which in turn required larger amounts of copper. Urbanization boosted residential construction, with timber increasingly being replaced by stone and metal, and food-processing industries expanded, e.g. breweries and sugar refineries, in which copper kettles were used. More copper coins had to be minted for the small daily expenses of growing numbers of people and to pay ever greater numbers of wage earners. In addition to promoting the manufacture of utensils made of copper or brass, socio-cultural changes increased production of clocks, medals, sculptures, and other bronze *objets d'art*.[63]

From the middle of the fifteenth century onwards, application of a new technology, the *Saigerprozess*, which made it possible to separate small amounts of silver from copper,[64] boosted production in Europe. The most important mines were in the region around Neusohl or Banská Bystrica in central Hungary (now Slovakia), the County of Mansfeld (now part of the federal state of Saxony-Anhalt), and the Alpine lands, comprising Tyrol, Styria, Carinthia, and Mühlbach. Everywhere technological improvement increased the impact of commercial capital on the organization of production. The Fuggers, the Welsers and other large South-German trading houses spared no effort to gain control of the highly lucrative silver and copper market. In return for lending substantial amounts to the highest political authorities, they obtained the exclusive right to sell the entire output of the mines in Tyrol and Hungary. In 1498 the Fuggers teamed up with four other South-German firms in a cartel that controlled the entire copper market in Venice; their use of Latin aliases proves how controversial their action was.[65] In 1515 Emperor Maximilian I brought about a cartel in the copper trade for the second time, and the Fuggers signed a contract with the Höchstetters to supply the European markets together. Tyrolean copper was reserved for the German and Italian markets, and Hungarian copper – commercialized by the Fuggers – was exported exclusively to Antwerp.[66]

Some of the copper was not intended to be used in its pure form. It was smelted with another element at specialized centres far outside the mining regions: with tin to make bronze or with calamine to make brass. In this period brass became more popular than ever, as this alloy, known as 'coloured or yellow copper', had many advantages in processing compared with pure copper: 'It was easier to cast, to work cold, to solder, and to surface-finish, and it did not develop a toxic oxide film when it came into contact with food'.[67] Ideally, kitchen utensils were therefore made of brass. Wire too was one of the main products in the brass industry and was used to make hooks, buckles, rings, chains, and needles, as well as to manufacture timepieces. Other semi-finished products included plates and rods that could be processed in all kinds of other ways. In addition, a very broad range of objects was manufactured from brass: spoons, water pots, andirons, chandeliers, liturgical items, nautical instruments, handguns, and the like.

---

63 Schick (1957), 276; Irsigler (1979a), 15-16; Hachenberg (1992), 239-40.

64 See esp. Suhling (1976) and (1994); l'Héritier and Tereygeol (2010).

65 Ehrenberg (1896), I, 417-20; Blaich (1967), 107-17; Nehlsen-von Stryck (1988), 6.

66 The standard work on the Fuggers is still Pölnitz (1949) and (1958-1985). Häberlein (2012) provides a synthesis.

67 Hachenberg (1992), 230.

From the central Middle Ages onwards the centre of the brass industry was situated between the Meuse and the Rhine rivers, as that was where the oldest and largest calamine quarries in Europe were. This zinc carbonate was also present in the Thuringian Highlands, at Iserloh in Sauerland, near Lemgo in the principality of Lippe, in the Black Forest, in the Harz, in Carinthia, and in Galicia (Poland), but the mines around Aachen, Limburg, and Stolberg were the most productive and supplied the best quality. The brass producers appreciated calamine from this area not only for its extreme purity but also because it provided a substantial increase in weight, thereby increasing the profit margin.[68] Calamine from the Altenberg near Aachen was renowned for yielding the very best quality brass.

Between the Rhine and the Meuse rivers little copper ore was present, and so the basic raw material had to be brought in from more remote areas, thereby promoting the development of commercial networks. When the brass industry in Aachen expanded considerably in the second half of the fifteenth century, ever greater amounts of copper ore were brought in from Mansfeld County, as *Garkupfer*, which came from the area of the towns of Mansfeld, Eisleben, and Hetstedt, and was best suited for brass production. Manufacturers in Aachen were even required to use this raw material exclusively; otherwise their brassware would not be stamped with the town's eagle. In the mid-fifteenth century the brass industry was introduced into Aachen by immigrants from Dinant and expanded there after Dinant was destroyed by the Duke of Burgundy in 1466. The proximity of the Altenberg and the favourable geographic location were the foundations for ongoing growth that made Aachen a first-class brass production centre in Europe North of the Alps. In 1559, 69 *Kupfermeister* and a thousand journeymen operated over one hundred smelting works in the town, where *Garkupfer* and calamine were processed together for eight to twelve hours. Next, the brass sheets were cut into strips or pieces and were then hammered, generally using hydropower. Contemporaries placed the average annual output of such a smelting works at 13,500 to 15,000 kilograms of brass *per annum*, yielding an estimated total production of 1425 metric tons.[69] Nuremberg was the only German city that may have achieved close to the production volume in Aachen, although it did not exceed it.

That 69 *Kupfermeister* in Aachen employed over one thousand journeymen (i.e. averaging fifteen per workshop) was exceptional. Everywhere else – including in Nuremberg – the number of journeymen per master was tightly restricted, ranging from two to a maximum of five, and the *Kupfermeister* were subject to several other regulations as well. In the Aachen brass industry, on the other hand, workshop size was unrestricted, and labour was almost entirely free: the guild did not require an apprentice period, no accession dues were payable (except for whoever was not born in the city), and no masterpiece had to be produced.[70] This made capitalist organization of production possible, and that was precisely what happened – on a massive scale, as revealed by the fact that smelting works greatly outnumbered *Kupfermeister*. The need for fixed capital and the recurrent purchase of a relatively costly commodity such as copper led to such developments elsewhere as well, but in Aachen the concentration of operations and subcontracting occurred on a far greater scale.

68 Peltzer (1925), 202-3; Bruckner (1967), passim.

69 Peltzer (1908), 305 and 434, proposes the maximum: 1,5 million kg of brass. Also Pohl (1977), 230-2, 235.

70 Stahlschmidt (1970), 142, and Müller (2002), 77-85.

Schetz was perfectly informed. He knew that mining the Altenberg was not a massive operation and consequently did not require excessive investments. From the 1460s on, the authorities had imposed a maximum number of eighteen miners, and this restriction remained in effect until 1550, to avert overproduction and premature depletion of the best situated ore seams. Miners were exempt from military service. They also received tax benefits. Their average age of around 45 suggests that aside from physical strength, experience was considered very important. Oxidizing zinc ore required large amounts of charcoal, which the lessees could obtain from the nearby domain forest Hertogenwald, together with the timber they needed to support the shafts and galleries. One sole technician/manager was sufficient to oversee all the operations of the Altenberg mine and to supervise the workers.[71] Schetz therefore had ample reason to lease the Altenberg mine for twelve years from 1 April 1519. He did this together with Vleminck and Pruynen, who by then had been his partners for many years. For the first six years the firm had to pay Rg1300 and subsequently Rg1400 *per annum*, i.e. much less than in 1507, when the annual rent was Rg1600.[72] In the spring of 1519, the government of the Habsburg Netherlands was probably unable to negotiate a higher price, because the lease appeared to be risky or might in any case be perceived as such. There was great political uncertainty, not only in Flanders but throughout the Holy Roman Empire. The upcoming election of the new Emperor caused the greatest confusion and uncertainty, as the position of the Electors remained highly enigmatic for months. On 28 June 1519 Charles, Duke of Burgundy and King of Spain, was finally elected unanimously as King of the Romans, and Schetz had reason to congratulate himself on his decision to lease the Altenberg.

Five years later the partners ceded one sixth of the Altenberg lease to Jan de Cock and Gerhard Parijs, two brothers-in-law who had become business partners. De Cock was a merchant from 's-Hertogenbosch who had married Barbara van Kelmis, a sister of Ida/Isabella, while Parijs was married to Agnes van Kelmis and possessed operating systems for processing calamine and producing brass. Why Schetz & Co. ceded part of their lease remains unknown. They did not want for money. The relevant deed did not mention financial or other recompense. Schetz, Vleminck, and Pruynen stated that they were acting 'at the explicit request' of De Cock and Parijs, and that they were entering into the arrangement for 'reasons of encouragement'. Vaguer wording is impossible to imagine. One possible explanation is that the lease on the part of members of the Van Kelmis family, to whom the three partners were related, and who long remained closely involved in mining the Altenberg, was open to question. At any rate, it was explicitly stipulated that Schetz & Co. would remain fully responsible for operating the mine, and that nobody else was allowed to interfere in any aspect of extraction, processing, transport, or distribution. Once every year or two, accounts would be presented to De Cock and Parijs. The two firms agreed they would never lease or purchase calamine elsewhere, as long as Altenberg reserves remained, and that each violation would be liable to a penalty of two thousand Rg – a fine far in excess of the sum of

71 AGR, CC, Cartons 109 and 529; Van Uytven (2001), 199 and 201. In 1538, Erasmus Schetz paid Count Henry III of Nassau fl.525 for the right to fell 1/25 of a large forest in the County of Sankt-Vith every year for 25 years; this is also likely to have been intended for operations in the mine. SAA, SR 192, f° 338v°.

72 AGR, CC 637, f° 63, CC 2453, 1519-1520, f°15v°-16, CC 20786, 1522-1523, f° 18.

the annual lease.[73] While the motive underlying this agreement is unknown, no information is available about its termination either. Nor was it mentioned in any subsequent deeds.

In 1526, Schetz & Co. asserted that the richest ore seams were becoming depleted, and that they wished to fund a search for new veins at their own expense, if the Emperor would guarantee them a new lease and allow them to double the number of miners. The line of reasoning was not convincing and probably spurious. All the same, after extended negotiations the partners prevailed: the lease was extended on very favourable terms. Schetz and Pruynen – Vleminck had died by then – obtained a new twelve-year lease on the Altenberg from 1 April 1531. Despite the rising demand for calamine, they would pay 'only' Rg1300 for one third of the term and Rg1400 *per annum* afterwards. Although the number of miners was not increased, charcoal suppliers and transporters were exempt from military service, as were the miners, and they were allowed to let their horses or oxen graze in the Hertogenwald. Tolls were waived for all calamine transports in the Duchy.[74]

The Antwerp firm clearly received special preference. In early 1531, Nuremberg capitalists tried to take over the lease of the Altenberg. To this end, they contacted Count Hoyer VI von Mansfeld, who convinced Henry III of Nassau to put their case to the Emperor. They were informed that the lease would cost Rg1600 *per annum* for four years and Rg1700 for the next eight years, i.e. Rg300 more than what Schetz & Co. ended up paying, and thus it came to nothing.[75] On 1 April 1543 the contract was extended for another twelve-year term, without any public lease and on the same financial terms as before. Even though the value of the golden Rhenish guilders in Flemish groats had increased by then,[76] the rent remained very modest. This was also the case in 1550, when the contract was not only extended, but Schetz moreover received permission to employ six washers: men who extracted the calamine by washing piles of waste and were paid a percentage of the proceeds from the quantity they supplied.[77] Over the years several arguments were invoked to convince the authorities not to increase the Altenberg rent. Until 1543/4 the threat of the hostile Duchy of Gelre was invoked as a serious risk. Other arguments included the operating costs to be incurred, because the best-situated ore seams were becoming depleted, and that despite the prohibitions calamine was being imported illegally into the Habsburg Netherlands. Why did the central government accept these arguments without a murmur? The power Schetz wielded on the Antwerp money market was presumably decisive: as a banker he could be of great service to the Emperor, who was in perpetual financial difficulty. At any rate, continuous extension of the Altenberg lease at very attractive terms in effect entailed a calamine monopoly, rendering brass producers in all major centres between the Maas and the Rhine dependent on Schetz & Co.

Production figures are available only from a later period. Between 1561 and 1581, when the Altenberg was still operated by the Schetz firm, the average annual revenue was 2,015,750 pounds or *c.* 950,000 kilograms of calamine, of which 832,000 kilograms were

---

73 Text edited by Correns, Rau and Van de Cruys (2014), 167-70.

74 AGR, CC 294, f°43v°-51v°. See also Rössner (2012), 356-7, 500-1 (with references to the literature).

75 Möllenberg (1911), 77-9.

76 The Rhenish gold florin had a market exchange rate of c. 42 Flemish groats in 1490, c. 56 in 1500, c. 59 in 1521, and c. 60 in 1550.

77 AGR, CC 2458, 1550-1551, f°23v°-25, and PEA 139, f°201-202.

mined and roasted.[78] Production capacity was in fact much higher, because in this period the firm was coping with issues arising from excess ground water, and from 1578 military operations and an outbreak of the plague made working there all but impossible.[79] As no technical innovations were introduced in the sixteenth century, and the number of miners remained constant, an average annual production of one million kilograms of mined and roasted calamine may be regarded as a minimum in the period 1520-50, when the operations were continuous. The most substantial market was in Aachen. The amount of calamine delivered to this city is impossible to quantify precisely, as the number of smelting works is unknown before 1559. Assuming that between 1520 and 1550 about 75 were operating on average, which seems plausible, based on an annual output of *c.* 13,500 kilograms per oven, the combined brass production would have been *c.* 1,012,500 kilograms. Calculating the amount of calamine requires knowing both the copper content of the brass and the zinc content of the calamine. The first proportion, according to most authors, was about 70 percent in the sixteenth century. The second proportion is generally estimated at 25 percent, in which case manufacturing 100 kilograms of brass with a 70 percent copper content would have required 120 kilograms of calamine.[80] As calamine from Altenberg was the very best, calculations may be based on a zinc content of 40 percent, so that 65 kilograms, or slightly more than half, would have been sufficient.[81] Using this calamine was therefore economically advantageous. Based on this ratio the average annual output from each oven of 13,500 kilograms of brass would have required 8775 kilograms of calamine, yielding a total of 658,125 kilograms for 75 ovens. About two thirds of the annual Altenberg production, estimated at one million kilograms, would therefore have been intended for the Aachen brass industry between 1520 and 1550.[82]

The brass industry in Bouvignes, Dinant, and Namur– easily accessible via the Meuse – was a second, less substantial market. In the period 1519-22 the coppersmiths from these centres agreed with Schetz that they would purchase *c.* 280,000 kilograms of calamine every year. At the time Bouvignes had over 250 coppersmiths, who were allowed to work on only one anvil and were restricted to having only one journeyman and one apprentice at a time.[83] Whether this market along the banks of the Meuse expanded or contracted during the second quarter of the sixteenth century is impossible to ascertain because of lack of data. In the period 1561-81, at any rate, supplies to coppersmiths in Dinant, Namur, and Bouvignes (in this sequence here) amounted to 157,000 kilograms *per annum.*[84]

Nuremberg was a third market. In the late fifteenth and early sixteenth centuries, Peter Wolff exported calamine to Cologne, where his brother Karl had settled, but the mineral was most probably intended for Nuremberg. Van Richtergem, who leased the Altenberg from 1507, also supplied merchants in Cologne, especially the Struysses, who had close ties with large firms in Nuremberg.[85] In the period 1561-81 the average annual export to

78 I.e. without the calamine extracted by the six washers.
79 Van Uytven (2001), 197 and 201-2.
80 Pohl (1977), 230 (with references to the older literature), and Halleux (2015), 325.
81 Hachenberg (1992), 232. See also Thomas and Bourgarit (2018).
82 In the period 1561-81 *c.* 69 percent was destined for Aachen: Van Uytven (2001), 197.
83 Henri (1904), 832.
84 Calculation based on Van Uytven (2001), 197.
85 Irsigler (1979b), 120-1.

Table 1. Distribution of Altenberg-calamine around 1550

Proccessed in	Metric tons *per annum*	% of total
Aachen		
– by Schetz & Co.	*190*	*18.9*
– by other brass producers	*468*	*46.6*
Subtotal	658	65.5
Dinant, Bouvignes, and Namur	218	21.8
Nuremberg	128	12.7
Total	1004	100.0

Sources: estimates calculated from data provided by Peltzer (1908), 305-6, 434; Möllenberg (1911), 77-9; Pohl (1977), 230-2, 235; Van Uytven (2001), 197.

Nuremberg, where the manufacture of scientific and musical instruments thrived, was 128,000 kilograms, i.e. less than a fifth of what was sent to Aachen. Nuremberg obtained a supply from elsewhere too, but the discrepancy was so vast that the dominance of Aachen in brass manufacture was undisputed.[86]

Mining the Altenberg was highly profitable. In the period 1561-81, when the economic circumstances were less favourable than in the first half of the sixteenth century, calamine sales yielded a net profit of 47 to 55 percent.[87] That trade in calamine was intrinsically profitable demonstrates how crucial the monopoly position of the Schetzes was. This was indeed the outcome of the leases: they kept getting their monopoly extended, consistently on very favourable terms. They succeeded only because Erasmus and later on his eldest son Gaspar established and maintained close ties with the centre of political power by providing financial services to Charles V and Philip II, respectively.

During the second quarter of the century calamine had figured as part of an integrated industrial and commercial system for Erasmus Schetz and his partners. At the time they used their monopoly to gain control of the brassware producers in Aachen. They were not the only wholesalers to manufacture export items. From the second half of the fifteenth century onwards, merchant capitalists in Europe engaged increasingly in different kinds of industrial production with a view to maximizing profits. They devised putting-out networks in rural regions for weaving woollens, linens, and fustians, and they invested ever more heavily in mining and the metal industry, using various types of organization.[88] Some set up companies to make finished products directly for the market. Cosimo de' Medici owned two wool shops and one silk shop in Florence, all large enterprises. The firm Gruber-Podmer-Stromer from Nuremberg owned several mills for metalworking.[89] There are other examples, but centralized production financed by merchant capital remained rather exceptional in the fifteenth and sixteenth centuries. Putting-out or subcontracting were generally preferred in order to tie up as little capital as possible. The objective was

86 Peltzer (1908), 371; Stahlschmidt (1970), 129.
87 Calculated from Van Uytven (2001), 199 and 201.
88 Holbach (1994).
89 De Roover (1963); Von Stromer (1963).

essentially to coordinate industrial processes and to control the distribution of manufactures, which might entail organizational innovation and/or product innovation. The tendency to relate production to circulation was an important development, however, since even if labour was not subordinated to capital directly, industrial investments by merchant bankers were conducive to the development of capitalist relations of production.

Three factors combined afforded Schetz the opportunity to maximize profits as a 'merchant-industrialist': his calamine monopoly, his thriving trade with Portugal, and the rising demand for brassware in West Africa. He was unable to compete with the large scope of trading companies in Augsburg and Nuremberg that combined production of silver and copper and supplemented their mining activity with trade in Asian spices, but by focusing on brass goods intended for the West-African market he could create and expand an extremely lucrative niche, integrating calamine mining, trade in *Garkupfer*, and brass manufacture.

From the 1470s, when they were exploring the Gulf of Guinea, the Portuguese used copper and copper alloys as payment currency in trade with West Africa, first mainly unprocessed copper and copper goods, but from the 1500s on, mostly brass goods. Ore seams in this part of Africa were relatively small, and the supply of copper from the North by Arab traders along the trans-Sahara caravan routes was by definition limited.[90] Several areas had an established tradition of working copper. In the Yoruba city Ife (in what is now southwestern Nigeria) naturalist brass busts had been made since the early fourteenth century. The sophisticated lost-wax casting technique was probably introduced from there to Benin, which had become a large military and commercial power by the time the Portuguese arrived. Another Yoruba Kingdom renowned for brass casting was Ijebu, situated on the coast. The title of the ruler conveyed the close symbolic link between copper and power: Olurin, meaning 'Owner-of-the-Metal'. The Portuguese discoverer Duarte Pacheco Pereira, who travelled to the area in the 1490s, described the thriving trade based on exchanging manillas or bracelets for slaves; the rate at the time was twelve to fifteen brass manillas for a slave.[91]

The importance of copper or brass in West Africa was comparable to that of gold in Europe; it was a rare luxury commodity and was all the more valuable, because it was credited with magic powers. The Portuguese quickly understood that the market for 'red gold' was enormous. All along the coast, they could use manillas and alternatively basins and other utensils as currency. The Crown long attempted to control trade in both manillas and in malagueta pepper. Such control proceeded via the *Casa da Guine*, following the construction of Fort São Jorge da Mina, St. George of the Mine, on the Gold Coast (presently Ghana) in 1482, also called *Casa da Mina* or simply Elmina. In addition, Fort Arguim on an island near Cape Blanco served as a checkpoint. After a few decades commercial activity was concentrated in three places: the Gold Coast (with Elmina as its hub), the kingdom of Benin, and the island São Tomé in the Gulf of Guinea. The monopoly of the Portuguese monarchy was not the most efficient strategy from an economic perspective.[92]

---

90 Blanchard (2005), 1150-3.

91 Ezra (1992), 8, 11, 23, 299; Duchâteau (1994), 35-40. For Pereira's account, see Hodgkin (1960), 95-7.

92 Dias (1964) qualified the policy of the Crown in connection with its African ventures as a typical manifestation of *capitalismo monárquico português* ('Portuguese royal capitalism').

Direct control was therefore gradually abandoned, and trading rights were leased to *contratadores* in various coastal areas, or exclusive, renewable contracts were signed with private entrepreneurs, entitling them to export or import specific merchandise.[93]

The Europeans soon found that African demand for metal goods was highly complex: not all types, forms, and sizes were accepted everywhere, the selection had to very broad, and standards were very high. Manillas were always open and horse-shoe shaped with flared ends, but there were many varieties.[94] They were assessed according to thickness, diameter, flare at the tips, weight, shape, and, last but not least, their colour and the sound they made when tapped. Preferences varied widely depending on the region and possibly over time as well. Thorough knowledge of metalworking led to fastidious tastes and was deemed all the more important, because the objects imported by Europeans had to be suitable for reuse. Bracelets, for example, were worn by women as jewellery, as tokens of wealth, and were widely used as monies of account, but they were often also melted and recast into objects of local designs.

Imports of copper and brass goods in São Jorge da Mina on the Gold Coast during the first half of the sixteenth century are estimated to have averaged 45 metric tons *per annum*. Nothing is known about the size of the Portuguese transports to Arguim, Senegambia, Upper Guinea, Benin, and São Tomé. Nor are data available on the quantities brought in by merchants attempting to circumvent the Crown's monopoly. The Portuguese claimed the exclusive right to trade on the coast of Africa, a right that was acknowledged by the Pope in 1455 and ratified by agreements with Spain, but the monopoly was not airtight. Not only did ships from other countries or equipped by unlicensed merchants sometimes arrive in the Gulf of Guinea, but Portuguese based in São Tomé or the Cape Verde Islands are known to have traded illegally. In the early sixteenth century officers of the Crown deplored the success of these *lançados*.[95] Even assuming that the impact of interlopers was minimal in this period, total imports must have been considerable. By around 1530, the trade was highly profitable. Manillas that cost 10 réis apiece in Antwerp sold for ten to twelve times their value in gold in Elmina, and the rate for basins was also 10:1 to 12:1. Gigantic quantities of metal goods were exported to Africa. Between 10 June 1529 and 31 August 1531, i.e. within less than 27 months, over 280,000 manillas and over 9,000 basins were brought to Elmina alone.[96]

The phenomenal demand in West Africa led to a surge in European trade in brass goods, which were exported first from Bruges and thereafter from Antwerp to Portugal. Accurate figures are available only for 1498-1505, when Tomé Lopes, the commercial agent for the Portuguese Crown, shipped the following amounts from Antwerp to Lisbon: 300,655 kilograms of crude copper, 957,586 manillas, and 66,488 basins,[97] i.e. an average of *c.* 37,600 kilograms of unprocessed copper, *c.* 120,000 manillas, and *c.* 8300 basins *per*

93 Herbert (1984), 123-5; Elbl (2007), 95-6, 102, 106-8.

94 For descriptions and photos of different types of manillas, see Denk (2017).

95 Thornton (1992), 58-61, and Thornton (2009), 107, who refers to the Ph.D. dissertation of Ivana Elbl, 'Portuguese Trade with West Africa, 1440-1520' (University of Toronto, 1986). See also Ebert (2008), 53-4, 64-5.

96 Vogt (1973) and (1975), 642; Herbert (1984), 126 and 131; Ballong-Wen-Mewuda (1993), 372. The Portuguese *cruzado* of 360 *réis* was nearly the equivalent of the Spanish ducat, so that 10 réis = c. 2.2 Flemish groats.

97 Dias (1964), II, 290-1.

annum. Calculating the total weight would be pointless, as the manillas and basins could be made of either pure copper or brass; generally, however, the weight of the different types of basins varied from 1.5 kilograms (*bacias de mijar*, urinals) to 1.75 kilograms (*bacias de barbeiro*, shaving basins). The designations the Portuguese and other Europeans gave to basins, bowls, and similar brass goods obviously reveal nothing about how these receptacles were ultimately used in West Africa. The standard brass manilla sold by the Portuguese at Elmina in 1529-31 was said by one source to have weighed about 600 grams,[98] but ten years later the average seems to have ranged from 250 to 300 grams.[99] At any rate, the manillas and basins combined weighed over twice as much as the unprocessed copper.

Trade in brass goods offered huge profit opportunities. If the transactions by Nuremberg merchant-entrepreneurs Hans Walther, Wolfgang Perger, and Nicolaus Finck are representative, no single branch in the precious metals trade was more profitable in the first quarter of the sixteenth century: in 1512-13 their firm in Antwerp generated a 68 percent profit on the sale of brass goods, compared with only 5 to 8 percent on the trade in copper and silver.[100] In the 1520s, Schetz & Co. understood that to maximize profits, in addition to trading in calamine, they would need to engage in brass production as well. This required two steps on their part. First, they had to supply the brass producers in Aachen not only with calamine but also with the best copper, so that they controlled the entire commodity chain. To trump potentially competing copper suppliers, they needed their raw material to be of very high quality: *Garkupfer*, i.e. tough-pitch copper,[101] which was especially suitable for manufacturing brass. Second, they had to be able to supply the Portuguese Crown with brass goods continuously for trade with and in West Africa. To guarantee a sufficient and regular supply in Lisbon, they needed to control a large share of the production in Aachen.

As they required copper of high quality, they needed to be in Mansfeld Land, where mining and metal processing were intensive.[102]From the second decade of the sixteenth century on, economic relations there were changing dramatically. By the 1520s merchant capitalists dominated the industry.[103] The powerful Count Albrecht IV von Mansfeld facilitated and even actively promoted this course of events. In 1524 he teamed up with merchant banker Jakob Welser of Nuremberg and Leipzig banker Heinrich Scherl to found the Leutenberg *Saiger-Handelsgesellschaft* to produce *Garkupfer* at their own smelting works. They quickly became market leaders in Thuringia.[104] For Schetz & Co. the progressive concentration of production in the Mansfeld Land offered an opportunity to obtain their supplies from one single company. On 29 March 1526 they signed a contract with Ewald Knauss, who represented the Leutenberg *Saiger-Handelsgesellschaft*. This firm produced over 9000 *Zentner* or *c*. 450,000 kilograms of *Garkupfer* each year in the period 1526-34.[105]

---

98 Vogt (1973), 94.
99 Based on Strieder (1930), 351-2, 451-4.
100 Kellenbenz (1960), 315.
101 Refined and re-melted copper containing about 0.02 to 0.05 percent oxygen.
102 There are indications that Schetz & Co. may have tried to extract copper at the Wenau monastery in the area of Düren, about 25 kilometres from Aachen, but the benefits appear to have been minimal: Voigt (1961), 508; Bruckner (1967), 61.
103 On changing economic relations in the Mansfeld area, see Roper (2016), 24-8.
104 Strieder (1925).
105 The share of this Company in the total copper production in Thuringia was around 30 percent. Möllenberg (1911), 25-7; Westermann (1971b), 12-13.

In the contract with Schetz & Co. the Leutenberg Company agreed to supply *c.* 150,000 kilograms of copper yearly in Frankfurt for three years, at a global value of Rg6400. From Frankfurt Schetz & Co. were to transport the copper at their cost. Each year in Leipzig they had to deliver 100,000 kilograms of lead valued at Rg1600 and pay Rg4800 in cash.[106] The requirement that lead was to be supplied for one quarter of the total amount was very important for the Leutenberg Company: its inclusion in one of the stages of the *Saigerprozess* enabled extraction of silver from argentiferous copper, by smelting the copper with large amounts of lead or lead ore. Political conflicts in the free Imperial City of Goslar, the main mining centre in Central Europe, had driven the price of lead so high since 1527 that the Leutenberg Company preferred to obtain it from elsewhere in Europe. As large amounts of English lead were exported to Antwerp, Schetz & Co. may be assumed to have obtained it at attractive prices there.[107]

In the Central European mining industry, lead came to be considered so important that in England in the 1540s Schetz made an offer for 'the King's lead', i.e. the metal that was stripped from dissolved monasteries and of which there was an enormous surplus. When as a result of the critical war against France, Henry VIII had to take out new loans, Stephen Vaughan, his financial agent in Antwerp, suggested that large amounts of the metal might be brought to this city, as additional collateral in future transactions. However, few firms were willing to pay cash at the time. The best offer came from Schetz: he agreed to purchase 3000 fothers – *c.* 2755 metric tons – of lead *per annum* at £4 sterling per fother. That offer would most probably have been accepted, had Schetz not demanded in addition that the king appoint him permanent English factor for all lead sales on the continent. This was unacceptable to the Privy Council, as it would basically have granted the firm a monopoly on all future exports.[108]

How Schetz & Co. organized the purchase and distribution of *Garkupfer* in the 1530s and 40s is impossible to trace, but the activity indisputably remained essential to their economic operations. To this end, they maintained a permanent trading post in Leipzig, which because of its strategic location was crucial in the metal trade.[109] From the late fifteenth century on, an increasing share of copper produced in Central Europe was distributed from this city, which consequently superseded Erfurt as an economic centre. According to Christoff Fürer, a well-informed merchant entrepreneur from Nuremberg, the brass industry in Aachen required *c.* 700,000 kilograms of *Garkupfer per annum* in the 1530s,[110] and Schetz & Co. needed 200,000 kilograms for their own wire production, by which he meant that the Antwerp firm manufactured brass goods in Aachen on its own or had them produced.[111] While several Nuremberg firms were active in the copper trade, the available evidence demonstrates that Schetz & Co. were the largest importers of

---

106 *Urkundenbuch* (1915), 86-8 (No. 51).

107 De Smedt (1954), 368-9. Schetz & Co. imported large amounts of English lead: SAA, CERT 6, f°157v°.

108 Richardson (1954), 36-7, 42-3.

109 On the factors in Leipzig, see Fischer (1929), 15, 32, 374-5, 389; Unger (1963), 29; Kellenbenz (1970a), 111; Dietrich (1991), 175-8.

110 This estimate seems realistic, as 75 smelting works, each averaging 13,500 kilograms of brass *per annum*, containing 70 percent copper, would yield this quantity. Möllenberg (1911), 77-9.

111 On Fürer's strategies and projects, see Möllenberg (1911), 77-9; Strieder (1914), 159, 243-4; Westermann (1971a), 115-16.

Garkupfer in Aachen.[112] The continuous arrival of large amounts of *Garkupfer* and calamine necessitated permanent storage facilities. By 1526 the firm had already purchased two houses, soon combining them in one large unit, known as the *Kelmishaus*, later renamed *Das Grosse Haus von Aachen* (the Large House of Aachen). This impressive complex comprised a residential section, an office area, and storage facilities. Over the years that followed three more *Kelmishäuser* were purchased to use as additional warehouses.[113] In the *Grosses Haus* the partners installed as their factor Sebastiaan Vleminck, a nephew of Jan Vleminck the Elder and guardian of his young son; once Jan Vleminck the Younger came of age, he became the agent of Schetz & Co. in Aachen from 1540 to 1560.[114]

How Schetz & Co. organized processing 200,000 kilograms of *Garkupfer per annum* into *c.* 288,500 kilograms of brass, is impossible to ascertain. They may have had their own smelting works, operated by *Kupfermeister* with little or no capital, but they might also have signed contracts with independent producers or have used the putting-out system, a type of subcontracting where producers received raw materials in exchange for delivering fixed quantities of goods at set times for agreed prices. While they were not the only merchant entrepreneurs in Aachen who combined trade with manufacturing, nobody was more in control of local industry.[115] Some *Kupfermeister* also exported their products to Antwerp, but these were minor operators on a market dominated by Schetz & Co., not only quantitatively but also qualitatively. The superior quality of the brass goods that Schetz & Co. supplied was the basic reason why the firm remained so prominent in Portuguese-African trade for so many years. The extraordinary interest in quality among African buyers suited Schetz & Co. perfectly, as their manillas were consistently regarded as the very finest, especially because of their special reddish hue. Schetz manillas, known as the 'Schetz', became a brand name. They served as the standard of perfection, against which all other brass goods were measured.[116]

For several decades Schetz & Co. supplied the Portuguese monarchy with a large share – very probably most – of the manillas intended for West Africa. As far as can be determined, none of the partners ever set foot in Africa, and organizing transport between Lisbon and Elmina was left to representatives of the Crown. The data indicate that trade began to decline in the 1540s, because the price ratios in West Africa became less favourable for the Europeans. The Antwerp firm soon understood this and gradually stopped manufacturing brassware. Entrepreneurs in Aachen who aimed to sell their manufactures on their own now had free reign. In 1541 *Kupfermeister* Edmund Duppengiesser, who consistently appeared as a merchant, signed a contract with the Spanish merchant Diego de Villegas to supply 30,450 manillas with a total weight of *c.* 7500 kilograms; Villegas explicitly stipulated that the bracelets 'should be the same type and quality as the ones Erasmus Schetz had sold him thus far'.[117] In 1543-45 exports by Schetz & Co. to the Iberian Peninsula accounted

112 Schetz & Co. used the route along the Main river to Frankfurt and proceeded from there along the Rhine to Cologne: AGR, PEA 1666/1/A, f° 10.

113 Presently the site of the *Internationales Zeitungsmuseum*, International Newspaper Museum.

114 Correns, Rau and Van de Cruys (2014), 20-1, 42-3.

115 In 1531 they ordered brass weights at a total cost of Rg31 from the renowned bronze caster Stephan Godl: Pölnitz (1958), 557 n. 45.

116 Herbert (1984), 131.

117 Strieder (1930), 91, 277, 351-2; Kellenbenz (1970), 105. On manillas, see Denk (2017).

for only 4.6 percent of the total value of all their shipments, which most probably gives a distorted impression of their trade but nonetheless indicates the declining importance of their brassware exports. Clearly, the Antwerp firm would not accept a lower price for its brass goods. The Fuggers did agree to this, because they had vast stocks of copper and copperware, and because their trade with the Iberian Peninsula was intensifying around this time. The Portuguese contract with Schetz lapsed at the end of 1547 and was not extended. On 20 January 1548 João Rebello, representative of the Portuguese Crown in Antwerp, signed a contract with Christoph Wolf,[118] a factor for the Fugger firm, to supply massive quantities of copper and brass goods. Over the next three years the firm supplied a total of *c.* 435 metric tons of brass manillas,[119] of which 90 percent was intended for Elmina and 10 percent for the remaining trade with Guinea, which presumably meant Benin. In addition, 24,000 brass 'urinals', 10,500 brass pots with handles, 4500 barbers' basins, and 1800 large-rimmed bowls were to be supplied. The agreement stipulated explicitly that all brass goods had to be 'the same size, type, and perfection as had always been customary in this trade',[120] referring to the quality guaranteed by the Schetz firm. Shortly after the middle of the century, exports of copper and brass goods to the Gold Coast declined considerably, and the Fuggers discontinued their trade with West Africa,[121] supporting the idea that Schetz had accurately anticipated the reduced profits in 1547.

The calamine monopoly and everything related to trading copper and producing brass was a major windfall for Schetz. Net profits on calamine sales in the period 1519-50 cannot be quantified but are certain to have been substantial. The fee for leasing the Altenberg was never raised, mining continued without interruptions, operating expenses were relatively modest, and sales were guaranteed. Even during the severe economic slump in the period 1561-81, net profits were still about 50 percent. By supplying *Garkupfer* as well during the second quarter of the sixteenth century, Schetz & Co. gained solid control over the manufacture of brass goods in Aachen, the most important European centre of the industry. Smelted with Altenberg calamine, the Mansfeld *Garkupfer* yielded an ideal alloy. Deciding to manufacture manillas and other brass goods intended for export independently or to subcontract their manufacture was a master strategy. All information indicates that the firm sold about 288,500 kilograms of brass *per annum*, i.e. more than one quarter of the total produced in Aachen. No other brass manufacturer in Europe could hold a candle to Schetz & Co. In the period 1519-39 the Fuggers exported *c.* 530,000 kilograms of Hungarian copper via Gdansk and Stettin to Antwerp *per annum*,[122] but they were selling a commodity intended for India, whereas the Antwerp firm supplied a finished product intended for West Africa. This made the Portuguese connection especially attractive to Schetz & Co., because it connected brass goods exports with imports of both African pepper and Madeira sugar, with Lisbon once again serving as transit port.

---

118 Not a member of the Wolff family that was related by marriage to Claes van Richtergem.

119 Based on the 'new' Portuguese weight (1 arratel = 16 ounces) used in the copper trade: Westermann and Denzel (2011), 99-100.

120 Strieder (1938). See also Pölnitz (1967), 561-3, and Magalhães-Godinho (1969), 373-4.

121 Pölnitz (1971), 450-2; Herbert (1984), 130.

122 Calculated from Van der Wee (1963), I, 523.

1.3 Pepper and Sugar

From the start of his career, Erasmus Schetz positioned himself at the centre of the rising global economy and participated fully in early modern world trade. His earliest known transactions (in 1501) concerned mainly malagueta pepper from West Africa, and after 1510 he focused increasingly on purchasing Indian pepper from the Malabar Coast. His close ties with the Portuguese King were essential in this context, but he also benefited from the declining interest of Jakob Fugger in the spice trade,[123] thereby avoiding having to compete in Antwerp with the most important merchant banker in Europe. The scarce available figures demonstrate that he was very active in the spice trade. In Lisbon in 1522 Schetz & Co. purchased almost 31 metric tons of pepper on their own behalf, as much as the Imhof firm and 50 percent more than the Welser firm. That year the French merchant Jehan Bécud alias João Bicudo apparently owed the *Casa da India* a large sum of money for spices purchased on behalf of the Antwerp firm.[124] Schetz & Co. also sold loads of fruit in Antwerp supplied by other firms from Portugal. In 1525, for example, the representative of the Welsers in Lisbon chartered a ship loaded in the Algarve with figs, which were ultimately sold in Antwerp by Schetz & Co.[125] In this period, however, the partners mainly sold spices in bulk, as revealed in a transaction from 1525: in February that year they supplied Francisco de Olivera with a batch of cloves costing over £844 Fl.gr.[126] The available evidence suggests that he negotiated directly with the Portuguese Crown or its representatives with regard to these imports.

Schetz consistently gave special consideration to the Lisbon connection. Following the death of King Manuel I in 1521, he made every effort to forge equally close ties with his son João III. In his letter dated 17 March 1526 he asked Desiderius Erasmus why he had not yet dedicated a work to the King of Portugal, whom he qualified as 'an outstanding Christian prince and a man of exceptional benevolence and kindness, most generous towards those who serve him, and particularly generous to those who are able, by their words and writings, to make known the blessings of the gospel'. During the months that followed, he continued to pressure the humanist. On 18 March: 'I shall be happy if only you will give me hope that you will dedicate something to the King of Portugal'. On 8 September: 'Please, don't forget to write to Portugal'. Finally, on 4 February 1527, the mission was accomplished: 'I am glad you have decided to dedicate one of your works to the King of Portugal [...] for his royal highness deserves great praise'.[127] This correspondence demonstrates once again how deeply Schetz cared about being on good terms with the highest authorities in Portugal. Shared humanist contacts and interests were conducive to succesful relations with João Brandão, the factor of the *Casa da India* in Antwerp from 1499 to 1514 and from 1520 to 1525.[128] Brandão was a scion of an affluent Portuguese family and was deeply interested

---

123 Häberlein (2006), 52-3; Pohle (2000), 109.

124 Stols (1973), 21; Kellenbenz (1974) and (1990), I, 60. Bécud also traded large quantities of sugar around this time: Bréard and Barrey (1906), 271-2.

125 Geffcken and Häberlein (2014), 111 and 268. On the production of figs in late medieval Portugal and exports to Flanders, see Miranda (2015).

126 Strieder (1930), 31.

127 Erasmus, Ep. 1681, 1682, 1750, and 1783. Quotations in *Correspondence* (2003), 102-3, 106, 357, and 450.

128 See Braancamp Freire (1920), 93-100.

in both humanism and the plastic arts. In 1521 he invited Albrecht Dürer thirteen times to banquets and showered the artist with gifts. In addition to a great many engravings, he was rewarded with a magnificent signed portrait of his 20-year old black maidservant/ slave Katharina.[129] In 1529, two years after Brandão died, Schetz mentioned in a letter to Erasmus that this friend had frequently been of great service to him in Portugal.[130]

The spice trade required diplomacy, both in Portugal and in the Habsburg Netherlands. In 1527 Erasmus of Rotterdam learned the hard way how dangerous it was to write anything about monopolies when addressing the King of Portugal. In 1527, at the explicit request of his friend Schetz, he dedicated *Chrysostomi Lucubrationes* (a collection of Latin translations of works by St John Chrysostom), to João III. In the preface he praised first Manuel I, the father of the current King, because this 'wise man' had merely endeavoured to proclaim the faith overseas and had taken all measures possible to avert any suspicion of self-interest. The following two sentences, however, were less innocuous: 'I only wish that this remarkable record of generosity were not being spoilt by the monopolies held by certain people. Admittedly, it is easier now to import things, but people tell me that thanks to these monopolies, prices, far from falling, have actually increased, and some items, sugar, for example, have not only gone up in price but now reach us in a more adulterated state'. Erasmus was most likely writing 'certain people' to refer to large trading houses, but his words could be interpreted as a general condemnation of monopolies, which reflected badly on the Portuguese Crown. His dedication was indeed understood in this manner. In 1530 a well-informed visitor told him that his statement had led Portuguese courtiers to withhold the complimentary copy for fear that the King would take offence at the condemnation of monopolies.[131]

A few years later the spice monopoly of the Portuguese Crown was subject to criticism in Antwerp. This was caused by the arrival of Portuguese merchants who were suspected by the central government of being *marranos* (i.e. of continuing to observe Jewish religious customs). In 1532, Charles V ordered some high-ranking officials to arrest all New Christians in Antwerp and seize their goods. Diego Mendes, an extremely wealthy merchant, who figured prominently in the international spice trade, was placed under house arrest, which gave rise to vehement protests, not only on the part of the city council but also and mainly by King João III of Portugal, who wrote the Emperor to insist that the matter be addressed rapidly and according to 'the principles of justice and equity', adding that most of the goods confiscated belonged to him. Mendes went free. In 1534 António Fernandes, another New Christian, was arrested, officially because he did not have a residence permit but in fact because small and medium-sized Antwerp firms accused him and Diego Mendes, as well as twenty other New Christians, of monopolist practices in the spice trade. The case was a very sensitive one, because Gian Carlo Affaitadi and the Florentine Luca Giraldi were also labelled as monopolists in the charge, and they were both powerful merchant bankers who rendered great service to the highest authorities. Giraldi was one of the closest

129 Dürer (1978), esp. 13-14, 42.

130 Erasmus, Ep. 2243. Quotation in French: *Correspondance* (1979), VIII, 400, my translation.

131 Erasmus, Ep. 1800 and 2370: *Correspondence* (2003), 504, 506-7 (quotation), and (2016), 70-1. See also Bataillon (1974), 70-5.

partners and largest creditors of the Portuguese King,[132] while Affaitadi was crucial in international trade in Antwerp and acted as a creditor to the Emperor. Mary of Hungary instructed the members of the Privy Council and the Great Council of Mechelen (the highest court in the Habsburg Netherlands) to launch an investigation. The scholars of law ultimately concluded that while the Church decried the monopolies as *turpe lucrum* (dishonest gain), this practice was in fact standard in the Netherlands and in many other countries. If Mary of Hungary intervened, many foreign merchants would inevitably leave, which would have very serious consequences for the public interest and for the ruler. Stricter legislation might be considered, but that needed to be examined in depth by scholars of law. Fernandes was released, and no other individual involved in the spice trade was prosecuted. Meanwhile, Schetz had been instructed to estimate the value of the goods seized from the marrano Gabriel de Negro, who had gone into hiding. He had already vouched for Mendes and was now protecting de Negro as well: he reported that as the liabilities considerably exceeded the assets, the Emperor would suffer a loss, if he appropriated the estate. Gabriel de Nero was spared.[133]

In the 1530s and 40s Schetz retained his lead in the pepper trade in Antwerp. The one percent tax (Hundredth Penny) on all exports from the Low Countries, both by land and by sea, reveals that in 1544-45 he was a veritable pepper magnate: he was responsible for fully 13 percent of total pepper exports.[134] The vast majority was exported to the German areas, with Leipzig as the main destination. In the meantime, he had also entered the sugar trade, not on the Canary Islands, which belonged to Spain, and where other merchants from the Low Countries were active, but on Madeira, which was ruled by the Portuguese Crown. This trade led Schetz & Co. first to purchase a sugar refinery in Antwerp and then to invest in a sugar came plantation and the requisite technical facilities in Brazil. As in the metal trade, circulation was thus related to production. Colonial trade was always immensely important for Schetz & Co. In 1552-53, shortly after the founder's death, the firm, with imports totalling *c.* £64,700 Fl.gr., ranked seventh among the 489 merchants importing goods from the Iberian Peninsula and its colonies into the Low Countries.[135].

Sugar cane and all confectionery products made from it were exclusive products for which demand increased in the sixteenth century. The correspondence of Desiderius Erasmus reveals how popular they were, as the great humanist always expressed delight

132 See Marcocci (2014), 104-6.

133 Goris (1925), 562-70; Van Answaarden (1991), 259-68; Leone Leoni (2005), 3, 18-24; Servantie (2006). In December 1540, the entire consignment of the Portuguese spice fleet (about 35,000 quintals or *c.* 1800 metric tons of pepper and 20,000 quintals or *c.* 1030 metric tons of ginger) was sold to Gian Carlo Affaitadi, Diego Mendes and Beneto de Negro. See Edler-De Roover (1938), 214-15.

134 Jeroen Puttevils' database 'Hundredth Penny Tax on Export', based on AGR, CC 23357-23364. See Puttevils (2015b).

135 The eldest son, Gaspar Schetz, was assessed separately for an import value in excess of £6,000 Fl.gr. The largest importer was the Spanish merchant Antonio del Rio (£364,000 Fl.gr.), followed by Marcos Nuñez (*c.* £244,000 Fl.gr.), Gian Battista Affaitadi (£229,000 Fl.gr.), the Portuguese Antonio Palos and Andres Manricques (£160,000 and £154,000 Fl.gr.), and the Genoan merchant banker Giovanni Battista Spinola (£92,000 Fl.gr.). In the mid-sixteenth century Schetz & Co. while not the largest operators trading with the Iberian Peninsula, were still major importers; the Spanish merchant Diego Ortega de Carion, ranked eighth, imported 'only' £33,000 Fl.gr. in value and was followed by six merchants whose imports amounted to £20,000 to £30,000 Fl.gr. apiece; 23 others ranked in a still lower category at £10,000 to £20,000 Fl.gr. each, and they in turn were followed by hundreds of far smaller merchants. Bril (1962), 128-44.

whenever he received sugar, conserves, or a jar of candied fruit from some benefactor. In 1534, he asked his banker friend Schetz to send a few cones of good sugar from Antwerp to Freiburg, as such products were unavailable there.[136] In the mid-sixteenth century sugar remained a luxury commodity, even though the traditional Christian-held production regions in Cyprus, Crete, and Sicily had been complemented since the 1450s by plantations on islands in the Atlantic, first on Madeira and Porto Santo, settled by Portugal, and later successfully on the Canary Islands (Castile) and São Tomé (Portugal) as well. Massive imports from Portugal led market prices to fall substantially in Antwerp.[137] Nonetheless, for the vast majority of the European population sugar remained an unaffordable delicacy. Affluent families revealed their social prestige not only by their choice of sugar – Madeira was the quality standard – and the amount they served but also and especially by new, sophisticated preparations introduced via Iberian circles. The popularity of preserves – a veritable hype – led demand for this 'white gold' to surge.[138]

The magnificent celebration that Charles V arranged for his sister Eleonor, Queen of France, and her entourage on Sunday 26 October 1543 in Brussels demonstrates that confectionaries were considered very special, as purchasing the different types of *succades* accounted for the bulk of expenditure.[139] The same held true for the renowned Binche celebrations in August 1549, when Mary of Hungary hosted her brother Charles V, his son Prince Phillip, her sister Eleonor, and the aristocratic elite for nine days at magnificent banquets in her Renaissance castle in the County of Hainault. On the last evening of their stay on 30 to 31 August, she treated her distinguished guests to a wondrous 'dessert gala' in the *Cámara encantada* (the 'enchanted chamber'). Three times from above, an ingenious mechanism submitted the richly decked tables to thunder, lightning, and a hail of *comfits*. The tables featured all kinds of candied and crystallized fruits, delicious conserves, and life-size game, birds, and fish, all made of the finest sugar.[140]

Mediterranean sugar cane exports, long dominated by Venice, were no match for the growing production on the islands in the Atlantic, especially on Madeira, where for many decades massive amounts of excellent sugar cane were cultivated by slave labour. There were also many wage workers on Madeira and the other islands, and slaves toiled not only on plantations but were involved in other economic activities as well. Still, sugar and slavery evolved in parallel.[141] Madeira sugar exports were controlled largely by foreign firms. When King Manuel I limited the planters on Madeira to producing 120,000 *arrobas* or *c.* 1542 metric tons to stabilize prices in 1498, he also set sugar quotas for the different parts of Europe: 33 percent could be exported to Flanders, 30 percent to Italy, 12.5 percent to France, the same share to the Levant, and the remaining 12 percent in part to the Iberian peninsula and in part to England. That system remained in effect until 1508, after which free trade was restored. Henceforth, merchants could purchase all the sugar they wanted and export it to countries of their choice. Data from ships that sailed to European ports

136 Erasmus, Ep. 2511, 2593, 2704, 2955.
137 *Dokumenten* (1959), 330-2; Scholliers (1960), 39-40, 89; Van der Wee (1963), I, 318-20.
138 Stols (2004), 237-45.
139 ADN, B 2442, f° 609.
140 Calvete de Estrella (1552), 350-2, and (1883), III, 151-3. See also Glotz (1991), 143 n. 127.
141 Vieira (1996) and Moore (2010), 10-12.

loaded with Madeira sugar between 1490 and 1550 reveal that Flanders accounted for a substantial share: 39 percent of the total went to Bruges and (increasingly) Antwerp and was redistributed from there.[142]

The Portuguese wished to control the plantations on Madeira but had to work with foreign businessmen, because the sugar cane processing equipment required huge investments. Florentine and Genoese merchant financiers were very active in this domain. Some settled on the island and over time were integrated into local society.[143] Italian trading companies – including the Affaitadi – were prominent in sugar cane exports, but they did not dominate the European market. French, German, and Flemish merchants participated in the trade from the last quarter of the fifteenth century. Bruges was the most important import port in the Low Countries for a few decades.[144] By 1500 Antwerp became the commercial hub, however, structurally changing Flemish-Portuguese trade.

Van Richtergem and Schetz derived the greatest benefit from the new commercial constellation. Their insights enabled them to combine calamine mining with brass manufacture, export metal goods produced in Aachen and intended for West Africa to Lisbon (importing malagueta pepper and Madeira sugar from there), and subsequently re-export these to Central Europe. Van Richtergem founded this commercial-industrial network, but Schetz expanded and perfected the capitalist commodity chain. With support of the Portuguese King, he eventually managed to replace malagueta pepper with Asian spices. In West Africa, and more specifically in Elmina, Schetz manilas were henceforth used as currency for purchasing slaves. After his father-in-law died, Schetz & Co. traded Madeira sugar via two agents in Portugal: Diego de Hano and a certain Jorge; both had stayed in Funchal and had close ties with important economic operators in Lisbon.[145] After 1519, these men no longer served as representatives of Schetz, Vleminck, and Pruynen. Had the association failed to yield the envisaged results? Or were other factors at play? At any rate, Schetz & Co. intended to continue in the sugar trade, but they had no intention of representing their own business interests in Madeira and Portugal. In the early 1520s they teamed up with the substantial Bruges merchant Willem de Boodt, who knew Flemish merchants on Madeira. They installed Willem Van Lare from Bruges as their factor in Lisbon in 1522. He was paid £15 Fl.gr. *per annum*, i.e. hardly more than what a skilled worker earned, but was provided with a home, a small holiday cottage, a servant, and a horse. He was assisted by the Portuguese merchant Francisco Lobo, who initially handled customs formalities for exports and imports alike and addressed pending matters in Lisbon, when Schetz sent Van Lare to Madeira in 1523.[146]

Excerpts remain from the financial records,[147] offering an impression of Van Lare's commercial activities. He recorded the most important transactions as factor of Schetz-De Boodt in the period 1523-26. On the one hand, these covered the traditional commodities

---

142 Vieira (2002), 81-3, and (2004), 71. The large share of Italian ports between 1490 and 1550, viz. 52 percent, is misleading, because the percentages for Italy, France, and the Levant were clearly combined.

143 Moore (2009), 363-6.

144 Mus (1964), 17-24, 41-9, 62-7.

145 WBA, BoZ 5270 (RPC392), f°135v°; Slootmans (1985), II, 998.

146 Everaert (1986), 450-1.

147 MPMA, no. 318.

trade in Lisbon, especially textile imports and olive oil exports,[148] and on the other hand the sugar trade, which consumed most of his time and energies. In addition to purchasing different varieties of sugar, directly on Madeira or via agents, he purchased delicacies prepared from sugar for which the island had become renowned: conserves, jams, syrups, and the like. He shipped the bulk of these products to Antwerp.[149] The available documents do not specify sales in the Low Countries, but comparing sugar prices in the production area with those on the market where they were sold reveals that this trade could be immensely profitable. While average prices on Madeira dropped between 1520 and 1523 and subsequently recovered in the period 1526-31 to near their level in 1520, they continued to rise sharply in Antwerp.[150] The growing discrepancy resulted largely from resumption of military and economic warfare between France and the Habsburg Netherlands, which coincided with embargos and piracy, complicating trade with the South in general and the supply of Madeira sugar in particular.

The actual profits in the sugar trade may be inferred from the calculations by Van Lare in his personal 'merchant's manual'. For the period around 1530 he carefully noted the prices of different types of sugar on Madeira, indicating how much was payable for storage, transport to the harbour, and export duties, and finally taking into account the cost of shipment to Antwerp, insurance at sea, import duties, and commission fees. Net profits equalled at least 12 percent and might reach 36 percent, with an extreme of 143 percent for the *rescumas* (the least appreciated unrefined variety).[151] Since Van Lare negotiated particularly low purchase prices in the period 1523-26, the profits of Schetz-De Boodt would have been even higher at that point.

During the first half of the sixteenth century sugar processing soared in Antwerp. While only one refiner was listed until 1508, at least 25 were active in 1556, refining an estimated one third of all sugar imported each year. According to contemporaries, the quality of their finished products was such that the town became internationally renowned as a sugar refinery centre.[152] Schetz & Co. did not restrict their business to trade in sugar and operated refineries for many years. In 1531 they purchased two large adjacent houses behind the City Hall, on what soon afterwards was named *Suikerrui* (Sugar Canal); both houses had belonged to a sugar refiner unable to pay his debts. After Pruynen died, this business was continued. Only in 1549 did Erasmus Schetz and the heirs of Arnold Pruynen sell the complex, equipped with two sugar boilers, to the sugar refiner Jan de Ribaucourt for fl.6,400, i.e. over seventy times the annual wage of a skilled worker.[153]

Why did the firm become involved in industrial processing in 1531 and why were these activities discontinued in 1549? Both decisions related to changes in the European economy on the one hand and geographic shifts in sugar production and sugar distribution on the

148 In this period Schetz & Co. also sold large quantities of pepper and olive oil to Bruges merchants without direct intervention by De Boodt. See AGR, GRM 822, no. 22 (1 August 1522).

149 Everaert (1986), 452-4.

150 Van der Wee (1963), I, 320, 323-4; Pereira (1969), 492-3, 734-7, 742.

151 Everaert (1986), 456 and 468. Van Lare's calculations seem reliable, as the purchase prices on which they are based correspond with those in other sources: Vieira (2002), 73. On the different qualities of sugar cane, see Nunes (2002).

152 Thijs (1979), 23-6. Also Stols (2004), 268-70.

153 SAA, SR 181, f° 466, 469, 491-3, SR 184, f° 453a, SR, 207, f° 188, SR 232, f° 359.

other. Like other trading companies in the late 1520s and 30s, Schetz & Co. had to reckon with continual economic changes, both favourable and unfavourable. The rapidly growing trade with the South greatly benefited Antwerp, as is clear in part from the massive import of sugar cane from the Canary Islands, Spanish wool, and silk and silk fabrics from Northern Italy. One setback for trade in Antwerp was the resurgence of Venetian trade with Alexandria, weakening the Portuguese spice monopoly, given the steady rise in imports from the Levant of Asian pepper and ginger. It revealed the vulnerability of a commercial centre formed from outside. Moreover, growing difficulties in the German areas, in both silver mining and copper production and in textile manufacturing,[154] undermined further expansion of Antwerp's transcontinental trade. If residential construction by individuals may be considered a barometer for the urban economy overall, Antwerp was in a state of crisis from the late 1520s, when the number of new homes built each year declined rapidly and continuously: from 75 in 1527 to fewer than 25 in 1532 and 1533, after which the decline continued.[155] Merchant capitalists sought new investment opportunities, and they interfered with industrial production, sometimes only by coordinating it but in other cases by directly engaging in the manufacture of export goods or starting their own enterprises. Schetz & Co. devised both strategies, not as alternatives to their commercial activities but specifically with a view toward strengthening them.

Little is known about the precise nature and scope of their sugar trade in this period. Jacob vander Straten (alias Jacob von Strassen), who had replaced Willem van Lare as factor in 1526, was still resident in Lisbon in 1534, but whether he continued to work for the Antwerp firm by then is unknown; he had probably been replaced by Jan van Hilst, a brother-in-law of Erasmus Schetz. Quantitative data are unavailable, but the imports of Schetz & Co. are known to have changed during the second quarter of the sixteenth century. Production on Madeira declined from the early 1520s, and over the next decade the sugar economy on the island lapsed into a severe crisis. Increasing ecological problems and internal socio-economic deficiencies were the main causes,[156] but competition from the new production areas on São Tomé and the Canary Islands exacerbated the crisis. By the middle of the century, 51 percent of all sugar imported in Antwerp came from São Tomé. Though far superior in quality, the share of Madeira sugar fell to 20 percent of the total imported, because demand for cheap sugars from the new production areas surged.[157] During the first half of the sixteenth century ties between Antwerp and the Canary islands became closer than they had ever been with Madeira, because German merchants settling in Antwerp operated sugar cane plantations on La Palma. Merchants from Cologne had been very active in the sugar trade from the late fifteenth century. Initially they merely

---

154 Westermann (1986), 188-94. In 1529 the giant Augsburg firm of Ambrosius and Hans Höchstetter, which had controlled significant parts of the intercontinental silver and spice trades via Lisbon, went bankrupt. See Safley (2020).

155 Daems (1976), 66-8. The economic decline was also reflected in the annual income received for letting stalls at the Our Lady's *Pand*, where luxury commodities were sold: Ewing (1990), 565, 582-3. The 1530s have been characterized in very different ways: Van der Wee (1993), 87 and 101, places the start of the second period of economic growth in Antwerp in 1535, while Puttevils (2020), 35, even mentions 1530 as the year it began. In my opinion, they underestimate the unfavourable developments in this period.

156 See esp. Moore (2010). Also Pereira (1969), 158, and Vieira (2004), 48-9.

157 Brill (1962), 17-8; Materné (1993), 57; Everaert (2002), 198-9, and (2008), 139-40; Vieira (2002), 83.

purchased sugar in Antwerp and sold it in German cities in the West and South, but from the early sixteenth century they established direct connections with Spain and its colonial territories. Jakob Groenenberg(h) evolved into a true merchant entrepreneur. In 1513, together with his uncle, Johann Bysse, mayor of Cologne, he purchased the plantation that the Welsers had acquired a few years earlier on La Palma. His timing was excellent, as sugar prices soared. The plantation was organized on capitalist principles and was expanded significantly over the years that followed, under the aegis of members of the Groenenberg(h) family, known on the island as Monteverde. By 1526 Jakob controlled one sixth of the total surface of La Palma (729 square kilometres). Sugar was and remained the foundation of the family fortune.[158]

Erasmus Schetz does not appear to have considered running plantations on La Palma or on any other island of the Canary archipelago. After all, he would have had to deal with competition from Cologne-Antwerp merchant-entrepreneurs. Nor was he on the same terms with the Spanish rulers as with their Portuguese counterparts and would not have been granted special privileges. The sugar grown on the Canary Islands was moreover inferior to Madeira sugar, making his ongoing preference for the 'traditional' production area understandable. He realized, however, that the crisis in Madeiran sugar cane cultivation was not temporary, and that it was necessary to explore alternatives. Setting up his own refinery in Antwerp in 1531 figured in this context: importing unprocessed sugar had become more lucrative than trading white sugar. A few years later his established contacts with Portugal opened up a new opportunity: Brazil.

In 1530 King João III instructed the nobleman Martim Afonso de Sousa, who had demonstrated both military and diplomatic talents, to organize and lead an expedition to Brazil. The objective was threefold: drive out the French and Dutch pirates, look for precious metals in the newly discovered areas, and explore the coasts to the Rio de la Plata. In two years' time, Martim Afonso had accomplished his mission, establishing a pattern that the Portuguese colonists would follow for a very long time: on the one hand exploration and raids inland and on the other hand founding settlements and setting up sugar cane plantations along the coast with a view to exports to Europe. In 1532 Martim Afonso founded the harbour of São Vicente (south of what is presently São Paulo), the first permanent Portuguese colonial settlement in Brazil. He divided the land among the new inhabitants, two of whom immediately set up sugar cane plantations, as the soil and climate proved suitable; both had an *engenho* (a water mill).[159] Two years later he launched his own initiative in the sugar economy: teaming up with his brother Pero Lopes de Sousa, Jan van Hilst alias João Veniste or Vaniste, Francisco Lobo, and Vicente Gonçalves, he formed the company known as the *Armadores do Trato* (the Ship-Owners' Trading Society), which started a plantation and constructed a sugar mill on the Island of São Vicente. From the outset they had close ties with Schetz: Van Hilst was married to his sister Maria and had represented Schetz & Co. in Lisbon, while Lobo had served the firm many times before as well. Presumably, therefore, they were both operating on instructions from Schetz. This is all the more likely, because around 1540 – the exact date is unknown – Schetz acquired

158 Mollwo (1899); Gramula (1972), 319, 321-4; Coornaert, Kevin (2000), 76-8; Everaert (2009a), 141-3; Viña Brito (2012).

159 Sousa (1839); Teixeira (2011).

legal ownership of the plantation and the sugar mill.[160] From that point onward, the firm was no longer named after the high office of Martim Afonso *Engenho do Senhor Governator*. Instead, it was named *Engenho São Jorge dos Erasmos*, which still appears on the remaining ruins of the operation, now designated as a National Monument.[161]

Although many studies – both archaeological and historical– have been conducted on the *Engenho São Jorge dos Erasmos*,[162] its appearance is impossible to describe. Accounts from contemporaries indicate that there were many buildings in the mid-sixteenth century: a very large residence, slave quarters, and two houses, all well-built and fortified, making the complex easy to defend with three or four light canon. The technical facilities consisted of a smithy, a mill with a water wheel to crush the sugar cane, and workshops to purify it. A few years later the estate also had a chapel dedicated to Saint George, the patron saint of Portugal. No information remains about the precise location of all these buildings or their appearance. Fortunately, an eyewitness account is available from 1548,[163] as well as a few other documents,[164] which describe how the enterprise was organized and operated. At the time it was run by a factor of Erasmus Schetz: the merchant Pierre Rousée, alias Peter Roesel or Rössel, from Arras, who had represented Schetz & Co.'s business interests in Antwerp from the mid-1530s,[165] and who made use of an ocean vessel of the firm in Brazil. Remarkably, family members did not represent the economic activities of the firm outside Europe. Managers from the commercial circles that Schetz & Co. knew and trusted liaised with Madeira and ran the Brazilian sugar cane plantation.

Rousée was expanding the plantation and intended to repair the mill and the water wheel, as his predecessors had neglected to maintain them. He also complained that settlers had unlawfully appropriated premises on the estate and were now operating there as cane planters. The court could not be expected to intervene against these practices. Despite all the problems, Rousée explained that production would exceed one thousand arobas (*c.* 14,700 kilograms) the next year, and that this amount was certain to increase in the near future, thanks to the newly planted groves. On the *engenho* were 130 slaves, men and women alike, all indigenous rural inhabitants, half of them children and elderly, who according to the eyewitness report did not work. There were also seven or eight '*negros* from Guinea', all *offica[l]es*, i.e. skilled men performing specific tasks. Three were *caldereiros*, coppersmiths, and another was a 'sugar master', the most prestigious position on the *engenho*; every month they received a substantial portion of sugar, which was the most frequent payment currency in early-colonial Brazil.[166] The presence of a few free male blacks – in addition to a great many enslaved native Americans – comes as no surprise, as in the New World

160 Laga (1963).
161 https://www.youtube.com/watch?v = H7bA19csRas (accessed 15 December 2020).
162 See esp. Andreatta (1999).
163 First published and translated from Flemish into Portuguese by Stols (1968). For an English translation, see Schwartz (2010), 198-202.
164 AGR, FU, L 199; Laga (1963), 26; Stols (1973), 21; Schwartz (1985), 23, 57, 66; Everaert (2009b).
165 In 1535 Pierre Rousée had formed a company with four other merchants residing in Antwerp to trade with Spain and possibly with Peru. The company had a capital of £300 Fl.gr., of which Rousée put up one third. So, at the time he was already interested in the New World. Strieder (1930), 79-89.
166 Only during the second half of the sixteenth century did black slaves gradually start to replace the native American labour force on Brazilian sugar cane plantations.

nobody had acquired any experience with sugar processing, while on Madeira and other Atlantic islands many freedmen had the requisite technical knowledge.[167]

Since the report from 1548 followed a period of mismanagement, it does not disclose the true economic prospects of the firm. It does, however, reflect the challenges facing Schetz & Co. Sugar plantations and sugar mills required not only large tracts of land, for growing sugar cane as well as for chopping wood to use as fuel, but also a substantial, permanent labour force and several technicians and specialists. In the early stage of the Brazilian sugar industry, owners of *engenhos* were on the one hand unable to use African slaves as yet, while on the other hand they faced serious resistance from the indigenous population to forced labour. Such resistance might be reduced if families were kept together, which would explain the large numbers of women, children, and elderly on the *Engenho São Jorge dos Erasmos*. What about the returns? If half the 130 slaves and the 7-8 black technicians worked full-time, then hypothetically 19 to 24 metric tons of sugar cane could be produced every year, as annual productivity in the New World during the sixteenth and seventeenth centuries was said to have fluctuated between 260 and 330 kilograms per labour-year.[168] According to Rousée, production the next year would equal only 14.7 metric tons, i.e. considerably below the average levels. This low productivity probably resulted from the deficiencies noted as regards the technical facilities. Other factors may have come into play as well, in particular the declining fertility of the soil. It is not purely coincidental that Rousée had new groves planted and announced yet more. At any rate, efforts were made to boost productivity and production alike.

During this period sugar was in any case transported from São Vicente to Lisbon, apparently on ships belonging to partners of the Schetz firm or equipped by them. How many ships the firm owned or leased remains unknown. Nor is it known whether they were also used for transport from Lisbon to Antwerp. In 1549, i.e. in peacetime, Erasmus Schetz had a ship equipped in Middelburg with three pieces of artillery, 99 cannon balls, and 5 vats of gunpowder, indicating ocean voyages. In 1533 in São Vicente the German *Landsknecht* and explorer Ulrich Schmidl boarded a vessel bound for Lisbon that was owned by Jan van Hilst and was loaded with Brazil wood and sugar.[169] In the meantime, some South-German merchants followed the example set by the Schetz firm and started sugar cane plantations in Brazil. Members of the Lins or Linz family, originally from Ulm, were active in the Pernambuco region from the late 1530s, and entrepreneurs from Erasmus Schetz pioneered sugar cane cultivation and processing in the New World. Around 1550 his *Engenho São Jorge dos Erasmos* was probably the largest plantation in southern Brazil. He had assessed the opportunities of the new production area correctly and despite the logistical problems and a period of mismanagement, he was optimistic about the future prospects of the plantation and the mill on São Vicente. His sons understood what the *engenho* could offer and were happy to continue this branch of their father's firm as well. Since they easily found a partner with plenty of capital,[170] the proceeds in the 1550s and 60s

167 See Vieira (2004), 56-61.

168 Moore (2010), 10. Note, however, that data for the early sugar industries are sparse and inconsistent: Schwartz (2004), 19.

169 AGR, PEA 1417/28, *Extract*; Obermeier (2005), 127.

170 Kieckens (1883); Harreld (2003), 153; Correns, Rau and Van de Cruys (2014), 135-9.

are sure to have been substantial. Moreover, the quality of Brazilian sugar was excellent, and Schetz & Co. were for a long time among its few importers in Western Europe. In 1570, *c.* 9000 arrobas or *c.* 132.3 metric tons were imported from Portugal to Antwerp.[171] Assuming that the *Engenho São Jorge dos Erasmos* was operating at full capacity by then, which seems plausible, the owners would have accounted for about a fifth of total sugar imports from Brazil.[172]

1.4 Diversification and Focus

Diversification was a key concept in the world of big business in the late Middle Ages and the early modern period. Capitalists moved capital between trade, finance and manufacturing. Only in exceptional cases did they specialize and usually only temporarily. On the one hand, they were aware of the precarious nature of Lady Fortune, which made versatility advisable and even necessary, and on the other hand they had sufficient financial means to seize every promising new opportunity to make a profit. This does not alter the fact that the top commercial operators would nonetheless concentrate on specific products and directions of trade within their broad spectrum of business activities. The aim of capitalists was to integrate their most essential business activities and to improve their core strengths, neither of which was easily attainable. The available data reveal that Schetz & Co. succeeded brilliantly in this endeavour.

Pepper and other spices always constituted the bulk of their imports to Antwerp and their exports to Germany (Leipzig), while brass goods were their main export to Lisbon. But they did not limit their business to these products. Like other large firms in the sixteenth century, their commodities trade comprised a great diversity of products, sent in many different directions. The lack of accounts precludes a comprehensive list of their commerce. Shifts in the relative importance of different merchandise are therefore impossible to pinpoint. Fragmentary data reveal, however, that they always traded large quantities. In most cases the aim was to strengthen the two trade directions crucial for the firm, i.e. with Portugal and Germany, but efforts were made to involve other markets as well. Schetz consistently instrumentalized his good relations with the highest political authorities. This was especially true in the 1520s and 30s, during fundamental shifts in Antwerp's international trade, with wars, natural disasters, and soaring grain prices increasing the negative effects. Some firms used the events and developments to increase profits over the shorter or longer term. Schetz & Co. did this successfully. They perceived the opportunities that either brief crises or structural economic changes offered and benefited fully from them.

In the early 1520s they teamed up with substantial merchants from La Rochelle in exports and imports between Antwerp and the Atlantic coast of France. At the time La Rochelle was one of the most important French harbours. The city attracted traders from all parts of the kingdom and had longstanding commercial ties with Bruges and Zeeland, in particular with Middelburg and other Walcheren ports.[173] From the early sixteenth

171 Pohl (1967), 353.
172 For a more skeptical view, see Everaert (2009b) and (2020).
173 Trocmé and Delafosse (1952).

century on contacts with Antwerp became more frequent, as La Rochelle was the main distributor for Poitou wines, which were especially popular in Flanders and Brabant. The merchants there also supplied the renowned Brouage salt and the dye indispensable for dyeing cloth blue: woad.[174] The most important exports to La Rochelle were spices and sugar, products that Schetz & Co could easily supply, and which made contracts with French merchants very profitable. From 1521 on, the war between Charles V and Francis I had involved trade restrictions, although these do not appear to have bothered Schetz & Co., as in 1523 they were supplying French woad to dyers in both Bergen op Zoom and Antwerp.[175] Probably Schetz & Co. had obtained permission despite the war to trade with Bordeaux or the harbour of La Rochelle. That was certainly the case in 1525. After the Battle of Pavia (24 February 1525) no obstacles remained to resuming trade between France and the Habsburg Netherlands. As long as peace had not been reached, however, such trade was with the enemy, and the central government in Brussels proved disinclined to grant the special permissions required. Charles V, did, however, grant passports to French merchants before the Battle of Pavia. On 21 February the governor, Margaret of Austria, wrote that his attitude gave rise to great indignation: many merchants from the Low Countries were ruined, as they were prohibited from trading with the enemy, whereas 'foreign firms' had clearance to import wine and salt from France and to bring spices to that country. In those circumstances, his subjects threatened to refuse all new requests for funds.[176] While the governor did not disclose the names of foreign firms, they may be assumed to have been the partners of Schetz, as he had enough leverage to convince the Emperor to issue passports. On 13 May 1525 Charles V officially granted him and Pierre Gérart of La Rochelle, their partners, and their representatives permission to purchase spices, sugar, wax, linens, tapestries, leather, and herring in the Low Countries as often and in whatever quantities they wished and to convey them to France, over sea or by land. They merely had to present passports bearing their name and the names of their partners. In France they were allowed to purchase unlimited quantities of wine, salt, and woad, although for security reasons they were not allowed to enter any port in the Habsburg Netherlands with more than twelve French ships at once – suggesting trade in massive quantities.[177] Since merchants from La Rochelle exported large quantities of wine and salt to Zeeland in normal years, Schetz and Gérart are likely to have realized very high profits indeed in 1525 (and probably before that as well). They purchased their wares mainly from André Morisson, a substantial businessman, who operated as an agent for the Spanish firm Pedro Lopez & Co. and frequently dealt with the well-known Antwerp merchant Jacob Hoefnagel. Like many other merchants in La Rochelle, he was involved in viticulture and sold Poitou wines; in the 1530s he shipped large quantities to Arnemuiden, Middelburg, and Zierikzee in Zeeland, sometimes on his own account, at other times together with businessmen from Bruges and Antwerp.[178]

174 Coornaert (1961), I, 317-9; Concato (1975), 94-6.

175 Slootmans (1985), I, 452.

176 Lanz (1844-46), I, 84.

177 Craeybeckx (1958), 213.

178 AGR, GRM 826, no. 48; Sneller and Unger (1930), II, nos 36 and 50; Trocmé and Delafosse (1952), 99; Coornaert (1961), I, 320, and II, 51; Drost (1984), 23-4, 36-7, 43.

The years 1521-25/6, though difficult for many merchants, offered new prospects for Schetz & Co. The firm used the war with France to obtain a *de facto* monopoly on woad imports into the Low Countries, which Schetz accomplished thanks to his excellent connections with Emperor Charles V. Woad was an important trade commodity, as textile manufacturers needed it to dye cloth blue; this costly commodity was their greatest expense.[179] Schetz & Co. could maintain their woad monopoly only while peace with France was not official. The banker Gaspar Ducci used the resumption of the Habsburg-Valois conflict in the early 1540s to establish his own woad monopoly in de Netherlands. When he fell out of favour, Schetz & Co. once again expressed great interest in trading the dye, which at the time was produced mainly in the Toulouse area. Only after the death of Erasmus Schetz, however, were supply contracts signed with Pierre Assézat (the main dealer in woad for the south of France) and this substantial merchant became involved in other dealings with the Schetzes as well.[180]

Trade with France never became the mainstay of Schetz & Co. The export registers concerning the war years 1543-45 list shipments of goods from the firm to France, originating from both Antwerp and from Arras and Valenciennes, but they pale in comparison to exports to Germany (see below). Since trade with France was of course heavily affected by the new Valois-Habsburg conflict, the available data cannot be deemed representative. Still, there is no doubt that the primordial commercial interests of Schetz & Co. lay elsewhere. They did not hesitate, however, to sell products exceeding the scope of their core business, whenever profitable opportunities arose.

On several occasions, for example, they sold large quantities of grain. In 1530 Schetz stated that over the past two to three years, he and other merchants had leased ships in Holland or Zeeland and sent them with ballast to Bremen to be loaded with grain there, whence they sailed directly to England, Portugal, and Spain. Grain was no longer transported via Amsterdam or Middelburg in order to avoid the *congiegeld*, an export licence fee charged in Holland and Zeeland that greatly reduced the profit margin. In the summer of 1529 he had leased a ship of 350 *last* in Arnemuiden, Zeeland, and had sent it with ballast to Bremen to be loaded with wheat there and then to sail directly to Lisbon. The Antwerp firm was not the only one trading in grain at this period, but, at *c.* 10,500 hectolitres, it was among the main exporters. By comparison: Ruy Fernandez, the factor in Antwerp for the King of Portugal, had 1400 *last* or 42,000 hectolitres of wheat and rye purchased in Gdansk at the time.[181] Large merchants clearly benefited from the high cost of grain in Southern and Northwest Europe between 1527 and 1534, albeit at different moments and to varying degrees.[182] Schetz & Co. profited mainly from the opportunity to supply grain in Lisbon. The Portuguese monarchy had a longstanding practice of encouraging this trade, rather than promoting domestic grain cultivation. Under the governments of Manuel I and João III, agriculture went into a serious decline, and, even in 'normal' years, grain harvests were insufficient to meet basic needs. Grain therefore had to be purchased from abroad to feed the population. Participation in supplying the rapidly growing population

179 Thijs (1987), 80-4.

180 Craeybeckx (1958), 238; Coornaert (1961), I, 332-3; Brumont (2002); Puttevils (2015a), 70.

181 Meilink (1923), esp. 38-40, 49, 55. See also Van Answaarden (1991), 243-4.

182 Abel (1974), 47-54. In Antwerp grain prices peaked in 1530/1 (rye) and 1531/2 (wheat): Scholliers (1960), 7 and 14.

of Lisbon improved the leverage of firms such as Schetz & Co., which depended on the goodwill of the Crown for their trade in pepper and brass goods. Gratitude for the grain import also explains why the Portuguese King and his representatives enabled the firm to set up a sugar plantation in Brazil very early on.

Schetz also had good contacts in England, as is clear from his correspondence with his humanist namesake. Whether trade with this country in the 1520s and 30s consisted mainly of imports or exports is impossible to determine. In any case, the firm acquired great renown for reliable deliveries, as during the soaring prices in 1545/6, they were the preferred supplier of Stephen Vaughan. On 20 February 1546 he signed a contract with the firm for the purchase of 800 *last* of rye and 400 *last* of wheat from Gdansk, i.e. Polish grain, to be delivered 'with the first open water after mid-Lent', half the rye and one quarter of the wheat to Newcastle, the rest to London and Dover. The English admiralty was instructed to instruct all captains that the ships of the Antwerp firm were to be granted free, unobstructed passage.[183] That Schetz & Co. was willing and able to deliver 1,200 *last* or *c.* 36,000 hectolitres of grain to Henry VIII in a period of soaring prices was remarkable. In early March the Bremen city council wrote to the English King that grain had not been so scarce in the past hundred years,[184] and prices continued to rise, causing famine in several areas. When the English ambassadors solicited Mary of Hungary in mid-March for permission to transport 400 *last* of grain originating from the duchies of Jülich-Cleves-Berg from Dordrecht to Calais as provisions for the troops there, their request was denied. The ambassadors argued that these duchies were not territories of the Emperor, and that thanks to the delivery by Schetz & Co., the grain could be compensated within six weeks, but the governor was firm. She emphasized that the scarcity here is so great as to be beyond expression, poor people having died of famine. The English King had to understand 'that charity begins at home'. Her sole accommodation was to sign an export permit for 100 *last*.[185] But Schetz & Co. were not pressured by the government in Brussels to sell their much larger quantity of grain in the Netherlands. The firm appears to have been too influential to be opposed in any way, even when grain prices soared. On the other hand, comparison of the prices charged by the firm with those paid on the market in the spring of 1546 in Antwerp and in nearby Lier,[186] shows that Schetz & Co. did in fact profit from the grain transaction with Henry VIII, but not exorbitantly. While they were certainly not acting out of generosity, their strategy in business arrangements with rulers and their representatives was to be reasonable: moderation and reliability yielded the greatest benefits in the long run.

Antwerp had a long tradition as a centre of the grain trade, but the rising tensions between demographic expansion and available arable land made this trade progressively more important, and imports from France and Hesbaye were replaced by imports of

---

183 LPFD, Henry VIII, 21/1, nos 251 and 259. See also Häpke (1913), I, 799, 805-6, and Simson (1913), 20 February 1546.

184 LPFD, Henry VIII, 21/1, no. 352.

185 HHS, B-PA 59, Letters dated 14, 17, 24, 26, 27 March 1546, and 1, 5,6, 12, 17 April 1546. Also CSP, Spain, 8, nos 211, 212, 223, 224, 225, 232, 234, 236, 244, 248. In Europe grain harvests varied regionally in 1545 and 1546, leaving many areas with serious shortages: Abel (1974), 56-7.

186 Vaughan agreed to pay 300 Flemish groats for a quarter (291 litres) of wheat. Compare with *Dokumenten* (1959), 254, 257, 259, and Van der Wee (1963), I, 177, 187.

Polish grain from Gdansk via Amsterdam.[187] All the evidence suggests that the crisis of the late 1520s and the 1530s encouraged large firms in Antwerp to seek new opportunities for earnings. The Saint Felix flood of 5 November 1530 had disastrous consequences, sweeping away large areas of Zeeland and what is now Zeeland Flanders. The polders of Lillo, Stabroek, Berendrecht, Zandvliet, Ossendrecht, and Woensdrecht north of Antwerp were also severely flooded. The next year, the central government and the city authorities launched initiatives to restore the dykes and reclaim the submerged lands from the sea but lacked the necessary funds. To make matters worse, on 2 November 1532 a new storm struck and caused major damage. The authorities now appealed to private investors and were highly successful. The merchant-brokers Georg Meuting, Lucas Rem, and Lazarus Tucher convinced many businessmen to lend large sums to both governments and aristocratic families toward new embankments. International merchants and bankers from Antwerp and high-ranking officials purchased land and built dykes, mainly on South Beveland. The High Germans were the most active, but Italian and Spanish businessmen participated as well. Speculation was their chief motive. Land prices had plummeted in the areas flooded. Since this had been very fertile farmland, however, they hoped that rebuilding the dykes would lead to vast harvests to sell on the market, or that they might sell the land at a substantial profit.[188]

On the basis of a letter he wrote to Desiderius Erasmus, the rising grain prices were Schetz's main reason for purchasing farmland. In October 1531 he wrote that prices had soared, but that he could not sell grain on the market, because his fields had yielded nothing but straw.[189] He did not invest in building dykes in Zeeland, where South-German, Italian, and Spanish merchants were active. As always, he avoided participating in enterprises in which many other capitalists were involved wherever possible. Instead, over the years 1534-37, he and Pruynen purchased nearly 400 hectares of polder land in Ossendrecht, about 25 kilometres north of Antwerp.[190] By 1549, Schetz also owned *c.* 25 hectares of polder land in Berendrecht, Zandvliet, and Lillo that he had purchased on his own in the 1530s, suggesting that such investments were profitable.[191]

He also purchased farmland around Lier, a small town fifteen kilometres southeast of Antwerp. He had good contacts there, as he had inherited houses and fields from relatives who had lived there for many years. In the period 1533-35 he purchased two farmsteads with a total of *c.* 30 hectares of arable land on the Donk near Lier and a farmstead with *c.* 8 hectares of arable land in nearby Boechout. While these were undoubtedly investments, he presumably hoped to benefit from the rising grain prices as well. He soon succeeded, as in 1535/6, 1536/7, and 1538/9 wheat prices soared. More importantly, all grain prices rose sharply from the 1540s on. Transport from Lier to Antwerp was not a problem, as both cities were connected by waterways. Schetz also purchased *c.* 43 hectares of forest land

187 Van der Wee (1963), II, 171-2, 177-86; Munro (2003), 307.

188 Dekker and Baetens (2010), 15, 21, 48-9, 66-7, 71, 84, 219-30.

189 Erasmus, Ep. 2558: *Correspondance* (1980), IX, 489.

190 Trading tracts of land with other owners yielded a vast contiguous area comprising two farms. The investment must have been profitable, because after Pruynen died in 1536, the land was not sold; in 1549 his heirs and Erasmus Schetz simply divided the complex in two. WBA, BoZ, HA 441; SAA, SR 191, f° 53, SR 232, f° 351-7, 359.

191 SAA, SR 197, f° 346, SR 203, f° 27v°-28, COLL 9, f° 13. See also SR 187, f° 135, SR 191, f° 53, SR 192, f° 85v°-86, and SR 195, f° 440.

near Lier, which had been planted with oak coppice. This timber served various purposes but was used primarily as fuel, suggesting that it was intended for the sugar refinery. The investment was in any case profitable, as prices for firewood rose significantly in Antwerp from 1542/3, thanks to both demographic growth and industrial expansion.[192]

In the early modern period large trading companies never missed an opportunity to make rapid and large profits, even if the transaction exceeded the scope of their usual range of goods or standard trading routes. In the spring of 1543, with a new war against France imminent, Mary of Hungary instructed Erasmus Schetz to supply the artillery masters in Mechelen with 5000 kilograms of copper as quickly as possible. Even though the Fuggers had far greater stocks, the Antwerp firm was commissioned to supply the canon foundries in the Netherlands. The firm also imported from Germany large amounts of saltpetre, the major and most active component of gunpowder. In April-May of that year Schetz complained to the central government that officials had blocked entry of the cargo that he had brought from Germany at his own risk and was valued at about fl.16,000, even though it was intended for the artillery masters in Mechelen.[193] The firm did not supply munitions only to the central government of the Habsburg Netherlands. Although in 1546 Charles V was in the midst of preparing to wage war against the German Protestants, Schetz & Co. were permitted to export 134 barrels or *c.* 12,000 kilograms of gunpowder to England.[194] After Erasmus died, his sons continued to sell munitions on a large scale.[195]

The prospect of profit was a major incentive, but it was not necessarily the sole or even the major motive, especially when supplying luxury goods to Charles V or Mary of Hungary. Indications suggest that Erasmus Schetz brokered the sale of tapestries between producers and the Spanish Crown. Around 1544 he supplied the governor with seven tapestries depicting the *Story of Scipio*.[196] These were a reissue of a series commissioned by Francis I of France in 1532 comprising 22 items. The seven new tapestries, consisting of five *Deeds* and two *Triumphs*, sold by Schetz, accurately reflected the preparatory sketches executed by Giulio Romano and his pupil Giovanni Francesco Penni for the original series in 1528. They were most probably woven at the Brussels workshop of Balthasar van Vlierden. Their number, size, and especially the fact that they were largely in silk explain their astronomical cost: £3,672 Fl.gr. This was not an isolated transaction, as in May 1547 Schetz received the first payment from the secretary to the governor, namely £810 Fl.gr., for another series of tapestries depicting the *Story of Tobias* and sold shortly before in Antwerp.[197] While he must have made some money from the two transactions, his profits cannot possibly have been exorbitant. Mary of Hungary was perfectly able to compare prices, as she was an expert on tapestries: when she departed the Netherlands in 1556, she took 254 tapestries with her to Spain.[198] Schetz is more likely to have brokered these sales to maintain good relations with the governor. Mary of Hungary showed a daily interest in

192 SAA, SR 185, f° 231v°, SR 188, f° 6, SR 218, f° 130v°, COLL 9, f° 14; RAB, RB, AG 596, f° 431. For prices of wheat and fire wood in Antwerp, see *Dokumenten* (1959), 253-9, 350-4, and Scholliers (1960), 13-15, 44-5.

193 AGR, PEA 1661/1; Pölnitz (1963), I, 231.

194 LPFD, Henry VIII, 21/2, no. 72.

195 SAA, COLL 8, f° 110-113v°; Roosens (1977), 212, 234-6. See also Lejeune (1939), 194-5, and Jeannin (1978).

196 Presently located in the Patrimonio Nacional, Palacio Real, in Madrid.

197 Buchanan (1992), 380-2; Van den Boogert (1993), 295; Campbell (2002), 281-2, 343, 349, 370, 414.

198 Beer (1891), CLVIII-CLXIII.

all important political and economic matters in the Habsburg Netherlands. Her countless letters demonstrate that she launched all kinds of initiatives and took commercial and financial decisions independently, which mattered greatly to a firm such as Schetz & Co. Remaining in her good graces was therefore important, and the best way to achieve this was to indulge her desire for luxury and her collector's frenzy.

Commercial diversification was necessary, but pepper and brass goods remained the mainstays of trade by Schetz & Co., who therefore retained Portugal and Germany as their main trade routes. Germany was also generally the most important destination from Antwerp. The Hundredth Penny tax records reveal that trade over land with Germany accounted for nearly 37 percent of all shipments. Italy ranked second with 22 percent.[199] One of the problems with this source is that the name of the person paying the tax reveals nothing about the ownership of the exported goods: he could be a transporter or a merchant owner. An additional complicating factor is that individuals or firms might ship goods on their own behalf but could also operate as agents for others. The value of the shipments by the Van der Molen brothers to Italian cities commissioned by third parties in this period, for example, was triple or quadruple the amount they exported on their own behalf.[200] While additional sources enable an accurate calculation for the Van der Molens, this is exceptional. Even with the principal exporters, little more can be done than an attempt first to distinguish transport operators from trading firms and then merchants who generally exported on their own behalf from those who usually operated as agents, which in many cases proves impossible for lack of supplementary data.

Who were the biggest exporters based in the Netherlands and especially in Antwerp? Schetz & Co. topped the list by a wide margin. The value of their shipments in the period 1543-45 was no less than £65,822 Fl.gr., of which 63 percent went to Germany, 25 percent to the Northern Netherlands (mainly to Amsterdam and Arnemuiden), 7.4 percent to England, and 4.6 percent to the Iberian Peninsula. The minimal export to the South, i.e. to Portugal, might be deceptive, because shipments to Arnemuiden were often transferred at this major outpost of Antwerp to larger ships bound for Lisbon. Additionally, a share of the shipments to Arnemuiden belonging to the Portuguese factor consisted of products he had purchased from Schetz & Co. Still, the firm may be assumed to have exported progressively less brassware in the 1540s.

The total value of shipments by other exporters was considerably lower than that of the Schetz firm. Willem van Montfort, who hailed from Aachen but had become a citizen of Antwerp in 1538, ranked second with £43,085 Fl.gr. He was repeatedly labelled a 'transport entrepreneur' and may therefore be assumed to have exported goods largely on behalf of other merchants. Little is known about Jan Ghieten, who came next with £36,7300 Fl. gr., except that in 1542 he was listed as a citizen of Cologne and at the time served as an agent of Jaspar Terlaen from the same city. Jan della Faille ranked fourth with £28,249 Fl. gr.; in this period he increasingly traded on his own behalf, but most shipments were still commissioned by the firm of Maarten de Hane, established in Venice. The exports of Mannaert & Co., from Mechelen but based in Antwerp in this period, amounted to

199 Puttevils (2015b), 1347. These percentages concern the period from 9 August 1544 to 11 August 1545.
200 Edler (1938), 133 and 144 n. 269; Brulez (1959a), 489.

£21,552 Fl.gr. (nearly 92 percent of which went to Italy). Little is known about Lodewijk Ferraryn alias Louis Fraryn, whose exports totalled £19,296 Fl.gr. (about 91 percent of which went to England). In 1546 he tried in vain, together with Gillis Hooftman, Jacques Le Prieur, and other wholesalers, to pay a large lump sum to be free of the *grote costuyme*, the high import duties levied in England. The two firms listed after him shipped goods valued at £12,858 and £10,285 Fl.gr., respectively (mainly to Italy). All other exporters shipped goods valued at less than £10,000 Fl.gr.

Trade routes were clearly subject to specialization: exporters to Germany and to Italy operated in two largely separate circles. Only two of the ten largest exporters to Italy did business with Germany as well, and this trade achieved significance only with Jan della Faille (amounting to 18 percent of his total export value). Conversely, regular trade by merchants from the Low Countries with Germany rarely coincided with export to Italy, and, when it did, these shipments tended to be of relatively little value.[201] Lack of business contacts cannot have been the reason, as Arnold Pruynen was related by marriage to the Van Bombergens, who traded mainly with Italy. The family connection never induced Schetz & Co. to venture into this market, perhaps because they did not specialize in textiles. While they sent large quantities of English cloth to Leipzig, they did not send English kerseys, Flemish serges, or other textile goods and therefore did not need specialized knowledge. Export to Italy on the other hand, required extensive knowledge of all aspects of textile manufacturing and trade, as the fabrics were highly diverse in name, origin, measurements, colours, and quality; in addition, changes in fashion required careful consideration.[202]

Since Schetz & Co. were focused mainly on Germany (in addition to Portugal), this trade direction merits special attention. Analysis of the data concerning the value of all goods exported to German areas in the period 1543-45 places Puschinger at the top of the list with £64,031 Fl.gr. In the 1540s this businessman, originally from Leipzig, became very active in Antwerp. However, he not only operated on his own behalf but was mainly an agent for the Augsburg firms Herwart & Co. and Herbrot/Hörbrot & Sons.[203] The same held true for Willem van Montfort, who ranked second with £41,166 Fl.gr. He exported almost exclusively to Nuremberg, mostly on behalf of other merchants. Ranked by the value of their exports, Schetz & Co. were in third place at £41,415 Fl.gr., but they did not operate for third parties. In other words, they were indisputably the largest of all *independent* operators. Jan Ghieten, who came next with £36,680 Fl.gr., exported almost exclusively to Germany. Anton Haug, who was fifth, ran a company together with Hans Lang(e)nauer and Ulrich Linck; all of them came from Augsburg. The total value of their shipments was £32,076 Fl.gr. The next nine merchants, all Germans, shipped goods valued at £10,000 to £20,000 Fl.gr.[204] Some were members of large trading companies, such as the Imhof(f)s and the Welsers, while others did not trade exclusively or even primarily on their own behalf. Bartholomäus Jenisch and Hartman Schmaltz, for example, both based in Antwerp, represented various firms from Augsburg, Nuremberg, and/or Leipzig.[205]

---

201 Brulez (1959a), 479-83, 487-8, 497, and (1959b).

202 See the pertinent remarks of Puttevils (2009), 36, and (2015b), 1356.

203 Ehrenberg (1896), I, 239, 256, 258; Thijs (1975b), 366; Harreld (2004), 73-4, 85.

204 Data taken from Brulez (1959a), 493. They differ slightly from those published by Harreld (2004), 193-4.

205 For more detail on the Augsburg merchant families, see Reinhard (1996), and *Augsburger Stadtlexicon Online*.

Table 2. Top five of 'Antwerp' exporters to Germany in 1544-45

Exporter Destination	Willem van Montfort	Wolf Puschinger	Erasmus Schetz	Anton Haug	Jan Ghieten
Hamburg	–	3291	2991	–	–
Cologne	6617	1000	–	2586	10,483
Frankfurt	1458	3625	1662	2073	3399
Augsburg	777	4595	–	2252	117
Nuremberg	14,589	5570	4503	6643	115
Leipzig	1874	6087	12,243	250	275
Other cities	958	1300	1429	1339	9
Total value in £ Fl.gr.	26,273	25,468	22,828	15,143	14,398

Source: Jeroen Puttevils' database 'Hundredth Penny Tax on Export', 1544-45

Schetz & Co. therefore topped the list of *independent* export traders with Germany. No other firm operating on its own behalf could match them. The value of shipments by the firm Haug-Lang(e)nauer-Linck was 23 percent below theirs. All remaining independent merchants/firms exported less than half the value of the goods that Schetz & Co. placed on the German market.

The bulk of exports from Antwerp to Germany went to five cities, in order of importance: Nuremberg, Cologne, Frankfurt, Leipzig, and Augsburg, together accounting for nearly 94 percent of the total value of all shipments. Thorough analysis of the Hundredth Penny tax records from 9 August 1544 to 11 August 1545 (i.e. over twelve months) shows the cities to which Schetz & Co. exported, as well as the value of the goods.[206] A small proportion went to Arnemuiden in Zeeland and Amsterdam. The goods sent to Arnemuiden were mainly metal wares and manillas, which were to be forwarded to Portugal and West Africa. Large quantities of pepper and sugar, as well as hides and mercery goods, were exported to Amsterdam.[207] In 1543 Schetz & Co. sent one of the largest sugar shipments destined for Germany via Amsterdam: 11,000 Antwerp pounds or *c.* 5.2 metric tons.[208] These shipments converged with far larger ones bound for Hamburg. Schetz & Co. had focused on this trade route for a long time for several reasons. According to a statement by Theobald Pruynen, probably related to Arnold, by the late 1520s ships from Holland were often loaded in Antwerp with goods from the firm to be transported to Amsterdam and from there on to Bremen, Hamburg, and further east.[209] The loads may be presumed to have consisted mainly of pepper, sugar, and mercery goods, as those were the main products that the firm also exported to Hamburg in the period 1543-45. Their other exports at the time consisted mainly of alum and glass. Conceivably and even probably, they exported far larger amounts

206 The following figures are taken from Jeroen Puttevils' database 'Hundredth Penny Tax on Export', based on AGR, CC 23357-23364.
207 Mercery goods were a very broad fashion category, comprising all types and prices.
208 Harreld (2002), 615. See also the interesting remarks of Lesger (2001), 44-5.
209 SAA, N 2073, f° 83-4; Strieder (1930), 218-19.

Table 3. Top five of 'Antwerp' exporters to Leipzig in 1544-45

Product category Exporter	Pepper	English cloth	Flemish cloth	Other textiles	Other products	Total value in £ Fl.gr.
Erasmus Schetz	4273	7785	–	170	15	12,243
Wolf Puschinger	1525	–	2715	600	1247	6087
Hans Spiegelberch	–	–	3752	352	96	4200
Brudegem Brs.	–	525	2340	–	–	2915
Willem van Montfort	–	–	1877	890	301	1874

Source: Jeroen Puttevils' database 'Hundredth Penny Tax on Export', 1544-45

of alum to Southern and Central Germany, as well-informed contemporaries stated.[210] Glass was in great demand among the elite in Northern Europe. From the early sixteenth century, Antwerp imported exclusive Venetian glass, and around 1537/8 entrepreneurs there started manufacturing a competing product known as *façon-de-Venise*.[211] Data on return cargoes are unavailable, but they may be assumed to have consisted largely of copper and especially grain. The growing importance of the export-import trade with Hamburg is reflected by the fact that Schetz installed a factor (Simon Kowangel) there in 1544 or 1545.[212] Shipments by Schetz & Co. to Nuremberg consisted almost exclusively of pepper, which was then redistributed by local wholesalers throughout Central and Eastern Europe. Some may also have been intended for the Nördlingen fair, with which Nuremberg had special ties.[213] The largest share of the firm's exports to Germany, however, was destined for Leipzig. No other firm exported as much as Schetz & Co. on this trade route. In 1544-45 the value of the goods they shipped from Antwerp to Leipzig was £12,243 Fl.gr. (i.e. 29 percent of total exports from the Netherlands to that city). At £6087 Fl.gr. Puschinger did not ship half that amount, and, moreover, he operated largely as an agent for local merchants. Exports by Hans Spiegelberch from Braunschweig and the Brudegem brothers from Leipzig were only one-third to one-quarter of the levels exported by Schetz, and all other exporters shipped much less.

Why Schetz & Co. focused on Leipzig is easy to understand. This city was at the crossroads of a North-South route (the *Via Imperii* or Imperial Road, extending from Stettin near the Baltic via Leipzig to Venice), and a West-East route (the *Via Regia* or King's Road), that went from Bruges/Antwerp via Leipzig to Breslau (Wroclaw). The second route became considerably more important in the fifteenth century. By 1500 Leipzig had become the central market in European West-East and East-West trade and was also attracting trade with Northern Italy via the Brenner Pass. In 1507 Emperor Maximilian I declared the Leipzig fairs to be *Reichsmessen*, Imperial Fairs, and moreover prohibited setting up another fair or staple for goods within a radius of *c.* 112 kilometres, making the city still more commercially and financially important. During the first quarter of the sixteenth century Leipzig became a

210 See Chapter 2.3.
211 For references to the literature, see Veeckman (2002), 84-7.
212 Häpke (1913), I, 430.
213 Harreld (2004), 135-6.

first-rate centre for trade in precious metals. The city was pivotal in operating and distributing the Mansfelder *Garkupfer*, which was crucial for the brass industry in Aachen. It was also in the middle of a thriving proto-industrial region based on linen weaving in the hinterlands and on fustian production in Silesia and the Oberlausitz. Whether Schetz & Co. brought these textile goods back to West-German cities or Antwerp is unknown, but the commercial expansion of Leipzig in any case offered good prospects for the firm. Not only did regional and interregional trade flourish there from the early sixteenth century onward, but international trade also became more significant over the decades that followed. Leipzig was in much closer proximity than Nuremberg to the expanding market in the East, thereby reducing transaction costs. It became the gateway for the growing Polish trade with the West. Towards the middle of the century it benefited from the convergence of the two main transit routes from Frankfurt an der Oder and from Breslau (Wroclaw) and had optimally expanded trade connections with North Germany, especially with Hamburg and Lüneburg. Trade and finance evolved together, leading Leipzig and Frankfurt am Main to dominate all other German *Messen*, trade fairs.[214] Merchants who settled in Leipzig during the first half of the sixteenth century or installed a factor there traded mainly in metals, textile, and spices,[215] the same areas in which Schetz & Co. operated. From there the Antwerp firm had copper brought to Aachen and the Netherlands. Aside from small quantities of other products, their shipments to Leipzig consisted of cloth and pepper, respectively accounting for 65 and 35 percent of their total export value. These same products also dominated shipments by other merchants sent to Leipzig, whence a part was conveyed to Breslau (Wroclaw), which was the distribution centre for Poland.[216]

With regard to textiles, Schetz & Co. exported almost exclusively fine English cloth. They never shipped sayes, demi-ostades (half worsted, half-linen cloth), or satins from the Southern Netherlands to Leipzig, for two reasons. On the one hand, trade in Flemish textiles was far more competitive than in high-quality cloth. Some substantial merchants exported a broad range of fabrics, but most specialized, and many small firms were active in the market for less costly textiles.[217] On the other hand, capitalists such as Schetz & Co. might reach agreements in Antwerp both with major English importers of unfinished cloth and substantial master cloth dressers. In the mid-1540s the commercial tripod that had made Antwerp great remained the cornerstone of Schetz & Co.: Portuguese spices, German metals, and English cloth. The names of the Merchant Adventurers that supplied textiles to Schetz & Co. are not listed anywhere, but Thomas Gresham was presumably among them. In this period he exported considerable quantities of unfinished broadcloths to Antwerp each year, and he was friends with the Schetzes.[218]

Major exporters of English broadcloths in Antwerp worked with the more substantial master cloth dressers, as the quality of the finished product depended largely on their

214 Straube (1979); Brübach (1994), 432-9; Eiden (2002); Straube (2012), 64-7.

215 Fischer (1929), 18-20; Brübach (1994), 447.

216 Direct contacts also existed between Breslau (Wroclaw) and Antwerp, with Flemish and English cloth being the chief commodities traded: Thijs (1975).

217 Harreld (2004), 142-51.

218 In 1546 Melchior stayed with the Greshams in London and visited them several times afterwards. The Greshams and the Schetzes – father and sons – presented each other with costly gifts: Guy (2019), 35-6, 61.

expertise, while the size and organization of their workshops were crucial to pricing and delivery schedules. Commercial operators were reluctant to run their own workshops, which required major capital investments and additional risks on their part. Nor did they wish to be responsible for the supervision or to incur the transaction costs arising from subcontracting to a great many artisans. A statement by the deans of the Antwerp cloth dressers' guild from 1536 reveals that the Schetzes, Fuggers, Welsers and Van Bombergens concluded contracts with master cloth dressers who each employed fifteen, twenty or more journeymen in order to ensure that everything would be ready to ship on time. The small masters objected to the 'abuses' that were inherent in such arrangements: those who entered contracts with the trading houses would also hire 'unfree' workers (i.e. persons who were not part of the guild system). The large entrepreneurs insisted that this was necessary in order to meet their contractual obligations to the trading houses in all cases. They refused to observe restrictions on the number of journeymen per workshop, arguing that if they did so, their principals might switch to a different textile centre. The dominance of the large entrepreneurs also led the guild officials to recognize sons far younger than eighteen as full masters, enabling their fathers to install an additional *scheerdis* (workbench). The strategy of the Schetzes and other merchant capitalists basically gave rise to deregulation and flexibilization.[219]

Several German rulers, including the Dukes of Brunswick, purchased fine cloth exclusively from firms that were based in Leipzig or had a factor there. In the 1530s and 40s Schetz & Co. supplied Duke Albert of Prussia and John Frederick I, Elector of Saxony, both strong supporters of Luther. Schetz considered religious affiliation and commerce to be entirely separate pursuits. At Easter in 1540 his firm sold the Elector English cloth for a total sum of 3024 gold florins or *c.* £743 Fl.gr. (i.e. about 10 percent of the value of all cloth they exported to Leipzig each year), and another large shipment followed a few months later.[220]

Shipments to Leipzig were highly profitable. After Erasmus Schetz died, his sons Gaspar, Melchior, and Balthasar continued this trade. In 1552, however, Balthasar, who until then had taken charge of the trade with Germany, travelled to Spain to represent the financial interests of the firm there, while financial matters in the Netherlands kept Gaspar and Melchior fully occupied. Accordingly, the brothers entrusted trade with Germany to Christoffel Pruynen (the son of Arnold) and to Adriaen van Hilst, who lived in Leipzig in a house owned by the Schetz brothers. Both were partners of the brothers, who together invested £4000 Fl.gr., while Pruynen paid in £3000 Fl.gr. and Van Hilst £2000 Fl.gr., amounting to £9000 Fl.gr. in social capital, with the explicit stipulation that the names of the brothers were never to be disclosed; the company was to continue operating under the names of Pruynen and Van Hilst. This is not the place to discuss the activities of this company. What matters is that net profits in just over five years between 1 January 1553 and 17 March 1558 were so high that the social capital increased to £24,777 Fl.gr., i.e. nearly threefold.[221] An excellent result, especially considering the serious commercial difficulties of the period, which had not been the case in the 1540s.

219 SAA, GA 4029; Thijs (1987), 220-1.
220 Häpke (1914), 50; Brübach (1994), 435; Schirmer (2006), 447 and 503.
221 IISH, NEHA 2.5.11.4; Génard (1882), 483-90.

Erasmus Schetz always regarded international trade as central to his economic activities. He set up an import/export network in which Lisbon, Antwerp, Aachen, and Leipzig were essential hubs. The Altenberg operations and brass manufacture in Aachen would never have been so profitable without the export of manillas and other metal wares to Lisbon. Conversely, the same held true: without pepper imports via Lisbon, trade with Leipzig would never have been so profitable. From the 1520s the product selection was diversified, and trading was extended to other areas to instrumentalize profit opportunities arising from wars and price increases, as well as from long-term trends, especially the ongoing price increases for grain. The commercial strategies of Erasmus Schetz were successful. In the mid-1540s no firm based in the Netherlands exported goods with a higher total value to other parts of Europe. Covering 13 percent of total pepper exports, Schetz & Co. surpassed all other trading companies in the Low Countries. They were also the largest firm trading independently with Germany. That they had their most intensive commercial relations with Leipzig of all German cities was no coincidence: in addition to being a centre for purchasing Mansfelder *Garkupfer*, Leipzig was a growing market for pepper and English cloth, as it was a gateway for trade with Eastern Europe.

1.5 Finance as Investment and Speculation

The complex relation between capitalist development and state formation in early modern Europe has led historians to adopt highly divergent and often incompatible positions. I therefore need to research to what extent and in what ways political rulers and Antwerp capitalists served, helped, and favoured one another during the first half of the sixteenth century. Clearly, the peculiar nexus between Schetz and the Portuguese Crown derived essentially from mutually beneficial commercial deals. In addition, the Antwerp capitalist had the highest political authorities in the Low Countries on his side. The explanation for his effective calamine monopoly lies in his role as creditor of Charles V. The Habsburg-Valois wars, which started in 1521 and continued with some interruptions into the 1550s, could not be funded by the central government of the Habsburg Netherlands through regular income, subsidies, or new taxes and continuously necessitated raising new loans. Like other bankers, Schetz saw the Emperor's need for money as an opportunity, but his objective was not so much to obtain huge profits quickly as to secure his mining rights. In that respect, he was no different from the Fuggers, who applied the same strategy during the reigns of Maximilian I and Charles V.[222]

Schetz did not build his business on speculative finance. Commodity trading always remained central to his economic activities. He was aware that banking in general and exchange operations in particular might yield far higher short-term profits than trade in commodities, but that they entailed greater risks. Even a merchant who was well-informed about 'monetary standards, mint regulations, shipping charges and insurance rates, commercial practices, the credit standing of business firms', and, 'above all 'the ebb and flow' of the exchange, that is to say, 'the pattern of seasonal fluctuations in the money

222 See the synthesis by Graulau (2008).

market' could suffer serious losses, if he assessed market conditions incorrectly.[223] Schetz was an astute and experienced businessman. His letters to Desiderius Erasmus reveal his skill in explaining monetary and financial matters. The advice his learned friend received from Schetz always turned out to be correct and to yield a profit.[224] Yet, as far as can be ascertained, Schetz gained mainly from the actual commodities trade itself, i.e. from price differences between countries and cities, not from speculation on exchange rates.

His caution did not deter him from serving as banker to Charles V and the government in the Habsburg Netherlands. He knew that the support of the Emperor and his representatives was indispensable in obtaining the economic benefits that were crucial to him. The most important of these was of course the continued lease of the Altenberg mine at favourable terms. Exemption from the import and export prohibitions imposed from time to time on trading companies was also very important, as was providing the central government with copper and saltpetre for the arms industry, not only because of the profits to be made, but also because doing so facilitated the import of commodities intended for commercial use in wartime. On the other hand, anybody with sufficient cash available to provide the public authorities with short-term loans could profit nicely. Even though interest rates on the Antwerp money market declined significantly between 1515 and 1550, they often fluctuated considerably, and even their far lower level in the 1540s (averaging 12 to 13 percent *per annum*) was itself very attractive.[225] While Schetz did not miss out on favourable opportunities to profit from loans to public authorities, he was extremely cautious throughout most of his career and regarded financial operations mainly as investments. This is clear from what appears to have been his very first loan to Charles V in 1522.

In the years following his election, the Emperor was seriously short of money. In addition to his massive debt to the Fuggers, the Welsers and the Italian bankers, who had paid the German Electors large sums to vote for the Habsburg candidate, he also faced rapidly rising expenditure on military campaigns, as the changing balance of power inevitably led to war with King Francis I. The first Habsburg-Valois conflict, which broke out in 1521 and dragged on – with an interruption in 1525-27 – until the Peace of Cambrai in 1529, had serious consequences for the Low Countries. The opposing forces included two partisans of France, Robert de la Marck, Lord of Sedan, and Charles II, Duke of Gelre, requiring deployment of armed forces along both the southern border and in the North. By the end of 1521, Charles V had taken Tournai, and the imperial-papal troops had achieved victories in Northern Italy and Navarra.[226] Since the two sides were basically evenly matched for the time being, the Emperor decided to leave for Spain, where following the recent *comunero* revolt in Castile he hoped to restore good relations between the Crown and the insurgent cities. First he travelled to England to discuss a 'Great Enterprise' against France with Henry VIII, after which in mid-June he instructed

223 De Roover (1949), 166.

224 Erasmus, Ep. 1993, 2001, 2014, and 2527. See also Godin (1987), 543-5.

225 Van der Wee (1963), I, 527, and II, 362-3. The official figures were misleading: the standard interest rate often came with various special charges, which might amount to 2 to 4 percent: Braudel (1959), 196.

226 Rodríguez-Salgado (2004), 24-35.

the fleet moored in Arnemuiden, Zeeland, to sail to Spain.[227] The sailors and the 3,000 *Landsknechte* (mercenaries), however, refused to embark until they received their back pay. The Emperor could not pay them. Head of Finance Antoine I de Lalaing, Count of Hoogstraten, went to Antwerp and tried to obtain loans there. Despite pledging the jewels of the Emperor and Governor Margaret of Austria as collateral, he was ignored by the financial community. Even the Fuggers adamantly refused. The commercial and industrial situation was abysmal. In 1522 and 1523 no Spanish, Portuguese, or Italian ships entered the Scheldt. The ongoing threat of war obstructed trade with France, even though some firms – Schetz & Co. among them – were allowed to trade with the enemy. Political-military prospects were so bleak that rapid economic recovery appeared impossible. The conflict between Christian II of Denmark and the Hanseatic cities, moreover, disrupted the grain trade, while crop failures and destruction on the part of the French army led prices to soar, instigating riots and pillaging in several cities. Rural and urban impoverishment considerably delayed payment of the *aides* (the subsidies granted to the ruler by the Estates). Devaluation by the King of France disrupted the tenuous monetary system in the Netherlands. A crisis of confidence ensued.[228]

Erasmus Schetz saw the opportunity emerging from financial disillusionment, uncertainty, and mistrust. Able to lend money without jeopardizing his commercial activities, he had good reasons to be of service to the Emperor. He agreed to put up an interest-free loan of £10,000 Artois of 40 Fl. groats. Still, he took no risk, demanding a precious drinking vessel called 'Le Pavillon' and four golden necklaces that belonged to the wife of Lalaing as collateral. If the loan was not repaid the day it came due, he would be allowed to melt the necklaces and pass the gold on to other businessmen at a high interest rate.[229] Although in the sixteenth century precious jewels and silver were often used to obtain credit, it was unusual for a powerful aristocrat – let alone his wife – to agree to such an arrangement. Lalaing did so, because he owed Schetz & Co. fl.8437 ½ for a large shipment of pepper supplied by the Burgos merchant Fernandez Annez; if Annez did not receive payment within six months, Schetz & Co. could take possession of an annuity of fl.543 charged against the City of Antwerp.[230]

Compared with loans that the Emperor had obtained in previous years, the sum that Schetz provided in 1522 was relatively modest, but at the time there was a dire shortage of cash, and fundraising efforts by the central government appeared doomed.[231] Not only was he the sole businessman at that point willing to help the Emperor in his time of financial need, but he was also doing it without intending to make any profit – provided that the loan was repaid when due. The offer was exceptional, at a time when yearly interest rates were 20 percent and higher. As a result, he could do no wrong in the eyes of Charles V. No complete list is available of the sums he lent the Emperor over the course of subsequent years or of their terms. In the 1520s and 30s the *receveur général* of Charles V did keep

227 The ships were ordinarily equipped in Arnemuiden: Sicking (1998), 161.
228 Braudel (1959), 197; Van der Wee (1963), I, 144-8; Blanchard (2009), 31-9, esp. 38.
229 ADN, B 2309; AGR, PEA 872, Compte de Jean Micault, 1522, f° 28v°-30. See Henne (1858-60), III, 265-6; Ehrenberg (1896), I, 367; Noordam-Croes (1968), 67. Note that £1 Fl/gr. = £6 Artois.
230 SAA, SR 161, f° 234 and 351.
231 In 1522 military spending consumed 70 percent of the state budget: Van Cauwenberghe (1982), 345.

careful records of the sums he borrowed in Antwerp or received as gifts, but he rarely indicated the names of the creditors. In most cases he made do with vague notes, such as 'certain Antwerp merchants', 'German merchants', 'Genoese merchants in Antwerp', or 'various merchants', averting disclosure of the share of specific groups or individuals. Many credit transactions were moreover conducted by Gerard Stercke or Lazarus Tucher, who operated as brokers for unspecified businessmen.[232] Beyond any doubt, Schetz provided the Emperor with emergency assistance several times in the mid-1520s. He also offered financial services to many high-ranking officials in the Habsburg Netherlands. At the end of 1525, for example, he agreed to transfer the *douaire* (the Spanish funds) of Margaret of Austria to the Netherlands for two years: 16,000 ducats *per annum*, payable in monthly instalments of 13331/3 ducats. The agreement was that Schetz would regularly have the money brought to the Court, which was located in Mechelen. Since the governor was often on the move, the stipulation was that payment would be made, only if the Court was within a distance of 12 Flemish miles, i.e. 45 to 46 kilometres, from Antwerp, thereby also including delivery in Brussels.[233] These transactions provided Schetz with such immense prestige that he was ennobled for 'services rendered' on 20 October 1527.[234]

In the early 1530s financial transactions with the central government of the Habsburg Netherlands were back on the agenda, with the Nuremberg businessman Lazarus Tucher frequently acting as intermediary. The amounts were substantial but not exorbitant. The largest loan amounted to £21,000 Artois and was provided not by Erasmus Schetz personally but by the firm Schetz & Co.[235] The partners were also among those who at the request of Margaret of Austria issued loans immediately after the great flood of 5 November 1530 towards rebuilding the dykes in South Beveland. In March 1532 the central government therefore owed Schetz & Co. fl.16,890 on that count (i.e. 6.5 percent of the total capital involved). South-German firms and agents had lent far greater sums: together with the interest due, the total debt to the Herwart brothers and their heirs amounted to fl.79,623, nearly fl.61,200 to Georg Meuting, and fl.28,434 to Hans Pimel from Augsburg.[236] The willingness of the partners to help the government in the event of financial difficulties undoubtedly explains why they were able to continue to lease the Altenberg mine on the same favourable terms in 1531, and why the higher bids on the lease offered by Nuremberg competitors were not even considered.

Four years later they were willing to help out once again. The new Habsburg-Valois war – in fact the continuation of the old, ongoing hostilities – was so costly that the finances of both parties were depleted by 1537. Obtaining new loans proved impossible. On 16 March Lodewijk van Schore (a permanent member of both the Council of State and the Privy Council) and Willem van de Werve (margrave of Antwerp) were therefore instructed to pressure the Antwerp city government in any way possible to provide money and to convince merchant bankers to issue a loan of fl.100,000 for a year at a 'modest

232 See the *Comptes de la Recette générale des Finances*, stored in the *Archives départementales du Nord* (ADN) in Lille, *Série B*. Microfiches are available in AGR, D 9000. See the comments of Braudel (1959), 195-6.

233 ADN, B 2327, 21 November 1525; Veratelli (2013), 92-3, 358-9.

234 AGR, PEA 879. See also d'Ursel (2004), 55-6.

235 ADN, B 2363; Ehrenberg (1896), I, 368; Pölnitz (1958), 555 n. 42.

236 AGR, PEA 1627/1, Letter dated 13 March 1532.

interest rate', i.e. 10 to 12 percent.[237] They failed in this effort, and ultimately the warbattle was discontinued for lack of funds. On 16 November a three-month truce was agreed and was followed by peace negotiations soon afterwards. The time had certainly come. On 12 November Schetz had written Count Henry III of Nassau that the merchants – including himself – who the year before had advanced large sums toward the war efforts wished to be repaid, and that such repayment should be made urgently to avoid lawsuits.[238] Easier said than done, as Mary of Hungary had already informed her brother: 'Your finance and income are so heavily taxed, sold, and overdue [...] that all has been consumed and depleted until 1539, and the debts payable moreover exceed fl.400,000 or fl.500,000'.[239] Schetz understood the dire straits of the government and proposed an equitable solution. The amount payable to him, i.e. fl.19,451 ½, could be repaid in one instalment of fl.8,851 ½ within two to three months and the balance due (i.e. fl.10,600) over twelve years in twenty-four instalments, starting on 1 April 1538, to be subtracted every six months from the lease of the Altenberg mine.[240] The central government would therefore not have to put up the money to pay off the bulk of the loan, while Schetz & Co. could rely on continuing their lease for many years to come and could be reasonably confident that the price would not be raised (which it indeed was not).

Schetz & Co. essentially regarded loans to the Emperor and the government of the Netherlands as investments into the late 1540s. As they aimed primarily to secure basic economic interests, the firm was willing to provide loans on favourable terms. On the other hand, the recurrent, increasingly frequent, and ever greater financial needs of the Emperor provided the opportunity for short-term (generally within three or six, sometimes twelve months) low-risk profits. The only risk in the second quarter of the sixteenth century was that the Emperor might be unable to repay on time, and this rarely happened. It was precisely the fragmented nature of his vast empire that enabled Charles V to mobilize highly differentiated resources and to transfer money from one part to the other, which was not an option for the French monarchy. Moreover, Charles V was a ruler who communicated well with merchant bankers: he was aware of their expectations and understood the problems associated with repayment. He was therefore able to establish and maintain a relationship of trust with the financial elites in Europe. As a Spanish observer rightly noted in 1534: he was 'a better payer than any other prince'.[241]

Over the course of the 1540s financial transactions by Erasmus Schetz gradually increased. This was in part because the public authorities used his services more frequently, not only for loans from him personally but also to mediate with South-German bankers. In several respects 1542 was a turning point, as warfare and its consequences created financial difficulties for the Emperor, as well as for the government of the Netherlands and the Antwerp city authorities; and their financial problems became endemic. In June, French troops invaded Artois and Luxembourg, followed on 12 July by an official declaration

237 AGR, PEA 1652/1, Letter dated 16 March 1537.
238 AGR, PEA 128, f°132.
239 Quoted in Baelde (1963), 19 (my translation).
240 AGR, CC 138, f° 272-3. The method used in 1538 to calculate the interest is the first known example of repayment in constant annuities in the Low Countries. See De Groote (1968), 204-5, and Meskens (2013), 75-81.
241 Quoted in Pacini (2004), 183.

of war. The greatest threat came briefly from warlord Maarten van Rossum. He served William, Duke of Jülich-Cleves-Berg, who claimed the neighbouring Duchy of Gelre and was an ally of the King of France. In mid-July Van Rossum invaded Brabant with a large force, left behind a trail of destruction, decimated a government army, and held Antwerp under siege. Philippe II de Croÿ, Duke of Aarschot, had warned Mary of Hungary shortly before that the medieval fortified walls would not withstand systematic artillery fire for long. Fortunately, Van Rossum left three days later without giving battle, for reasons that remain unclear.[242] The aborted siege of Antwerp led to a major outcry and was to have important consequences, as will become clear later in this book.

Many international traders had been tempted to flee Antwerp, when they learned that Van Rossum was approaching,[243] as the *schuttersgilden* (armed citizen militias) were unable to repel a large, professional army, and the central government could not deploy troops in time. Gian Carlo Affaitadi, who had resided in the Scheldt town for quite a while by then and hoped to settle permanently in the Habsburg Netherlands, is said to have convinced many foreign merchants to remain in the city, armed a group of residents at his own expense, and urged his peers to follow his example. The foreign merchants did in fact heed his advice and formed companies of armed men.[244] Schetz manifested himself as *protector urbis* during these dramatic days. He equipped a great many soldiers and supported them at his own expense, thereby further enhancing his renown both locally and with the government.[245] In August of that same year, he moreover issued a zero-interest loan of fl.8000 to pay the army along the borders. In March 1543 Mary of Hungary asked him to mobilize 'German money' to cover the cost of armaments.[246] She obviously knew that Schetz had every interest in doing so, as he himself supplied materials for the imperial artillery. In the summer and early autumn the financial situation became so desperate that the governor sent Philip Nigri, member of the Council of State and a skilled negotiator, to Antwerp, instructing him to do all he possibly could to raise money. He was expected, for example, to convince the guardians of minors from wealthy merchant families to provide loans.[247]

The new Valois-Habsburg war created much tension on the Antwerp money market, climaxing in 1544, when the central government had to pay £217,385 Artois or *c.* £36,231 Fl. gr. in interest. As Lyon became increasingly attractive to South-German capital, the government grew more dependent on Spanish and Genoese bankers. Their ever greater role in European finance coincided with the supply from the Americas of silver, which benefited Medina del Campo in Castile, with Genoa serving as the main point of relay for Italy.[248] In August 1544 Spanish and Genoese bankers lent Charles V a total of 126,833 ducats or *c.* fl.253,666 at an annual interest rate of 13 percent, followed in October 1546, by

242 Gorter-Van Royen (1993), 73, 75, 80-2. See also the letter from the powerful aristocrat and statesman Louis of Praet to Mary of Hungary, 24 September 1542: Lanz (1844-46), I, 365.

243 The Governor of the English merchants fled the city. Henry VIII regarded this as dereliction of duty and had him imprisoned in London on 6 August 1542. De Smedt (1950), I, 160.

244 Henne (1858-60), VII, 368-71.

245 Servilius (1544); Papebrochius (1845), 247.

246 AGR, CMH, no. 35, Letter dated 24 August 1542, and PEA 1629/1.

247 AGR, PEA 1629/2-3: 28 and 29 September 1543.

248 Van der Wee (1963), II, 200-4.

an additional 74,667 ducats or fl.149,334, half of which came from Erasmus Schetz, who provided an additional 15,000 ducats or fl.30,000 as a personal loan.

Other businessmen from the Low Countries who lent the central government smaller amounts in this period included Aer(d)t van Dale (10,000 ducats), Pauwel van Gemert (5000), and Vincent de Smit (3000)[249]; all three merchants making their fortunes in Antwerp. Whether they had special reasons for lending the Emperor money is unclear, but this is likely to have been the case for Van Dale. Like Schetz, he primarily traded in commodities, but in the period 1533-40 he was one of the three city receivers and was consequently well aware of the public finances. The marriage of his daughter to Gerard Stercke, a scion of a Brabant family of bankers that arranged a great many loans for the Brussels Court via the Antwerp money market, was presumably an additional incentive for him to act as creditor.[250]

In the 1540s the Emperor and the government of the Netherlands were not the only one resorting to the Antwerp money market. Several European rulers became important customers, including the kings of Portugal and England. While Schetz & Co. operated as creditors on several occasions, their intention for a long time was to cultivate reciprocal relations that might be conducive to commercial contracts, lower taxes, or other economic benefits. The loan totalling fl.35,000 that they issued around 1540 to the Elector of Saxony is likely to have been connected to privileges they obtained for their trade in *Garkupfer*.[251] Although the amount of their loan to the King of Portugal is unknown, whose debts in Antwerp soared from 1543 onward,[252] they are certain to have granted loans to secure their business interests in Lisbon. The firm extended credit to the King of England for the same reason. When Henry VIII ran into financial difficulties in July-August 1546 and not only had to request Anton Fugger for an extension on the payment due but had to obtain new short-term loans as well, Schetz & Co. lent him £20,000 sterling or £26,000 Fl.gr. for six months at 6 percent via Stephen Vaughan, as had been promised and arranged by his eldest son Gaspar.[253] The firm agreed to lend Henry VIII such a substantial sum – far more than any previous loans to Charles V– because of the falling exchange rates caused by the 'great debasements',[254] as the firm benefited from them via its substantial grain and gunpowder exports to England.

From 1542 onwards, Erasmus Schetz and his two eldest sons (Gaspar and Melchior), sometimes together but in most cases individually, also extended short-term loans to the City of Antwerp, which soon became recurrent and steadily larger. Schetz & Co. regarded these loans as safe investments, at least until 1548, as they believed them secured by the 'extraordinary' income from the city and the value of the urban patrimony. The city used the money to finance the construction of new fortifications. After the siege by Maarten van Rossum, international traders had threatened to leave the town, unless the obsolete

249 AGR, PEA 1630/4, and 1641/1; Carande (1967), 334, 338-9. 1 Spanish ducat = fl.0.547.

250 AGR, CMH, no. 33, Letter dated 24 August 1542; Donnet (1895-96), 216, 234-9, 251; Ehrenberg (1896), I, 364-5; Strieder (1930), 38, 103, 164, 191; Pölnitz (1958), passim. In the 1530s Gerard Stercke was also receiver-general of the alum duties: AGR, PEA 1414/4, no. 1.

251 Schirmer (2006), 586.

252 Van Houtte (1952), 177.

253 LPFD, Henry VIII, 21/1, nos 1420-1, 1434, 1477, 1492.

254 Van der Wee (1963), II, 204. See also 2.14.

medieval city walls were replaced by an adequate defence system. On 16 August 1542 the Emperor, who two years previously had urged that new walls be built around the city, ordered that construction begin immediately. Starting demolition and excavation required the recruitment of about two thousand workers.[255] To raise funds to pay their wages, the city government turned to Erasmus Schetz on 13 September 1542. He agreed to lend them fl.8000 for six months at 6 percent. In the weeks that followed, loans were obtained from three other businessmen from the Low Countries, as well as from an Augsburg firm.[256] This marked the start of a long series of loans, for rapidly increasing amounts, which the city government was able to repay after a few years only by taking out new loans, leading its debt burden to become disproportionate by 1548.

A list of all loans obtained between September 1542 and November 1547 to finance building the new fortifications reveals that the local authorities obtained credit very easily indeed. Trade and industry were thriving, and moneylenders took comfort from the fact that all the possessions and income of the city were pledged as security. So great was this confidence that the city government was generally granted short-term loans at a lower annual interest than that paid by the central government. In 1544, when interest rates were at their highest, the city obtained three-month loans at 8 to 12 percent *per annum*, while the government paid 14 to 17 percent.[257] The rapid deterioration of the city's financial situation in 1545 and its nadir in 1548 did not appear to be a major concern, as hardly anybody was aware of the 'extraordinary' expenditures.[258]

Erasmus Schetz and his sons were among the chief moneylenders, providing 23.4 percent of all new loans taken out by the City of Antwerp between 13 September 1542 and 11 November 1547, totalling fl.1,876,235. Erasmus was the main creditor, usually as an individual financier but in some cases as the largest shareholder of the firm Schetz & Sons (15.8 percent), while Gaspar was second (5.8 percent), and Melchior had a supporting role (1.8 percent). Input from other creditors from the Low Countries was negligible: together, they provided a combined total of less than half the credit that Gaspar underwrote. The share of Erasmus Schetz and his sons surpassed that of all Italian (especially Genoese), Spanish, and Portuguese bankers combined (12.7 percent). The High Germans, however, greatly outdid all the other creditors, supplying 55.4 percent of the city's borrowings. Comparison with *individual* merchant bankers and firms from Augsburg and Nuremberg is difficult, because some High Germans served as intermediaries acting on behalf of others, whose identities were rarely disclosed. One such individual was Lazarus Tucher, who in August 1546 lent a total of fl.185,539 for six months. Other brokers were Ulrich Hainhofer, who acted first as a factor for Anton Haug & Co. and then for the Bimmel, Wolf Puschinger, and Franz Werner.[259] In any case, some firms from Augsburg lent large sums, notably Welser & Co., Herwart & Co., Haug-Lang(e)nauer-Linck, and the brothers

255 AGR, PEA 1629/3; SAA, PK 78, f°176v°-177, and PK 2242, no. 1.

256 Those concerned were: the excise collector Geert Bruynseels (fl.7500 for six months), the banker Gerard Stercke (fl.6785 for twelve months), the beer brewer Hendrik van Duysborch or Doesborch (fl.1141 for three months), and the South-German firm Hans Rosenberger & Co. (fl.3000 for 9 months).

257 Van der Wee (1963), I, 526.

258 See Part Three.

259 Franz Werner acted as an intermediary for many merchants: Strieder (1930), 130, 145, 147, 168, 198.

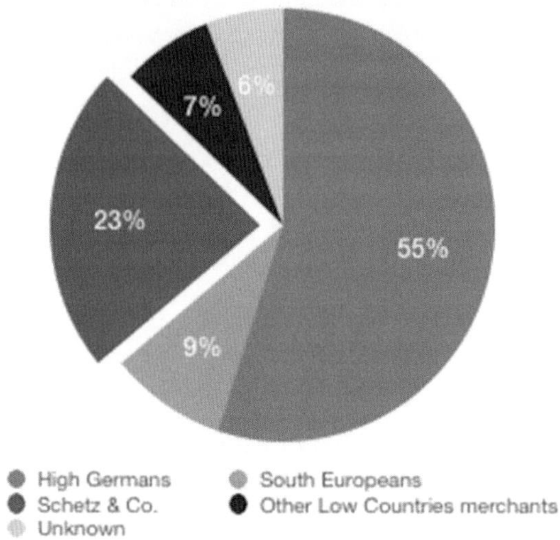

Figure 2. Lenders to the City of Antwerp, 1542-47

Source: SAA, T 724, no. 1
Note: Total sum loaned: fl.1,886,235

Hans and Erasmus Rot. Anton Fugger topped the list: in August 1544 he lent fl.100,000 at an interest rate of 12 percent *per annum*, fixed for four years. No other firm lent such a large sum for an equivalent period.

Erasmus Schetz refused to match the commitment that Anton Fugger underwrote. During the period under review, he issued loans to the City of Antwerp almost continuously, but nearly all were short-term loans ranging from three to six months. Only in exceptional cases did he provide loans for two or three years. Once, in August 1545, he provided a longer-term loan of fl.6000, without charging interest and stipulating explicitly that the money would go toward building a specific section of the fortifications. Did he wish to convey to the Emperor how deeply he cared about their progression? In April Charles V and Mary of Hungary had visited some of the walls and bastions under construction and were probably not impressed with the rate of construction. They had stayed with Schetz, who must have known that the Emperor was scheduled to return to Antwerp in the autumn, as indeed happened: on 25 November the Emperor officiated at the opening ceremony of the new and monumental (albeit as yet incomplete) Saint George's Gate; this beginning or end of the road to and from Mechelen and Brussels was promptly renamed 'Emperor's Gate.'

Erasmus Schetz long continued to be very cautious in the amounts he lent the city. At no point in the period 1542-46 did he have more than fl.42,000 outstanding. In February 1547 the firm Schetz & Sons issued its first very large loan: fl.100,000 for six months at 6 percent. Their reasons are unclear. Did they hope to extend their influence, where Lazarus Tucher was clearly the city's main loan broker? In August 1546 Tucher had raised fl.185,539, as has been mentioned above, and when the city proved unable to repay the full amount of this loan in February 1547, he agreed to extend the duration on more than half the amount by another six months. Tucher also served the central government on the Antwerp Exchange. He had already underwritten loans to the Emperor in the 1530s, but in the 1540s and early 1550s he became increasingly important as a broker, first for Charles V and later for Phillip II.[260]

Be that as it may, financial transactions were not Erasmus Schetz's main source of income. Accrued interest from all the loans he provided to the Antwerp city government between mid-September 1542 and mid-February 1548 amounted to fl.18,832, i.e. an average of fl.3477 *per annum*. A complete list of his loans to the Emperor and the central government during the same period is not available, but in any case in 1544 and 1545 his income from interest was 3721 fl., averaging fl.1861 *per annum*. In each of these two years the sum total therefore amounted to fl.5338. The very large loans to Henry VIII and Charles V, respectively, significantly increased overall revenues in the next two years: over fl.12,800 in 1546 and nearly fl.9500 in 1547. A fair revenue, though hardly spectacular when compared, for example, with the proceeds from the Altenberg: in the period 1561-81, when serious operational difficulties were common, annual net profits from the sale of calamine ran to between fl.8880 and fl.10,150.[261]

Toward the end of his life, Erasmus Schetz suddenly became far more active in the Antwerp money market. On 5 May 1548 – ten days before he drew up his last will and testament – he and his sons Gaspar and Melchior lent the Emperor fl.200,000, repayable by 15 May 1549 at 12 percent interest. In October of that year, the loan was extended by six months at the same rate of interest. By then, the firm had lent Mary of Hungary fl.20,335 as well, for a six-month period.[262] Why at this point Erasmus Schetz was prepared to lend the Emperor twice as much as ever before is unclear, as is his reason for lending the money for a much longer period.[263] Admittedly, both the political and the economic contexts were favourable. Perhaps he assumed that such loans would not entail any serious risk. The glorious victory at Mühlberg marked the start of a brief period in which Charles V seemed all-powerful. He had defeated the German Protestants, his two greatest rivals (King Francis I of France and King Henry VIII of England) had died in early 1547, and the Ottomans were posing no threat.[264] Trade and industry thrived, as manifested on the Antwerp money market by the low and stable interest rates for short-term loans.[265] Low interest rates, however, also meant lower profit margins. Another factor to be considered was that repayments of large loans could drag on. The question therefore remains as to why he invested so much capital in financial transactions, instead of spending it on commercial activities, which in these years would most probably have generated greater returns. He had already been elevated to the nobility some time previously, but perhaps he was looking for further reward. If such was his intention, then he succeeded in it, because on 8 June 1548 the Emperor awarded him the honorary title *Pfalzgraf*, Count Palatine, which though devoid of any political power did carry certain prerogatives.[266] The growing influence of his eldest, highly ambitious son Gaspar, however, undoubtedly played a role. From 1545

260 Ehrenberg (1896), I, passim; Strieder (1930), passim; Bauernfeind (2011), 25-6.
261 Calculated from Van Uytven (2001), 199.
262 AGR, CMH 63, and PEA 1661/1/B, f°100.
263 In February 1547 he had lent the Emperor fl.100,000 for six months, his highest amount ever.
264 Rodriguez-Salgado (2000), 105.
265 Van der Wee (1963), I, 527.
266 d'Ursel (2004), 61-2.

on, Gaspar had together with his brothers Melchior and Balthasar been a partner in the firm, henceforth officially known as 'Erasmus Schetz & Sons.'[267]

In the 1550 and 60s, Gaspar, Melchior, and Balthasar were highly prominent in economics and finance in the Habsburg Netherlands, as their father had hoped they would be. Six children had been born from the marriage of Erasmus Schetz and Ida van Richtergem: four boys (Gaspar, Melchior, Balthasar, and Koenraad) and two girls (Maria and Isabella). Father Schetz expressed the value he attributed to family ties in business and his high expectations for his sons in the names given to his three eldest: Gaspar, Melchior, and Balthasar. By reference to the three Magi (after whom the sons were named), father and sons were identified with the world of international (and exotic) trade, of which the city of Antwerp was the new centre. According to Christian tradition, the Magi, also known as the (three) Wise Men or the (three) Kings, all from distant countries in the Orient, visited Jesus immediately after He was born and presented the child with gold, frankincense, and myrrh – rare and valuable commodities.[268] The Medici had introduced this theme in Florence,[269] and in the mid-1470s Sandro Botticelli produced scenes of the Adoration of the Magi for various businessmen with close ties to the Medici.[270] The theme's attraction was that it enabled families to legitimate their newly acquired wealth and their civic prominence. Introduced in Antwerp at the end of the fifteenth century, its popularity there was phenomenal and between 1500 and 1530 became 'the defining subject of the Antwerp mannerist painting, its signature iconography'. The Magi scene tended to be the central panel in a triptych and nearly always depicted all kinds of luxury commodities transported by the retinue of the Kings, who were regarded as patrons and protectors of merchants. Comparison with contemporary long-distance traders quickly came to mind. In this period artists in Antwerp increasingly depicted themes related to the world of trade, in paintings and prints alike, but the Adoration theme dominated the market and was reproduced hundreds of times.[271] Erasmus Schetz therefore made a conscious choice between 1513 and 1520, according to what could be expected from an affluent businessman in Antwerp. As a newcomer, symbolic identification with this trading city was of great social import for him. At the same time his choice of names expressed his expectations for his three eldest sons: they were destined to become substantial businessmen.

Gaspar, Melchior, and Balthasar fulfilled their father's wishes, in that they became economic players, with Gaspar taking the lead from the outset, less because he was the eldest than because he undeniably had the keenest business acumen. Trade and finance were not the brothers' sole preoccupation, as contemporaries agreed that they also had artistic and/or scientific talents. The *artes liberales*, however, were always secondary. Once they completed their education, all the sons, except for the youngest, Koenraad, were included by father Schetz in the firm's activities. At 22, Gaspar was sent to Frankfurt am Main, the most important *Messe* (fair) in Germany for trade with Antwerp, to represent the

267 SAA, T 724, no. 1, sub anno.
268 See esp. Beer et al. (2014).
269 Acidini (2011), 108-9.
270 O'Malley (2010), 17.
271 Vermeylen (2001), 49, and (2003), 161; Ewing (2004/5); Van den Brink, Martens and Van Hout (2005).

business interests of his father.[272] From the mid-1530s he also operated independently, most probably facilitated by his marriage (in 1535) to Margriet (van der) Brugghe, the daughter of a wealthy merchant family from Mechelen. From the outset he was far more interested in finance than in the commodities trade. He lent money to individuals, always members of the higher nobility,[273] while underwriting mainly short-term loans to the Antwerp city government and to the central government.[274] Specializing in such transactions, he spent the 1540s continuously enlarging the network that his father had established. Melchior, who married the merchant's daughter Anna van Stralen, also began to pursue his own economic activities in this period, focusing, like Gaspar, mainly on finance. Balthasar was able to follow suit only after he came of age in 1545. At the end of that year the company name was changed to include the sons. Later documents reveal that Gaspar, Melchior, and Balthasar were the sole partners of their father, that Gaspar was responsible for the financial operations, and that he increasingly involved his father and brothers in the imperial finances. His impact on decision-making grew steadily. In April 1548 he travelled to Augsburg, where Charles V was trying to impose a political-religious settlement on the Protestant rulers, following his victory at Mühlberg. His plans were thwarted by his inability to raise enough funds, owing to the extant backlog of debt.[275] Gaspar assured the Emperor that Schetz & Sons would provide him with money as quickly as possible and in fact did so the next month (see above).

The increasing impact of the sons, especially of Gaspar, on the operations of the firm coincided with the death of their mother, soon followed by the second marriage of their father. On 7 June 1548, Ida van Richtergem died,[276] not unexpectedly, as on 15 May she and Erasmus had drawn up a last will and testament. This document stipulated that the 'large house in Antwerp', the House of Aachen, would go to Gaspar, Melchior, and Balthasar, as it was the head office of the partnership that Erasmus formed with them. The youngest son, Koenraad, and the two daughters, Maria and Isabella, were each to receive an annuity of fl.250 charged against these premises as compensation, amounting to a capital of fl.4000; the total value of the House of Aachen was thus estimated at fl.24,000.[277] The next year Erasmus indicated that he intended to remarry, this time to his cousin Catharina de Cock, daughter of Barbara van Kelmis. The marriage was her second one as well.[278] He was 69 or 70, and his future bride was much younger, as may be inferred from the fact that she ultimately survived him by more than twenty years. Did this second marriage come about because of the one-sixth share that her father, the late Jan de Cock, and his brother-in-law Gerhard Parijs had obtained in 1524 on the lease of the Altenberg, and was Erasmus hoping to end this arrangement before his own death? Or did other, non-material motives come

272 Erasmus, Ep. 3067: *Correspondance* (1982), XI, 322-3. On the Frankfurt fairs, see Dietz (1910), I, 37-8, and North (2014), 65-6.

273 NA, ND, Raad en Rekenkamer te Breda II, no. 1039 (Count Maximilian of Egmont, Stadtholder of Friesland); SAA, SR 241, f° 673-674v°; Gunn, Grummitt and Cools (2007), 179.

274 AGR, PEA 1661/1/B; Pölnitz (1967), 466.

275 Tracy (2002), 226-7.

276 Jasparus(1548).

277 Although the last will and testament no longer remains, some of its provisions are summarized in SAA, V 328, V 332, and V 338.

278 Her first husband was one Andries de Mil, about whom nothing else is known.

into play? In any case, his children did not approve of this marriage. Erasmus, however, was determined and was willing to pay a huge sum to receive dispensation for a marriage between cousins, for which only the Pope could give permission. Such a dispensation cost fl.12,000,[279] i.e. half the capital value of the prestigious House of Aachen. To appease his children, Erasmus had a notary stipulate in writing on 28 March 1550 that his second wife would have no legal claim to the movable items and properties relating directly or indirectly to his commercial, industrial, or financial interests. Two months later, on 31 May, Erasmus passed away. Immediately thereafter Kathelijne de Cock confirmed that she had indeed waived all rights that would have become hers from the business interests of her husband.[280]

The sons showed far more interest in financial matters than their father, even before he died. In 1546 Erasmus had issued Charles V two loans charged against the Treasury of Castile, but that was all. Gaspar, Melchior, and Balthasar, on the other hand, revealed themselves from 1550 on as major financiers of the Spanish Crown. On 10 May they contributed 20,000 escudos or 18,668 ducats towards an *asiento,* a short-term loan, of 95,000 escudos, with Spanish financiers covering the remainder. Two days later Gaspar joined these same Spaniards and a group of Italians in an *asiento* of 60,000 escudos. Such deals continued. On 31 August 1551 'Gaspar Schetz & Brothers', as the firm was then called, went so far as to lend 235,295 ducats. In May 1552 a new loan was issued for 221,760 ducats.[281] In August that year, to top it all, Gaspar met with Anton Fugger and proposed that they jointly underwrite a large loan for the Emperor. The Schetzes and the Antwerp representatives of the Fuggers had at times been competitors, for example in supplying the canon foundries in the Netherlands, but in the 1530s and 40s they had also done business with each other, with both parties supplying goods and lending money.[282] Anton Fugger considered Gaspar Schetz & Brothers to be a reliable and solvent partner and agreed to lend Charles V 600,000 ducats: 150,000 to be put up by the Fuggers and repayable in Naples, and 450,000 ducats to be provided by the Schetz brothers and charged against the Treasury of Castile. A few days later Balthasar underwrote two more loans totalling 158,415 ducats. The transactions were so important to the firm that Balthasar travelled to Spain, where in the spring of 1553 in Medina del Campo he underwrote a new *asiento* for the sum of 100,000 ducats.[283]

Some historians have calculated the share of the Schetzes in the loans charged against the Treasury of Castile based on the period 1521-55 at *c.* 4.5 percent.[284] Such a calculation is pointless, as until the middle of the century, Erasmus Schetz participated in such transactions only in exceptional cases. The years 1550-55 should therefore be taken as the standard. All new loans combined amounted to 10,302,564 ducats in this period, of which the Schetz firm provided 1,330,558, i.e. 12.9 percent of the total.[285] No wonder the brothers, under the

279 Butkens (1726), I, 287.
280 SAA, COLL 8, f° 13v°-14, 26, COLL 9, f° 17.
281 Lonchay (1907), 944; Carande (1967), 317, 344-5, 348, 381, 474; Kellenbenz (1970), 330, and (1990), I, 400. One ducat = 0.9334 escudos.
282 Pölnitz (1967), 92, 269, 340; Reinhard (1996), 138 and 142. The available sources list the amounts the Fuggers owed Schetz & Co. and vice versa but never indicate the reason.
283 SAA, T 628, no. 43; Carande (1967), 478, 480, 488; Pölnitz (1967), 576.
284 Kohler (1999); Tracy (2002), 101.
285 Calculated from Carande (1967), 344-51, 472-97.

undisputed aegis of Gaspar, soon became so famous that contemporaries automatically identified them as the main economic actors in the Low Countries.[286]

As a moneylender in international finance and a broker, Gaspar Schetz became so indispensable that in 1555 Phillip II appointed him factor: his official representative on the Antwerp Exchange. He was authorized to agree to loans on behalf of the monarch and to manage all monetary transactions, except for money transfers from Spain, which were arranged by the wealthy nobleman Juan Lopez Gallo, who settled in Bruges. Schetz was also allowed to enter into all types of contracts for purchasing goods intended for the armed forces in the Netherlands. His position of power was therefore exceptional. According to Governor Margaret of Parma, he did not misuse this power for his own benefit or that of his brothers, although this seemed highly improbable to other high-ranking persons, including Frédéric Perrenot de Granvelle, the brother of the Cardinal. Nevertheless, Phillip II heeded the advice of his stepsister and in 1561 appointed Gaspar Schetz treasurer-general of finance, enabling him to influence all financial and commercial decisions by the central government in the Habsburg Netherlands.[287] On 15 April 1568 the Duke of Alba wrote to Phillip II from the Netherlands that Schetz 'arranges all financial matters here; he is the God whom they all worship.'[288]

While the careers of the Schetz brothers are not our main preoccupation here, they did not follow their father's lead. They did not focus primarily on trade in commodities and did not regard finance as an investment. They remained partners in all firms in which their father had made a fortune, and they also launched new initiatives, including in the alum trade, but entrusted their commercial operations to partners. Their involvement in trading companies remained limited to capital investment. They were first and foremost financiers, granting short-term loans to public authorities. Gaspar circumvented the prohibition on providing interest-bearing loans independently or via intermediaries, resorting to front men. The brothers took major risks and turned a blind eye to the distinction between public and private money.[289]

1.6 Wealth and Prestige

During the first half of the sixteenth century, Antwerp indisputably offered opportunities for social advancement, especially for those engaging directly or indirectly in international trade. Large-scale foreign businessmen, however, were the ones making huge profits. The archival data gathered by Renée Doehaerd demonstrate that many merchants, transporters, and industrial entrepreneurs from the Low Countries were active in Antwerp between 1488 and 1514, but the vast majority had little capital. Some started companies, but nearly all were transitory associations. They did not set up large, more enduring firms, such as those

286 See SAA, V 332, no. 1.

287 Lonchay (1907), 945-7.

288 Quoted in Gachard (1955), II, 23 (my translation).

289 See *inter alia* SAA, V 322; V 324, f° 50v°-51v°; V 331; AGR, MD 809; De Groote (1972); Correns, Rau and Van de Cruys (2014), 63-5, 67-81, 104-16, 139-46; Puttevils (2015), 67-70, 74-5, 90-3, 98-100.

of the Italians and the High Germans.[290] The Venetian ambassador Gaspare Contarini was probably referring to the local elite, when he remarked in 1525 that 'few Antwerp citizens invest in large businesses; they derive their income from taxes, letting their houses, and similar pursuits', but his subsequent comment made perfectly clear what he wished to convey: 'The wholesale trade is run by foreigners'. A quarter century later, Cavalli (one of his successors) argued that nothing fundamental had changed.[291] Yet, according to Jeroen Puttevils the situation was most certainly different. Based on the export tax registers of 1544-45, he infers that growing numbers of 'local' merchants had become active in international trade. The source does in fact indicate 'the presence of a multitude of smaller and middle-sized merchants', who 'traded in products similar to those of their large-scale colleagues, albeit in smaller volumes'. The author does not, however, specify the relative importance of these 'local' merchants. That most of them were not 'generalists' but 'specialists', as he emphasizes, suggests that their commercial endeavours were most likely modest, because substantial merchants nearly always aimed to diversify. In any case, Puttevils fails to demonstrate that by the 1540s merchants from the Low Countries operated 'just like all other successful merchant groups'.[292] It would appear more likely that substantial 'local' merchants became prominent on European markets only in the 1560s and 70s, as Brulez has argued.[293] In any case, 'local' merchants who advanced to the upper echelons in business appear to have been exceptional before the middle of the century, as the zero-interest loan of 1552 shows.

In December 1552 the Emperor ordered the economic elite of Antwerp to grant a zero-interest loan. In what turned out to be a miserable year for him, he was experiencing the greatest difficulty in obtaining loans, and in his view the substantial businessmen in the commercial capital of the Low Countries should help fund the defence of the realm. The chancellor of Brabant and the treasurer-general of finance personally ensured that nobody escaped. They raised fl.253,650, of which nearly 80 percent was paid for by businessmen. The Genoese and Florentines were assessed as a group, for fl.15,000 and 8,000 respectively. Among the merchants/financiers and firms registered separately, Aer(d)t van Dale and his son Pauwel, who largely traded Canary sugar and grain, and were important creditors of the English Crown, topped the list with a combined loan of fl.13,000.[294] As for Gaspar, Melchior, and Balthasar Schetz, the authorities took into consideration that half of the estate of their recently deceased father was destined for three other children (see below). This was why they were instructed to contribute 'only' fl.8000. Even so, the amount was exceptionally high, as twelve to fourteen Florentine firms together paid as much.[295] A wide margin separated the Schetzes from the other contributors. Two members of the higher nobility each contributed fl.4000, followed by sixteen firms and individuals that each lent fl.2000 to fl.3000, including the Fuggers, Welsers, Lazarus Tucher, Wolfgang

290 Doehaerd (1963); Pitz (1966), 56-7, 74-5, 83-4, 88.
291 *Relazione* (1840a), 22, and *Relazione* (1840b), 202.
292 Puttevils (2015a), 47, 167-8, and (2015b), 1360. On the problems with this source, see 1.7.
293 Brulez (1959), 365-9, 458-9.
294 On the Van Dale family, see Donnet (1895-6); Ramsay (1975), 4; Coornaert, Kevin (2000); Arbelo García (2005); Guy (2019), 94.
295 For the names of the Florentine firms in Antwerp in 1552, see Goris (1925), 618 and 619-20.

Table 4. Principal contributors to the Antwerp zero-interest loan of 1552

Name	Occupation/Origin	Contribution in fl
Genuese 'nation'	Genuese merchants/financiers in Antwerp	15,000
Aer(d)t and Pauwel van Dale	Low Countries merchants and financiers	13,000
Florentine 'nation'	Florentine merchants/financiers in Antwerp	8,000
Gaspar, Melchior and Balthasar Schetz	Low Countries merchants and financiers	8000
Magistracy	Burgomasters and aldermen	7000
Jehan de Bourgogne	Aristocrat	4000
Evrard Cot(t)ereau	Knight; Lord of Malle	4000
Fernando de Bernuy and family	Spanish merchants	3000
Conrad Beyer 'and others'	Merchants from Augsburg	3000
Fuggers	Merchant bankers from Augsburg	3000
Andreas Ligsaltz	Merchant from Munich	3000
Wolf Puschinger	Merchant-broker from Leipzig	3000
Lazarus Tucher	Merchant-broker from Nuremberg	3000
Johann Welser and brothers	Merchants from Augsburg	3000
Johann Kaltenhofer & Co.	Merchants from Nuremberg	2500
Widow Fernando Dassa	Merchant from Aragon	2500
Diego de Villegas	Merchant from Burgos	2400
Gerard Stercke	Low Countries merchant-broker	2000
Alexius Grimmel	Merchant and financier from Constance	2000
Pauwel van Gemert	Low Countries merchant	2000
Widow Michiel van der Heyden	Widow of burgomaster	2000
Widow Jan Scheyff	Low Countries merchant	2000
'Lombards'	All Lombard financiers in Antwerp	2000

Source: Papebrochius (1845), 384-94. Identifications based on Goris (1925); Strieder (1930); Soly (1977); Fagel (1996); Häberlein (1998a).

Puschinger & Co., Andreas Ligsaltz & Co. (from Munich), and Fernando de Bernuy Jr. (of Spanish-Jewish descent). Only two businessmen originally from the Low Countries belonged to this category: Gerard Stercke and Pauwel van Gemert.[296]

The 1552 zero-interest loan demonstrates clearly that the two companies that had long traded in colonial products had amassed the greatest fortunes: the Schetzes (pepper) and the Van Dales (sugar). They topped the city hierarchy of wealth, followed at a very great distance by all other merchants and financiers. Capitalists in Antwerp were no different

296 Papebrochius (1845), 384-94.

from their counterparts in Augsburg: truly great fortunes could be made only by those who were active in specific, highly profitable economic sectors, suggesting that they made the right choices at the right moment and were able to raise the capital required to do so – and to continue raising it in the event of difficulties or setbacks.

Erasmus Schetz's fortune is impossible to quantify accurately. In a deed signed after his death for the Antwerp city government, his children stated that all movable goods and properties that belonged to the firm – including the houses in Aachen and Leipzig – were to remain the property of Gaspar, Melchior, and Balthasar, and that Koenraad, Maria, and Isabella had received a 'vast sum of money' as compensation.[297] Regarding the furniture, jewellery, and cash unrelated to the firm, the record disclosed only that the heirs had divided everything out of court. Information about the properties was provided in this record and in other sources, but in many cases their value was not specified. Such information is available only on the House of Aachen in Antwerp and the seigniory of Grobbendonck: their combined value was fl.60,000. Nothing is known about the value of the other properties.[298] Since the three youngest children received properties as compensation for the houses in Germany, the House of Aachen in Antwerp and the seigniory of Grobbendonck, the value of all properties combined may be estimated at approximately fl.120.000. Erasmus Schetz had indeed invested heavily in properties, but in this he was not exceptional among substantial merchants in Antwerp: upon their deaths in the 1570s or early 1580s some owned houses, land, and annuities representing 10 to 20 percent of their assets.[299] Applying these proportions to the legacy of Erasmus Schetz places his fortune at a minimum of fl.600,000 and a maximum of fl.1,200,000. He could not hold a candle to the Fuggers, but then could no other businessman or company in Europe. The Augsburg giant was in a league of his own.[300] Schetz's fortune, however, was many times that of the wealthiest inhabitant of Leipzig in 1537 (*c.* fl.185.000), the richest citizen of Lübeck in 1541 (*c.* fl.55,500), the merchant banker Sebastian Welser in Nuremberg in 1567 (*c.* fl.260,850) and the Spanish merchant André Ruiz, the most affluent resident of Nantes in 1577 (*c.* fl.205.000).[301] In terms of his assets, Schetz was therefore at the top of the urban economic elite in Europe.

Wealth was not a sufficient basis for social prestige: *nouveaux riches* were expected to spend their money on forms of *magnificentia* to elevate their status. Schetz was keenly aware of this. He therefore always cherished the House of Aachen. Between 1536 and 1539 he expanded the complex of buildings on Spuistraat that he and his wife had inherited from van Claes van Richtergem in 1516.[302] Nearly all buildings were demolished and replaced

---

297 Deeds were drafted in different languages, in which the heirs stated that all possessions of and transactions by the firm Schetz & Co. in Portugal and other countries belonged exclusively to the brothers Gaspar, Melchior and Balthasar. See, e.g., SAA, COLL 8, f° 12.

298 The complex of buildings at Koepoortbrug and on Minderbroedersrui in Antwerp, purchased in 1533 (SAA, SR 183, f° 80); the house in Maastricht that Erasmus inherited from his brother Willem; the large houses on Ballaarstraat in Lier (also a legacy); the two farmsteads, agricultural lands, and forests in the area around the same city; and the farmsteads and vast polder lands in Ossendrecht and Zandvliet.

299 Brulez (1959), 186; Soly (1977), 61-6.

300 See Ehrenberg (1896), I, 122-5, 144-9.

301 Brulez (1959), 236. André Ruiz was the brother of the famous Simon from Medina del Campo.

302 Adding two adjacent houses, the warehouses pertaining to them, as well as a smaller house. SAA, SR 191, f° 402, 485v°-486, 488, SR 192, f° 468v°-469, SR 195, f° 293v°-294v°.

by the new 'House of Aachen'. Significantly, private rooms, offices, and warehouses were combined in a single complex. Erasmus Schetz had no wish to conceal that he was first and foremost a businessman. He may be presumed to have retained the name 'House of Aachen' as a tribute to his late father-in-law and as a token of acknowledgment that this city provided the mainstay of his economic activities: brass manufacture. He also knew that this name was certain to meet with the approval of the Emperor, the most powerful man in Europe, as this was the city where Charles had been crowned King of the Romans (i.e. Holy Roman Emperor) on 22/23 October 1520.

None of the private residences built in Antwerp's Golden Age could hold a candle to the palaces of merchant bankers in Florence or Genoa in their design, size, and exclusive residential purpose, but the House of Aachen was among the very finest of urban residences available to businessmen in those days in the Low Countries.[303] This was why, as noted above, Charles V stayed there, as did many members of the aristocracy, including William of Orange, who was a guest there repeatedly between 1556 and 1567. In his last will and testament of 1548, Erasmus Schetz assessed its value at fl.24,000, an estimate that all his children accepted, when they divided the inheritance two years later.[304]

Why did Erasmus Schetz commission the construction of such a stately building? Owning a valuable property obviously greatly enhanced his reputation for solvency, but by 1540 he owned vast tracts of land and many houses, and the House of Aachen tied up a great deal of capital. His objective is likely to have been twofold. On the one hand, he wanted to match the opulence of the large South-German and Genoese trading companies based in Antwerp. The Fuggers, for example, owned an elegant mansion on Steenhouwersvest, a stone's throw away from where the House of Aachen was situated. On the other hand, he wished to convey social prestige. He was a merchant banker, that was very clear, but his home also showed that his lifestyle reflected the ideal of '*vivre noblement*' (living like a lord). Owning a city palace was indispensable for hosting the Emperor, Mary of Hungary, aristocrats, and senior government officials, and these personal contacts were immensely important to Erasmus Schetz in his business dealings.

This also explains why he purchased a seigniory. In the eyes of the aristocratic elite, being elevated to the nobility carried little weight, not even if the House of Aachen manifested a material culture suggesting a costly noble lifestyle. The key element in the Duchy of Brabant was probably the same as in the County of Flanders: seigniorial lordship. '[A]t the turn of the sixteenth century, being or becoming noble [in Flanders] was entwined with the possession of a seigniory, a property right which entailed the exertion of public power over its inhabitants'. Seigniorial lordship was at the heart of nobility. No other element conferred such prestige on its owner.[305] Was the purchase of a seigniory by Erasmus Schetz

303 The first known images of the building are from the mid-nineteenth century, after the façade had probably undergone extensive changes; they are by the Antwerp painter-engraver Jean Théodore Joseph Linnig, who sometimes added imaginative late medieval or sixteenth-century touches to cityscapes he depicted. J. Linnig, *Het Huis van Aken*, Painting, Collection of the Museum Vleeshuis, Antwerp.

304 SAA, V 338, and SAA, COLL 9, f° 11-12. In 1574, when the Jesuits purchased the complex to open their college there, they paid 17,000 gold Crowns or fl.34,000, about 42 percent more than the original estimated value. Poncelet (1927-28), I, 226-8. The nominal price index of house rents in Antwerp rose by c. 50 percent between 1545-49 and 1570-74: Scholliers (1962), 610-11.

305 Buylaert, De Clercq and Dumolyn (2011), 395-6, 410-11, 413 (the quotation on page 396).

one month after the Emperor had stayed with him purely coincidental? On 18 May 1545 Schetz purchased from Count Philibert de Mastaing, Lord of Sassegnies, the seigniory Grobbendonck, with high jurisdiction, situated in the bailiwick of Zandhoven, *c.* 25 kilometres east of the centre of Antwerp.[306] While the price was not disclosed, following the death of Erasmus, the other children agreed whith Gaspar's statement of its value as fl.36,000. The amount appears reasonable, as the *dénombrement* (official description of the seigniory), transmitted on 10 July 1545 by father Schetz to the Emperor as feudal overlord of Brabant, made clear that it contained a large and complex set of buildings, land, rights, and prerogatives.[307]

While purchasing a seigniory was a costly undertaking in all cases, it was within the means of various wealthy merchants in sixteenth-century Antwerp. Potential buyers were of course only those who settled in the Low Countries permanently. Among these only a limited group was in fact eligible: good connections with representatives of the ruler or aristocratic families were a *sine qua non*. Merchants might purchase a *hof van plaisantie* (a summer residence) or a manor in the area around the city, but until 1585 very few succeeded in acquiring a seigniory. Nearly all those able to do so were great businessmen involved in the royal and/or municipal finance, representing the interests of the highest officials in other ways, and/or providing loans to aristocratic families. The banker Gerard Stercke, who arranged loans for Charles V on the Antwerp market and was knighted for his services, inherited a castle from his mother, together with all the associated rights, at Deurne near Antwerp (now Sterckxhof) and later purchased more prestigious properties: the seigniory of Bucquoi in the County of Artois, a castle at Niel, ten kilometres south of Antwerp, and the seigniory of Wijnegem, five kilometres east of Antwerp.[308] Gian Carlo Affaitadi, who in 1542 had served with great merit in the defence of Antwerp and had been of financial service to Charles V on several occasions, purchased in 1545 the Barony of Gistel, ten kilometres from Ostend, for fl.40,000; this seigniory came with the hereditary aristocratic title of chamberlain.[309] The merchant banker Gaspar Ducci, who in the 1540s figured in the upper commercial and financial echelons in the Low Countries, subsequently purchased the seigniories of Schoonsel (part of the present Hoboken) and Kruibeke, both near Antwerp.[310] Pauwel Van Dale, who was knighted by the Emperor for services to the Crown in 1554, purchased the Seigniory of Lillo situated on the Scheldt, amid the polders north of Antwerp in the following year. In 1567 Guicciardini listed him explicitly as Lord of Lillo and described him as a man of great wealth.[311] The Antwerp merchants and financiers who purchased seigniories in the decades that followed also had close ties with the central government and/or members of the higher aristocracy. François Schot became Lord of Waarlooos, Kontich, and Reet after many years of supplying rations and textiles to the army, Gerard Gramaye became Lord of Schoten and 's-Gravenwezel after

306 SAA, SR 216, f° 90-91v°, 133. See also AGR, CC 20788, f° 13 and 34v°, and d'Ursel (1984).

307 There was a *borch*, castle, in Ouwen parish near Herentals, a ban mill, and two farmsteads. The estates covered 135 hectares. In addition, there were many *cens et rentes* and all kinds of hunting and fishing rights. SAA, COLL 9, f° 10; AGR, FU, R 78.

308 Pölnitz (1958), passim; Correns, Rau and Van de Cruys (2014), 85 and 94.

309 Denucé (1934), 67-8.

310 See Chapter 2.4.

311 Guicciardini (1567b), 192; Donnet (1896), 234-7.

serving as war treasurer, and Jacob van Hencxthoven became Lord of Hemiksem after successfully completing the works on the citadel, built on the orders of the Duke of Alba along the south side of Antwerp.[312]

Owning a seigniory did not lead these new lords to cease their economic activities. Although Erasmus Schetz was 65 when he bought Grobbendonck, he saw no reason to hand over the firm to his sons. While he made them official partners, the name he chose for the firm shows that he remained *primus inter pares*: 'Erasmus Schetz & Sons'. Other merchants/financiers who purchased seigniories remained economically active as well. One case is unclear: in the last will and testament drawn up shortly before his death in 1555, Gian Carlo Affaitadi stated that he had retired from business a few years earlier, and at the time his Antwerp firm was indeed run by his brother Giovanni Battista. An inventory compiled in 1568 reveals, however, that Gian Carlo remained a partner in the firm.[313] In the 1550s Ducci was forced to retire, because no-one on the Antwerp exchange or in government circles trusted him any longer. He was the exception to the rule. As long as commercial and financial operations were sufficiently profitable, businessmen in Antwerp remained economically active. So there was no 'betrayal of the bourgeoisie', at any rate not before 1585. Only when political-military circumstances brought about commercial changes that made investments in land a rational alternative, did living in retirement and the associated lifestyle become more widespread.[314]

Erasmus Schetz remained a businessman throughout his life and always declared himself as such as well. His reputation was that of a reliable, discreet, and cultured businessman. When he was elevated to the nobility, he selected a coat of arms featuring a raven rising and spreading its wings,[315] which in heraldry denoted both abundance and generosity. The decision was carefully considered, as the raven referred to Erasmus of Formia, a Christian saint and martyr, who at the end of the third century had fled to Mount Lebanon to escape the persecution of Christians by Emperor Diocletian and was brought food there every day by a raven. He was one of the Fourteen Holy Helpers to be honoured as intercessors between God and the pious. He represented all that a person such as Schetz considered to be important: a namesake he shared with his friend Erasmus of Rotterdam, a patron saint of sailors, related to international trade, and an attribute denoting generosity, a Christian and aristocratic virtue.

His reliability and discretion, together with his excellent political contacts, ensured his high standing in commercial circles. He was first among the sixteen merchants testifying on behalf of Ambrosius Höchstetter in Antwerp in 1531; Ruy Fernandez signed the affadavit as well, probably at the request of his friend Schetz.[316] In 1536 the governor of the Merchant Adventurers asked him to mediate with the alderman Aert Schoyte and the merchant Anthonis van Bombergen in the ongoing dispute between the English merchants and the

312 On Schot, see Strieder (1930), passim; Van Passen (1964), 431-2; Soly (1971). On Gramaye, see Baetens (1982), 8-9, and Wijnroks (2003), 73-80. On Van Hencxthoven, see Soly (1976b), 566-70, and (1977), 70-1, 332-4, 354. See also Part Three.

313 Denucé (1934a), 73-7.

314 Soly (1976a). For a European perspective, see Kamen (2000), 112-19.

315 *'Argent, on a mount vert, a raven rising, wings elevated and displayed, sable'.* See Duerloo and Janssens (1992), IV, 441-3.

316 Niedermayer (1980).

receiver of the Great Water Toll of Brabant.[317] In 1537-39 he served as spokesperson for a large group of merchants and financiers who argued that the terms of payment at the annual fairs at Antwerp and Bergen op Zoom needed to be tightly regulated, because the matter had frequently given rise to disputes, as the Merchant Adventurers had emphasized shortly before. After consulting the most prominent businessmen, he asked Adriaan Herbouts, pensionary of the city of Antwerp, to convince the highest authorities in Brussels that they also needed to take measures to acknowledge as legal both payments through assignments and payments in cash. The central government honoured the requests formulated by Schetz and issued ordinances to enact appropriate legislation.[318] In 1542/3 merchants from the Low Countries asked him to intercede with Mary of Hungary who had seized ships coming from Hamburg loaded with their goods during the war with Denmark; Schetz stood surety for them, after which the governor released the ships.[319]

In January 1549 Mary of Hungary made clear her appreciation of Erasmus Schetz, when she asked him to serve as one of the three commissioners who would inspect all income and expenditures by the *Fortificatiekas* (Fortification Fund) of Antwerp and keep the central government informed of any possible problems. The governor had learned of persistent rumours about malversations,[320] and she requested the most reliable and respected men to look into the matter. At least one of them moreover needed to have experience with financial matters. Schetz, though reluctant to accommodate this request, was in no position to refuse. On 21 February the *Seigneur de Grobbendonck, ridder* Willem van Halmale, *amman* of Antwerp, and *ridder* Godevaart van Enckevoort were appointed by the Emperor as 'principal commissioners for the new defence works in the city of Antwerp', and on 15 April they were sworn in by the city magistrate. Two weeks later, Van Enckevoort had to resign from his position for health reasons and died soon afterwards. In mid-April 1550, Schetz also asked to be relieved of his duties, as he felt too ill to continue. The governor urged him to stay on another year,[321] but Schetz was unable to comply with her request: he died on 11 May.

---

317 AGR, CC 20788, f° 3.

318 De Smedt (1940-1). On the practice of transferring bonds through assignment, see esp. Van der Wee (1963), II, 345, and (1993a), 152-3. Also Puttevils (2015a), 119, 125-6.

319 Häpke (1913), I, 395-6.

320 See Chapter 3.1.

321 SAA, R 1756, f° 1v°-3v°, 6-7v°; AGR, PEA 1633/3, Letter of 17 April 1550, and PEA 1666/1, f° 1.

Plate 2. Stained-glass window offered by Gaspar Ducci and depicting Archangel Michael slaying the dragon, Pescia, San Michele, c. 1545

PART 2

Gaspar Ducci, 1495-1577

2.1 Creative Banking

When Gaspar Ducci,[1] born in 1495, arrived in Antwerp in his early twenties, he was unable to establish himself as an independent merchant. Nobody in his family was commercially active; instead, they held municipal office. His father Lorenzo repeatedly served on administrative bodies in Pescia, a small town under the aegis of Pistoia, which was in turn controlled by Florence and was annexed in 1530, so that Ducci could claim to be Florentine. His paternal uncle Francesco was an apostolic protonotary and a provost of the cathedral in the same city. His family was therefore well respected. No further information is available about his two brothers (Antonio and Ludovico) or his sister (Caterina), but Gaspar at least received instruction in grammar and arithmetic in Pescia, after which he was apprenticed to Niccolò Nobili & Co., a fairly large firm from Lucca, indicating that as a youth he was considered to have an aptitude for rational economic reasoning and conduct. Around 1515 he joined the Antwerp branch of this firm, where he remained, although he never lost contact with his family in Pescia. He bought English cloth from the London merchant John Gresham (who was a factor for his brother Richard), and his instructions came from both Niccolò Nobili and Jacopo Arnolfini, also a merchant from Lucca,[2] who often traded jointly. At the same time he represented another merchant (Bartolomeo Gondecini).[3] In other words, at first he operated as a commodity broker and a commission agent, but by 1526 he was trading on his own behalf with England.[4] Over the years that followed he also became involved in marine insurance and especially in finance. In 1531 he was among the 44 underwriters of an insurance policy that covered a ship and its cargo for a journey from Lübeck to Arnemuiden; the value of the cargo was estimated at £1883 Fl. gr.[5] The underwriters included several Italian merchants with whom he already had close ties (e.g. the Arnolfini), or with whom he would soon set up commercial ventures (e.g. Gian Carlo Affaitadi and the brothers Giovan Battista and Lorenzo Guicciardini). His participation in this oldest extant Antwerp insurance policy shows that Ducci was interested in new commercial techniques and sectors.

1 His name is spelled in very different ways in the sources: Docci, Douche, Douchi, Douchy, Doucy, Doulci, Dowche, Dozzi, Ducci, Duche, Duchy, Tutzi, Tutzy. He consistently signed letters and other documents as 'Gaspar Ducci.'

2 He came from the same powerful family as Giovanni Arnolfini, who in the second quarter of the fifteenth century lived in Bruges and had two portraits painted there by Jan Van Eyck of himself with his wife.

3 Stumpo (1992).

4 Denucé (1934b), 28.

5 Hofmeister (1886). See also De Ruysscher (2015), 83-4, and De Ruysscher & Puttevils (2015), 32.

In 1533 Ducci – by then already 38 – married Elisabeth Stegemans, widow of Antonio Frescobaldi, a merchant-banker from an old, elite Florentine family.[6] Frescobaldi was in debt at the time of his death, but the family continued to be highly respected in Antwerp. By marrying his widow, Ducci improved his position among the Florentine merchants and bankers who had left Bruges permanently around 1510 and had settled in Antwerp, where they had become very influential. Anna Stegemans, Elisabeth's sister, may have indirectly provided Ducci with business connections, as her son-in-law was the merchant Sebastiaen van Utrecht who specialized in the woad trade. Considering Ducci's monopoly on pastel imports in 1543 and 1544,[7] agreements between the two family members seem likely.

In this period he was still respected in Antwerp commercial circles. He was asked to testify as a 'Florentine merchant' in a dispute about an Italian bill of exchange, and was qualified as *circumspectus vir*, a deliberate and cautious man.[8] One of the parties was Alexis Grimmel, from Constance, factor of the powerful trading company Bartholomäus Welser & Co. from Augsburg. It was probably Grimmel who put Ducci in contact with Hieronymus Seiler/Sailer, with whom he arranged loans in subsequent years. Seiler was from St. Gallen and belonged to a prominent family with close ties to the Welsers. Seiler was the same age as Ducci, but in the 1520s he became far more experienced in international trade and credit operations. He did business for the Welser firm in Portugal and Spain, signed contracts on its behalf for colonial ventures in Venezuela, and issued large loans to the Spanish Crown. In 1533 he married a daughter of Bartholomäus Welser.[9]

Ducci acted increasingly as a broker in financial matters, in which he involved both Grimmel and Seiler from 1536 onward. Whether these were temporary joint ventures or actual partnerships remains unclear. Nor are the parties to whom they issued loans known – was it to the Emperor or also to foreign rulers? Fragmentary data suggest that they focused on exchange-arbitrage between Antwerp and Lyon that was entirely distinct from the commodity trade. In other words: they were speculating. According to contemporaries the monetary/financial operations of the three created an acrimonious dispute with Bartholomäus Welser, who via his son-in-law Hieronymus Seiler had become involved in these complex transactions and lost vast amounts, severely straining family relations. Grimmel and Seiler were forced to sever all ties with the Welser firm for a while. Ducci does not appear to have suffered any damage to his own reputation and even emerged as a successful and shrewd financier.[10] It was only the beginning of his spectacular and turbulent career as a master-speculator.

During the *Bamismarkt* (St. Bavo's Fair) of 1539,[11] which opened at the end of August and lasted six weeks, he caused major upheaval on the Antwerp Exchange by playing on the fluctuating ratio of gold to silver coins. For many years the Netherlands in general

6 Antonio Frescobaldi died between 12 July and 6 November 1532. See SAA, PK 481, no. 6, and RAB, RB, AG 594, no. 151.

7 See Chapter 2.3.

8 Strieder (1930), 21, 33, 52-4.

9 Kellenbenz (1993); Kellenbenz and Walter (2001), 30-2; Häberlein (2005).

10 Ehrenberg (1896), I, 221, 311-2.

11 *Not* 1540, as Ehrenberg (1896), I, 313, and many other historians have argued. Their incorrect dating derives from the testimony that Gilbert van Schoonbeke, who was twenty in 1539, provided six years later: Génard (1888), no. III/4.

and Antwerp in particular had experienced a continuing shortage of gold coins, which led their free-market values to soar well above the official rates set by the Emperor. The war against France drove the exchange rate of gold coins still higher on the free market in the period 1535-38. Since the official rates were lower than those prevailing in trade, gold became even scarcer in the Netherlands. Commodity traders gradually adjusted to the situation and increasingly paid commercial debts with silver coins. Repaying large loans and transferring huge funds from one place to another, however, still required gold coins. The imperial policy of Charles V implied that sums of money had to be paid in different currencies throughout Europe, requiring exchange transactions and currency transfers, in which the Antwerp money market was pivotal. In April 1539 the government of the Habsburg Netherlands issued an ordinance intended to halt or at least curtail the soaring exchange rates of gold coins on the free market. Protests ensued. Bankers argued that all gold would be diverted to other countries. In June the government reversed the measure, restoring the old arrangement with respect to the official rates,[12] but serious unrest persisted. Ducci viewed the monetary insecurity as his opportunity. The measures taken by the government did not in themselves create a *strettezza*, a shortage of money, but Ducci's manipulations caused the scarcity of gold coins on the Antwerp money market to become even greater.

How he staged the *strettezza* operation, and who his partners were, is impossible to ascertain, but the gist of it can be reconstructed. He and other speculators had piled up an enormous sum by selling bills of exchange to accomplices abroad, most probably in Lyon. Thanks to its favourable location along travel routes and its geopolitical advantage, Lyon was experiencing strong commercial growth during the first half of the sixteenth century.[13] Many merchants from Italy, Southern Germany, and the Netherlands visited its four fairs, held in March, May, September, and December, enabling Lyon to become a centre for exchange transactions as well. As the Genoese bankers were granting loans to his enemy during the Valois-Habsburg war, Francis I prohibited them from trading with France. As a result, they asked merchants from other countries to conduct their business transactions in Lyon.[14] South-German merchant bankers seized this opportunity. Grimmel and Seiler were especially well-positioned, as they came from Swiss cities that were neutral in the Valois-Habsburg conflict. Since they remained active on the Lyon money market even after 1539, Ducci presumably used their services, as well as those of Sebastian Neidhart, born in Ulm and married to a daughter of the substantial merchant Christoph Herwart, who operated a branch in Lyon. Neidhart had been active on the Antwerp Exchange since 1530, had granted several loans to Charles V, and knew the exchange market in Lyon very well.[15]

12 Edler (1937), 667-9, has argued that the two government ordinances promulgated in 1539 reduced the face value of gold coins by 10 percent, causing an outflow of gold and rising interest rates. Van der Wee (1963), II, 203, and Li (2015), 1210, have adopted this interpretation. De Smedt (1950-54), II, 505 n. 21, has noted, however, that the measures made no difference in the end, except that in 1539 no businessman would have considered selling gold or silver at the official rates.

13 See the seminal work of Gascon (1971).

14 Kellenbenz (1959), 194-5. On banking in sixteenth-century Lyon, see Matringe (2016).

15 He also participated in several colonial ventures, including in pearl fishing off the coast of Venezuela and in silver mining in Mexico: Häberlein (1998b).

Ducci & Co. instigated a panic on the Antwerp Exchange. Gold coins became so scarce that the factor of the Portuguese King could find nobody with sufficient funds to finance the maturing debts of his sovereign – nobody, that was, except Ducci, who set exorbitant conditions. In September 1539 the average annual interest rate for short-term loans to the central government was 18 percent, and during the *Koudemarkt* (Winter Fair) in Bergen op Zoom, in October it even rose to 19.5 percent. Foreign rulers and individuals undoubtedly paid still higher interest rates. The *strettezza* had severe consequences for all those whose financial reserves were depleted and were in urgent need of money. The Portuguese factor and several merchants were ruined.[16]

Such anger and indignation arose from Ducci's manipulations that the city council launched an investigation. He ended up being expelled from the Exchange for three years. Some of the aggrieved were not satisfied. In April 1544, government commissioners were told that the Lucchese broker Francisco Francesqui, nicknamed Franca, was suspected of conspiring to assassinate Ducci in late 1539 or early 1540. According to the Florentine merchant Michel Bonsignori, Franca could not tolerate the release of somebody 'who so greatly disrupted the Exchange and true commodities trade, that he was universally considered to be a pest.' Franca had offered him a vast sum to help eliminate Ducci; two other merchants – one Lucchese and the other Portuguese – were already prepared to support such an attack.[17] The evidence is questionable, but that is not the point. The testimony of Bonsignori (and other Italians) proves that a plot to murder Ducci was held to be credible.

The cycle of *strettezza* and *larghezza* – contraction and expansion of credit – was well established, and exploiting a contraction of the money market was presumably not a new phenomenon, but the speculations of Ducci & Co. were of a different order. The events caused so much unrest that the States General demanded legal measures. On 4 October 1540, with their support, Charles V issued an ordinance stipulating that interest was lawful only up to an annual rate of 12 percent; all 'contracts and bonds' with higher rates were to be qualified as usurious.[18] The objective was clearly to curtail exchange-arbitrage not directly linked to commodity trading. At the same time, the imperial ordinance from its inception established a legal basis for relatively high profits from financial transactions, as 12 percent was nearly double the standard interest on annuities based on urban real estate, i.e. 'penny 16' or 6.25 percent *per annum*.

Mary of Hungary believed that additional measures were necessary to contain the monetary chaos, especially because she attributed the sharp fluctuations essentially to speculation, but speculation by whom? She mentioned 'fraud' by merchants.[19] The problem, however, was that the monetary interests of commodity and currency traders could diverge considerably, and the governor consulted only those who in her view knew the money market best: Ducci and other bankers in Antwerp. Following their advice, provided 'in the general interest', Charles V promulgated an ordinance on 10 December

16 Génard (1888), no. III/4; Ehrenberg (1896), I, 312; Goris (1925), 375; De Roover (1949), 159-60.
17 '[…] gastoit la bourse et empeschoit le vrai train de marchandise tellement qu'il estoit estimé en tel endroit comme une peste'. AGR, RB, OF, PPG 326.
18 Munro (2012), 169.
19 Baelde (1965b), 174.

1541 stipulating that all bills of exchange were henceforth payable at a ratio of two-thirds gold and one-third silver. The merchants felt cheated, as the masters of international finance had succeeded in obtaining privileges for the currency trade at the expense of the commodity trade. Businessmen in Italy understood that the measure would compromise international trade. A partner at the Genoese firm Doria (operating in Milan) stated bluntly that only a tiny group of Antwerp merchant bankers would benefit. The fierce opposition in commercial circles led the governor to assign two commissioners to investigate in Antwerp. They consulted the Balbani (from Lucca), the Guicciardini (from Florence), and the Vienmoranti (from Milan). Although little is known about the Vienmoranti, the Balbani and the Guicciardini both did business with Ducci (see below). Understandably, they considered the ordinance to be 'highly beneficial for the general interest'. Soon afterwards, representatives of the 'nations' of foreign merchants in Antwerp and the factor of the Portuguese King argued precisely the opposite: Mary had been 'falsely and poorly' informed. The gold shortage in the Netherlands made paying two thirds of trade debts in gold coins impossible. Many merchants would need to obtain loans from bankers or request extensions on their payments, leading interest rates to rise and commodity prices to increase. The ordinance favoured a few large merchant bankers, who would 'monopolize' the gold more than they had previously, thereby enabling them to cause *larghezza* (abundance) or *strettezza* as they pleased. Mary of Hungary dismissed all objections. She announced that she would have the 'anti-speculation' measures enforced and … achieved the opposite of what she had intended. The ordinance of 1541, which remained in effect for nine years, had many negative consequences, especially giving rise to a clandestine exchange market, connected to a 'black market' in gold, and leading to the proliferation of all kinds of fraudulent practices.[20]

The Antwerp city government had Ducci expelled from the Exchange, but Mary of Hungary overruled the ban and instructed Ducci to obtain short-term loans for the central government. She argued that state interests were at stake, and that in such circumstances the City of Antwerp had little or no authority. The support of Mary of Hungary was of the utmost importance for Ducci. The Emperor had granted his sister exceptional powers, when he appointed her governor, and he ratified nearly all her decisions, even those she took without consulting him.[21] She cared not only about political affairs and everything related to them (including matrimonial issues) but was also very closely involved in economic, fiscal, and monetary matters.

How could a businessman of ill repute have gained the trust of the governor and her chief advisors? After all, that is precisely what happened: in 1542 Ducci was entrusted with all the financial transactions of the central government, and soon afterwards was appointed Receiver-General of both a 6-percent tax on trade with France (1542-1544) and a 1-percent tax on exports to all countries (1543-1545). He also gained control of imports of Toulouse pastel and alum, two very important raw materials used in the manufacture of textile goods, the main export industry in large areas of the Low Countries. State interests might not have become so closely linked with individual ones, had the political-military

20 For a more detailed analysis, see Coenen (1990), 832-3, 835-41. Also HHS, B-PA 41, f° 186.

21 Parker (2019), 215.

context not been so precarious and the financial needs of the Emperor so great. The Fourth French-Habsburg War (1542-1544) offered Ducci a dream opportunity to appear in government circles as the most inventive merchant-banker in the Netherlands – and the opportunity to make a fortune.

In June 1542, the King of France launched two offensives, one in the north and one in the south, indicating a large-scale and therefore very costly war.[22] This was especially problematic, because the Emperor also faced dangerous allies of King Francis I in the north, while the central government of the Netherlands had immense difficulty raising enough money to finance large-scale military campaigns. Ducci seized his opportunity. While Anton Fugger hemmed and hawed, or in any case did not commit himself outright, Ducci agreed to provide the central government with short-term loans and at the same time proposed new ideas that would fill the war chest. Mary of Hungary instructed Margrave of Antwerp Willem van de Werve to encourage the magistrate of the Scheldt town to accommodate Ducci in a business dispute with an Italian firm 'taking into account the good services he renders us daily'.[23]

His good services consisted mainly of the short-term loans which he had arranged on the Antwerp Exchange from January 1542 onward, even before the overt hostilities with France: *c.* fl.152,000 from 2 February for six months at 6 percent, followed by other short-term loans on 12 February and 15 March, each for the same period and on the same terms. The Receiver-General for all Finances in the Habsburg Netherlands recorded in his account: *affaires secrètes* (secret matters), which given the amounts could only mean preparations for war.[24] Ducci was also pivotal in arranging loans to the Spanish treasury. Did he operate independently? Or was he a broker for other bankers? The second option seems the most likely, as the Fuggers had huge financial interests in Spain and in this period concealed quite a few monetary transactions with governments, either by demanding that the name of their firm not appear in the accounts, or by involving an intermediary. Since Ducci had been engaging in massive business transactions with them for a few years by then, he was the obvious choice.[25]

He was a very inventive banker. At the maximum interest rate set by imperial ordinance at 12 percent, he was able to raise large sums on the Exchange based on what were known as *rentmeestersbrieven*, bonds of the receivers-general, which the officials concerned issued in various provinces of the Netherlands – especially in Flanders, Brabant, and Holland – in their own name but on behalf of the government, guaranteed by the future income to be obtained from the province. Ducci was the first to place large numbers of these government bonds on the Exchange, enabling the central government to obtain short-term loans more easily. The *rentmeestersbrieven* were fixed-income securities and bearer bonds. As such, they could be redeemed by whoever held them and could therefore be traded on the Exchange. Eager to speculate, Ducci seized the opportunity to become a major player

22 Brandi (1964), 393-5; Parker (2019), 284-5.

23 AGR, PEA 1661/1, Letter dated 16 June 1542.

24 ADN, B 2430. In the first half of 1542 the central government also approached Lazarus Tucher and the Spanish merchant Dimas Ferrer, but both lent smaller amounts at higher interest rates.

25 In late August 1540 Ducci was the largest creditor of the Fugger factory in Antwerp at £25,145 Fl.gr. He was also a debtor for the sum of £12,219 Fl.gr.: Pölnitz (1963), II/1, 175, 488 n. 191, and II, 3, 55.

and set up a large-scale operation: he informed the governor that if she wished to work with him, he would be able to raise up to three million florins within eighteen months. As for the current year, he would start by obtaining bills of exchange amounting to 500,000 ducats on the Lenten fair at Villalon in Castile. By May, this sum could be dispatched to Antwerp on the ordinary fleets.[26] In April, May, and June each, he would raise fl.300,000 for a six-month term, totalling fl.900,000, and then the same amount again in July, August, and September, all at 12 percent *per annum* and a 'gift' of 3 percent, also *per annum*, assessed from Easter for the first segment and from Pentecost for the second segment. He would cover all these sums with *rentmeestersbrieven*, meaning that tax revenue had to be sufficient to cover the government bonds.[27]

Ducci could obtain large sums in return for *rentmeestersbrieven* on the Antwerp Exchange only if he convinced the creditors that the provincial receivers-general in whose name they were issued would be able to pay them on time, in other words: that they would be reimbursed when the *rentmeestersbrieven* matured. The government hoped to raise fl.1.3 million by requesting *aides* (subsidies) from the Estates General,[28] but the enormous sum could clearly not be generated through the usual measures. New, regular sources of income were necessary. Mary of Hungary and her chief advisors, Lodewijk van Schore and Louis of Praet, did everything possible to convince the Provincial States. They succeeded. On 1 December 1542 three new taxes were introduced: a Tenth Penny (i.e. 10 percent) on the proceeds of real estate and annuities, a Tenth Penny on the annual earnings of native businessmen (i.e. not *les marchans estrangiers*, the foreign merchants), provided they had operating capital of at least one thousand florins,[29] and, last but not least, a Hundredth Penny (i.e. 1 percent) on the value of all exports from the most important provinces of the Habsburg Netherlands, both over land and by sea.[30]

Meanwhile, Ducci continued his arbitrage transactions. While visiting Antwerp on 12 October 1542, Mary of Hungary was told that businessmen with international banking activities and financial operations who participated in the fairs of Lyon were manipulating the Antwerp money market to the detriment of many merchants. While no names were recorded by Mary of Hungary, this clearly involved Ducci & Co., who had remained active on Lyon's exchange market. The governor appointed a commissioner, who consulted merchants who (at that moment) had no ties with Ducci: Erasmus Schetz, Veit Hörl as factor for the Fuggers, Anthonis van Bombergen, Diego Mendes, Alonso de Sancta Gadea, Fernando Dassa, and Martin Lopez. They argued that everyone in the Low Countries should be prohibited from performing arbitrage transactions at the Lyon fairs, and that

---

26 Ducci needed cash, not only to earn the trust of the merchants on the Antwerp Exchange, but also because the government had to pay the troops in cash. The available data reflect transfers of at least 400,000 ducats.

27 AGR, PEA 1661/1, *Moyens*. See also Ehrenberg (1896), I, 252-3, 312, and II, 27, 50-1, 118, 128; Van Werveke (1944), 129; Bindoff (1958), 67-8; Pölnitz (1963), II/1, 232, 253.

28 The three core provinces of Flanders, Brabant, and Holland provided about 75 percent of the subsidies from all the Low Countries provinces: Tracy (2004), 71.

29 The government and the Provincial Estates ultimately agreed that trade profits would be taxed at 6 percent, which on an operating capital of fl.1000 amounted to fl.60, one tenth of which (equalling fl.6) then became payable. Soon afterwards, the government had to accommodate the Provincial Estates by taxing foreign merchants as well (AGR, PEA 819, f° 182v°), but this tenth penny was soon waived.

30 Verhofstad (1937), 58-64. With respect to 'trade with the enemy' (France) the special 6-percent tax, introduced in October 1542, obviously remained in effect.

this injunction should apply to all merchants from Spain, Naples, Sicily, Milan, Florence, and other territories ruled by the (Spanish) Habsburgers. If Lyon were to be replaced by another exchange market, the close ties between commodity trade and arbitrage transactions needed to be taken into account. Favourable geographic accessibility was therefore essential. As an alternative to Lyon some suggested Milan and others Strasbourg, two cities submitted to imperial rule. Mary of Hungary, however, had no wish to resort to this course of action and merely proclaimed that merchants who had exchanged money at the previous Lyon fair had a duty to adhere to the exchange rate she had set. To prevent gold coins from being channelled out of the Netherlands to Lyon and at the same time to promote cash transfers from Lyon to Antwerp, the governor secretly told a few substantial businessmen in Antwerp that they should restrict their visits to the fairs of Lyon to the time necessary to withdraw their money and merchandise from there.[31] At no point did Ducci become concerned. Was Mary of Hungary reluctant to cause problems for the man who turned out to be better than anyone else at arranging money for the central government?

Ducci's launch of the *rentmeestersbrieven* was highly successful: the government bonds enabled him to borrow nearly one million florins before the summer of 1543, especially from South-German, Italian, and Spanish merchant bankers and brokers based in Antwerp.[32] Mary of Hungary was delighted and praised him repeatedly. In the summer, however, the problems increased. By late July, Ducci could no longer raise vast sums. The Antwerp governement was urged to offer financial aid but was unable to assist, because the enormous expenses on constructing the new city walls had depleted their coffers. In August Ducci stated that no money could be found on the Antwerp Exchange. In September he managed to raise only fl.130,000; soon afterwards, he informed the governor that he could no longer obtain any money on the basis of *rentmeestersbrieven*. They were insufficiently covered, precluding the issue of new series.[33] The taxes allocated by the Provincial Estates added far too little income. The government sought alternatives and following tedious negotiations with the representatives of the Provincial Estates introduced *nieuwe middelen*, new ways & means, which no longer depended on payments by the property-owning classes in general and the merchants in particular. Instead, the new consumer taxes affected mainly wage workers and segments of the social middle groups. They included different elements, widely varying in importance, both regionally and temporally, but they consisted largely of excises on beer, wine, and retail sales of textile goods. Accepted by the Provincial Estates in October 1543, they were in fact a vast source of income.[34] Only in the second half of the next year, however, did these *nieuwe middelen* start to reach the public coffers, rendering the transition period extremely difficult for the central government.

By late 1543, the government's outstanding debt had soared to an unprecedented fl.850,000.[35] Repayment was not an option. Moreover, new funds were needed, as the war was being waged on several fronts, and the Emperor started to raise new armies in March

31 Kellenbenz (1959), 196-7.
32 AGR, PEA 132, f° 48, PEA 1629/2-3, and PEA 1661/1, Letter dated 19 October 1543; Pölnitz (1963), II/1, 243, 253, 267, 279-80, 283-4.
33 AGR, PEA 1661/1, Letters dated 26 July and 17 August 1543; Ehrenberg (1896), II, 51-2.
34 Maddens (1979), 873-9; Tracy (1985), 83-9, and (2002), 263-7.
35 Ehrenberg (1896), II, 51. See also Braudel (1959), 196-7.

1544. As long as income from the provincial taxes was not forthcoming, no large series of *rentmeestersbrieven* could be introduced on the market. The government had no choice but to approach Anton Fugger directly. A substantial short-term loan had to be obtained immediately, argued Ducci, because if redeeming the *rentmeestersbrieven* proved impossible to postpone at the upcoming fair, 'half the Exchange' would go bankrupt. Complex negotiations and equally complicated transactions followed, whose precise mechanism is impossible to trace, ultimately leading to a solution, by which the central government could once again obtain short-term loans.[36] These loans were issued at the official maximum rate (i.e. at 12 percent *per annum*), but the letters from Ducci to the governor reveal that the creditors were not satisfied with the arrangement. The surcharge they assessed was ordinarily 2 percent or more, in addition to which the anticipation fee could be as high as 2 percent. Ducci also felt entitled to a *gratuité* (gift) of 3 percent on loans he arranged for the central government.[37] Given the large sums involved, such 'gifts' were obviously substantial. In Ducci's view, these earnings were well-deserved, as nobody else issued so much credit, and he worked very hard indeed.[38]

During the first half of 1544, the King of England desperately needed money to finance military reinforcements and the defence of Boulogne and instructed his financial agent Vaughan to obtain loans in Antwerp. This was the first time he issued such an order. The task proved highly challenging, as the royal credit was deeply mistrusted, and Vaughan was a merchant with little experience in international finance. The mere rumour that he was looking for a major loan drove the already high interest rate on the Antwerp Exchange up to 16 percent *per annum*. The subsequent course of events is somewhat obscure. After all kinds of entanglements, Vaughan reported to Henry VIII in July that he had obtained a loan via Ducci of 122,778 crowns or *c*. fl.221,000 (including interest). In August a second loan followed, this one for £22,000 Fl.gr. or fl.132,000 at 7 percent, to be repaid on 15 February 1545. Anton Fugger is very likely to have been involved in these transactions, but to what extent and in what way is impossible to determine. Nor is anything known about Ducci's profit. In this case we know that he received 0.5 percent commission per quarterly fair (i.e. 2 percent *per annum*), but he may have participated in the loans as well.[39]

In difficult financial circumstances Ducci thus convinced international businessmen to lend money to the central government (Fugger) or to Henry VIII (Welser). While the actual interest rates were relatively high, he was still more successful than Tucher or other brokers. Why? Several elements may have come into play. His arbitrage transactions with Spain and money transfers from there to the Netherlands may have indirectly benefited Fugger. Whether Welser had motives other than purely financial considerations remains unclear. Perhaps the Habsburg-Tudor alliance formed in 1543 offered economic prospects. At any rate, the vast network that Ducci mobilized comprised not only Fugger and Welser but Italian bankers as well, such as Bonvisi and Vivaldi.

36 AGR, PEA 1661/1, Letters dated 29-31 October 1543, and ADN, B 2436.

37 He charged 4 percent for loans to Henry VIII on the Antwerp Exchange: LPFD, Henry VIII, 19/2, no. 66.

38 See AGR, PEA 1661/1, Letters dated 16-18 November 1543, and 21 January 1544.

39 AGR, PEA 1661/1, Letters dated 4, 7, 13, and 14 June 1544, and 6 July 1544; LPFD, Henry VIII, 19/1, nos 630, 725, 822, 887, 911, 988, 1017; De Smedt (1928), 232-5; Richardson (1953), 52-3; Pölnitz (1967), II/2, 47.

During the second half of 1544 Ducci once again managed to arrange favourable short-term loans for the government of the Habsburg Netherlands. He extended *rentmeestersbrieven* series for six months at 6 percent and then placed new series on the market on the same terms. He worked with Anton Fugger at some points and with Neidhart and Grimmel at others. Gian Carlo Affaitadi and Stephan Kaltenhofer surfaced as creditors as well. In some cases Ducci operated as the broker or in any case acted as such, while in other cases he participated in the credit operation.[40] The *Comptes de la Recette générale des Finances*, however, do not reveal information such as to who belonged to 'Neidhart and company' or to the respective input by different creditors in a loan. The problems were not limited to this area.

The many different initiatives that Ducci launched in the period 1542-45, both in serving the highest state representatives and on his own behalf, complicate insight into his economic activities. Lack of transparency – to put it euphemistically – was a reproach that his contemporaries consistently directed at him and may be a still more serious problem for current researchers, due to inadequate source material. The increasingly intertwined economic and political interests offered huge opportunities for profit, which to a certain extent were perfectly legal but also entailed fraudulent practices that appear to have been decisive in many cases. Moreover, Ducci used his positions as financial agent of the government on the Antwerp Exchange and as Receiver–General of new commercial taxes to obtain advantages in business akin to monopolies. His success in financial and commercial networks alike was in part attributable to his dealings with other businessmen. In some cases the names of the partners are known, but the amounts of capital they contributed remain a mystery. In other cases the available data suggest that merchant bankers who stayed in the background were closely involved in certain transactions and may even have been in control. 'Firm' conclusions are therefore not always possible. But historians must work with what is available. Let us try, as far as the available data allow, to shed light on three closely related issues in the period 1542-45: the benefits that Ducci derived from the commercial taxes he introduced and organized, his profitable trade with the enemy, and his monopoly of the alum trade and its distribution in Northwest and Central Europe.

2.2 New Commercial Taxes and War-Time Monopolies

Ducci was both a master in credit operations on the Antwerp Exchange and highly ingenious in tax-related and commercial matters. He was the first to advocate assessing taxes on trade between the Habsburg Netherlands and other countries. This concept was unprecedented. In the late Middle Ages some cities and provinces had assessed import or export duties on specified commodities, and the central government had tried once – unsuccessfully – to introduce customs duties on trade between Flanders and England & Ireland.[41] No other efforts had been made. In England and France, on the other hand, customs duties were levied from the late Middle Ages onward. In England the standard rate was 5 percent of the nominal value of most imports and exports; only grain and leather exports were

40 ADN, B 2442.

41 Blockmans (1978), 402-10.

assessed at a higher rate.[42] In France, taxes *ad valorem* were gradually introduced on various commodity exports, albeit not systematically, and during the first half of the sixteenth century import duties were levied on silk fabrics, expensive cloth, jewellery, and spices. In 1544 Francis I established the office of *Contrôleur général des traites*, with the intention of supervising the organization of taxes on trade with other countries. In practice such trade was mainly from Lyon, where the first real *douane* (customs authority) was opened and then closed again the following year.[43]

In the past, hostilities with France had already led the government of the Habsburg Netherlands to take economic steps.[44] Still, Ducci's proposal, launched in September 1542, to levy a 6-percent tax on trade with France marked a turning point, as this was the first systematic action and was aimed specifically at deriving income from 'trade with the enemy'. Ducci agreed to organize the operation, which was not a sinecure, as it required setting up and staffing offices in Antwerp and several border towns, with Arras as the most important centre.[45] The plan met with great enthusiasm. Trade with France was prohibited, except by means of a safe-conduct from the central government, in which case a 6-percent tax was payable on the value of the commodities imported or exported, plus an additional 2 to 6 percent for many types of merchandise. The tax was introduced on 20 October 1542, and Ducci was officially appointed Receiver-General the next day. He was authorized to control trade with neutral areas, such as the Duchy of Lorraine and the County of Cambrésis, since commodities could easily be transported from there to France. Shipments to or from Germany, Italy, and England could not ordinarily be blocked, except in the event of indications that they came from, or were going to France, in which case they could be inspected. Two-thirds of the proceeds from all confiscations would go to the Receiver-General and one third to the Emperor.[46]

Discontent at the 6-percent tax on trade with France paled in comparison to the protests, disputes and conflicts that resulted from introducing the Hundredth Penny, the 1-percent tax on exports to all countries (1543-1545). Trade with France constituted only a small share of total imports and exports, no more than 10 to 12 percent,[47] and merchants based in the Netherlands involved in this trade were neither well-organized nor part of the business elite. Matters were by definition entirely different with respect to trade with all other countries. International merchants objected vociferously. On 31 January 1543 Ducci wrote to Mary of Hungary that a large crowd had gathered on the Grote Markt in Antwerp: 'I assure you, Madam that the populace will not judge me lightly, nor will others', as rumour has it 'that I have devised all the new measures'.[48] Although the trading companies' objections

---

42 Jones (2017), 98.

43 Coornaert (1961), I, 48-50, 71-9.

44 See Fagel (2005) for an account of the legislative activity.

45 Since the Central Middle Ages, Arras had been an important trade city and during periods of war in the sixteenth century was the main transit centre between the Netherlands and France: Coornaert (1961), I, 197-200; Blockmans (2010), passim.

46 AGR, CC 23497-23508, 49871-49873, 49967, and SAA, T 55. See the comments of Goris (1925), 320-3; Craeybeckx (1958), 214-18; Coornaert (1961), I, 77-8, 89.

47 Brulez (1975), 123-4, 126. See also Puttevils (2015), 1347, 1351.

48 'Et vous promets, Madame, que je ne usce point en bonne sentence du commun et generalement de beaucoup d'aultres', and '[la rumeur] court que je suys de touttez aultres nouvellites'. AGR, PEA 131, f° 235. On the protests, see Verhofstad (1937), 58-64; Posthumus (1971), 5-8; Maddens (1979), 861-4; Tracy (1985), 79-83.

were supported by the city government, they were futile,[49] revealing once again how little impact Antwerp had on government policy, even with regard to measures that affected the foundation of its economy: international trade. The next day, in exchange for the urgent payment of fl.200,000, the governor of the Habsburg Netherlands entrusted Ducci with collecting the proceeds of the Hundredth Penny. Various sources reveal that an undisclosed part of the sum was raised by Affaitadi, Neidhart-Welser, and Seiler.[50]

For two and a half years (until 24 September 1545), Ducci controlled exports from the most commercialized part of the empire of Charles V.[51] Collecting the 1-percent tax was a monumental operation: altogether sixty cities and smaller centres were ultimately involved. The bulk of exports by sea of course passed via Antwerp, together with its ports at Walcheren, with Amsterdam in second place, while export over land was concentrated in Antwerp on the one hand and in Arras and Valenciennes on the other hand. In secondary centres such as 's-Hertogenbosch, Maastricht, Mechelen, Namur, and Utrecht, however, additional offices had to be opened or inspectors stationed. In less than two months, Ducci managed to set up the entire organization – an impressive achievement.[52] Ducci was certain that there would be attempts to commit fraud. Above all, he needed to be able to inspect ships on the Scheldt, as the overwhelming majority of exports proceeded via this river. The existing infrastructure of what was known as the Toll of Iersekeroord or the Toll of Zeeland, based in Antwerp from 1532, offered many opportunities for inspection, as there were offices and checkpoints on the isles of Zeeland, especially at the ports on Walcheren. He therefore leased this toll on 3 October 1543, teaming up in this effort with Jan Moys, the Receiver-General of the *aides* (subsidies) in Brabant. Ducci and Moys hoped that trade and shipping would soar, once the war ended, and the results exceeded their wildest dreams.[53]

Despite the sound organization and ample authority for inspection, the Hundredth Penny was not collected flawlessly. Ducci encountered opposition from a great many provincial officials, aldermen and civil servants,[54] but he deplored in particular the *tromperies* (deceit) that he and his staff encountered. The export values reported by freight-managers and merchants were often considerably lower than the inspectors' estimates, instigating endless debates and implying widespread fraud.[55] He experienced continual difficulties along the eastern border,[56] but his chief worry was a southern escape route, especially the opportunities that the neutral Duchy of Lorraine offered to avoid export taxes and of course the safe-conducts required for trade with France. From the Habsburg Netherlands

---

49 Only the Merchant Adventurers were granted an exemption but they had to pay the government £1000 Fl.gr.: De Smedt (1950-1954), I, 161-3, and II, 238-9.

50 Tracy (1985), 83 n. 26.

51 AGR, CC 23357-23430, 49870, 49963, 50245-50249; Goris (1925), 329-34; Posthumus (1971), 6-8, 100.

52 Mary of Hungary granted him and the inspectors he appointed the right to open all bales, baskets, packages, and barrels being exported.AGR, PEA 819, f° 284, and PEA 1661/1, Letter dated 18 April 1543.

53 In 1544 and 1545 they paid fl.16,500 each year, of which fl.10,500 went to the Emperor and fl.6000 to the City of Antwerp, and in 1546 only fl.13,840, but the lease fee increased substantially afterwards: fl.27,000 in 1547 and fl.32,000 in 1548, and these sums paled in comparison to the increase in income: Unger (1939), 137-41, 162.

54 AGR, PEA 1629/1, *Mémoire*, PEA 1629/2-3, and PEA 1661/1, Letter dated 24 September 1543; Coornaert (1961), I, 78 n. 1.

55 See HHS, B-PA 71, passim.

56 AGR, PEA 1661/1, Letter dated 7 November 1543; SAA, T 55, *Remonstrance*.

and in particular from Antwerp, the Duchy was easily accessible via a network of rivers and roads. The large village of Fontenoy-le-Château southeast of Vittel became a transit point for international shipments along a North-South route connecting Antwerp via Lorraine with Northern Italy. This was thanks mainly to the entrepreneurial initiatives of the dynamic *conducteur*, freight-manager, Pierre Thierry, who organized convoys to and from Antwerp, where he had correspondents, and also guaranteed shipments to France, England, Germany, Switzerland, and Northern Italy, specializing in transports from Antwerp to Ancona. He did business with many Italian firms (including the Guicciardinis and the Salviatis), with Spanish and Portuguese merchants, and with Bartholomäus Welser.[57] In late 1543 he invoked the neutrality of the Duchy to import and export merchandise without requesting safe-conducts. This practice was intolerable, argued Ducci, as most commodities imported via Mézières in the Ardennes came from France and not from Lorraine, as Thierry claimed, and the same held true in the opposite direction. Moreover, merchants were exporting textile goods manufactured in Lyon via Lorraine to Germany, Switzerland, or Northern Italy. Others had vast quantities transported via Antwerp, first to Germany, where their sale was staged, after which they were brought to France via Lorraine without a safe-conduct.[58]

The report drafted in May-June 1544 by Thomas Gramaye, brother of the Receiver-General for Brabant, revealed additional issues. Although large quantities of merchandise were exported daily to the Prince-Bishopric of Liège via Namur and from there were transported to Aachen and Cologne, the authorized official had received hardly anything. Much of the export to Germany went via Maastricht, where another problem arose: according to the local aldermen, the Hundredth Penny was payable only on raw materials and finished commodities from the Low Countries, i.e. '*not* on commodities imported from other countries, such as Rhine wine, Spanish wines, English cloth, spices, oils, and the like.' Maastricht was under the sovereignty of both the Duke of Brabant and the Prince-Bishop of Liège, and merchants used this dual status to transport transit goods first via the Meuse River to Liège and from there to Aachen, without paying the Hundredth Penny.[59]

When the Treaty of Crépy marked the end of the war, merchants throughout the Netherlands refused to continue paying the Hundredth Penny. Since Ducci had not yet recovered the 200,000 fl. he had advanced, he objected vehemently to discontinuing the export tax.[60] Mary of Hungary had no objections and extended the tax until 24 September 1545. The total collected for the entire period 1543-45 amounted to *c.* fl.201,650,[61] certainly less than what Ducci had expected. According to the tax registers, from 9 August 1544 to 11 August 1545, when the military operations had ceased, and the proceeds were at their highest level in comparative terms, the value of exports from Antwerp exceeded fl.6 million, i.e. three-quarters of the total exports from the Netherlands, which are estimated to have

57 Brulez (1959a), 411, 413, 469-70, and (1959b), 468-9; Coornaert (1961), I, 266-9; Yante (1998), 385-9.
58 AGR, PEA 1661/1, Letters dated 30 November 1543, 15-16, 24 January 1544, and 3, 8-11 February 1544.
59 SAA, T 55, *Remonstrance*.
60 AGR, PEA 1661/1, Ducci to Mary of Hungary, September-October 1544.
61 Goris (1925), 329-34.

amounted to about fl.8 million.[62] Even considering that the Merchant Adventurers were exempt from the Hundredth Penny, and that exports to France had not yet resumed, Ducci can hardly have been jubilant about this result. Estimates place the value of exports from the Netherlands at about fl.16 million *per annum* for the 1550s and early 1560s.[63] While trade had presumably increased considerably by then, the value of exports is unlikely to have nearly doubled. In other words: evasion and fraud are extremely likely to have kept income from the Hundredth Penny lower than what should in fact have been received. Had Ducci done poorly? Not at all. He profited from both the taxes he introduced.

The new war against France, which placed the Emperor in dire financial straits, offered opportunities. Thanks to his excellent relations with the central government, Ducci obtained exceptional import permits, even entitling him to trade with the enemy, France. He initially opted for a raw material that was indispensable for dyeing English cloth in Antwerp and crucial at various textile centres in the Low Countries and in neighbouring countries: Toulouse pastel. In addition, he obtained permission to import massive quantities of Bordeaux wine and, conversely, to dispatch a fleet of herring busses to France. Once again, the desperate financial need of the state was the substrate on which this widespread trade with the enemy thrived.

No single industry in late medieval and early modern Europe had such an immense economic and social significance as textile manufacturing. The supply and pricing of raw materials necessary for manufacturing textile goods were therefore carefully monitored, not only by merchants and producers but often by public authorities as well. In the event of shortages or soaring prices, municipal authorities feared social unrest, while central governments obtained income from import and export duties. Customs duties or embargoes on wool, flax, or raw silk might be instrumentalized to protect local industry or as weapons in conflicts with other states but never influenced pricing in large parts of Western Europe. In important commercial centres no single firm gained complete control of the trade in such raw materials. Even control of a substantial share of the market was difficult. This was possible to some degree for certain dyes, however, because the highest quality was available only in select areas. Woad was a case in point.

Woad or pastel (*Isatis tinctoria*) was an indispensable pigment for dyeing cloth blue. Cultivating the plant required a combination of soil properties and weather conditions present only in very specific regions, and production was relatively complicated. There was no substitute. Indigo from India gradually became available from the sixteenth century on, but this pigment long remained prohibited in several European countries, including the Netherlands.[64] Woad was one of the three staples in the European textile industry, in addition to weld for yellow and madder for red. By the Middle Ages blue was the base colour used for dyeing most woollens, after they were often immersed in a tub with still more woad or another dye, which could produce a broad range of colours. During the

62 Calculated from Puttevils (2015b), 1346, and Brulez (1975), 119.

63 Brulez (1970), 37-43.

64 The prohibition applied not only in woad-producing countries such as Germany and France, where political and religious authorities long regarded indigo from the New World as a 'rotten colour', a 'harmful colour', or even as a 'colour of the devil' (Vázquez de Ágredos Pascual et al. (2007), 134), but also in other parts of Europe, where using indigo correctly presented technical problems.

first half of the sixteenth century light and dark blue fashion garments became still more popular, at first in France, but also in Italy and the Low Countries.[65]

In this period Antwerp evolved into a first-rate textile dyeing centre, because English merchants often found it less costly to transport their valuable broadcloths undyed to the Scheldt town and to have them finished there and subsequently re-exported.[66] Cloth exports from London to Antwerp 'surged', as a contemporary rightly stated: broadcloths averaged *c.* 43,000 *per annum* between 1496 and 1500, *c.* 62,000 between 1516 and 1520, *c.* 92,000 between 1536 and 1540, and nearly 124,000 between 1546 and 1550.[67] Based on the *blauwkuipaccijns*, i.e. the excise tax payable by the Antwerp cloth dyers for each woad tub, calculations indicate that in the early 1540s about 22,400 cloths were dyed for the first time. This figure is merely an estimate. The actual number of cloths dyed blue could have been either higher or lower, as the number in each tub also depended on the desired colour intensity, which could vary considerably. At any rate, a quarter to a third of all imported English broadcloth was dyed blue in Antwerp, which required importing *c.* 9000 bales of woad, as one bale of *c.* 160 kilograms was enough to dye 2.5 cloths with an average length of 40 els. This output represented a capital of £13,500 to £15,000 Fl. gr.[68] Woad imports intended for the Antwerp cloth dyers alone could therefore generate substantial revenue.

Woad was cultivated in several regions in Europe. In the late Middle Ages Antwerp merchants obtained their supplies in Picardy and in the Rhineland, but after the the middle of the fifteenth century both production areas declined.[69] While the slump in local wool industries was an important factor, the main cause was the rising competition from the region around Toulouse, the capital of Languedoc. Pastel from the Toulouse-Albi-Carcassonne triangle (the *pays de cocagne)* entered a veritable heyday in the sixteenth century, not only in France, but also in Spain, England, and, last but not least, the Netherlands, where Antwerp evolved into the main distribution centre in Northwest Europe. The phenomenal growth of trade in Toulouse pastel rendered the import of all other woad in the Scheldt town superfluous. From the 1520s, the available sources in any case rarely mention blue dye from other production areas.[70].

Exports of Toulouse pastel were dominated by a small group of substantial businessmen from the outset. Local capitalists controlled both woad production and exports. They made farmers dependent on them by granting loans, demanding in return that these farmers sell the entire harvest to them at a price fixed in advance. Transport was arranged via the Garonne to Bordeaux, the port city whence wine had been shipped to England and the Netherlands for centuries. Until the early 1540s, firms from Toulouse organized the pastel shipments from Bordeaux to Rouen, London, Antwerp, or Bilbao, often stopping in Rouen *en route* to the Low Countries. Given the weight and the high price of the woad, this was

---

65 Pastoureau (2000); Hayward (2015).

66 Thijs (1987), 65-7. Indications suggest that a great many *dyed* English kersey cloths were exported in the mid-sixteenth century: Peacock (2006).

67 Munro (2003), 294, 306-7.

68 Calculations based on Thijs (1987), 77-81, 438.

69 Asaert (1973); Irsigler (1979), 89-93.

70 Significantly, the deans of the Antwerp guild of cloth dyers accepted only Toulouse pastel for the master's test in 1563. Thijs (1974), 190-1.

the most efficient transport method.[71] By 1530 pastel ranked first and wine second in exports from Bordeaux. This very important trade was highly capital-intensive, as pastel was an expensive product: the value of a barrel filled with this dye was six to seven times that of a barrel of wine.[72] Increasing quantities were exported: the average number of bales *per annum* rose from 13,380 in 1520-29 to 24,650 in 1530-39 and later soared to an unprecedented 38,325 bales in 1540-49. The sources available list Bilbao, Rouen, London, and Antwerp as destinations, but, except for London, the figures concerned do not reveal the *final* destination. According to the official figures annual pastel transports directly from Bordeaux to Antwerp averaged *c.* 3400 bales in 1520-29, *c.* 6200 in 1530-39, and *c.* 13,300 in 1540-49.[73] A large (perhaps the largest) share of the pastel shipped from Bordeaux to Rouen was undoubtedly intended for Antwerp, and there are indications that Bilbao often served as a transhipment port as well. Many ships loaded with pastel that arrived in the Scheldt town came from Rouen or 'Spain'.[74] Far greater amounts of pastel were therefore imported to Antwerp than the above figures suggest.

Trading companies from Burgos and increasingly from Toulouse long arranged pastel shipments to Antwerp on their own account. Firms based in the Scheldt town tended to purchase substantial amounts, which they re-exported to other textile centres in the Low Countries and Northern France. In the years 1521-25/6 Schetz & Co. benefited from the war with France to control most of the woad imports in the Low Countries,[75] but that had been an exceptional and passing phenomenon. As far as can be determined, in about 1540 firms based in Antwerp did not yet import Toulouse pastel directly. The same held true for Giovan Battista and Lorenzo Guicciardini, brothers of Lodovico, author of the renowned 'Description of the Low Countries'. Together, they traded extensively in pastel and Bordeaux wine, but up to that point they were exporters, not importers.[76] This changed when the 6-percent tax on trade with France was introduced. From that point onward, merchants wishing to 'trade with the enemy' had to apply for licenses, and such permits would be issued or refused by the central government exclusively on the recommendation of the Receiver-General, who thus became pivotal. The cost of licences varied according to the product and could be high, but Ducci obviously had opportunities to evade the tax: after all, he controlled imports and exports. He took advantage of the system in other ways as well. Since he had become virtually indispensable, he could easily obtain licences for very large quantities, thereby excluding competition. Associating the licences with all kinds of additional conditions effectively gave him a monopoly. Of course he had to import commodities for which demand was substantial and continuous, and for which substitutes were not readily available during the war. Woad was the obvious choice.

71 Many aspects of the classical study by Caster (1962) have been complemented and corrected – including the chronology – by Casado Alonso (1991) and Brumont (2009).

72 Craeybeckx (1958), 145. One barrel (*ton*) of French wine = *c.* 824,4 litres.

73 Calculations based on Brumont (2015), 859, and (2016). These 'large' bales weighed about 160 kilograms.

74 See Craeybeckx (1958), 147-8; Brulez (1959), 453 n. 2; Coornaert (1961), I, 219, 239, and II, 79 n. 5; Brumont (2009), 420.

75 See Chapter 1.4.

76 Goris (1925), 160, 258, 619; Craeybeckx (1958), 37, 285-6; Brulez (1959), 468, 470; Coornaert (1961), I, 351. For biographical notes on Giovan Battista Guicciardini, see Jacqmain (1977), and Aristodemo (2004).

From 1540 on (and possibly even before that), he had participated in the commercial operations of the Guicciardini firm and knew that trade in Toulouse pastel was profitable even in normal years. He was acquainted with all the international firms involved in this trade. He was also related by marriage to the Delft-born merchant Sebastiaen van Utrecht, who had settled in Antwerp around 1540 and specialized in trading woad, had a factor in Bordeaux, and owned installations for processing the dye.[77] Ducci was therefore well-positioned to know how great demand was in the Netherlands for pastel, and at what price it would sell. Of course he had to operate discreetly and needed partners to import the commodity for him, using the licences he obtained. These partners also needed to have organizational skills and/or capital. The Guicciardini brothers, who had a good reputation, were useful partners, because they could serve as exporters for distributing the woad. Their fairly modest financial means did not present a problem, as Gian Carlo Affaitadi funded the purchase and sale of massive amounts of woad. He may have been the actual initiator and may have had Ducci apply for the required licences. As is often the case with other commercial and financial ventures, his role in pastel imports is impossible to specify. At any rate, he was an ideal partner (or principal). In early November everything was arranged. Ducci got what he wanted: Charles V had the Guicciardini brothers provided with safe-conducts to import 20,000 bales of Toulouse pastel and 10,000 barrels of Bordeaux wine, on the condition that they pay Ducci the 6-percent tax.[78]

That Ducci was allowed in 1542 to import or arrange the import of 20,000 bales from France and to sell them in the Netherlands proves that he was exceptionally influential.[79] After all, such a quantity was enough to supply both the Antwerp cloth dyers and most of their counterparts in other textile centres in the Netherlands. When in 1567 Lodovico Guicciardini wrote that 40,000 bales of woad were imported annually into the Low Countries,[80] it is unclear whether he was referring to 'small' or 'large' bales, but even if he meant large ones, his figure would have concerned a later period. That Ducci requested and was granted permission in 1543 to import the same amount of Toulouse pastel again (i.e. another 20,000 bales) proves that this amount was considered to be sufficient for the Low Countries at the time.

For two years Ducci effectively held a monopoly on pastel imports in the Netherlands, as the central government agreed to withhold permission to anyone else until Ducci had sold his stock. Nor was he expected to pay for safe-conducts, thereby further increasing his profit margin. He later stated that each bale had cost *c.* fl.9 to import in 1542/3 (including transport fees). This seems plausible, as in 1545 he sold a batch of Toulouse pastel in Antwerp at fl.10 fl. per bale, and the price is unlikely to have been any lower two years earlier.[81] Importing 20,000 bales therefore required a capital of *c.* fl.180,000 or £30,000 Fl. gr. Ducci was not about to advance such a large amount himself and reached an agreement with Affaitadi. While most aspects of the Ducci-Guicciardini-Affaitadi agreement remain obscure, the partners were in any case willing to have shipments for which the 6-percent

77 Soly (1977), 132-3.
78 ARCHV, PERG 147/21.
79 AGR, PEA 1414/4, no. 36.
80 See Brulez (1970), 26.
81 AGR, PEA 1661/1, *Sur la despesche*, and letter dated 29 January 1545.

tax was payable registered in their names. They understood that if it became known that the Receiver-General of all people was importing an indispensable raw material on his own account, as well as virtually monopolizing it (which was indeed the case), there would be an uproar. According to the official figures reported by Ducci during the first war year, however, the Guicciardini brothers reported only two-thirds of the 20,000 bales.[82]

The Guicciardini brothers imported both Toulouse pastel and Bordeaux wine, for which they also obtained licenses via Ducci – and were the only merchants in the Netherlands credited with doing this during the first year of the war. Additionally, they paid import taxes on only 1187 of the 10,000 barrels they shipped. A few years later the Florentine merchant-banker Renaldo Strozzi charged Ducci with venturing into this wine trade via front men, which was indeed the case.[83] Transporting massive amounts of pastel and wine led the Guicciardini brothers to charter ships, sometimes with Affaitadi, in other cases with Ducci, purchasing marine insurance in some – but not all – cases to this end.[84] These precautions were by no means superfluous, as the war situation was complex, and privateers roamed the North Sea. By the summer of 1542, French privateers were already boarding English ships in the Channel. Henry VIII and Charles V negotiated an alliance, but signed a formal treaty only on 11 February 1543, agreeing to invade France in the summer of the next year. Henry VIII, however, was fighting a war on two fronts, as Scotland, traditionally allied with France, remained an enemy. On the one hand this led to repeated warfare on land and on the other hand to privateering on the North Sea. Importing woad from France was also complicated because Henry VIII regarded such imports as trade with the enemy. Aware of this situation, Ducci discussed various options with Mary of Hungary for transporting pastel and wine on French ships. He argued that the English were not allowed to impede this, if the ships had an imperial safe-conduct and were unarmed.[85]

In early March 1543 Mary of Hungary instructed the imperial ambassador Eustace Chapuys to request the English ruler to provide the Guicciardini brothers with a safe-conduct for the transit of French woad and wine. Henry VIII was far from accommodating. On 2 April Chapuys reported that he was unable to obtain safe-conducts in England. His Majesty continued to object, arguing that French ships could use such shipments as a cover for sailing to Scotland, and that, even if that was not the case, funds should certainly not be added to the war chest of the enemy. He preferred hurting the French by not buying their woad harvest: 'It would be better to let the French lose their crop (*denrée*), and so molest the people with the war, than to send them money'. He informed me, reported Chapuys, that he would agree to issue safe-conduct only for a 'reasonable' amount, and if Flemish ships handled the shipment. Mary of Hungary tried a different approach, asking Chapuys to explain to Henry VIII that the military campaign by the Emperor against the Duke of Cleves, ally of Francis I, prevented trade in German wine. She had therefore authorized importing 10,000 barrels of Bordeaux wine, 3000 of which had already been loaded onto twenty French ships. She guaranteed that not a single ship would sail to Scotland, and she assured the King that henceforth only wine and woad would be transported on Spanish,

82 AGR, CC 23497-23499; Craeybeckx (1958), 235.
83 SAA, PK 1012; Craeybeckx (1958), 37, 214-5, 235.
84 See, e.g., Goris (1925), 641-2.
85 AGR, PEA 1661/1.

Flemish, or English ships. Henry VIII ignored all entreaties. On 18 April Chapuys reported that no safe-conduct could be obtained for the French ships. The King refused to change his position: this practice would bring far too much money to the country of the enemy, and wine was not indispensable: '[He] would himself rather drink beer, indeed water, than permit his subjects to have wine from France as usual'. He was astonished at this request for a safe-conduct for 10,000 barrels; after all, in peacetime, the combined consumption in England and 'Flanders' did not exceed 3000 barrels.[86] That was nonsense, as in normal years in the middle of the century 20,000 to 23,000 barrels of French wine was imported in the Netherlands,[87] but the mistaken estimate by Henry VIII is not the point here. What mattered was that Mary of Hungary allowed Guicciardini & Co. to import 10,000 barrels, and that such import actually took place, even though during the first war year Ducci recorded only 1187 barrels in the tax registers on behalf of the Guicciardini firm. This not only proves beyond any doubt that these registers distort the importance of trade with France but also indicates the additional profits that the partners could realize by not having to pay taxes on nearly 9,000 barrels of wine at £10 Fl.gr. per barrel: savings of £7,200 Fl.gr.[88]

Surprisingly, in 1542/3 Charles V allowed the Guicciardini brothers to import 10,000 barrels of Bordeaux wine. Even before the war, the government of the Habsburg Netherlands had expressed concern about the relentlessly rising French wine prices, which senior officials and aldermen attributed to 'monopolist' practices in well-documented reports: wholesalers based in Antwerp made 'pre-emptive purchases' in the production areas and funded the costs of transport to the Netherlands. French merchants had by then all but disappeared from this import trade. The government had taken the wave of complaints seriously and had prepared legal measures but had postponed ordinances due to the outbreak of war with France.[89] Entrusting the import of a massive amount of Bordeaux wine to one single firm in 1542/3 was hardly a check to 'monopolist' practices! Mary of Hungary was well aware that Ducci was involved in this trade, and she also knew that he was the chief participant, as their correspondence reveals.[90] The only possible conclusion is that in 1543 she saw no other solution and/or believed that the general interest – supplying the Netherlands – coincided with a private interest in this war year. Notwithstanding the initial objections from Henry VIII, Ducci imported 10,000 barrels of Bordeaux wine via partners and front men.

During the war, trade with France obviously entailed risks. In 1543 the Guicciardini brothers 'and their partners' tried to claim insurance compensation for two ships that were seized by the Spanish after departing from Bordeaux and the nearby port at Blaye carrying nearly 4,000 bales of Toulouse pastel valued at £6,000 Fl.gr.[91] The captains concerned had a letter of marque, i.e. were authorized by the government to capture and conquer merchant vessels of the enemy. In their view French ships were a legitimate prize, even when transporting commodities with a safe-conduct from the Emperor. More

86 LPFD, Henry VIII, 18/1, nos 282, 353, 385, and 416.

87 Craeybeckx (1958), 29-30; Brulez (1970), 25-6.

88 On wine an additional 2 percent was payable, on top of the regular 6 percent in taxes: Coornaert (1961), I, 77 n. 5.

89 Craeybeckx (1984), 382-3, 391-6.

90 See AGR, PEA 1661/1.

91 AGS, SE 8336-3°; ARCHV, PERG 147/16 and 19; SAA, PK 1012; Goris (1925), 641-2.

losses followed. Over the course of 1544, seven ships loaded with Toulouse pastel and wine, insured by Ducci, were captured and diverted to Spain, while some months later six other ships loaded with herring and one carrying 700 bales of woad, all belonging to Ducci, were seized by the English.[92]

Ducci managed to obtain damages for the uninsured woad and wine seized. In Spain Charles V, as requested by his sister, pressured the relevant institutions, and in England Henry VIII soon relented and agreed to pay damages for these two products. He considered the seizure of herring busses legitimate, however, because herring was a food product and should therefore not fall into the hands of the enemy. Ducci protested vigorously. Vaughan warned Henry VIII that no banker in Antwerp would ever issue him another loan, if Ducci objected, but the King would not budge.[93] He felt he had been abandoned, after Charles V signed the Treaty of Crépy with Francis I on 18 September, and he was in the unenviable position of fighting a war against the French, making him intransigent with respect to trade with the enemy. Ducci believed he had struck gold, when he received permission in 1544 from Mary of Hungary to export 2,000 *last* or *c.* 2 million kilograms of herring from Dunkirk to a French port, requiring at least 50 vessels (known as busses).[94] Dunkirk was one of the three Flemish ports, and its fleet of fishing boats comprised about sixty herring busses, able to supply 2000 *last* of salt herring and 1200 *last* of fresh herring annually.[95] Ducci could therefore export the vast majority of this catch. Even in normal years, herring was by far the largest export from the Netherlands to France.[96] As one of the few merchants who had a safe-conduct for the product in wartime, Ducci could realize a substantial profit. The loss of six ships was of course a serious blow. Vaughan tried to negotiate, but Ducci stood his ground. As the negotiations about compensation dragged on, Mary of Hungary and Van Schore read the English diplomat Sir Edward Carne the riot act in January 1545, informing him that the Emperor felt entitled to detain the English merchants and their commodities in Antwerp until the Ducci matter was settled. The trade conflict in fact involved far more serious issues. After the Treaty of Crépy, Henry VIII had continued the war against France and had seized a great many ships from the Netherlands loaded with food *en route* to or from France because they were 'aiding the enemy'. The Emperor had subsequently ordered that all ships and goods of the Merchant Adventurers in Antwerp and Bergen-op–Zoom be confiscated. That the governor and the pivotal figure from her government should summon an ambassador to discuss this conflict and during this discussion to Carne's utter amazement should focus on the Ducci case attests to the immense influence of the banker on decision-making. He had penetrated the inner circles of power and had their unconditional support. Vaughan failed to understand, since the Emperor's reprisals were a source of loss for many merchants in Antwerp, leaving unemployed all those who subsisted from finishing English cloth as long as the Merchant Adventurers' goods remained confiscated: 'Great numbers of fullers, shearmen, dyers and

92 AGR, PEA 1414/4, no. 36, and LPFD, Henry VIII, 19/2, no. 365.
93 LPFD, Henry VIII, 19/2, nos 4 and 266, and 20/1, no. 43.
94 One *last* was about 1,000 kilogram of herring. Busses had a capacity of 30 to 40 *last*. Tracy (1993), 253.
95 Sicking (1998), 74, and (2015), 166.
96 Coornaert (1961), I, 218, 228, 314, 319, 324, and II, 109.

others thought their livings were utterly bereaved from them'.[97] This was no exaggeration, as large numbers of artisans were indeed involved in finishing the English broadcloths. In 1540 the Antwerp cloth dressers' guild comprised at least 1200 masters and journeymen. Because they played a major role in employment and consequently had a significant impact on local social relations, the Merchant Adventurers were the only 'nation' to be granted substantial commercial advantages by the city council.[98]

The social consequences of the reprisals against the Merchant Adventurers mattered far less to the government than the damages claimed by some substantial merchants, led by Ducci, as state and private interests once again overlapped. The government needed Ducci and insisted that 'appropriate' treatment of his case was an absolute priority, as the English diplomat Nicholas Wotton was told soon afterwards. Van Schore and the influential politician Nicolas Perrenot de Granvelle tasked Wotton with investigating how the conflict could be resolved and made clear to him that until Ducci was provided with adequate compensation, the Emperor would refuse any agreement. On 28 February state secretary William Paget and Wotton wrote to Henry VIII that Charles V would not relent. The losses suffered by Ducci and some Spanish merchants had to be compensated, or a settlement was out of the question. The conclusion was obvious: 'These merchants almost direct the Emperor'. Henry VIII was forced to concede. In May 1545 Ducci's bill was accepted. He was paid £10,251 Fl.gr. in damages for the loss of 542 *last* of herring.[99] The amounts he listed indicate that he ordinarily expected net profits of 50 percent. Taking into account expenses for packaging, transport, safe-conducts, and customs duties, exporting 2000 *last* of herring to France would have yielded net profits of nearly £12,000 Fl.gr.

In the meantime, Ducci had entered the international grain trade as well, as had Schetz & Co., who also regarded the rising prices in 1545 and 1546 as an opportunity. In June 1545 he requested Mary of Hungary for permission to import 300 *last* of grain from the Prince-Bishopric of Liège and the Duchy of Jülich (not controlled by the Emperor) and to transport them to Lisbon. He urged a rapid decision, as he was receiving information that a lot of grain was being loaded (onto ships) in the Baltic area for transport to Portugal. Moreover, the harvest within a few weeks would lead to a fall in prices.[100] In other words, this was the moment to realize maximum profits. He was granted the permit requested, which was highly unusual.[101] He was granted another export permit in 1546, when the grain shortage in the Netherlands was even greater than the year before. As a measure of how exceptional such a permit was, in March the governor refused to allow the grain that Henry VIII had purchased in Cleves and Jülich to be transported from Dordrecht to his troops in Calais.[102] Permission had been requested for 1200 *last*, which the governor found unacceptable, because exporting such a large amount would

---

97 AGR, PEA 1661/1, December 1543 and January 1544; LPFD, Henry VIII, 19/2, no. 723, and 20/1, nos 4, 65, 70; De Smedt (1952-54), I, 164-6.

98 De Smedt (1952-54), II, 128-57, 304-27. See also Thijs (1987), 220.

99 LPFD, Henry VIII, 20/1, nos 229, 281, 711; AGR, PEA 1661/1, Letter dated 11 May 1545. See also Wegg (1916), 276.

100 AGR, PEA 1661/1, Letter dated 11 June 1545.

101 See Scholliers (1960), 52 and 54.

102 Grain exports from Cleves and Jülich to the Netherlands were generally modest, but in the years 1544-1546 large shipments of wheat were transported to Dordrecht: Weststrate (2008), 274.

very much worsen the already serious food shortage in the Netherlands.[103] Ducci did obtain a permit, albeit for a much smaller quantity (225 *last*). However, he succeeded where an ally had not… The irony of the story was that his two ships loaded with grain were seized by the English *en route* to Portugal, after which Ducci wrote to Henry VIII expressing his confidence that the King would undoubtedly cover the damages. He was indeed paid compensation.[104]

Ducci indisputably made vast profits from the woad trade, although the amount is impossible to estimate even by approximation. On the one hand, Affaitadi's share in this venture is unknown, and on the other hand the Guicciardini brothers are very likely to have been deceived. Vaughan was convinced that Ducci and Affaitadi 'ha[d] great intelligence', and he was right. Affaitadi's firm, for example, sold 16,000 bales of Toulouse pastel during the war, which was resounding evidence of their pivotal role in its import.[105] This venture was no coincidence, nor was it an isolated incident. It has already been noted that Affaitadi raised part of the capital that the government required for collecting the 1 percent export tax. He was also involved in other commercial and financial ventures by Ducci, as will be shown below. Their alliances, however, were always shrouded in secrecy. Nor was the Guicciardini brothers' venture in the woad and wine trade possible to specify, but they appear to have served mainly as front men. It is impossible to determine how much Ducci invested personally in the 40,000 bales of Toulouse pastel that he was allowed to import in 1543 and 1544. In a letter to Charles V in June 1544, he described *all* the confiscated ship cargoes as personal losses, but only for strategic purposes since he was best placed to convince the Emperor to intervene in Spain and in England, which is exactly what happened. At the same time, he asked the Emperor to compensate him for the losses suffered by granting him exclusive rights to import Toulouse pastel into the Habsburg Netherlands for an indefinite period. Charles V did not grant this request. In 1535 he had signed a contract with the Welsers, granting them a monopoly for fifty years on woad cultivation near the harbour of Veracruz in New Spain. In exchange for land, labour and livestock, the Emperor was to receive one third of the envisaged earnings. The project was part of the political-economic struggle with France.[106] Its ultimate failure was impossible to anticipate in the 1540s, and the Emperor did not want to antagonize the Welsers by granting Ducci a monopoly on woad imports in the Netherlands in peacetime. Mary of Hungary was instructed to inform Ducci that such a monopoly would give rise to massive resistance and might lead the Provincial Estates to withhold a new *aide*. Ducci replied immediately with a new option: wait until the Provincial Estates have approved the subsidy. He would then provide the central government with a huge loan, after which he would be granted a commercial monopoly for ten years. It need not be for pastel imports. It could also involve the exclusive right to purchase all alum brought to Antwerp, another raw material for the textile industry.[107] The government opted for an alum monopoly.[108]

---

103 HHS, B-PA 71, March 1546, passim.
104 LPFD, Henry VIII, 21/1, nos 766 and 786.
105 LPFD, Henry VIII, 20/1, no. 96; Denucé (1934a), 57.
106 Priotti (2018).
107 AGR, PEA 1414/4, nos 36 and 40.
108 See Chapter 2.3.

Ducci did not abandon the woad trade immediately. First, he intended to recover all shipments seized or taken by privateers or to receive damages. Second, he was also serving the interests of Affaitadi in this import.[109] In 1546 he was still selling large quantities to Baudouin Barbier, a substantial merchant from Toulouse who lived in Antwerp. The sale consisted of 5515 bales supplied by Eustachius Kaltenhofer and Hans Welser & Co., 2300 bales loaded by Thomas Balbani in Bordeaux, and 3200 bales belonging to the Guicciardini brothers that were seized by privateers and had to be brought from Spain by Affaitadi. Altogether, Ducci provided Barbier with 11,015 bales of pastel.[110] These were his final dealings in Toulouse pastel. Several French, Italian, and especially South-German firms based in Antwerp or with permanent representatives there saw the profits that could be made and started importing massive quantities of Toulouse pastel (and Bordeaux wine). Apart from the rising competition Ducci faced from other large firms, he had good reason to quit a trade in which the Guicciardini brothers had been closely involved.

Giovan Battista and Lorenzo had to abandon their commercial activities when they were declared bankrupt in 1544.[111] A few years later Ducci alleged that their debt amounted to 150,000 *écus d'or* or £47,500 Fl.gr., without specifying who the creditors were.[112] How they ended up so deeply in debt remains a mystery. The brothers accused Ducci of cheating them, and they are very likely to have been right.[113] After their bankruptcy, the Guicciardini brothers sued Ducci. The case dragged on for a quarter of a century, and the final outcome is unknown. It is possible that no judgement was rendered. In any case, the brothers withdrew entirely from business and failed to convince the members of the elite to support them, even though Giovan Battista was the correspondent of Cosimo I de' Medici, Duke of Tuscany, in Brussels from 1559 on.[114] Did the pastel trade cause their ruin, and had Ducci played a role in their downfall? This seems plausible, as the nature of the Guicciardini-Affaitadi-Ducci association was central to the case that Strozzi brought against Ducci in Valladolid in the mid-1540s, leading to the appointment of a commission of investigation in Antwerp a few years later. According to Strozzi's lawyer, Ducci had been involved in both the pastel and the wine trade of the brothers and had illegally sold Gian Carlo Affaitadi a cargo of 4000 bales that had been shipped to them – both Florentines, as was Strozzi – without ever paying for it. After futile efforts to speak with Affaitadi in Antwerp, the lawyer resorted to the city government, which appointed commissioners to investigate the matter. Together with the lawyer, they searched for Affaitadi, first in Lier, where he often stayed, and then at his castle in Wommelgem, where he welcomed them but refused to let them examine the accounts relevant to the dealings with Ducci, invoking the Antwerp *Consuetudines*. He agreed only to show the ledger indicating the total purchase of 16,000 bales. The lawyer contacted the city authorities again, demanding

109 See esp. LPFD, Henry VIII, 20/1, no. 1194.
110 Craeybeckx (1958), 236. Eustachius Kaltenhofer was probably related to the more widely known Stephan. See Strieder (1930), 382 n. 1; Pöllnitz (1963), I, 253.
111 Jacqmain (1977), and Aristodemo (2004).
112 AGR, PEA 1414/1, no. 37.
113 In 1543, for example, Ducci allowed his 'good friend' Tommaso Corbinelli, director of the Salviati Bank in Antwerp, to import Bordeaux wine on the sly, even though the Guicciardinis held an exclusive licence: Matringe (2016), 127 n. 172.
114 *Lettere* (1950); Goldthwaite (1968), 148-9.

disclosure of the books kept by Affaitadi to learn exactly what had happened to the 4000 bales of pastel. Affaitadi persisted in his refusal, insisting that nobody in the Habsburg Netherlands could be forced to disclose the secrets of their accounts.[115]

The entire case ground to a halt, as the Antwerp aldermen were loath to offend a powerful businessman such as Affaitadi, who had been of great service to the city already and might help them again in the future. Nor did they wish to set a legal precedent. In this period, various aspects of Antwerp commercial law remained unclear. The legal scholars drafting the compilation of customary law of 1547 may have known little or nothing about trade, but the obvious question is why the city authorities made no effort whatsoever to address this aspect. The reason is probably that during the first half of the sixteenth century Antwerp's political elite had few ties to business circles. In any case, compilations from later dates indicate that Antwerp commercial law did not stipulate any obligation on the part of debtors to provide ledgers that would confirm a claim against them.[116] Affaitadi could invoke this point, although his argument concerning 'commercial confidentiality' did not figure in any sixteenth-century legal treatise. He expected, however, that in a metropolis such as Antwerp, the public authorities would respect this argument, and he was right. The city government could not afford to offend powerful economic operators – even less so in the late 1540s than before, as the city was carrying an astronomical debt.[117] As a senior official noted: 'No people on earth are less inclined to have their accounts examined than merchants', and this was especially true in a city where 'many businessmen trade not only with their own money and goods but also secretly with those that belong to others'.[118]

While many questions remain, the Fourth Habsburg-Valois War (1542-44), like the first one (1521-26), clearly offered merchant bankers exceptional opportunities for earnings, not only on the money market but also in terms of trade in commodities for which substitutes were unavailable or insufficiently available. In 1543 and 1544 this held true not only for imports of Toulouse pastel but also for those of Bordeaux wine, as well as to some extent for herring exports to France. In each of these cases, Ducci took the initiative, although he teamed up with other firms for both woad and wine. Only his single foray into the herring export was organized entirely on his own account. Ducci and Affaitadi were undoubtedly in complete control of importing and selling woad and wine during the war. They did not lift a finger to help their partners Giovan Battista and Lorenzo Guicciardini when they ran into problems. Although they operated mainly as front men, the two brothers invested money, apparently very imprudently. They always insisted that Ducci's manipulations had driven them into bankruptcy. This is of course impossible to verify – nor could their contemporaries do so – but the documents concerning the Strozzi-Ducci conflict indicate that the key figures had a lot to hide. Secrecy was inherent not only in the strategies of a capitalist such as Ducci, who obtained exceptional import permits but also put his stamp on the policy of a government that allocated such benefits out of financial necessity. Without active support or at least tacit cooperation from the State, nobody in Western

115 ARCHV, PER, Carpeta 147/1-7; SAA, PK 1012; Denucé (1934a), 57-8; Ruiz Albi (2018); Druwé (2020), 175-9.
116 De Longé (1870).
117 See Part Three.
118 SAA, T 199, *Redenen*.

Europe could control the import and sale of a dye such as woad. An official or effective monopoly was, moreover, possible only in times of war, because the finest quality dye (i.e. Toulouse pastel) could at that time be supplied only by those who held a licence to 'trade with the enemy'. But such monopolies did not endure. The strategies devised by Erasmus Schetz and Gaspar Ducci in the 1520s and early 1540s, respectively, clearly demonstrate their ephemeral nature. Only one raw material intended for the textile industry was suited to a long-term monopoly: alum.

2.3 The Alum Monopoly

No other product in medieval and early modern Europe was as economically interesting and at the same time so easy to monopolize as alum.[119] It was indispensable in the textile industry, the most important non-agrarian sector in medieval and early modern Europe, because it was the best mordant for fixing certain dyes. It was also used in tanneries (e.g. for dyeing gloves and leather garments), in glass-blowing, in painting, and in pharmaceuticals, but demand for alum was greatest in the textile industry. To produce a black hue in fabrics pre-dyed blue or to apply related colours to them, such as purple or violet, they had to be stained with alum and subsequently immersed in a tub of madder. Alum was also indispensable for red, yellow, and green dyes.[120] Understandably, therefore, the alum market was subject to close scrutiny, not only by dyers and wholesalers but also by the political authorities in textile-producing regions. International merchants tried to control the alum market from the thirteenth century, and such efforts nearly always met with great resistance; they could instigate trade wars and even political conflicts. Monopolization was not really so difficult, because the main sites where alum was present were geographically concentrated. There were mines in North Africa, in Italy, in Sicily, and on some Greek islands, but they were of little significance. From the thirteenth century onward, the largest quantities of alum came from Phocea in Asia Minor, and this very high-quality alum was mined and distributed by Genoese merchant bankers, who held a virtual monopoly of the trade; their ships carried it to Genoa, Catalonia, Flanders, and England.

When Phocea came under Turkish control shortly after the mid-fifteenth century, alum prices began to rise on western markets. By the early 1460s its price was nearly fivefold what it had been in 1453. Reopening small, known mines in the West was an option, although the alum produced there was substandard.[121] In 1462 the discovery of the mines at Tolfa near Civitavecchia in the Papal State – of all places! - was a turning point, as they contained vast deposits of excellent quality. The next year Pope Pius II prohibited trade in Turkish alum, and in 1465 his successor Pope Paul II proclaimed that the proceeds of Tolfa alum sales were to be used toward financing the crusades, meaning that Christians could purchase, sell, and process only *Allume della Crociata*. This policy soon proved difficult to enforce and had to be abandoned after a few decades. In the meantime, in 1470, the Pope

119 Natural aluminium sulphate, ammonium alum, or potassium alum, i.e. a double aluminium salt.

120 De Poerck (1951), I, 168-75, and Struckmeier (2011), 70-1, 79. On dyeing techniques in sixteenth-century Antwerp, see Thijs (1975a), 656-76.

121 Heers (1954); Weber (2013); Basso (2014).

had formed a cartel with King Ferdinand I of Naples, who owned a small alum mine on Ischia, to avoid mutual competition.[122]

Until 1501 the popes tended to separate the Tolfa mining from alum distribution and leased each of the two activities to different bankers, including the Medici, who exported vast quantities to the Low Countries.[123] Contractees in charge of the mining operations could also take over the mines in the southern part of Tuscany and at Agnano near Naples, but they had no control over production outside Italy.[124] In the Kingdom of Murcia substantial alum mines were discovered at Mazarrón and were operated from the 1460s, to be complemented soon afterwards by the smaller mines of Cartagena and Lorca. In Andalusia alum was also mined at Rodalquilar.[125] Although Spanish alum was not initially sold in the same quantities as Italian alum and was of inferior quality, it nonetheless made for stiff competition.

In the period 1501-53 the popes entrusted both production and distribution of Tolfa alum to a consortium of bankers for ten to twelve-year periods. Until 1531 the Apostolic Camera maintained contracts with companies from Siena, in which members of the Chigi family were pivotal, and afterwards with the Genoese firm Grimaldi & Co, which was dominant until 1553. In production, the bankers involved in Italy had full control; sometimes these Italian bankers also took over in Spain, where the mine owners nearly always leased them to Italian companies. The contractees, however, arranged sales to other countries via intermediaries: merchant bankers based there and more familiar with the relevant markets and therefore able to ensure distribution from there. The Tolfa contractees often encountered problems enforcing the papal monopoly, as several European rulers reserved the right to purchase alum elsewhere in 'exceptional circumstances', not only in Christian areas but if necessary in the Levant as well. The fall of Constantinople did not end Turkish alum imports. The mines in Anatolia remained in operation, and their output was also purchased by Christian merchants, notwithstanding all papal prohibitions.[126]

Alum was sold mainly to the Burgundian/Habsburg Netherlands. This was primarily because of the highly developed textile industries in various provinces, but also because at first Bruges and subsequently Antwerp served as a commercial redistribution hub in Northwest Europe. Political motives and tax interests led Emperor Maximilian I to favour Antwerp. Following the revolt by the Flemish cities, he transferred trade in all papal alum from Bruges to Antwerp in 1491. The alum staple made Antwerp very attractive as a commercial centre. With this in mind, the city authorities agreed to pay the ruler 25 Flemish shillings per last of alum sold. All importers were henceforth required to offer the mineral for sale in Antwerp first.[127] This windfall greatly boosted cloth dyeing in the city, as well as the local economy overall. In addition to having large amounts of alum

122 Strieder (1925), 171-6; Liagre (1955), 196; Delumeau (1962), 20, 23, 79, 128.

123 Delumeau (1962), 26-7, 90-4; De Roover (1963), 152-6; Boone (1999), 41-7. For a survey of the alum market in late medieval Bruges, see Dumolyn and Lambert (2018), 245-50.

124 Boisseuil (2005); Feniello (2005). See also Günster and Martin (2015).

125 Córdoba de la Llave, Franco Silva and Navarro Espinach (2005), 125-7.

126 Boisseuil and Ait (2014), with references to the literature.

127 SAA, Charters, no. 322; Mertens and Torfs (1847), III, 327. One last = 3.75 cantara.

on site for dyeing increasing numbers of English cloths, the staple was needed in a great many textile centres in Flanders, Brabant, Hainault, and Holland. A regular supply of alum was therefore indispensable for the economy of the Burgundian/Habsburg Netherlands. The rise of Antwerp as an international market also favoured increasing exports to other countries, especially to Germany and England. No other centre in Northwest Europe was as crucial for alum distribution in the sixteenth century.

Consequently, discussion of the legitimacy of papal interference in the alum trade and the monopoly of the Tolfa contractees was heated in the Netherlands. When Tolfa alum prices took off in 1504, Philip the Fair, Duke of Burgundy, entered a contract with the Florentine Jeronimo Frescobaldi to supply Turkish alum at a far lower price. The next year, Henry VII of England followed suit and reached a similar agreement with the Florentine Antonio Gualterotti to supply Turkish alum.[128] Pope Julius II retaliated on 17 May 1506 with a papal bull recalling that Christians were prohibited from trading with infidels. Whoever purchased or sold Turkish alum therefore risked excommunication. The representative of the Apostolic Camera delivered the papal bull in person to all merchant bankers trading in alum. The threat of excommunication created such an outcry that Archduchess Margaret of Austria, governor of the Netherlands, consulted the Council of Flanders on it in 1507. In a detailed and well-substantiated report, the lawyers argued that the Tolfa contractees, who controlled all the alum mines in Italy, were driving prices up artificially and causing serious harm to the textile manufacturers. Importing Turkish alum had put an end to this 'disgraceful' state of affairs. No longer able to reap exorbitant profits, Agostino Chigi & Co. had asked the Pope to impose a (new) import ban. Such a ban 'had nothing to do with Christian tenets', as it 'catered exclusively to the *secular* interests of the Pope'. Ultimately, negotiations got under way and yielded a compromise on 18 October 1508: the representatives of the Apostolic Camera were guaranteed that only 'their' lessees would be allowed to import Tolfa alum in the Netherlands for two years, but they had to agree to a maximum price of 72 Flemish shillings per last and to pay the government a toll of 12 Flemish shillings per last.[129]

It was not the last serious dispute about papal involvement in the alum trade. Rulers could undermine the monopoly of the Tolfa contractees by authorizing the import of Turkish alum officially or by tacitly tolerating it. They could also thwart the system in other ways, for example by granting permission to sign contracts with the lessees of Spanish alum mines or, far more important, awarding merchants active in their country a monopoly on alum imports without taking into account any existing commercial agreements that the Tolfa contractees had reached with other firms. Political support was indispensable but was also very uncertain, because a wide variety of factors could lead to contracts and monopolies being granted, enforced, or broken: ties between the Pope and certain secular rulers, balances of power between and within states, the financial position of the Crown, the influence of merchant bankers, and the weight carried by socio-economic lobbies. Since a fortune could be made here, the alum trade was a continual subject of dispute and speculation.

128 AGR, PEA 1414/4, no. 81; Delumeau (1962), 46; Setton (1984), 49.

129 Finot (1902). See also ROPB, 2nd ser., I, 87.

The successive contracts that the government of the Burgundian/Habsburg Netherlands entered into with the Tolfa contractees between 1508 and 1528 stipulated that each year a minimum amount of Italian alum – generally 4000 last – had to be delivered to the Antwerp staple market and in some cases – but not all – at a maximum price. Mazarrón alum is known to have been imported in ever greater quantities in the 1520s, causing Tolfa alum prices to decline. From 1528, prices started to rise again, which Mary of Hungary attributed to a cartel agreement between the Pope and the Marquis of Villena, who owned half the alum mines in Spain. While they could not be prevented from earning a profit, she wrote to Emperor Charles V, 'accepting and tolerating monopolies that seriously harm your subjects in the Low Countries is not reasonable'.[130] The Emperor did not respond. The government of the Habsburg Netherlands was powerless to stop the continuous rise in prices, which in 1536 soared to 100 Flemish shillings per last, i.e. 150 percent higher than in 1525-27. Gerard Stercke, Receiver-General of the alum duties, warned the governor: 'This price is excessive, and the common people are disgruntled that the ruler permits this'.[131] Since the cloth dyers and shearers already had difficulty selling their products because of the general economic slump, the central government feared that higher spending on a basic raw material would exacerbate their discontent, possibly jeopardizing the precarious social order. Moreover, higher alum prices affected the profit margin of merchants exporting large quantities of English cloth, such as the Schetzes and the Van Bombergens. They could not recover the additional costs they had to pay the dyers entirely from their customers, without risking a substantial drop in sales. Emperor Charles V became so alarmed that he instructed his sister to launch a thorough investigation.

Mary of Hungary sent Van Schore, her most trusted senior official, to Antwerp in July 1536 to discover 'the secrets relating to alum' and to propose adequate measures. According to Van Schore, both the firms operating the Italian and Spanish alum mines and some Antwerp wholesalers (among whom was Pauwel van Gemert) were responsible for the soaring prices: the former profited the most, while the latter also achieved substantial earnings by buying up all cargoes immediately on arrival and then reselling them in small quantities. The cloth dyers were still more disgruntled, because they knew that alum prices in Italy and Spain had hardly increased since 1527-28. Aware that these affluent entrepreneurs were central to the main branch of Antwerp's textile industry, Van Schore understood that caution was advisable.[132] Since the main Turkish alum quarries had been seriously damaged (possibly by earthquakes), the dyers were forced to purchase South-European alum at any price and refused to accept the situation. Van Schore achieved nothing in his talks with the factors of the Genoese banker Ansaldo Grimaldi and the Sienna banker Girolamo Venturi,[133] who leased the Tolfa mines, and Gaspare Rotulo from Milan, who operated the mines at Mazarrón and Rodalquilar. They accused each other and unspecified Antwerp firms of underhanded practices and mentioned that marine insurance was

130 Quoted in Gorter-Van Royen and Hoyois (2009), no. 276, my translation.

131 'Que led. pris est excessif et que le commun peuple se plaint de ce que le Prince permect ainsi vendre lesd. alluns a si chier pris'. AGR, PEA 1414/4, no. 1 (see also nos 4, 5 and 81). For more detail, see Soly (1974b), 807 and 844.

132 AGR, PEA 1414/4, nos 1, 2, 4, and 10. A cloth dyeing works cost fl.8000 to fl.10,000, and weekly woad and alum supplies amounted to about fl.250: Thijs (1987), 284-7.

133 On these bankers, see Guidi Bruscoli (2007), 169-70.

becoming increasingly expensive as a consequence of ongoing warfare. When Van Schore resorted to threatening that the government would decree a maximum price, the factors replied that such a measure would be very unwise. After all, their masters would in that case have no choice but to start shipping the alum to a different market (e.g. London instead of Antwerp), which would entail a major loss of income for the Emperor. Such an intervention by the government would moreover have a heavy impact on trade in the Habsburg Netherlands in the long run, because all international merchants would regard the measure as a dangerous precedent. In the words of the factors: 'The merchants come to the Low Countries to enjoy the freedom there [and they] the merchants will choose other destinations without this freedom of trade'.[134] Van Schore is unlikely to have taken the threat seriously. Still, he must have understood that the argument 'infringement on freedom of trade' could not be dismissed out of hand.

Maximum prices for bread and – more rarely – grain were sometimes set by municipal authorities or the central government, but only in times of crisis and always for brief periods. No such measure had ever been taken with respect to industrial raw materials or other commodities traded internationally. That the representatives of the Italian merchant bankers considered setting a maximum price for alum as an unacceptable infringement of the freedom of trade is therefore understandable. Presumably, they were also referring to 'freedom tied to privileges', and they tended to interpret their privileges very broadly. Measures by the central government that might complicate or impede trade in Antwerp for certain groups in some way had until then been exceptional. Recently, however, the local authorities had taken measures that he Merchant Adventurers had perceived as infringing on their privileges. In the 1530s they had a great many complaints indeed on this issue: about loading and unloading goods with the harbour crane, weighing goods at the *Stadswaag* (the Urban Weigh-House), and measuring cloth,[135] as well as about the municipal administration of justice, about the excise exemption on beer and wine, and the like. They informed the aldermen that they would leave the city, unless their demands were met.[136] The factors of the Tolfa and Mazarrón lessees must have known about this. Their threat to divert alum shipments to a secondary but nonetheless important market such as London therefore came at a time when the central government could not afford to antagonise international merchants.

The extreme scarcity of capital became even more acute, as the long-expected war with France had broken out and was being waged in the North and South alike. Only in July 1538 did Emperor Charles V and Francis I agree to a reconciliation; by then they had depleted all financial reserves. Mary of Hungary and her advisors saw no possibility of economic intervention, and alum prices remained extremely high. The Antwerp city government warned the government of the increasing protests. Paradoxically, however, new wars and harmful monetary measures caused a gradual but consistent decline in prices from 1539. The wars between Venice and the Ottoman Empire (1537-40) and between Emperor Charles V and Francis I (1542-44) had a heavy impact on the textile trade and

134 'Les marchans hantent le pays de pardecha pour la liberté qu'ilz y ont sans laquelle ilz charoireront aultres lieux'. AGR, PEA 1414/4, no. 5: 28 July 1536.

135 All these inspections and procedures were mandatory and payable.

136 De Smedt (1950-1954), I, 147.

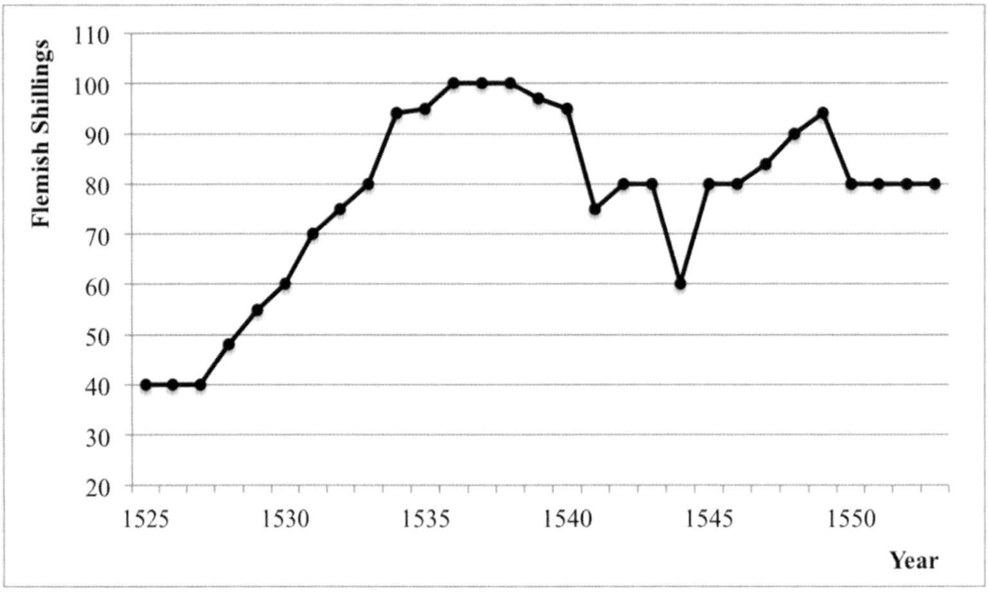

Figure 3. Wholesale price of alum (in Flemish shillings per last) in Antwerp, 1525-53

Sources: AGR, PEA 1414/4, and SAA, T 622 and 629.
Note: One last = 400 Antwerp pounds = *c.* 188 kilogram = 3.75 cantara.

manufacturing, which in the Netherlands was also affected by the Emperor's financial policy.[137] The steep fall in textile prices (i.e. plummeting demand) drove decline in the alum price: in 1543 in Antwerp a last cost only 70 Flemish shillings, i.e. 30 percent less than in 1536-38. Ducci later stated that the price would have declined far more, had the banker-contractees of Italian and Spanish mines not formed a cartel.[138] He was probably right, as a few years later price agreements did indeed come to light.

Prices depended not only on supply (i.e. on the contracts that the Tolfa and Mazarrón lessees entered into with firms responsible for transport from Spain/Italy to the Low Countries) but also on distribution in Antwerp: which firms purchased the alum on arrival, on what terms did they offer it on the local market, and how much did they re-export? On the Antwerp market large and small amounts were not ordinarily sold at the same price per last. In 1540 the nobleman Christoph von Gersdorf wrote to King Ferdinand, brother of Charles V, that the '*Schotzische Gesell[s]chaft* largely controls Italian and Spanish alum and keeps prices high'. He was referring to the Schetz firm.[139] While no factual data confirm his statement, it seems very plausible, at least as far as distribution of Tolfa alum in the Low Countries is concerned. In 1540, the Florentine firm Salviati, a major operator at the fairs of Lyon, had convinced Ansaldo Grimaldi & Co., the lessees of the Tolfa mine, to provide them with 12,000 cantara or 3200 last of alum each year for twelve years. They had exclusive authorization to sell this alum in Antwerp and thus had a monopoly on Tolfa alum in the

137 Edler (1937), and (1938), 119-22; De Smedt (1950-1954), II, 501-5; Van der Wee (1963), II, 203-4.
138 AGR, PEA 1414/4, no. 81.
139 Quoted in Strieder (1925), 181-2. See also Ruiz Martín (2005), 70-1.

Low Countries. The contract was so important that Averardo and Piero Salviati opened a branch in Antwerp. The Antwerp *compagnia* traded in various products, but alum sales appear to have been its *raison d'être*. The Salviatis did not run this trade on their own. They covered one quarter of the alum contract and shared their monopoly with Spanish merchants, including Francisco del Castillo, and probably with other firms as well. From the outset the Salviatis in Antwerp relied on other investors, and major depositors in their bank turn out to have been Schetz and Ducci.[140] Why would they have been interested in a new medium-sized *compagnia*, if they had no opportunity to purchase vast amounts of alum at favourable terms and resell it at a profit, in the Netherlands or elsewhere? It has been argued that the Salviatis wound up their Antwerp branch in 1544, because they were insufficiently successful in economic terms,[141] and that is true. But the underlying reason is very likely that after losing their alum contract, they no longer had a compelling reason to remain there.

Until then, the banker-contractees of the Tolfa and Mazarrón mines had been granted monopolies, in that they had entered into contracts with firms given the exclusive right to sell alum in a certain country or region. On 16 August 1544 the Emperor introduced an entirely new policy, which had vast consequences. He granted Ducci a ten-year exclusive right to purchase all Italian and Spanish alum brought to Antwerp at 60 Flemish shillings per last; Ducci was to sell everything at a maximum price of 80 Flemish shillings per last. Ducci thereby obtained a monopoly on the alum trade, both in the Low Countries and in the rest of Northwest Europe, for which Antwerp was the distribution centre. If Ducci charged the maximum price of 80 Flemish shillings per last, he would be operating legally, though he would in fact be charging 15 to 30 percent more than the standard market price in 1543 and 1544.[142] While this was already a cause for complaints, a far more serious problem was that Ducci's monopoly undermined the position of the Tolfa and Mazarrón contractees, who were no longer in full control, rendering the contracts they had entered into with their distributors worthless. The Emperor's advisors, however, did not take possible threats to sell the alum elsewhere seriously: no other port city in Western Europe offered the commercial opportunities that Antwerp did in this period. While they expected objections from the main operators in the European alum trade, their main concern was the Emperor's dire financial straits of and the 'solution' proposed by Ducci, i.e. a huge loan in exchange for a monopoly.

The many loans that Charles V contracted on the Antwerp Exchange to finance the war drove interest rates up to 16 percent *per annum* in May-June 1544. Since the government was unable to repay its current loans on time, a crisis ensued. Worse, because Ducci informed the governor on 15 May that the Emperor would be unable to obtain new loans, unless he repaid the heirs of the Portuguese marrano Diego Mendes the amount payable very quickly: £16,666 2/3 Fl.gr. In fact, no financiers were prepared to advance money, even at high interest rates, and in June some creditors started calling in their capital. Prospects seemed grim. Then Ducci offered to lend fl.100,000 (i.e. £16,666 2/3 Fl.gr.) for

140 Lang (2014), 110-11, 114-17; Matringe (2016), 104. See also Brulez (1959), 468 and 496. On contacts between Francisco del Castillo and Fernando Dassa: Fagel (1996), 99.

141 Lang (2014), 114.

142 AGR, PEA 1414/4, no. 28; Soly (1974b), 844.

an indefinite period at an annual interest rate of 16 percent, provided that he was granted a ten-year monopoly on the alum trade in the Habsburg Netherlands. Mary of Hungary agreed immediately, signed the contract drafted by Ducci, and informed her brother that she saw no other solution.[143]

In addition to putting up the capital needed, Ducci had contacted the German/Swiss merchant-financiers Grimmel, Neidhart, and Seiler, with whom he had set up various financial ventures in the past, and had convinced them to participate in this one. Each took up a fifth of the loan in exchange for an equivalent share in the alum contract. The stipulation was that their names would not appear anywhere.[144] In other words: Ducci would be the only visible operator in a field carefully watched by the entire European business community. The authorities were similarly discreet. Mary of Hungary was aware that Ducci's monopoly would elicit vehement objections and ordered that the name of the Tuscan banker be omitted from the imperial ordinance of 16 August 1544. The ordinance was even presented as a measure *against* monopolization. 'Some merchants only interested in their own earnings' were said to have entered contracts to 'gain control' of all Italian alum in the Netherlands, and others were said to have done likewise with Spanish alum, forcing cloth dyers to pay exorbitant prices: 120 to 140 Flemish shillings per last (i.e. triple what had previously been the usual rate). Worse: these merchants were not content with usurious profits on alum but would sell only to wholesalers who were also prepared to purchase other overpriced commodities from them. In the interest of ending these 'monopolies', nobody was allowed to import or sell alum, unless it was sold to the Receiver-General of the alum duties; he was to be the only one setting purchase and sale prices, but these would be 'reasonable'.[145]

Immediately after the text of the ordinance was made known, a wave of protest ensued. Fearing the reactions of substantial merchants who would feel that they had been wronged, the Antwerp magistrate refused to publish it officially. On 25 August he wrote to his representatives in Brussels that they should use all possible means to urge the central government to reconsider the whole matter. In addition to the danger that the proposed arrangement would have an important impact on international trade, granting a distribution monopoly and setting a maximum price could set a dangerous precedent. The government needed to be made aware that such a policy was 'far more likely to benefit individuals than to make the commonwealth more affluent'.[146] The argument in favour of the public interest was probably sincere, but the opposition by the city government was not based solely on social considerations. In 1540 Fernando Dassa, Martin Lopez, and other powerful Spanish merchants, who resided permanently in Antwerp, had entered into a contract with the Tolfa lessees Luca and Giovanni Battista Grimaldi.[147] According to the terms of this agreement, the Tolfa lessees would supply them with alum in Antwerp every year for twelve years, enabling them to sell the alum independently. Dassa and Lopez

143 AGR, PEA 1414/4, nos 18, 19, 22, and 28.
144 AGR, PEA 1414/4, no. 37.
145 ROPB, 2nd ser., V, 83-5.
146 'Meer tot proffyte van particuliere persoonen dan tot welvaert van den gemeyne best'. SAA, T 629, no. 3.
147 Members of the Genoese Grimaldi family, all merchant bankers, had been operating the Tolfa mines since 1531: Bruscoli (2007), 169-70.

had teamed up with the Salviatis – and probably with the Schetzes as well.[148] By August 1544, however, they were for reasons which are unclear the sole party remaining. The new imperial ordinance rendered their contract worthless. They refused to accept this turn of events and had the means to resist, as wealthy merchants with close ties to the Antwerp political elite: Fernando Dassa was the brother-in-law of burgomaster Lancelot van Ursel. Martin Lopez, heir to a considerable fortune, was active as a merchant but had studied law and had sufficient legal connections to know which procedures to use (and their viability) to challenge measures by the central government.

Thanks to their close ties with the city council, these Spaniards knew that Ducci was the driving force behind the ordinance on 16 August. The news spread rapidly. On 28 August Ducci wrote to Van Schore that the Spanish signatories of the alum contract with the Tolfa lessees were doing everything possible to tarnish his reputation. One had even told him directly 'that if I were to be killed, all my novelties would cease'.[149] In his defence Ducci turned the tables: the merchants accusing him of devious practices had in previous years abused their strong market position by driving alum prices up and profiting at the expense of the 'poor dyers'. Dassa & Co. retaliated by stating that they would not lend the government another penny, if the ordinance were proclaimed, as it would render their alum contract impossible to enforce, leading to such a serious financial loss that they would no longer be able to obtain credit on the Exchange. Despite their remonstrations, they were no match for Ducci, who thanks to his resourcefulness and efficiency in financial matters was trusted and effectively supported by Mary of Hungary. On 30 August the Antwerp authorities were obliged to proclaim officially the – now notorious – ordinance.[150]

The matter did not end here. Dassa & Co. argued that the 'alum ordinance' had rendered their contract with Grimaldi & Co. null and void and refused to accept any more shipments from Tolfa. The Genoese firm rejected this argument and seized the property of the Spaniards in Rome, leading the Spaniards to complain to the Pope. Since the interests of the Holy See were at stake, Paul III dispatched a lawyer from the Apostolic Camera (Alessandro Palantieri) to the Netherlands to investigate. The views expressed by the papal nuncio were very different from those of Mary of Hungary. Palantieri argued that the Tolfa lessees were being forced to sell their alum to Ducci for 60 shillings per last, whereas previously their wares had fetched a far higher price; this meant a violation of freedom of trade and in his view conflicted with the tenets of the Church. The governor replied that the ordinance had been proclaimed 'to curtail the profits of merchants, who thanks to their monopoly were trying to drive up the alum prices'. The government had therefore determined a 'reasonable price'. Precisely because the alum trade was being monopolized, 'rulers do not want alum to be traded freely and are regulating it'.[151] While the agreement that the government had reached with Ducci might be disadvantageous to

148 Ducci suspected that Schetz had teamed up with Dassa and Lopez. Several documents reveal that they certainly did business with each other. See, e.g., AGR, PEA 1661/1, Letter dated 30 May 1546.

149 ''Que sy je soys fait tuer cessoient toutes nouvellités de ma part'. AGR, PEA 1414/4, no. 23.

150 AGR, PEA 1414/4, nos 24-27, 46.

151 'Pour reprimer l'avarice des marchans qui par leurs monopoles voulloient mectre lesd. alluns a trop hault pris', and 'ce a cause que l'on seet que es contractz d'alluns l'on commect communement monopoles parquoy les princes n'ont volu permectre vendre les alluns librement mais y mis ordre'. AGR, PEA 1414/4, no. 31.

the lessees of the Tolfa mine and the Holy Father, this was of no concern to the Emperor, as these were only the secular interests of the Pope. That Ducci purchased alum for 60 shillings per last and sold it for 80 was no business of the Pope. The governor did agree, however, to convene a meeting to instruct the highest government officials and prominent legal scholars to investigate the papal complaint.

The meeting was chaired by Van Schore, who since 1540 was president of both the Privy Council and the Council of State. The other participants were: Louis of Praet and Charles II de Lalaing (heads of the Council of Finance), Engelbert van den Daele, chancellor of Brabant, Lambert de Briarde, president of the Great Council of Mechelen, the supreme legal authority in the Habsburg Netherlands, as well as a great many lawyers, including Viglius, Aytta van Zwichem, one of the most prominent legal scholars of his day. Palantieri argued that 'secular rulers must not take legal measures to the disadvantage of the Pope or other ecclesiastical authorities',[152] that the contract between the Grimaldi firm and Dassa & Co. did not qualify as monopolization (since it exclusively concerned the Tolfa alum), and that whether such contracts were valid or void was to be determined in Rome. Van Schore replied that the Grimaldi firm controlled both the Tolfa alum and the bulk of the Spanish alum; only the Cartagena and Lorca mines were still outside their reach, but very soon they would have eliminated all competitors. 'Perhaps the contract between His Majesty and Ducci is also a type of monopoly', continued Van Schore, 'but that does not render the contract void, as a ruler is entitled to enter into a monopolist contract, if doing so serves the *common good*, as is the case here'. He invoked the spice trade monopoly of the Portuguese King as a case in point: since 1506, the King had rigidly controlled pepper and spice imports.[153] And was the contract between the Pope and the Grimaldi firm not a 'true monopoly, since the Pope was allowed to sell alum only to them?' All advisors subscribed to this view that the ordinance of 16 August 1544 allowed the interest of the ruler to coincide with the public interest and personal interests. It was not infringing on the privileges of the Church. After all, 'if the ruler orders that no grain is to be exported, or that it must be sold at a certain price or in a certain place, or that a certain tax is payable on it, then his ordinance applies in equal measure to the grain that the clergy intends to sell as to the grain of lay people'. The advisors concluded by noting that the contract between the Pope and the Grimaldi firm was far more monopolist than the agreement with Ducci.[154]

In 1544 the government officials and lawyers were far more radical and outspoken than their predecessors had been in 1507, who had merely noted that the Pope had to operate as a secular ruler when trading alum, not as the head of the Church. Now they distinguished not only between the ecclesiastical and the secular domain of the Pope but also made very

152 'Les princes seculiers ne peulvent riens statuer au prejudice du Pape ou aux gens d'église'.

153 'Et combien que le contract fait entre Sa Majesté et led. Jaspar Duchi contient aussi quelque monopole, ce ne peult invalider led. contract en tant que ung prince peult faire et aussi permectre ung contract monopolieux quant il [le] fait principalement en faveur de la *chose publicque*, que a esté fait au cas present' (my italics). Related to the royal monopoly in Portugal was the Estado da India's effort to monopolize the Asian spice trade, but this 'monopoly' was far from complete and exhibited ever more signs of weakening in the 1530s and 40s.

154 'Si le Prince ordonne que on ne peult tirer nulz bledz hors de son pays ou les vendre a certain pris ou en certain lieu ou soubz certain impost, telle ordonnance apprehandt aussi bien les bledz que les gens d'église veullent vendre que les bledz des gens seculiers'. AGR, PEA 1414/4, no. 31.

clear that rulers had the right to grant monopolies, when they served the common good by doing so. The representative of the Apostolic Camera could hardly counter this view, let alone refute it. The theologians and moralists from the School of Salamanca had yet to publish their great treatises, but their views on commercial contracts were undoubtedly known in 1544: a ruler was entitled to decree in the public interest that any subject could purchase and sell certain merchandise.[155]

The 'public interest' was obviously open to interpretation. Paul III assigned the confessor of Mary of Hungary to take Ducci to task and to use arguments different from those of Palmieri. Ducci subsequently reported to the governor that the clergyman had told him that the alum contract might burden the conscience of the Emperor and would be disadvantageous for many merchants, because his profit margin was excessive. He was certain to make fl.500,000 from the transaction. Ducci replied that this was patent nonsense, and that his contract would in fact safeguard against excessive profits being realized, as had happened all too often in the past.[156] Mary of Hungary accepted his arguments without question. She continued to support Ducci, not only because she desperately needed him as a financial agent on the Antwerp Exchange, but also because Paul III refused to accommodate the Emperor on important matters.[157] Whether the attitude of the Pope tipped the scales remains unclear, but it did help resolve any doubts about granting an alum monopoly.

Mary of Hungary did not want the discussion about Tolfa alum to jeopardize the supply to the Low Countries and in an unusual move in March 1545 invited the Genoese banker Paolo Doria, the representative of Esteban Doria & Co. (the lessee of the Spanish alum quarries[158]) and Ducci to her castle at Binche (Hainault) to see whether they could reach an agreement about the stocks that Doria kept in Antwerp and about future deliveries. Her initiative demonstrates how important this matter was to her, and also how much she appreciated Ducci. Binche was her leisure retreat, where she mainly went hunting, and she grew ever fonder of this beautifully situated small town, when Charles V gave her the illustrious seigniory in February 1545.[159] An invitation to come to Binche was therefore a great honour and a sign of immense trust. She convinced Doria and Ducci to enter into an agreement: from 1 September 1545 Doria would provide Ducci in Antwerp with 4,000 last of alum *per annum* for six years at 67 Flemish shillings per last. Ducci argued that the price was exorbitant and as compensation received attractive payment terms.[160]

The governor did the right thing at the right time, as Dassa & Co. were by then negotiating with the English. They refused to sell their stocks of Italian alum in Antwerp at the price Ducci was willing to pay (i.e. 60 Flemish shillings per last). Aware that the negotiations between the English King and Erasmus Schetz about the sale of large quantities of lead had been fruitless, they offered Vaughan alum in exchange for lead.[161] The offer was accepted,

155 Rosolino (2013), 799-802.

156 AGR, PEA 1414/4, no. 32.

157 In 1543 and 1544 Paul III persistently refused to take sides in the Habsburg-Valois war, although Charles V repeatedly informed him that Francis I had entered an alliance with the Ottoman Turks.

158 Córdoba de la Llave, Franco Silva and Navarro Espinach (2005), 127.

159 Gorter-van Royen (1995), 292-3. At the end of 1545 she started to build a new Renaissance palace here.

160 HHS, B-PA 71, f° 208-209.

161 LPFD, Henry VIII, 20/1, no. 1009.

and on 28 July 1545 an agreement was signed: Dassa & Co. would supply 30,000 quintals or *c.* 7500 last of Spanish alum in Southampton or London at 66 shillings per last, totalling £24,750 sterling or *c.* £30,900 Fl.gr. Their price was only slightly higher than Ducci's (82.4 instead of 80 Flemish shillings), but they relied on the fluctuating exchange rate and especially on trading alum for lead to make a profit. And indeed, the King of England agreed to supply fothers of lead in London, Southampton, or Hull, depending on the amounts of alum imported, at £4.66 sterling or *c.* £5.80 Fl.gr. per fother; the Spaniards would pay the regular customs duties for both products.[162]

Ducci was 'in a great rage', when he learned about this agreement. He regarded it as an infringement of his monopoly, guaranteed by the contract with Doria. He was too sensible to take Dassa & Co. to court, which could drag on for years but as usual tried to benefit from the situation. In September he told the English secretary of state William Paget that he was willing to repurchase the alum supplied by Dassa & Co. Not wishing to offend Ducci or Dassa & Co., Paget provided an evasive response. When the London merchants authorized to market the alum discovered that selling the quantities supplied in England was far more difficult than they had expected, Ducci informed Vaughan again in January 1546 that he was willing to sell all the alum at cost and over the course of several years, offering favourable payment conditions. His offer was rejected, probably due to the growing mistrust in English political and commercial circles of a businessman who by then was described by Vaughan as 'a man of extreme greediness'. In any case, Henry VIII did not benefit from the agreement with Dassa & Co. On the contrary, the deliveries ran up against all kinds of problems, and sales incurred serious delays; by the end of 1546 the King faced losses of £8566 sterling.[163]

Meanwhile, the main operators on the continent hoped to reach a compromise. The representatives of Paul III, Mary of Hungary, and the Grimaldis started to negotiate, away from the public eye, as they were well aware that public statements about monopolies might create an uproar, especially given the persistent complaints about the 'exceptional privilege' Ducci had been granted, as Antwerp merchants cautiously described his monopoly in petitions to the central government. Dassa & Co. objected repeatedly to the course of events. In September 1546 they argued that both the bankers leasing the Tolfa mine and Ducci were making disgraceful profits, that their firm had been suffering serious losses since the imperial ordinance, and that the contract with Ducci conflicted with the public interest.[164] The parties continued to hurl accusations at each other. The Pope refused to recognize the contract with Ducci as legitimate. The Grimaldis and Dassa & Co. maintained their fundamental disagreement regarding the application of their contract and sued each other.

The spring of 1547 was a turning point. On 21 May Ducci wrote to Van Schore that he had a most amicable dinner with Archbishop Giulio Sauli, who served as papal nuncio. The Pope, the Grimaldis, and Ducci settled out of court, rendering the contract of Dassa & Co. null and void. The Spanish firm was even fined 9400 ducats or fl.17,860, 16.5 percent of

---

162 De Smedt (1928), 253-4; Richardson (1954), 44; Ruiz Martín (2005), 72. In 1545 Vaughan obtained £ sterling at an average rate of 25 Flemish shillings: De Smedt (1950-1954), II, 524. One fother = *c.* 919 kilograms.

163 LPFD, Henry VIII, 20/2, no. 153, and 21/1, no. 788; Richardson (1954), 45-7.

164 AGR, PEA 820, f° 95, 125-6.

which Ducci had to provide.[165] Three months later Ducci entered a formal agreement with Luciano Pallavicino de la Rocca, who represented the Grimaldis.[166] Grimaldi & Co., who by then had formed a cartel with Estoban Doria & Co., sold him 20,000 last of Italian and 28,000 last of Spanish alum, totalling 48,000 last, to be delivered in Antwerp in 24 equal instalments, distributed over six years, starting from 1 September 1547. The price of Tolfa alum was fixed at 60 Flemish shillings per last and that of Mazarrón alum at 59. The total purchase price, also payable in 24 instalments, was therefore £142,600 Fl.gr. Transport, insurance, and all other fees were payable by the Grimaldis, who for six years agreed to not to sell alum to anybody else in Northwest and Central Europe. Merchants and producers in England, Scotland, Ireland, Germany, Scandinavia, and the Baltic countries had to obtain their supplies from Ducci in Antwerp. An additional condition was that the Tolfa contractees would export alum to France only if the buyers agreed not to re-export the mineral to any other country in Northwest Europe. If they did, the cargo would be seized, and they would be fined two ducats or 12 2/3 Flemish shillings per last and would no longer receive any alum. The final stipulation was that if either party failed to comply with a specific clause, the aggrieved party was entitled to damages of 10,000 ducats or £3166 2/3 Fl.gr.[167]

Why did Paul III and the Grimaldis ultimately agree to grant Ducci the monopoly to distribute alum throughout Northwest and Central Europe on very favourable terms? The Pope probably believed that waiving all opposition was the wisest course of action. In late January 1547 he had abandoned Charles V and deeply regretted this, when the German Protestants suffered a crushing defeat at Mühlberg on 24 April; with this victory, the Emperor brought his chief adversaries in Central Europe to their knees for the time being. Nor did he have reason to fear anyone any longer in Western Europe, as his two greatest rivals, King Francis I of France and King Henry VIII of England, died in early 1547. Presumably, as a gesture of good will, Paul III pressured the Grimaldis to accommodate a financier clearly favoured by Charles V. The Grimaldis were apparently obliged to accept relatively low prices for both Italian and Spanish alum. Nor could they any longer control alum exports to Antwerp, as the contract stipulated that in Northwest Europe they were to supply exclusively to Ducci for six years. Ducci made a handsome profit, as the following comparison demonstrates. In 1540 the Grimaldis had sold the Florentine firm Benvenuto Olivieri & Co. the rights to export 3000 cantara or 800 last of alum *per annum* to French ports on the Mediterranean for twelve years, yielding average annual profits of 25 percent for the Florentines.[168] In 1547 Ducci paid a net purchase price of 59 to 60 Flemish shillings per last, which he was authorized to sell at 80, amounting to earnings of 33 to 35 percent, for a quantity tenfold that of the Florentines. Ducci and his partners Grimmel, Neidhart, and Seiler therefore came out on top, but Charles V and Mary of Hungary must have been satisfied as well: in exchange for the alum monopoly, Ducci had provided a large loan and gave the Emperor the prospect of a fixed and regular income. Moreover, securing supply

165 AGR, PEA 1414/4, nos 46 and 57, PEA 1661/1, 1 July 1547. Both parties calculated the ducat at 76 Flemish groats.

166 He came from a powerful Genoese family that had ties with the Apostolic Camera and was consequently an important operator in the alum trade: Delumeau (1962), 210, 233-6; Beck (1989), 783.

167 AGR, PEA 1414/4, nos 47, 55, 57, and PEA 1638/3.

168 Bruscoli (2007), 173-5.

and setting a maximum price were believed to serve the common good. The sole benefit for the Grimaldis was that the contract guaranteed that they would sell vast quantities for six years, although they had little cause to be jubilant about the deal.

Such a large contract for alum distribution was unprecedented in the history of Europe. Eight thousand last *per annum* could supply the textile industry throughout Northwest, Central, and Eastern Europe. Contemporaries estimated that alum demand in the Habsburg Netherlands in about 1550 was some 3000 to 4000 last or 564 to 752 metric tons *per annum*.[169] This figure seems plausible, as 3000 last was enough to dye only nine million ells of cloth, based on four pounds or *c.* 1.88 kilograms of alum for an average cloth with a length of about 30 ells, which is certainly within reason.[170] A total length of 9 million ells corresponds to very conservative estimates of the woollens to be stained and dyed in the Low Countries: 6.5 million ells for the products in the traditional and light drapery industry and 2.5 million ells for English cloth.[171] Ducci suggested that in England in about 1545 demand was unlikely to exceed 1100 last *per annum*, but he deliberately quoted a very low figure. Laurens Longin, treasurer-general of finance from 1551 to 1554, estimated total alum processing in England, Scotland, and Ireland at 1400 last, which other contemporaries confirmed.[172] In 1546 Ducci explicitly mentioned France among the countries to which much alum was re-exported from Antwerp, and fragmentary data attest to this, although the total amount cannot be ascertained.[173] A conservative estimate of about 500 last does not seem excessive, as in the period 1540-52 the Tolfa lessees shipped an average of 2800 last *per annum* to France, mainly to Rouen, La Rochelle, and other Atlantic ports, but this supply did not meet demand.[174] The amounts intended for the Low Countries, England, and Northern France would thus have been *c.* 5400 last. Additionally, in 1544/5 according to the Hundredth Penny tax, 550 last was shipped to Hamburg and Danzig, whence part was re-exported to Scandinavia, yielding a total of *c.* 6000 last for all areas mentioned. This would leave *c.* 2000 last for the Rhineland, South Germany, and areas further east.[175] Remarkably, according to the Hundredth Penny tax, only about 100 last was exported from Antwerp to Cologne and other German textile centres.[176] Demand for this raw material may have declined due to the fear of war, but the decrease cannot have been so great as to jeopardize production continuity. Merchants and cloth dyers in the cities concerned were unable to obtain large amounts in Central or Eastern Europe. Output from the mines in Thuringia and Silesia was very modest, and mining in Kuttenberg in Bohemia became significant only toward the middle of the century.[177] While alum is very likely to have been supplied via Venice, in the period 1531-53 imports from Tolfa to Venice averaged only 2575

169 AGR, PEA 1414/4, nos 4, 5 and 81. See also Ruiz Martín (2005), 203-4.

170 Thijs (1987), 84.

171 For more detail, see Soly & Thijs (1979), 40-1, and Stabel (1997), 30-2. In the 1540s the average import was 90,000 *broadcloths* having a total length of 3.6 million ells, of which 3 million ells were dyed in Antwerp; alum was needed for 2.5 million ells.

172 LPFD, Henry VIII, 21/1, no. 141, and AGR, PEA 1661/6.

173 Asaert (2019), I, 411-13, 418, 423?

174 AGR, PEA 1661/1, Letter dated 29 January 1546; Coornaert (1961), II, 114; Bruscoli (2007), 171-3. See also Bottin (2005).

175 Ducci took re-exporting alum to Germany for granted: AGR, PEA 1661/1, Letter dated 29 January 1546.

176 Jeroen Puttevils' database 'Hundredth Penny Tax on Export', based on AGR, CC 23357-23364.

177 Today Kutná Hora in the Czech Republic.

Table 5. Ducci's alum monopoly: Antwerp as distribution centre in 1547-48

Alum destined for	Estimated quantity in last per year
Antwerp and other cities in the Low Countries	> 3500
England	1400
France	500
Hamburg, Gdansk and Scandinavia	550
Other parts of Germany and Eastern Europe	2050 (?)
Total	*c.* 8000

Sources: see text and notes

cantara or nearly 690 last *per annum*[178], and a major share of this was intended for Venetian textile manufacturing. What about Turkish alum? Notwithstanding all papal prohibitions, it continued to be imported to the West, and the Ottomans granted monopolies, just as European rulers did. In 1546 they guaranteed Venice a three-year monopoly on alum mining in Anatolia in exchange for the substantial sum of 25,000 ducats.[179] This does not explain the minimal export from Antwerp to Germany in 1544/5, however, as massive imports of Turkish alum by Augsburg and other South-German cities would seem extremely unlikely at the time. Was alum smuggled directly from France to Germany during the Habsburg-Valois war? This would have been very risky indeed, and the quantities cannot have been very large.

Did the extremely low alum export to the Rhineland, South Germany, and areas further east, as recorded in 1544/5, arise from entirely different causes, i.e. illegal export by a few large firms with which Ducci made private agreements? This is less far-fetched than it might initially seem, as from the outset Ducci was rumoured to have sold the entire stock to a small group of wholesalers, and he may have wanted to privilege them by waiving the Hundredth Penny tax on alum they re-exported. Large merchants knew that Ducci could not easily sell substantial quantities without their support, enabling them to negotiate favourable terms. Since Schetz & Co. had probably been trading alum since 1540, they would have been interested in an attractive offer from Ducci in 1544. According to the Hundredth Penny tax, they were among the chief alum exporters to Hamburg, as was Pauwel van Gemert, who was identified as a stakeholder in several documents relating to Ducci's contract. The Affaitadi firm was involved in the alum trade as well, together with two other substantial merchants: Lambrecht van Kessel, who had close ties with the city council and later served as bailiff of Antwerp (from 1564 to 1575), and Vincent de Smit the Elder, who amassed a fortune in international trade.[180] Since Schetz & Co. traded intensively with Central Germany, they could easily include alum in their shipments in that direction. An additional factor in their favour concerned the escape routes via Maastricht – where they were well-known – and Namur. The same held true for other

178 Delumeau (1962), 303.
179 Inalcik (1977), I, 88.
180 AGR, PEA 1414/4, no. 55, and PEA 1661/1; Ehrenberg (1896), I, 372; Denucé (1934a), 60-1; Ruiz Martín (2005), 71.

major exporters. As Receiver-General of the tax, Ducci could moreover commit fraud when it suited him. His assistants are very likely to have taxed the cargoes shipped but not all those transported over land, as social control would have been present in the first case but not in the second. Lacking records and explicit listings in other sources, however, this scenario remains hypothetical.

2.4 Networks and Financial Deals

Late medieval and early modern merchant networks have received extensive attention, and the basic concept has taken on a wide variety of meanings and methods, from network as a metaphor to Social Network Analysis. Most economic historians agree that business networks served to mitigate insecurities and avert risks, obtain the best information available, enhance organizational efficiency, and improve competitive edge. Consensus is lacking, however, as to which factors were conducive to cooperation between members – i.e. internal cohesion – in the absence of institutions that could compel them by law to enter binding contracts.[181] Several authors have emphasized that such networks were based on interdependence and reciprocity, with trust and good repute as essential values. Other factors could also come into play, but they argue that the performance of business networks depended essentially on appreciation, on the 'credit' status of a merchant/banker, which was in turn derived from both his moral qualities and his economic leverage.[182] This certainly held true for Erasmus Schetz, who was regarded by other substantial businessmen and by the highest political authorities as an honest and generally trustworthy businessman who, moreover, had considerable financial resources. Whether he was indeed so honest is doubtful, considering Ducci's alum trade,[183] but that is not the point: the economic and political elites perceived Schetz's conduct as trustworthy. The contrast with Ducci could not possibly have been greater. In the 1540s most businessmen in Antwerp viewed Ducci as unscrupulous. Still, he set up smoothly functioning networks and he was the chief advisor to the central government on financial and commercial matters. Does Ducci's case support the argument made by Oliver Williamson concerning the relationship between trust and 'calculativeness'?[184] In other words: should the 'elusive notion of trust' in the economy and economic history be replaced by calculative explanations of human relationships? My intention here is not to discuss and evaluate the different positions in the debate. I will, however, note some issues that have received little or no consideration thus far.

Researchers who have reconstructed sixteenth- and seventeenth-century merchant networks nearly always assume that what they reveal reflects the reality at the time, in other words: that the known members of the network were also interested parties or agents who openly operated on their own behalf. Personal correspondence and judicial investigations nonetheless reveal that several members of some networks were front men:

---

181 For recent surveys of different approaches, see Molho & Curto (2003); Coulon (2010); Caracausi (2014); Antunes & Polónia (2016); Düring et al. (2016); Sánchez & Kaps (2017).

182 See esp. Studnicki-Gizbert (2003), and Trivellato (2003) & (2009).

183 See Chapters 2.3 and 2.6.

184 Williamson (1993).

they were instructed by substantial merchants or financiers who for many different reasons could not or did not wish to operate openly.[185] With Ducci, that was more likely the rule than the exception (as I will demonstrate), and he was certainly not the only businessman in sixteenth-century Antwerp who ensured that outsiders could not be certain who had what share in which transaction. Moreover, most authors assume that the networks they reconstruct involve merchants and financiers performing legal transactions. They note that some members engaged in deceit or fraud now and then, but they argue that laws and government regulations were not systematically violated with the awareness of other members. The networks they studied may well have been representative, but this does not alter the fact that some forms of cooperation were partially or even entirely focused on clandestine commercial and/or financial operations. Contraband is the most striking example. England's illicit trade grew enormously during the reign of Henry VIII. In the early 1540s Bristol merchants could achieve net earnings of 150 percent on illegal exports of food products and 80 percent on leather; many such were among the wealthiest and best-connected men in the local community.[186] What made such networks cohesive? Relations with public authorities may be assumed to have been important with clandestine or semi-clandestine economic activities, but what was the decisive factor: reciprocity or independence, active or passive cooperation? Finally, businessmen could nearly always participate simultaneously in several networks that were not connected with one another and might operate in entirely different ways. The interplay of all these factors explains why relations between Ducci and his business partners were in some cases more likely to be based on trust and in other cases seemed to derive from shrewd calculations. It was, however, always a question of degree. Calculative considerations and precedents figured in all his networks. Trust was at best calculative.

What was the basis for cooperation in Ducci's commercial-financial networks? Capital strength and the power of information were essential elements. The Fuggers were a special category in Europe, as far as capital was concerned, and the Affaitadi were among the top of the other trading companies; both firms were always solvent. Ducci on the other hand was a first-rate source of information. No one knew better than he what would be decided in Brussels, both commercially and on financial and monetary issues, as no other businessman could access the governor and the highest-ranking government officials with such ease. In 1543 Charles V had appointed him *conseiller* (advisor) for his meritorious service. As this title was not specified further, it presumably meant 'financial advisor' and later figured in all official documents. Also, Ducci was briefed by his partners Grimmel, Neidhart, and Seiler about the exchange market in Lyon, while the Bonvisis and the Vivaldis informed him about commercial and political developments in London. Capital on the one hand and information (linked to competition) on the other hand guaranteed reciprocity. In this period cooperation with Ducci also enabled Fugger and Affaitadi to solve possible marketing problems and more importantly: to arrange commercial and financial operations that might compromise them as the main creditors. The controversial, morally or politically scandalous, and sometimes even illegal nature of several transactions

185 See the pertinent remarks of Favier (2013), 125.
186 Jones (2017), 104-11, 223.

ensured that participants could rely on each other to do exactly as agreed and never to disclose anything. This was especially true for all those involved in exchange-arbitrage between Antwerp and Lyon.

Ducci boasted that he was 'master of the Emperor's finances', as Stephen Vaughan wrote to the Privy Council on 17 December 1544. Vaughan soon discovered Ducci's self-image to be largely true. His initial delight at the helpful disposition of the Tuscan banker quickly made way for deep mistrust of a businessman 'altogether given to his own lucre', admitting nonetheless that without Ducci's help he would not be able to make financial deals in the Habsburg Netherlands: 'Undoubtedly here there is nothing to be done without him'. In his letters Vaughan attributed Ducci's dominant position on the Antwerp Exchange to a combination of three elements: resourcefulness, lack of scruples, and networking. He considered this last element to be especially important, as he was convinced that no transaction on any major money market in the Christian world went unnoticed by Ducci.[187]

Frequent personal contacts with Mary of Hungary, high-ranking government officials, aristocrats, and representatives of foreign rulers required refined forms of self presentation. Ducci was familiar with the *magnificenza* that the Medici and other Florentine bankers had presented since the *quattrocento*. His financial means were ample for purchasing or constructing a stately mansion, but he aimed mainly to show that he was not merely wealthy but had taste as well. According to a later chronicler, on 23 August 1542 after leaving Antwerp to travel back to Brussels, Mary of Hungary and her entourage were invited to a memorable banquet at Ducci's *hof van plaisantie* (his summer residence) in Schoonsel: gold-covered oyster shells were placed on the platters lined with valuable pearls.[188] At his Schoonsel estate, situated on the border of Wilrijk and Hoboken, 7 kilometres from the centre of Antwerp, he built a 'very costly and beautiful residence', with a *warande*, a park, as he later stated.[189] On 26 November 1545 Ducci welcomed a select company of diplomats and aristocrats in Schoonsel: the English ambassadors Sir Edward Carne, Bishop Stephen Gardiner, and Thomas Thirby, and several representatives of the highest aristocrats in the Netherlands, including Philippe II de Croÿ, Duke of Aarschot, Maximilian of Egmont, Count of Buren-Leerdam and Stadtholder of Friesland, and Sir Jean de Hénin-Liétard, Count of Boussu, the *grand écuyer* of Charles V. That same day, Gardiner wrote to Paget after seeing the mansion that Ducci had built, that he found it to be 'of such cost and elegance as under the King [Henry VIII] no man has attempted in England'.[190] Meanwhile Ducci had bought Hoboken near Antwerp from the guardians of young Prince William of Orange. His sole aim was to acquire the title of 'lord', as the seigniory came without a residence: the castle opposite the Church belonged to the Antwerp patrician family Van Berchem. William's guardians were trying to settle the debts on the house, where his uncle, René de Châlon, Count of Nassau and Lord of Breda, had died. The price was fl.20,000, but the sale included the condition that 'if he [Ducci] was ever repaid the purchase price,

187 LPFD, Henry VIII, 19/2, no. 755, 20/2, nos 677 and 1044, 21/1 no. 1187.

188 Papebrochius (1845), 271. See also Mertens and Torfs (1848), 167.

189 SAA, PK 645, f° 16v°-17. In the early twentieth century these grounds became the site of the Schoonselhof park cemetery.

190 LPFD, Henry VIII, 20/2, nos 875 and 876.

he would be required in that case to return the domain to the Prince or his descendants'. On 12 December 1545 the *Cour féodale de Brabant* approved this provision.[191]

The interior of the large city mansion that Ducci acquired in September 1547 and expanded in 1548 must have amazed his contemporaries.[192] The façade of the complex with a main entrance on the prestigious Huidevettersstraat was built in a traditional Brabant-Gothic style, which Ducci left virtually unchanged. Inside, however, renovation and modernization enabled him to create a Renaissance-style city palace, very probably the first in Antwerp.[193] He had a gallery built with nine bays featuring Tuscan columns under rounded arches with profiled archivolts and scrolled consoles. There were three large reception areas. All rooms, including the panels or cassettes in the ceilings, were painted in the mannerist style propagated by Pieter Coecke van Aelst, Hans Vredeman de Vries, and Lambert Lombard. The twelve circular scenes painted on the ceiling of the great hall exuberantly glorified Emperor Charles V.[194] The decoration in general and the motifs, such as grotesques, strapwork, and the *putti* in particular were deeply influenced by the first School of Fontainebleau, epitomized by the Florentine painter Rosso Fiorentino. That Ducci had his city palace decorated entirely in this new style shows both his strong sense of artistic innovation and his desire to emulate Renaissance princes.

In his relations with the governor, Ducci operated with exquisite finesse. He was well aware that presenting Mary of Hungary with expensive gifts would be unwise and delighted her with niceties that from the perspective of a Queen with a considerable private fortune would be appreciated purely and exclusively because they were exotic and special, not because they were very costly. Ducci sent her mainly exotic fruits, such as 'beautiful, soft oranges', 'raisins from Damascus', 'fine melons', Italian fruit', 'some artichokes, ...' He might also bring her an outstanding Italian gardener. The governor could regard even his costliest gifts as tokens of friendship: satin damask from Florence or Granada silk.[195]

In discussions with international representatives of the Pope, Henry VIII, or international businessmen about financial or commercial matters that involved Ducci in some form, Mary of Hungary and Van Schore automatically sided with 'their' banker and in nearly all cases let him handle important financial transactions. In 1544 and 1545 Mary obtained some short-term loans from South-German merchant bankers on the Antwerp Exchange, sometimes directly and sometimes via brokers (including Tucher), but in most cases Ducci was in charge. From 1546 'his' *rentmeestersbrieven* helped the government find the money needed. Thanks to the backing by the new provincial taxes (which made for a regular source of income), confidence grew in these government bonds traded by individual

---

191 Quoted in Dierickx (1954), 33-4. Two years later Ducci acquired the Kruibeke seigniory (with high justice) on the right bank of the Scheldt, across from Hoboken, and then purchased a complex of buildings and estates for fl.14,400 there. AGR, GRM 849, no. 111.

192 SAA, SR 226, f°353, and SR 230, f°244, 249-250v°.

193 See the well-documented article by Maclot and Grieten (2002). Also Goldstein (2013a), 136. Ducci's city palace was demolished in 1952 to make way for a shopping mall.

194 In 2018 this ceiling was transferred from Sterckshof Castle in Deurne to Museum Hof van Busleyden in Mechelen.

195 Some examples: AGR, PEA 1661/1, letters dated 6 June and 18 July 1545, 28 January, 8 September, and 11 December 1546, and 18 August 1547. In this connection, see Heal (2014), 35-40.

businessmen and trading companies alike. Indicative of its success, the nominal interest rate – aside from a few brief spikes – remained below 12 percent *per annum*, even dropping below 10 percent, not including commission.[196]

In addition to his credit operations for the government in Brussels, Ducci provided short-term loans to Charles V, sometimes operating as the banker and putting up the required capital himself but more frequently as a broker on the Antwerp Exchange or within a temporary partnership with other bankers. He arranged large loans for the Emperor, whose debt to Anton Fugger climbed to 317,508 ducats or fl.603,265 by May 1545. Repayment was not an option, as financing the imperial policy required vast sums. Big business in Antwerp refused to grant new loans. The only solution, according to Ducci, was to strike a deal with Fugger. How he succeeded in doing so remains a mystery, but he had the payment deadline extended and even provided the Emperor with new money.[197] In 1546 he arranged yet another loan for the Emperor with Fugger. The balance sheet for that year reveals the profits Fugger made on the Antwerp Exchange: the firm obtained the money at 8 to 10 percent, while the *rentmeestersbrieven* yielded 12 percent, and the interest rate on the government's debt in Brussels was 13.5 percent.[198] In most of the loans that Ducci arranged for the Emperor in the period 1545-1548, he involved either Anton Fugger or merchant bankers with whom he had worked very closely in previous years: on the one hand Gian Carlo Affaitadi, who could call on family members in Spain (Giovanni Pietro and Giovanni Battista),[199] and on the other hand the partners Grimmel and Neidhart, with whom he had a consortium or temporary partnership at first and later a joint company by contract. Capital transfers at the Spanish fairs were considerable: 110,328 ducats in November 1544 (Affaitadi '*y otros Flamencos*'), 280,000 ducats in the summer of 1546 (Affaitadi-Grimmel), and 205.265 ducats in December of that year (Affaitadi-Neidhart). In the next two years loans were registered to Fugger: nearly 227,000 ducats in 1547 and 150,000 ducats in 1548.[200]

As 'master of the Emperor's finances', Ducci tolerated no interference. He and no one else was allowed to negotiate with Anton Fugger on behalf of the Emperor and the government in Brussels, as he repeated time and again, including in his letters to Mary of Hungary.[201] While he worded his message to the governor diplomatically, he adopted a much harsher tone toward Vaughan in similar circumstances. Upon meeting Vaughan at the Antwerp Church of Our Lady on 28 August 1545, Ducci confronted him with the 'unconscionable' fact that the South-German envoy and financier Christoph Haller von Hallerstein had been contacted without his knowledge about a loan of 60,000 crowns at 13 percent from Anton Fugger for Henry VIII. He exploded in 'a cold fury', shouting that such action was unacceptable. The Emperor had appointed him and him alone to supervise

196 ADN, B 2442, B 2448, B 2454, and B 2460. The financial statements for 1547 and 1548 are missing. See also Ehrenberg (1896), II, 313; Braudel (1959); Van der Wee (1963), II, 527.

197 Pölnitz (1967), II/2/2, 94-5, 99.

198 Ehrenberg (1896), II, 53-4.

199 See Bauer (1936), 46-7, 51.

200 AGR, PEA 1661/1, Letters dated 2 July, 22-24 August, and 9 December 1546, and 28 July 1547; AGS, SE 502, f° 25, 40-41, 109-112; HHS, B-PA 61, Letter dated 31 October 1547, and B-PA 71, Letters dated 26-28 June 1546; Carande (1960), 40, and (1967), 330-43; Pölnitz (1967), II/2, 199; Matringe (2016), 285-6.

201 AGR, PEA 1661/1, Letter dated 7 March 1545.

such financial transactions. He would block this transaction, as he would not tolerate loans to foreign rulers about which he had not been consulted.[202]

Fugger must have appreciated Ducci's services as a broker in this period, because Veit Hörl, his factor in Antwerp, while skilled in commercial transactions, had insufficient information to respond quickly and adequately to new financial challenges.[203] In addition, Fugger was facing a complex political context in the mid-1540s and therefore operated more cautiously than in the past as far as loans to the government in the Netherlands or to Henry VIII were concerned. He was aware that he was known to favour the Emperor and remained loyal. In the great political-religious conflict between Charles V and the German Protestant rulers and cities united in the Schmalkaldic League, however, Fugger weighed every move carefully, especially because his home town of Augsburg was religiously divided. He knew that he was being scrutinized by the other South-German bankers (especially on the Antwerp Exchange) and therefore preferred Ducci to serve as an intermediary. Ducci also proved a highly skilled negotiator, generating high profits for Fugger – without neglecting his own benefit. This is also clear from the loans Vaughan obtained for Henry VIII in 1545 and 1546.

Never before had the King of England needed so much money at such short notice as in 1544-1546, as the expense of the war against Scotland and the invasion in France was far higher than expected, ultimately reaching £600,000 and £700,000 sterling *per annum*.[204] By 1544 Ducci was widely mistrusted. Vaughan suspected him of fraud, and his suspicion was probably justified, but Ducci proved indispensable. In 1545 and 1546 he arranged two new loans, each after tough negotiations. He used Henry VIII's financial predicament to force deals through that yielded huge profits for himself and for the main moneylender Anton Fugger.

In late July 1545 Henry VIII obtained a twelve-month loan of 300,000 ducats from Ducci and Fugger at 'only' 10 percent, of which 40,000 ducats was to be taken up in jewellery. The transaction was carefully planned by Ducci, who knew the jewellery trade. In 1543 he had sold Charles V jewels valued at fl.17,000, which the Emperor presented to his sister Eleonor, Queen of France, and the noble members of her entourage in Brussels on 26 October. At the time, Ducci had also supplied fl.1746 worth of gold plate and buttons encrusted with precious stones from India to distribute to her entourage.[205] Since the most valuable jewellery was adorned with diamonds, rubies and/or pearls, he presumably purchased them from Affaitadi, whose firm bought and sold considerable quantities of precious stones and pearls.[206] In December 1544 he had informed Vaughan that he was willing to come to England, provided that he could bring along a 'gold plate' and jewels and take them back to Antwerp toll-free, if His Majesty the King declined to purchase them. In January 1545 he was granted permission to import and sell 'all manner

---

202 LPFD, Henry VIII, 20/2, nos 243, 258, and 362. See also AGR, PEA 1661/1, 18 July 1545.

203 See Pölnitz (1967), II/2/2, 84.

204 Richardson (1954), 36.

205 ADN, B 2442, f° 597 and 604. Unlike Henry VIII and Francis I, who both dressed very ostentatiously, with especially Henry VIII making a great display of his love for jewels, the Emperor was striking in his lack of magnificence. The jewels he purchased served mainly as ceremonial gifts: Burke (2000), 409.

206 Denucé (1934a), 63.

of jewels and precious stones, as diamonds, rubies, emeralds, pearls, plate of gold and silver, cloths of gold and silver' in England for twelve months. He did so a few months later, although the true supplier of the jewels (Affaitadi or Fugger) remains unknown. In any case, the underwriters of Henry's loan profited nicely, as the jewels which they assessed at 40,000 ducats were appraised by an Antwerp expert at only 30,000 ducats. The sole concession that Vaughan obtained was that the Fugger-Ducci loan, issued in crowns and Carolus florins, could be repaid in current money, albeit at a premium of 2 percent for the King of England. Ducci also agreed that half of the actual cash amount would be paid out in Frankfurt in September, which entailed an unhedged one-month loss of interest for the borrower. Additional costs included Ducci's commission and the currency exchange loss on converting the coinage received. The total interest rate thus in effect amounted to 18 percent or more.[207] Creating such a vast difference between the 'nominal' (10 percent) and the 'real' (18 percent) interest rate may be qualified as 'bilking' the Crown.[208] And the markup did not take into account the complications that arose in August, as Ducci managed to reap extra monetary profits, while at the same getting his own back against the English government for both the Haller deal and the alum contract with Dassa and Lopez.

In 1542 the Great Debasement had started, and in 1544 and 1545 this 'profit-seeking, aggressive, fiscal enterprise' was continued.[209] Henry VIII reduced the fineness of silver and gold coins, which of course created turbulence on all financial markets. Ducci capitalized on the devaluation of the English currency. When informing Mary of Hungary about his loans to Henry VIII, he qualified the Haller transaction as supplementary. Ducci spread doubt and confusion: did the English perhaps intend to buy up as many imperial gold coins as possible, so as to have them re-melted in London into less valuable pieces?[210] His suspicion was taken seriously, as such a currency policy could cause serious harm to international trade in the Low Countries. Mary of Hungary acted without hesitation. On 13 September 1545 Vaughan was summoned to the Margrave of Antwerp, who impressed upon him that without the explicit permission from the Emperor, he was no longer allowed to receive or export gold coins anymore. The government obviously did not intend to impede the Ducci-Fugger credit operation and lifted the embargo a few weeks later, provided, however, that Vaughan agreed not to export any gold coins minted in the Habsburg Netherlands. Vaughan had to exchange the coins supplied by Ducci-Fugger for French crowns, which were sold to him at a premium. In addition to being a waste of time, the exchange thus became very costly.[211] He was very certain that he had been duped: 'In all the days of my life was I never so craftily handled'.[212]

The loan provided in February 1546 was similarly questionable. Henry VIII needed money urgently to finance the construction of fortifications in Boulogne, resupply the

---

207 LPFD, Henry VIII, 20/1, no. 125/11; De Smedt (1928), 238-9; Richardson (1953), 66-7; Pölnitz (1967), II/2/2, 100-1, 113-14.

208 Expression used by Blanchard (1996), 65.

209 Munro (2011), 450-6, 464, 457.

210 AGR, PEA 1661/1, Letters dated 6 June, 18 July, and 24 July 1545.

211 See the remarks of Outhwaite (1966), 296. On moving large amounts of cash from Antwerp to Calais in this period, see Guy (2019), 29-30.

212 De Smedt (1928), 240-2; Richardson (1953), 67-8 (the quotation on p. 68)

troops in Calais, and prepare a new offensive. Vaughan rejected an offer from Affaitadi of 100,000 crowns or fl.180,000, because the loan would include a large table diamond in a gold setting, with an eastern pearl at the bottom, estimated to be worth 40,000 to 50,000 crowns. He approached the Fuggers, the Welsers, and other South-German bankers, but all set conditions he could not possibly meet. Ducci made various alternative offers. Some were dismissed as unrealistic, but in February the Privy Council basically accepted his offer of a loan of £30,000 Fl.gr. or fl.180,000 from Anton Fugger, to be repaid within six months at 6 percent, and to accept one third in white fustians. The deal was a wonderful opportunity for Fugger to unload a stock of textile goods at a decent price.[213] Henry VIII had to pay fl.3.15 apiece for the fustians, which were selling for only fl.2.4 to fl.2.5 on the Antwerp market around this time, a difference of more than 25 percent.[214] Little wonder that Fugger stipulated that the fustians were not to be sold below the purchase price in England. At any rate, just as in July 1545 (the 'jewellery deal'), the actual interest rate in February 1546 (the 'fustians deal') turned out to be far higher than it had initially been presented. The Ducci-Fugger team did have to make one concession: Henry VIII refused to provide an Act of Parliament as a state guarantee.[215] Just as they had with previous loans, the creditors had to accept bonds from the City of London. As for the currency export, Vaughan had learned his lesson and had requested a licence from the governor on time. He was granted one, on the condition 'that the money be not of the Emperor's coinage', and that only a limited number of coins would be involved. This time, however, Ducci explained to Vaughan how to use a single licence to take double or triple the officially authorized amount across the border.[216]

During the negotiations for the 'fustians deal', Ducci was presented by Vaughan on behalf of Henry VIII with a grant for services rendered: an annuity of £250 sterling, 'which he appeared to esteem far more for the honour than for the large fee', reported Vaughan.[217] Aware that acceptance was not to be taken for granted, Ducci consulted Mary of Hungary, telling her: 'I would not do anything without informing Your Majesty for all the silver or gold in the world'.[218] The reply from the governor has not been preserved but is certain to have conveyed disapproval. Ducci sent Henry VIII a letter, maintaining that the gift not only astonished but shamed him, 'for if it were made for anything he had done or could do, it was far too much, but if recompense of the loss to him in herrings and jewels, surely the King could easily compensate a loss of this kind by some other means'. What he meant by the loss of the jewels is unclear. In any case, Henry VIII was astonished and asked his representative in Antwerp for the cause of this unexpected and strange refusal.

213 The firm had developed fustian weaving as a putting-out operation in Weissenhorn near Ulm, but the imminent war between Charles V and the Schmalkaldic League created supply and sales problems; in the course of 1546 manufacturing was even halted several times: Pöllnitz (1964); Holbach (1994), 191-3. See also Harreld (2004), 133.

214 Calculations based on LPFD, Henry VIII, 21/1, no. 401, and Brulez (1970), 32. See also Westermann and Denzel (2011), 475. The King did not suffer heavy losses in this case, as the price at which the fustians were sold in London approximated the purchase price: Richardson (1954), 46 n. 3.

215 As the Privy Council wrote Vaughan on 8 March: the King will not 'seem unto the world to be brought so low as he should need, for that sum, to make them [the Fugger] assurance by Act of Parliament.' LPDF, Henry VIII, 21/1, no. 354.

216 De Smedt (1928), 247-8; Richardson (1953), 72; Pölnitz (1967), II/2/2, 140-1, 149-50.

217 LPFD, Henry VIII, 21/1, no. 142.

218 AGR, PEA 1661/1, Letter dated 27 January 1546.

Since Vaughan still needed the banker's services, he replied that Ducci had definitely not acted of his own volition, as the man's glory and his insatiable hunger for money would have led him to decide otherwise. He was undoubtedly acting on instructions from above, possibly given by Van Schore or even by the Emperor.[219]

By the spring of 1546 Henry VIII was in need of additional funds to repay the bonds that would mature that summer in Antwerp. Ducci informed him that Fugger was willing to lend him 600,000 crowns, but only if a substantial share of this amount could be provided in jewels or copper. Vaughan tried in vain to negotiate better terms, in particular a loan *without* components in kind and an extension of an old debt to the Augsburg firm, but Ducci assumed that the King of England would in any case have to repay his debt and did not budge. This time, however, Henry VIII stood his ground and contacted Anton Fugger directly, which he had never done in the past. Vaughan had always warned against this approach, as he did not expect Fugger to lift a finger on the Antwerp Exchange without approval from Ducci.[220] But now the situation had changed. The Schmalkaldic War had started, and Fugger understood that defeat would entail a massive financial loss for him and his family. With this prospect in mind, he did his utmost to recover capital on other fronts. Obtaining guarantees regarding the English debt was his top priority. At the same time, he tried to liquidate a considerable amount of copper, for which no market existed at that point. Following tedious negotiations, an agreement was reached in July-August. Henry VIII was to repay £92,180 Fl.gr. of his debt to Fugger and would receive a six-month extension at 6.5 percent for the balance due, i.e. £60,000 Fl.gr. He would also receive a new loan of £20,000 Fl. gr. but had to accept payment in copper. The Privy Council provided airtight guarantees.[221]

Fugger instructed his representative in Antwerp not to inform Ducci about the specifics of his agreement with Henry VIII.[222] He feared that Ducci would feel he had been circumvented and would notify Mary of Hungary. Considering the very precarious political-military situation, such action was ill advised. On the Antwerp Exchange victory by the Emperor was considered highly unlikely. Moreover, the Emperor was perpetually short of money and kept needing new loans. In such circumstances, anything that remotely resembled accommodating the King of England – both a short-term loan and supplying copper – would cause indignation. At any rate, the transaction did not lead Fugger and Ducci to stop working together, as demonstrated by several loans to the government of the Habsburg Netherlands and Charles V in 1546 and 1547.[223]

Ducci had several irons in the fire and had no objection to serving multiple masters at the same time, not only Charles V and Henry VIII, but also the French King. He had previously worked with Grimmel, Neidhart, and Seiler on exchange-arbitrage in Lyon; following the Treaty of Crépy, however, he was able to engage in lucrative deals directly with Francis I.[224] Although it is impossible to verify whether Vaughan was right when he

---

219 LPFD, Henry VIII, 21/1, nos 199 and 296.
220 LPFD, Henry VIII, 20/2, no. 333.
221 De Smedt (1928), 249-50; Richardson (1953), 73-4; Pölnitz (1967), II/2/2, 173, 176, 187, 219, 223-4.
222 Pölnitz (1967), II/2, 198-9.
223 See also AGR, PEA 1661/1, Letter dated 22 August 1546; Ehrenberg (1896), I, 147; Pölnitz (1967), II/2, 273.
224 LPFD, Henry VIII, 20/1, no. 1026.

reported to Henry VIII in February 1545 the rumours circulating in Antwerp that the King of France had asked Ducci to help him obtain short-term loans, it seems plausible. In the early 1540s Francis I had started to obtain loans in Lyon. This was important and major news, as in 1543 the Antwerp merchant Jan Ympyn, author of the first Dutch manual on double-entry accounting, wrote that exchange rates in Lyon would henceforth depend largely on whether the King of France borrowed large or small amounts.[225] Fragmentary financial records prove that the royal loans were substantial, and that they soon gave rise to massive speculation.[226]

Ducci used the information provided by Grimmel, Neidhart, and Seiler to pressure the English. In June 1545 he presented Vaughan with letters from merchant bankers of Lyon asking him to arrange a loan of 400,000 French crowns for Francis I; he was offered 5 percent per (quarterly) fair, i.e. 20 percent *per annum*. Vaughan believed it to be true 'and not a device to drive forward our present bargain.'[227] He was right, as Ducci also informed Mary of Hungary at about the same time. The problem is that – as is often the case in matters involving Ducci – no concrete data are available on his role in transactions with Lyon in 1545. Undoubtedly, however, he worked with Neidhart and Seiler to improve the financial situation for Valois.[228] This must have been very lucrative, as on 4 August 1546 in Antwerp Neidhart (represented by Grimmel) and Seiler, together with the Florentine Simon Pecori, factor of Alessandro Antinori,[229] founded a company with the aim of performing regular exchange-arbitrage between Antwerp and Lyon and with arranging short-term loans for three years to benefit from the interest rate differences between the two markets that resulted from the loans obtained by Charles V and Francis I, respectively. The aim was to profit from speculation, as exchange-arbitrage was entirely separate from the commodities trade. Aware of the political risks, the partners appointed Pecori (who had not contributed any capital) 'director' of the company in Lyon and entrusted him with performing all transactions on behalf of the company. Ducci and Neidhart were not listed in the company contract but were represented by Seiler in all transactions. Caution was indeed advisable, as loans to the King of France were nearly always to the disadvantage of Charles V. Neidhart and Seiler did not object, as political and religious divisions were no concern of theirs. Only when a financial venture was very risky was *conscientia* invoked as an argument. In August 1546, when members of the Schmalkaldic League intercepted letters revealing that Neidhart was providing financial services to the Emperor, did he rapidly propose that half the company capital be used toward loans to Francis I to avoid being labelled as favouring Charles V. Grimmel replied from Antwerp that he preferred to lend money to Lyon merchants, but his advice was not based on principle considerations. Rather, such a policy was simply less risky. Grimmel was outvoted.[230] Yet he was right in the long run, as the Antwerp-Lyon game did indeed entail risks.

---

225 Ympyn (1970), f° 15.

226 Hamon (1994), 166-70.

227 LPFD, Henry VIII, 20/1, no. 1045. In Lyon an interest rate of 5 percent per fair was standard for loans to the king in June-July 1545: Matringe (2016), 223.

228 Ehrenberg (1896), II, 89-90; Pölnitz (1967), II/2, 232-3.

229 The Florentine firm Antinori had branches in Antwerp, Lyon, Medina del Campo, and Valladolid.

230 Ehrenberg (1896), I, 222-4; Bauer (1936), 131-3

The war was waged not only on the battlefield but also on the money markets. Currency was manipulated in some cases. The *écus d'or*, for example, were over-valued in the Habsburg Netherlands to draw them out of France and thus increase the cost of the war to Francis I. Other measures included a ban on exporting precious metals or using letters of exchange. Francis I spared no effort in complicating access to capital for his adversary, even taking out huge loans intended mainly to deprive Charles V of the cash he needed to pay the troops in Germany.[231] In turn, the imperial advisors discussed strategies to disrupt or even completely disable the Lyon exchange market. In the spring of 1544 a secret commission convened in Spain to discuss the options for economic warfare against France. In addition to unnamed scholars, those consulted comprised the merchant bankers Rodrigo de Dueñas from Medina del Campo and Francisco de Burgos from Valladolid, representatives of the Fuggers and the Welsers, and the Genoese bankers Niccolò Grimaldi, Francesco Lomellin, and Pantaleón de Negro. They agreed that businessmen in Spain, the Netherlands, and Germany should be prohibited from engaging in arbitrage transactions at the Lyon fairs, and that this exchange market should be transferred to Besançon, to deprive the King of France of rapid access to large sums. Besançon was favourably situated for the Genoese, the Flemish, and the Germans. To maximize its effect, however, this economic policy required the support of the Duke of Florence, the Doge of Venice, and the aldermen of Genoa. Firms trading with Lyon were to be notified in time for them to withdraw their goods before the measure took effect. The Italians, however, warned that this initiative might harm the Emperor, since de-activating the Lyon exchange could disturb financial traffic between Spain, Antwerp, Milan, and Naples.[232] The plan did not move forward.

Although the warning from the Genoese bankers was justified, it is unlikely to have been the reason the plan was not implemented. The end of the war was surely the main factor. The Treaty of Crépy made commercial transactions with Lyon impossible to prohibit, since the King of France did not officially side with the Protestant German rulers united in the Schmalkaldic League. That the Habsburg side had even considered prohibiting trade on the Lyon money market for the second time within a few years, however, was a clear message. Both in the Netherlands and in Spain, advisors to the Emperor understood that Lyon was becoming increasingly important in the European exchange system, and that its participants needed to be observed carefully. In 1551 prominent South-German, Genoese, and Florentine merchant bankers stated that at each of the four Lyon fairs in normal circumstances letters of exchange worth 4 to 5 million *écus de marc* were traded, of which one fifth consisted of transfers between Antwerp and Lyon.[233]

While commercial transactions in Lyon posed no threat, financial speculation could cause major damage to the Emperor. The danger was all the more real in that, in the event of armed conflict, members of the Schmalkaldic League were expected to approach South-German bankers active in Lyon for loans. The need to operate safely between the political and religious fronts was precisely why Seiler's citizenship of a Swiss city was so important. Since his background ruled out affiliation with any side in the conflict – neither with

---

231 Spooner (1956), 128-30; Knecht (1994), 506.

232 Pöllnitz (1967), II/2, 31-2. On the role of Lyon in the European exchange system in the mid-sixteenth century, see the clear explanation by Matringe (2015), Ch. vi.

233 RAB, OF, PPG 223.

Habsburg or Valois, nor with the Emperor or the Schmalkaldic League – he was basically free to work the Lyon money market. This was exactly why the Augsburg businessman Hans Paul Herwart asked him to arrange loans in Lyon as well. Many other South-German merchant-financiers had relatives or factors who were born in a Swiss city or had acquired citizenship there perform transactions in Lyon on their behalf, or they approached the merchant-banker Hans Kleberg (known in France as Jean Cléberger), who resided in Lyon and was a citizen of Bern. Anton Fugger, who in 1544, even before the Treaty of Crépy, sold copper and fustians in Lyon, also operated via merchants who were citizens of Bern; he avoided any personal correspondence with these front men.[234]

That Pecori settled in Lyon together with a son of Neidhart shows that the partners intended to remain active on the Lyon money and exchange markets for several years and to conduct important business there. The start-up capital was 20,000 *écus de marc* or *scudi*, i.e. the equivalent of or just under £6400 Fl.gr., half of which was contributed by Neidhart, while Seiler and Ducci put up one quarter each. The objectives were twofold from the outset: to engage systematically in exchange-arbitrage between Antwerp and Lyon and to provide loans to the King of France. According to the founding charter, no more than half the authorized capital was to be used toward the second aim. The condition was soon waived, however, as Ducci and his partners regarded the death of Kleberg on 4 September 1546 as a window of opportunity. For years Kleberg had arranged all short-term loans for Francis I, and the King now had no comparably knowledgeable financial agent. Speculators therefore had far greater latitude. Ducci, who had been carefully observing all that transpired in Lyon, found Kleberg's death sufficiently important to merit special mention in a letter to Mary of Hungary four days later.[235] He wrote nothing about his alliance with Neidhart and Seiler, however, as financial speculation by the firm could hardly be regarded by the central government of the Habsburg Netherlands as evidence of loyalty. In December he informed the governor that the Antwerp Exchange was suffering from an extreme shortage of gold coins, and that the situation was worsening by the day, explaining to her that France increasingly favoured silver, which had negative consequences for the Antwerp money market.[236] He was careful not to tell her that Lyon was becoming progressively more attractive to South-German capital, or that exchange-arbitrage had caused serious disruption, as he was involved in this scheme as well. Cunning speculators could reap huge profits in Lyon at the time, as the deeply indebted Francis I and his successor Henri II were perpetually in need of new loans.[237] Based on the accounts that remain from Neidhart, it may be inferred that the partners made profits of nearly 45 percent in 1547 and nearly 42 percent in 1548.[238] The record earnings resulting from the combination of exchange-arbitrage and providing credit did not curtail their desire to speculate or prevent them from taking still greater risks, as soon came to light.

234 Pöllnitz (1967), II/2, 32-3; Häberlein (1998a), 129-30. On Kleberg's economic activities, see esp. Ehrenberg (1896), II, 87-90; Vial (1914), 23-51; Pfeiffer (1967), 415-16.

235 AGR, PEA 1661/1, Letter dated 8 September 1546.

236 AGR, PEA 1661/1, Letter dated 11 December 1546. In this connection, see the interesting comment by Spooner (1956), 129-34.

237 On the royal debt, see Hamon (1994), 169.

238 Bauer (1936), 178-9.

Ducci – elected 'consul' of the Florentine 'nation' in Antwerp in 1546[239] - and his Lyon partners also provided loans to Cosimo I de' Medici, Duke of Tuscany. In March 1548 Niccolò di Giunta and Tommaso Corbinelli represented the Duke in negotiations with Ducci and Neidhart, who in turn approached other merchant bankers, as a loan of 112,000 to 200,000 ducats was requested. Anton Fugger was among the potential creditors from the outset, as he already did business with the Duke, supplying large amounts of copper via Venice and Pisa. The Florentine businessman and Maecenas Bernardo Vechietti was pivotal in the complex negotiations between Cosimo I de' Medici, Ducci, and Fugger. Together with Ducci, he contacted Florentine firms with branches in Antwerp and/or Lyon, including Capponi, de Nerli, de Nobili, Ricci, Rucellai, Salviati, and Torrigiani. At the end of 1548 the Duke borrowed 330,000 ducats through these channels: 160,000 from 'various Antwerp merchants', 100,000 from Neidhart, and 70,000 from Fugger, who provided part of the loan in jewels. In addition to operating as the broker, Ducci put up capital on his own via Neidhart (and perhaps also via Florentine merchants in Antwerp), but the amount is impossible to trace. Over the next few months the participation by Ducci and his Lyon partners in loans to Cosimo I de' Medici grew still more obscure.[240]

The financial deals of Ducci & Co. had never been models of transparency, but in the late 1540s non-disclosure became the guiding principle. This was understandable, because several rulers were being served in complex political and religious contexts, and they operated on various money markets simultaneously. Ducci managed to remain in control, which was an impressive accomplishment in its own right. He appeared not only as 'master of the Emperor's finances' but also as the indispensable broker-banker for other European rulers who urgently needed money. Little wonder that he felt omnipotent on the Antwerp Exchange.

2.5 'Among Such Wolves'

In his letters and reports to the King of England and the Privy Council in 1545 and 1546, Stephen Vaughan emphasized over and over again that without Ducci's aid he could not obtain credit on the Exchange. In the event of a dispute no support would be forthcoming from the Emperor or his sister, as they concurred with all Ducci's proposals. Still, he argued, Ducci was so acquisitive that he consistently pursued maximum personal profit everywhere, even in transactions on behalf of the Emperor. Vaughan was deeply annoyed with this 'wicked fellow', 'wily fox', 'lewd man', 'troublesome fellow', concluding that he was 'evil contended'.[241] He had no illusions anymore about the manipulative or even malicious nature of many transactions on the Antwerp money market. He no longer believed anyone where financial/monetary proposals were concerned. In June 1546 he wrote to Henry VIII that operating 'among such wolves' and obtaining loans on the Exchange was fraught with danger. In August he stated that in London it was impossible to imagine how

239 AGR, PEA 1661/1, 2 July 1546.

240 Pölnitz (1971), III/1, 561 n. 25, 572 n. 83, 572-3 n. 83, 581 n. 82, 600 n. 134, 604-5, n. 39; Parigino (1999), 61-2, 64.

241 LPFD, Henry VIII, 19/2, no. 30, 20/1, nos 171 and 1010, 20/2, nos 333, 416, 552, and 21/1, nos 82, 962, 1335.

cautiously he had to approach financial matters in Antwerp, 'the world being so evil here'.[242] Around the same time the Venetian ambassador Bernardo Navagero, who had spent years at the imperial courts, wrote that Ducci was one of the most despised businessmen in the Netherlands: *odiosissimo*. Ducci, he stated, 'is aware of all financial transactions in Antwerp and of all resources and wealth of Flanders, which has placed him as much in the good graces of Queen Mary of Hungary as he is despised by the population'.[243]

It was not only representatives of foreign governments who expressed such blunt views. In November 1546 a pamphlet was distributed in Brussels, cynically signed 'your *friends* from the community of Ghent'. Its authors attacked Ducci and four high-ranking government officials as 'those whose pointless mischief instils evil in the Queen', referring to the new type of commercial taxes introduced on Ducci's initiative and to the new *aides*, provincial subsidies.[244] Naming a businessman in a pamphlet that was moreover offensive was extraordinary. In the Habsburg Netherlands the world of big business was subject to intense scrutiny, both in moralizing treatises and literary texts and in illustrations, but wrongdoings were rarely associated with specific occupational groups; and when they were, they hardly ever cited individual merchants or bankers.[245] Those who drafted the anti-Ducci pamphlet moreover directed their caustic criticism at four prominent officials: Van Schore, who was pivotal in the government system, Engelbert van den Dale, chancellor of the Duchy of Brabant, Jean Ruffault, treasurer-general of the Council of Finance, and Philip Nigri, member of the Council of State and chief negotiator. It was suggested that they were being manipulated by Ducci, or, even worse, that they were colluding with him, in other words: that the highest authorities were collaborating with a banker mistrusted by other businessmen. The reference to Ghent in the signature gave the pamphlet an ominous tone, because in 1539 the city had refused to pay the taxes imposed by Mary of Hungary, and groups of artisans and craftsmen had adopted a far more radical stand than the aldermen. Van Schore had reported in detail on this political-fiscal revolt. On the basis of his interpretations and advice, Charles V had had 25 'rebel leaders' executed the next year, while the aldermen, municipal officials, prominent citizens, the deans of the guilds, and many others underwent exemplary punishments.[246] The memory of this was still fresh in 1546.

Was Antwerp representative of upcoming commercial and financial centres? Did competition between capitalists augur a new era? This question is difficult to answer, because the research to date on speculation and competition in the fifteenth and sixteenth centuries is insufficient to enable systematic comparisons. Moreover, the available data appear contradictory. In the 1540s the Salviati in Lyon were quick to diabolize their competitors. Although they never hesitated to cheat other businessmen, they depicted the Bonvisi from Lucca, who were also active in Lyon, as shameless con-men, interested only in making easy money.[247] Merchant-bankers in sixteenth-century Florence, on the

---

242 LPFD, Henry VIII, 21/1, nos 1018 and 1420.
243 Quoted in *Relazione* (2005), my translation.
244 Text edited by Van Peteghem (1972), II, 140-2 (my translation). See also LPFD, Henry VIII, 21/2, no. 465.
245 Soly (2016), 211-12.
246 Dambruyne, Decavele and Van Peteghem (1990).
247 Matringe (2016), 162 and 167.

other hand, were not driven by a stiff competitive spirit, according to Richard Goldthwaite, except for those seeking to obtain huge government contracts elsewhere. The author contrasts their attitude and that of the Venetians with the Antwerp capitalists: 'The cut-throat competition practiced by the new generation of merchants coming out of Antwerp must have been as foreign to these Florentines as it was to their Venetian colleagues'.[248] Was this a contrast between a traditional and a new economic centre? Or was this (also) the difference between a homogeneous economic elite with local roots and a city where different groups of foreigners were engaged in international trade and finance?

At any rate, the 1540s offered unprecedented opportunities for speculation in Antwerp and Lyon, as both the second stage in international trade expansion and the rising demand for credit among central and local authorities were highly conducive to financial and currency transactions. This trend peaked in the years 1544-46, because the three main operators in the European political arena contracted huge loans at the same time – Charles V and Henry VIII in Antwerp and Francis I in Lyon - with each transaction inevitably influencing the others. While in 1540 the Emperor had indeed restricted the interest rate to 12 percent, permissible only on commercial loans,[249] this limit could easily be exceeded in various ways. Nominal interest rates often differed considerably from real ones, as Ducci's short-term loans demonstrate. On the other hand, many merchants benefited from the rapidly growing trade with Southern Europe. Ocean-going vessels, however, experienced privateering on the Channel, thereby suffering major losses as well.[250] Speculations, high expectations, risks: all made for great instability.

The Antwerp Exchange was dangerous, not only in terms of financial risk but also with regard to the physical integrity of its visitors. The city authorities were aware that concentrating large numbers of merchants in one place entailed a risk of violent interpersonal conflicts. The rules of procedure from 1513 indicated that conversations between merchants at the (Old) Exchange often culminated in 'riots, brawls, and invectives'. These would henceforth be severely punished: whoever had the temerity to draw a knife would be fined fifty gold Burgundian guilders or would lose a finger. Anybody injuring another person would be subject to double that penalty or would have his hand chopped off.[251] Whether the most severe punishments were in fact carried out is unclear. Still, the ongoing mention of them in the 1520s suggests that the problem persisted. The new *Bursa* or *Bourse*, Exchange, between Lange Nieuwstraat and Meir, which opened in 1532, was far more spacious than the Old Exchange. The building measured 51 by 40 metres, had an open courtyard that could be accessed along four sides, and was surrounded by four wings with a gallery upstairs and a low gable roof. The lower level consisted entirely of galleries as well. At the top of the main entrance on Meir,[252] the inscription read *In usum negotiatorum cuiuscumq. nationis ac linguae*: 'For the benefit of those doing business, irrespective of nation or language'. Although the different groups of merchants were not assigned official stations, the Italians, Spanish, and

248 Goldthwaite (2009), 589, referring to Tucci (1973).
249 ROPB, IV, 235.
250 Asaert (2019), I, 354-60.
251 Denucé (1931), no. III.
252 Meir was already a major thoroughfare in the sixteenth century. Today it is the busiest shopping street in Antwerp.

Portuguese were ordinarily positioned to the right of the main entrance and the French to the left. The Germans were at the front, the English in the middle, and at the back the Burgundians, the 'Flemish' – i.e. those originating from the Habsburg Netherlands – and the merchants from Northern Europe. The New Exchange was dedicated mainly to exchange and credit operations, as commodities were increasingly traded elsewhere in the city. Still, above the galleries in the New Exchange the city government set up booths that were leased to various persons to display and sell paintings and other 'small items'. A great many retailers also tried to sell their wares on the side streets. These were new, straight, and fairly wide streets intended to make the central financial area of Antwerp safer, but the New Exchange was open to everybody, regardless of age or origin, and the vast open space in the old city centre was a virtual magnet to all those seeking diversion, relaxation, or entertainment.[253] As a consequence, it was always crowded.

More than in the past, the city authorities tried to prevent disturbances of the peace. Shortly after the New Exchange opened, the rules of procedure from 1513 were reissued, announcing several additional prohibitions. Nobody was allowed to play ball in the inner courtyard of the building; violations would lead to a fine of fl.3, with parents being held liable for their children; nobody was allowed to set up a booth there without permission, and used goods vendors were prohibited from selling their wares there; again, violations were subject to a fine of fl.3. The new procedures were ineffective, as 'the insolence and noise' became even worse, 'causing the merchants great nuisance, torment, damage, and discomfort'. In 1536 and 1537 the prohibitions were published again. The magistrate further stipulated that playing dice and other games of chance was strictly prohibited at the New Exchange and decreed a penalty of fl.6 for carving in the benches with knives or leaving litter on the steps. The continued rise in the number of brawls was still more worrying and led in 1538 to violations of the regulations being punished more severely. Perpetrators of violence henceforth risked being banned, and insulting another person was heavily fined as well. The ordinance also applied to those committing crimes on a side street, *en route* to or leaving the Exchange.[254] The city government was concerned that many kinds of crimes were being covered up in and around the New Exchange, but in practice did not take drastic measures or make efforts to figure out a more enduring solution. In 1547 a high-ranking government official – most likely a member of the Privy Council – proposed having representatives of the merchants and bankers in Antwerp set up their own tribunal to rectify the wrongdoings on the Exchange. The Germans, Portuguese, Spanish, Italians, and local businessmen would elect representatives from their midst, who would be grouped in four *bourses*, each with a consul in charge: '*Les bourses des quatre consuls de la Bourse d'Anvers*' ('The exchanges of the four consuls of the Antwerp Exchange'). Together, the consuls would meet three days a week with a member of the city council to settle disputes and disagreements between businessmen on the Exchange.[255] The plan never crystallized. The city council was probably averse to a tribunal that would curtail the municipal judicial authority.

253 Materné (1992b), 59-61, 73, 75.
254 Denucé (1931), nos VIII-XI.
255 AGR, PEA 1191/41, no. 43.

Altercations and brawls were not the only problem. In November 1540 the magistrate proclaimed that anyone able to provide information about the assassination attempt at the New Exchange of the Portuguese merchant and insurance salesman Loys Mendez, who was seriously wounded, should contact the officers of the court. A compatriot, the pepper merchant Loys Fernandez, 'and his cohorts' were believed to be the culprits. In February 1541 in the vicinity of the Exchange the Spanish merchant Juan de Haro 'and his consorts' attacked Simon van de Werve, a scion of a prominent family. They wounded his servant, who later died of his injuries.[256] These were not isolated incidents. On 17 October 1542 the city authorities reported that 'ever more merchants and other persons in the Exchange threaten, beat, injure, and abuse each other daily, as happened again only yesterday'. Accordingly, such offences would henceforth be subject to the severest penal provisions.[257] Less than four months later, Simon Turchi, factor for the large Bonvisi firm from Lucca, was attacked and injured upon leaving the Exchange at around six o'clock in the evening; he sustained a gash to his face. According to some Italian merchants – including Ducci – the attack was planned by the Lucchese broker Francisco Francesqui.[258] The altercations and discord among the merchants in Antwerp caused such frequent disorder that on 14 May 1544 Mary of Hungary urged the Margrave and the city council to put an end to these incidents. Having 'merchants strolling the streets with concealed weapons and receiving assistance from their servants and others they hire and maintain' could no longer be tolerated.[259] Increasingly, substantial merchants did indeed have themselves escorted by bodyguards, who were supposed to protect them from attacks but were in some cases also used to threaten, beat, or even murder others.[260] Ducci was the worst of these offenders. He employed 15 to 20 *bravi*, nearly all Italians, who operated in groups of 3 to 6, both during the day and at night, always armed with clubs and knives. They easily terrorized others, as their master was so powerful that nobody in Antwerp would dare stand in his way. After a serious altercation in the Church of Our Lady with Jacob Maes, pensionary of the City of Antwerp, Ducci instructed one of his *bravi* to teach this lawyer a lesson; in the cemetery next to the Church, Maes received a thrashing. In January 1545 Ducci had some of his *bravi* ransack the Lange Gasthuisstraat residence of Maria van de Werve, who came from a prominent patrician family. Maria, age 43 and nicknamed *Bionda Maraviglia* for her beauty, was still unmarried and, according to Matteo Bandello, a well-informed contemporary, had a great many suitors, most of them Italians. Had Maria van de Werve offended Ducci? At any rate, the incident set many tongues wagging, especially because it once again proved the arrogance and impunity of Ducci, as noted by another of his victims, Gilbert van Schoonbeke.[261]

Van Schoonbeke's stepmother Anna Stegemans was the sister of Ducci's wife Elisabeth. The uncle harboured a grudge against his young nephew with regard to the problems that

256 SAA, PK 915, f° 9, 10v°-11.

257 Quoted in Denucé (1931), no. III/12 (my translation).

258 SAA, PK 915, f° 51v°-52v°; AGR, RB, OF, PPG 326.

259 'Gaende lancx de straten bedeckelyck gewapent ende gesterckt mit hueren dieneren ende anderen die zijl[ieden] huyren ende onderhouden'. AGR, PEA 1652/1, Letter dated 14 May 1544.

260 On 24 December 1544 Margrave Willem van de Werve wrote to Mary of Hungary that some merchants openly had themselves escorted by armed soldiers, when they went to the Exchange. AGR, PEA 693, f° 101.

261 Génard (1888), no. III/5, 8-9, 20. On Maria van de Werve, see Schmitz and Bousse (1988), 96-8.

arose in weighing the large quantities of alum he imported and sold. As master of the Weighing House, Van Schoonbeke was responsible for ensuring that no goods weighing over fifty pounds (*c.* 23.5 kg) were sold, unless they had been processed at the City Weighing House first, and a fixed amount paid.[262] Exactly what went wrong remains a mystery, but Ducci must have felt severely thwarted. He knew that Van Schoonbeke secretly did business with burgomaster Michiel van der Heyden,[263] brother-in-law of Lancelot van Ursel, also a prominent member of the city council and brother-in-law of… Fernando Dassa, who had challenged the alum contract. Did he suspect Van Schoonbeke of conspiring with his greatest enemy (at the time), whether or not on instructions from Van der Heyden? At any rate, on Sunday 22 February 1545 at nightfall he arranged for an attempt to be made on the life of his nephew. Shortly afterwards Van Schoonbeke reported in a written accusation that Ducci had seen him unarmed at the Exchange and had told his servants Antonio Ceusi and a certain Rosse or Rosseau to 'get rid of him' or words to that effect, while indicating Van Schoonbeke. Another servant of Ducci had tried unsuccessfully to reason with his master, after which the two *bravi* mentioned above positioned themselves at the exit of the Exchange, Ceusi at one end and Rosseau at the other. As Van Schoonbeke was leaving the Exchange, the two *bravi* had called out to each other and had charged him with their swords drawn. One would have run him through had Van Schoonbeke's servant not taken the blow, while the other would have split his head, had he not been wearing very solid headgear, but he did sustain injuries. Taken by complete surprise and without offensive or even defensive weapons, Van Schoonbeke had fled back into the Exchange.

In his accusation, Van Schoonbeke did not merely accuse Ducci of attempting to assassinate him. He described his uncle as a serious troublemaker, a man who tolerated no dissent whatsoever and was consistently heavy handed in dealing with his adversaries. His *bravi* were common criminals, who would stop at nothing, and would even resort to murder and manslaughter. Ducci never gave instructions to murder anybody. Rather, he might say 'give him a good thrashing', which depending on the context meant: beat him up, injure him, or kill him. The merchants Francesco Juliani and Francesco de Barros were threatened so often and suffered so much abuse that they left Antwerp. This accusation certainly did not lack foundation, because in April 1544 several witnesses had told government commissioners of rumours that Ducci and Joan Ambrosio had ordered the murders of Francisco de Barros and other Portuguese merchants.[264] Were the rumours false, a threat, or sincere? In any case, the result was that those concerned fled the city.

Ducci was financially untrustworthy, argued Van Schoonbeke, as he was 'the inventor and creator of all the evil practices and abuses that infest the Antwerp Exchange', as the demise of the Portuguese factor had demonstrated. He caused the ruin of many other merchants. Why had he ordered this new assassination? Simply because he refused to have the alum, which he monopolized (a public secret), weighed 'according to the rules' at the City Weighing House. He would not tolerate such a principle, and he had tried to destroy Van Schoonbeke's reputation in all possible ways, even spreading 'the disgraceful and false

262 Soly (1977), 133-4, 149. Van Schoonbeke served as master of the Weighing House from 1540.
263 See Chapter 3.1.
264 RAB, RB, OF, PPG 326.

rumour that he had made him a cuckold'. Worst of all, continued Van Schoonbeke, Ducci got away with everything. Relying on his excellent relations with the Court, he openly proclaimed that his power was so great that the governor would always protect him. He was full of confidence. He paraded around the city with his armed bodyguards and had sent Lazarus Tucher to convince Van Schoonbeke that he had better adopt a low profile or risk yet greater harm.[265]

The municipal authorities took the charge seriously and summoned Ducci to appear in court on 27 February. The accused neither appeared nor sent a representative in his place. This happened four more times.[266] The magistrate then banished all those involved in the assassination attempt from the city, including Ducci, who set off to Brussels to complain in person to the central government. He argued that Van Schoonbeke had started the altercation, that he had merely instructed his servant to give Van Schoonbeke a thrashing, and that the Antwerp city authorities were being unreasonable, even though his lawyer had explained the true circumstances of the case in a petition. The aldermen were acting out of 'vengeance and bias', incited by the inner burgomaster Lancelot van Ursel, who held a grudge against him. While this position was not mentioned in any written document, Ducci undoubtedly told the governor that Van Ursel was the brother-in-law of Dassa, who had challenged the alum contract. By March 1545 that contract was still in dispute. Mary of Hungary believed that state interests were compatible with personal ones and did exactly as Van Schoonbeke had alleged in his charge: she protected Ducci. The Tuscan banker was indeed indispensable in the eyes of the highest authorities. On 21 March 1545 Charles V instructed the Antwerp city council to urge Gilbert van Schoonbeke to abandon all legal proceedings against Gaspar Ducci immediately or risk heavy sanctions. If the aldermen or Van Schoonbeke wished to protest, their only recourse was the Council of Brabant, where the Chancellor would personally examine the arguments and counterarguments from both sides.[267] The message was clear and was understood by all: Ducci would in any case go unpunished. Nobody else filed any charges.

While Ducci was an extraordinary case, his practice of resorting to violence against persons did not differ significantly from many other merchants in Antwerp. In the afternoon of 27 November 1545 the Exchange was the scene of a massive brawl, in which the merchant-pharmacist Simon de Chosa together with many others attacked the substantial exporter Gabriel Tersago and a man named Jan Baptist Waryn. The next year three Genoese who had murdered Bernardo Bucio at the Exchange were declared outlaws. In February 1549 the Genoese Domenico Bassadonio, a member of the Pallavicino family, was beaten up in public and sustained severe injuries. In 1551 Leonardo Ronco, a merchant from Cremona, was murdered by Mario Antonio Bonsignori from Siena while leaving the Exchange.[268] Some resorted to ingenious torture or murder devices. In April 1544 Bernardino Pisani of Pisa and other merchants testified that the Lucchese broker Francisco Francesqui had shown them an iron or steel collar manufactured in Nuremberg with spikes containing

265 Génard (1888), no. III/ 3-4, 11-15, 17-18, 22-3, 32-3, 37-8, 43, 46-7, 50.

266 Génard (1888), nos IV-VIII.

267 SAA, IB 2168/2, and SR 214, f° 475; Génard (1888), nos IX-X.

268 SAA, PK 915, f° 61v°-63, 87v°-88v°, 118v°-119, 125v°, 138v°. On Tersago, see Goris (1925), 279, 360; Brulez (1959), 489. On Bassadonio, see Beck (1989), 766 and 783.

gunpowder; the victim was unable to open the clasp.[269] Whether this device was indeed used in Antwerp remains unknown, but Simon Turchi in any case acquired another sophisticated mechanism to immobilize a rival. In 1551 he killed another merchant from Lucca, Jeronimo Deodati, who had lent him a huge sum and had spread rumours that Turchi was in dire financial straits. Financial problems and amorous rivalry – involving Maria van de Werve! – led him to invite Deodati to his home, where he had him sit in a chair equipped with shackles that snapped shut the moment Deodati touched the armrests. Trapped in this position, Deodati was killed by one of Turchi's bodyguards. His remains were buried in the garden. Turchi, however, was arrested on suspicion of murder and confessed under torture. He was placed in the Death Chair on Grote Markt and burned alive.[270] The case caused quite a stir and was depicted at length in a *novella* by the Italian Dominican and writer Matteo Bandello, who had many good friends in the Netherlands and in 1550 was appointed Bishop of Agen (southwest France). The murder and execution were among the most spectacular in Antwerp's Golden Age. Exceptional though this case may have been, it resembled other acts of violence in the city, in that it arose from a conflict between Italian businessmen.[271]

Court records suggest that businessmen from Southern Europe, in particular those from Italy, were far more inclined to resort to violence than those who came from other countries. Italians, Spanish, and Portuguese together accounted for 90 percent of all foreigners prosecuted for crimes of violence in Antwerp in the 1540s and 50s. The overwhelming majority was Italian. Nearly all cases concerned confrontations and conflicts among compatriots: Italians fought Italians, and the parties involved generally originated from the same city.[272] Was the conduct of Florentine and other Northern Italian merchants in Antwerp – where they generally resided only temporarily to conduct business – the same as in their city of birth? The high rates of interpersonal violence in Italian cities seem to have closely correlated with 'the propensity of social elites to employ violence in pursuit of their political and economic interests'.[273] In the mid-sixteenth century about 200 merchants from different Italian cities were active in Antwerp. Did new commercial and financial rivalries add to 'imported' conflicts? In any case, in Antwerp the merchant nations from Florence, Genoa, and Lucca were clearly unable to resolve mutual conflicts on their own.

Those who were active in the interest of the large South-German firms that figured prominently on the Antwerp Exchange in the 1540s do not appear to have resorted to violence. The Fuggers, the Welsers, and most other Augsburg firms, however, had a factor representing them, whereas Northern Italian merchant bankers themselves lived in the Scheldt town and generally acted on their own behalf, even though they were a branch of a very widely dispersed family network, thereby increasing the likelihood of conflicts. Feverish speculation and cut-throat competition were in any case conducive to acts of violence. While fortunes could be made in this period, severe losses were sustained as well. Success stories and bankruptcies were both inherent in speculative market conditions,

---

269 RAB, RB, OF, PPG 326.
270 Laenens and Leemans (1953), 163-4; Sabbatini (1985), 123-6
271 For an English translation, see Bandello (1895).
272 Van Dijck (2007), 439-43.
273 Carroll (2016), 107.

which entailed serious risks.[274] Business failure was often the consequence of shipwrecks, piracy, war, illness, or other calamities, i.e. acts of God, but in some cases poorly chosen speculations were decisive, and such failure was easily attributed to commercial or financial manipulations by more powerful peers. This was all the more likely in that merchant bankers used monopolist practices, engaged systematically in exchange-arbitrage, and did not hesitate to commit large-scale fraud. Ducci was unsurpassed in such wrongdoings, but nobody could touch him: he was backed by the highest political authorities. In addition, he challenged everyone in Antwerp by surrounding himself with a small army of *bravi*, thereby openly flaunting his power.

2.6 The Fall

In the 1540s Ducci had immense freedom and could operate as a bully with impunity, because Charles V and Mary of Hungary greatly appreciated his organizational skills and commercial and financial acumen. Time and again, he managed to raise money for them at difficult moments on favourable terms, thanks to both his resourcefulness and his international networks. He was highly successful at making, and making use of, contacts with renowned merchant bankers such as Affaitadi or Fugger; it was one of his great trumps in negotiating commercial and financial deals alike. The Emperor was grateful. On 16 December 1547 he awarded Ducci the honorary title of *eques aur(e)atus Sancti Romani Imperii*: Golden Knight of the Holy Roman Empire, elevating his social standing substantially. This personal honour was not hereditary. As a member of the Order of the Golden Spur, he was authorized to wear golden spurs, which were restricted to noblemen; in practice he was also entitled to wear a gold collar. Ducci thus acceded officially to the public elite of the Holy Roman Empire. This elite comprised mainly members of the lower nobility and the urban patriciate, as well as substantial merchants and bankers.[275]

That a merchant-banker also benefited materially from his services to the Emperor and the government of the Habsburg Netherlands was taken for granted. That Ducci – sometimes? often? – applied sly strategies to enrich himself or achieved his objectives through violence was overlooked or even forgiven because of his contributions to the treasury. Under no circumstances, however, were his activities allowed to threaten, let alone cause harm to state interests. The legitimacy of the highest authority was not to be compromised in any way. Ducci therefore had to be very cautious about implementing the alum contract he had signed with the Grimaldis thanks to the support from the Emperor and his sister in 1547. Bringing about the agreement had required political-diplomatic pressure, as powerful parties had been involved, both directly and indirectly. New problems and conflicts were to be avoided. This proved impossible. The first attack came from an unlikely source.

Luis Fajardo de la Cueva, marquis of Los Vélez, who owned half the Spanish alum mines,[276] felt – as did Dassa and Lopez – that the agreement between Ducci and the Grimaldis was

274 Bankruptcy and insolvency *laws and procedures* in sixteenth-century Antwerp have been well studied: De Ruysscher (2008) and (2013). No research has been conducted, however, on the number of bankruptcies.

275 Stumpo (1992); Schmitt (2000).

276 The other half belonged to Diego López Pacheco, third Marquis of Villena.

disadvantageous to him, because he was no longer able to determine his selling price. In the spring of 1548 he instructed his factor, Pedro de Limpias, to contact Mary of Hungary and inform her that the price Ducci was paying was far too low. The marquis was now forced to sell alum at 59 Flemish shillings per last, whereas prior to Ducci's contract he was getting 62 shillings. The marquis was losing money this way, as production costs in Spain had risen sharply, owing to the increased cost of living and higher wages. Ducci had refused to accept two ship's cargoes of Mazarrón alum, unless the representatives of the marquis agreed to the price he was offering. Surely, it was unacceptable that Ducci 'purchased alum for the price that he set himself and whenever he chose'. Pedro de Limpias did not mention that the alum price was fixed in Ducci's contract with the Grimaldis and asked the governor to intervene. He proposed two measures: permission to employ 200 convicts in the mine to reduce operating expenses and a price increase of at least 10 Flemish shillings per last of alum. Forced labour was in demand, because operating the Mazarrón mines required about 350 workers, whereas the region concerned was very sparsely populated.[277] Mary of Hungary consulted Ducci, who categorically refused to consider raising the purchase price, unless he was allowed a commensurate increase in the selling price in Antwerp, which he of course strongly discouraged. In fact, he believed that the alum price should be reduced: production was higher than ever, while demand was declining, because the conquest of areas of Hungary by the Ottomans had led exports of coloured textile goods to fall since 1541.[278]

During the second half of 1548 complaints about the alum monopoly grew more vociferous, and the Grimaldis joined in. They had complied faithfully with the terms of the contract, although they were disgruntled that they had to supply alum in their chief selling area at a relatively low price, but Ducci was causing problems. He refused to pay for some cargoes within the period agreed in advance, because they had arrived very late or were defective. The Grimaldis explained that the transports had been delayed due to the extreme weather conditions, and that the stocks accumulated in Antwerp had been ample, but that Ducci was very headstrong and would not listen to reason. His ongoing refusal to pay led the Grimaldis to accuse him of breach of contract and to demand high penalties, which Ducci dismissed as unlawful. The Genoese firm then addressed the central government, which instructed the attorney general of the Great Council of Mechelen to investigate the supply of alum. In March 1549, the attorney general concluded that Ducci 'had formed a monopoly to the great disadvantage and detriment of the subjects', because he was selling the alum exclusively to a limited group of wholesalers, and refused to supply cloth dyers and retailers directly. As a consequence, the market price in Antwerp had soared to 94 shillings per last, i.e. way above the maximum of 80 shillings set in the imperial ordinance. Ducci replied that he respected the maximum price and was not responsible for the profits made by the resellers, but the attorney general rejected his argument: Ducci had taken 'bribes' from four wholesalers or had in any case made secret agreements with them; he supplied nearly all his alum to them, after which they would offer small quantities of

277 The Tolfa mine offered twice as much employment: Delumeau (1962), 77; Ruiz Martín (2005), 164-6. Working in alum mines primarily required great physical strength, but technicians and skilled workers were needed as well, as is clear from the pay scales. See Boisseuil and Chareille (2014).

278 AGR, PEA 1414/4, nos 35, 43, 44, 49, 81.

their stock for sale at a much higher price. The attorney general was very clear about the number of buyers, although he did not mention any names, suggesting that the parties were large firms that could be of service to the central government and therefore remained nameless.[279] According to Pallavicino, who represented the Grimaldis, Schetz & Co. were among the buyers, and he notified the members of the government, but the information he provided did not lead to an investigation.[280] High-ranking officials merely blamed Ducci for everything that went wrong. Laurens Longin, *commis* in the Council of Finance, stated bluntly that Ducci was not observing the spirit of the contract, since he refused to sell small quantities of alum, thereby driving the market price in Antwerp well above the ceiling established by contract. The implicit conclusion was that the Grimaldis were entitled to feel seriously aggrieved, since they were forced to sell alum far too cheaply in comparison with the actual market price in Antwerp. Pensionary Jacob Maes also found the complaints expressed in commercial circles to be entirely justified. No matter how much Ducci insisted that both officials were biased, his remarks carried progressively less weight. In may 1549 he wrote to Mary of Hungary: 'Rumour has it that I am a lost man'.[281] While this observation was somewhat premature, he was inundated with insinuations and accusations concerning not only his alum monopoly but also his financial dealings. The campaign against the alum contract had to be stopped, as it was turning – unnamed but presumably Genoese – merchant bankers against the government and was causing other tensions as well: high alum prices increased the operating costs of the cloth dyers, who passed them on to the merchants, resulting in all kinds of disputes. Ducci's monopoly was in danger of casting a shadow on the Joyous Entries that the Emperor and Prince Philip were to hold in September in Antwerp, and to which the 'nations' of foreign merchants, including the Genoese, were expected to contribute substantially.

On 1 August 1549 Charles V terminated the alum contract, retroactively to 1 December 1547. Ducci would be repaid the fl.100,000 or £16,666 2/3 Fl.gr. that he had lent three years earlier, although his subsequent earnings were to be subtracted from that amount.[282] Pallavicino continued to sue Ducci on behalf of the Grimaldis at the Great Council of Mechelen. The chairman, Lambert de Briarde, summoned both parties and tried to convince them to settle. Ducci agreed, but his opponent refused: he would never advise the Grimaldis to do such a thing, 'because I am dealing with a man who has manipulated me far too long'. Both parties claimed damages, one because shipments had not arrived in time, or because the alum quality had been substandard, the other because deliveries had been refused, or payment had been late, with the Grimaldis demanding a penalty of 10,000 ducats for each violation, as the contract provided. The case dragged on. The interim judgements were largely against Ducci, but both parties invoked new arguments and counter arguments against each other.[283]

For Ducci, the dispute about the alum contract, culminating in its nullification, was a serious blow, not merely because he lost out on future profits and was forced to pay fines,

---

279 AGR, PEA 1414/4, nos 65 and 82.
280 AGR, PEA 1414/4, no. 85.
281 'Le bruyt court tel qui semble que je soys ung homme perdu'. AGR, PEA 1414/4, no. 62.
282 AGR, PEA 1414/4, no. 95.
283 AGR, GRM 847, f° 52v°-57v°, GRM 849, no. 104, and GRM 851, nos 37-39.

but also because losing this monopoly reduced his commercial leverage. It demonstrated clearly that the support of Charles V and Mary of Hungary was no longer unconditional. This was especially ominous, because he was teaming up with Neidhart and Seiler increasingly often and for ever greater sums in the light of currency and exchange-arbitrage dealings between Antwerp and Lyon. There had been rumours about his financial speculations and their unfavourable consequences for the Emperor for a long time, but by the late 1540s these finally permeated the highest political echelons. Were competitors gaining influence, or were advisors at the Court becoming suspicious? In any case, some of those around Charles V started to urge closer scrutiny of Ducci's financial transactions. In January 1548 – before the disputes started about the alum contract – the Emperor informed his sister that Ducci's role on the Antwerp Exchange needed to be examined, as no other explanation was available for the sudden spike in the exchange rates. At the time the Emperor still resided in Augsburg, the centre of South-German banking, and therefore had a great many well-informed sources of information. When the governess made inquiries with 'her' banker in early February, he turned out to have been *par delà*, abroad, for a while, most probably in Lyon. He responded to the insinuation that he was to blame for the shortage of money on the Antwerp Exchange. He admitted that on returning he had been involved in arbitrage transactions, but the money shortage was already serious by then. He promised to have Neidhart bring money to the Scheldt town as quickly as possible – an 'offer' that at the very least seemed to confirm the rumours about speculation.[284]

Lack of evidence made the insinuations impossible to substantiate: Ducci and his partners had always been careful not to disclose details of how a deal was done, how the business was organized, who held what share in a partnership, and who was responsible for what. In 1548 and 1549 they were no longer worried and continued their exchange-arbitrage deals between Antwerp and Lyon. Of course they understood that their actions were risky and took care to put as little as possible in writing, thereby also preventing historians nowadays from shedding light on their dealings and profits. Their role in short-term loans to rulers remains similarly obscure. As long as no new Habsburg-Valois war broke out, they incurred no legal or moral liability in issuing loans to Henry II, although discretion in such transactions was advisable since they risked calling attention to the progressive flight of capital from Antwerp to Lyon. Ducci & Co. easily found South-German financiers willing to participate in loans to the King of France, as he offered higher interest rates than Charles V, and granted foreign creditors commercial privileges in Lyon. The 1549 loan of 100,000 *écus d'or* or *c.* £31.675 Fl.gr. to Henry II involved, in addition to the role of Neidhart and Seiler as representatives of the company, underwriting by Wolfgang Langemantel, Georg Mülich, and Matheus Pflaum from Augsburg.[285] Royal finance was a very dynamic investment market because of the accruing debt. In addition, the continued commercial expansion of Lyon boosted demand for credit and currency transfers, providing high and rapid profits.[286] Unfortunately, the sources available reveal nothing about the business

284 AGR, PEA 1661/1, Letters dated 4, 5, and 10 February 1548.

285 Ehrenberg (1896), II, 92-3, 95; Kellenbenz (1993), 44; Hamon (1994), 148 n. 75. See also Van der Wee (1963), II, 204.

286 Matringe (2016), esp. 330-1.

transactions of Ducci & Co. in Lyon in the middle of the century or about their financial strategies and practices. Even the data on their loans to Henry II are incomplete.

The nullification of the alum contract gave Ducci a stronger incentive than ever to engage in financial speculation as a way of offsetting his loss quickly. This move led to his downfall. In early 1550 he found that the circumstances favoured the creation of an artificial money shortage in Antwerp or Lyon as a way of making an extraordinary profit. He and Pecori explained to the Lyon partners the steps that would be necessary to this end. Neidhart hesitated and even criticised such action as 'irresponsible toward God and the world'. He was also aware that many South-German bankers were annoyed at Ducci's 'ostentatious behaviour and arrogance' and were deeply suspicious of his activities on the money markets in Antwerp and Lyon. Ducci's partners knew they would be in serious trouble, if the arrangement backfired. Still, Neidhart was tempted by his greed and participated in the *strettezza* plan which proved disastrous. The partners were betrayed. Although the informant is impossible to identify, he enabled government officials to intercept a great many letters from the company containing remittances for Lyon. Even a cursory glance revealed clearly that the partners were engaged in financial manipulation, providing the legal evidence for prosecuting Ducci, Grimmel, Neidhart, and Seiler.[287] The case became so serious that all four were arrested. Ducci, Grimmel, and Seiler were held in a Brussels prison, Neidhart was placed in custody at Augsburg.

The Emperor ordered the central government in Brussels and the Augsburg magistrate to conduct a thorough investigation. Everything happened very quickly. On 31 January 1550 Mary of Hungary dispatched high officials to Antwerp to ascertain which *subtilz espritz*, perfidious souls, had arranged a money shortage on the Exchange, leading to the extraordinary spike in interest rates. The governor did not believe that a 'reasonable' explanation existed for this pattern. It was surely the result of pernicious human interventions, *praticques illicites et monopoles*, illegal and monopolist practices. Fourteen days later, she also sent Jacob Boonen, a member of the Council of Brabant, to Antwerp, where he was to present a personal letter from her brother, ordering that all merchants in the Scheldt town who had signed bills of exchange drawn on Lyon be convened, and that they be prohibited from paying the exchanges. The total amount was estimated at 300,000 *écus d'or* or £95,000 Fl. gr. They were given one hour to draft letters informing their factors and were to present these letters personally to Boonen, who would send them to Lyon by express courier.[288]

The arrest of the main operators in the financial markets, judicial investigations, writs of summons to international merchants, and an imperial ban on exchange operations between Antwerp and Lyon: the measures reverberated throughout the business world. Putting the Ducci-Neidhart-Seiler group on trial for the scandal might taint the reputation of all South-German bankers and weaken their position on the Antwerp Exchange. Anton Fugger undoubtedly felt fortunate that his contacts with Ducci had not been as close in recent years as they had once been, although he still occasionally used Ducci's services and had done business via front men in Lyon as well. As such, he also came into the investigators' sights. Bartholomäus Welser, Neidhart's father-in-law, had still greater

287 Häberlein (1998a), 131.
288 AGR, PEA 1633/2, Letters dated 31 January and 13 February 1550; Pölnitz (1971), III/1, 615 n. 52.

cause for concern, as Ducci had contacted him with a view to arranging deals in Lyon, and he was moreover rumoured to be involved in the speculations of his son-in-law Neidhart on the Lyon money market. That Grimmel had once been his factor and was now representing Neidhart strengthened these rumours. The suspicions were justified. Letters that the Florentine merchant Niccolò Nettoli, an acquaintance of Ducci, sent to Cosimo I de' Medici in March indicate that Fugger and Welser were far more involved in the Antwerp-Lyon speculations than the authorities ever learned. Nettoli also mentioned contacts with the South-German firms Herwart, Herbrot, Paumgartner, Rehlinger, and Vöhlin.[289] At about this time, Grimmel and Seiler succumbed to pressure. Although at first they dug in their heels and refused to offer any explanations about the exchange-arbitrage, the testimonies they eventually gave confirmed that their financial speculations had generated enormous profits. Mary of Hungary understood that Charles V would not accept token sanctions and charged the attorney general of the Council of Brabant, and the most important members of the Council of Finance with conducting a thorough investigation of the matter, instructing them to pay special attention to currency and exchange-arbitrage between Antwerp and Lyon.[290]

Anyone who had even the slightest involvement in the affair or felt threatened in some way immediately activated their networks of substantial businessmen and influential politicians. On 20 March 1550 Nettoli informed Duke Cosimo of the 'great scandal' in the Netherlands. He regarded Ducci as a confidant of the Duke and was convinced that the banker could rely on him in difficult situations, just as 'Martha helped Lazarus during his illness'. Ducci also expected that the Duke, for whom he had often arranged short-term loans, would ask the Emperor to help him, as is clear from a letter that, as a 'subject and servant of the Duke', he sent Bernardo Antonio de' Medici, bishop of Forli and Cosimo's ambassador to the Emperor's court. Not wanting to jeopardize his excellent relations with Charles V, however, Cosimo behaved with extreme caution. He was the more cautious, because Niccolò Rondinelli, consul of the Florentine nation in Antwerp, told him that Mary of Hungary had been requested to intervene on Ducci's behalf, but that reticence was advisable, because the banker had been involved in dealings 'that cannot be mentioned and are regarded as *lèse majesté*'. His ambassador also urged Cosimo to be discreet, as he feared that Ducci's defence would become very sensitive and difficult. In this period the Duke of Tuscany certainly did not need extra complications, as he faced complex political, economic, and financial problems.[291]

In May the Antwerp factors of Fugger and Welser went to Brussels to 'assist' Grimmel and Seiler, as they stated in a letter. In practice, they probably talked about how both the accused partners and the members of firms that had not (yet) surfaced in the investigation could 'help', i.e. protect each other. Over the following months, Antwerp and Augsburg were abuzz with rumours about Florentine and South-German businessmen suspected of involvement in the financial manipulations by the Lyon firm. Interest in the matter extended beyond business circles and gave rise to massive indignation, especially in Augsburg. In his chronicle, city official Paul Hektor Mair wrote that Ducci, Grimmel, and Seiler – he

289 Pölnitz (1971), III/1, 115-16, 614 n. 52; Häberlein (1998a), 132.
290 AGR, PEA 1633/2, Letter dated 24 March 1550; Mair (1917), 200.
291 Pölnitz (1971), III/1, 614 n. 52, 616 n. 60, and 622 n. 86.

did not mention Neidhart – had been arrested *um dieses grosses Wuchers wesen*, 'for their dire usury'. The physician and historian Achilles Pirmin Gasser, who had been working in Augsburg since 1546, described their speculations as 'cunning and very rapid *Fürkauf*', i.e. speculative brokerage that raised prices, which was strictly prohibited.[292]

Ducci did not deny that his actions were wrong, but he mentioned nothing about them in his letters to Mary of Hungary and begged her to help him, because his 'enemies were using his imprisonment to organize his downfall'. To make matters worse, the suit that Pallavicino had brought against him on behalf of the Grimaldis regarding the alum sales was in danger of being decided against him. In early July he pleaded with the governor to urge Engelbert van den Daele, chancellor of the Duchy of Brabant, to release him from his pre-trial detention, so that he might better prepare his defence against all the accusations.[293] On 20 July he was released, together with Grimmel and Seiler. He had to put up 25,000 ducats bail and was prohibited from selling or pledging commodities pending the definitive outcome.[294] He still hoped to win his case, although prospects became ever grimmer, as several Florentine businessmen turned against him, and Neidhart was, moreover, trying to gain acquittal for himself by blaming Ducci, Grimmel, and Seiler for all that had gone wrong. Soon afterwards, Ducci begged the governor for sympathy because of his 'misfortunes': he was overwhelmingly described in public places as bankrupt, he encountered bailiffs daily, people sought to dishonour and destroy him. Remarkably, he mainly deplored Pallavicino's position on the alum issue. 'All I ask', he argued, 'is that he be reasonable, but he is unwilling [to accommodate]'.[295] Mary of Hungary again intervened personally in this matter. She had helped bring about Ducci's alum contract and very much wanted to bring the matter to a close without damage to her own reputation. On 22 October 1550 she succeeded in convincing the adversaries to settle. The Grimaldis accepted a much lower sum in damages and agreed to terminate the contract, while Ducci had to pay more than he had deemed reasonable but was allowed to keep all the commodities that his opponents had seized in the interim.[296]

The first serious problem was solved. Ducci was no longer inundated with claims for damages, although he no longer had his profitable alum contract. This loss was permanent, as the governor refused to take any more risks at all. Since the ongoing lawsuits had seriously jeopardized deliveries to the Habsburg Netherlands, she asked Pallavicino to deliver all alum shipments in Antwerp to Gilles Sorbreucq, who would offer them for sale in the Scheldt town at 80 Flemish shillings per last. Little is known about this substantial merchant-financier, except that he was highly respected in commercial circles and had been of service to the government since the early 1540s. At any rate, the governor trusted him.[297] The price soon fell to the agreed rate of 80 shillings per last. After the unpleasant experience of Ducci's monopoly, Mary of Hungary decided that entrusting alum imports again to a private entrepreneur from the Low Countries was unwise. She renegotiated with

292 Mair (1917), 199-200; Häberlein (1996), 54.
293 AGR, PEA 1661/1, Letter dated 3 July 1550.
294 Pölnitz (1971), III/1, 622 n. 86.
295 AGR, PEA 1661/1, Letter dated 9 August 1550.
296 AGR, PEA 1661/1, Document dated 22 October 1550.
297 AGR, PEA 1414/4, nos 88 and 91; Ehrenberg (1896), I, 183, 216; Brulez (1959), 497; Coornaert (1961), I, 344.

the Grimaldis and signed a new contract with them. On 5 September 1551 the lessees of the Italian and Spanish mines agreed to supply a representative of the central government in Antwerp with 4666 2/3 last of Mazarrón alum and 3333 1/3 last of Tolfa alum (i.e. a total of 8000 last) *per annum* at 80 Flemish shillings per last for three years. From this amount, they had to pay 20 shillings to the Emperor, and they were not allowed to pass this levy on to the buyers. The arrangement left them with a net amount of 60 shillings which, considering the dominance of Spanish alum, was a reasonable average price. Another new provision was the contractual stipulation requiring suppliers to maintain a reserve of 2000 last, which could be sold only in case of extreme shortages but was exempt from the imperial levy. Finally, the Grimaldis promised not to sell alum anywhere in northwest Europe outside of Antwerp (except to France). The representative of the central government there would also make their shipments available in 'small' quantities, on the understanding that the minimum purchase would be £100 Fl.gr. In return, the Grimaldis obtained a monopoly on alum imports in the Habsburg Netherlands.[298] Mary of Hungary negotiated a contract that benefited the Emperor, who henceforth derived yet more income from alum imports. She also managed to enforce the principle of a price ceiling, guaranteeing that it would apply to cloth dyers and retailers as well.

But the worst was yet to come for Ducci. In 1550 and 1551 his problems grew apace. The judicial investigation into his financial speculations proceeded on at an agonizingly slow pace, and the attorney general was inclined to demand very heavy sentences indeed; there was even talk of the death penalty. In addition, Ducci faced a new lawsuit from Strozzi, who continued to accuse him of fraud and non-payment regarding the pastel and wine trade; and Strozzi's friends were on good terms with Charles V and Prince Philip. Simultaneously, the Guicciardini brothers launched a veritable slander campaign against Ducci in both commercial and political circles, even contacting Cosimo I de' Medici. In June 1551 Ducci wrote to the governor that since his 'setbacks' everyone had the temerity to disrespect him and to make wild accusations against him. Regarding Strozzi and the Guicciardinis, he noted that the suit that Strozzi had filed against him in Valladolid was damaging his reputation, which might adversely affect his proceedings at the Council of Brabant. He asked the governess to write to the court in Valladolid, requesting that they 'consider the proceedings favourably and issue a judgment quickly'. Whether Mary of Hungary took such action is unknown, but the proceedings conducted at the Council of Brabant as regards the financial manipulations by Ducci & Co. in any case did not discourage her from continuing to rely on 'her' banker thereby expressing support for him in public. On the Antwerp Exchange, however, Ducci could no longer operate with the same leverage. He was regarded with still greater suspicion than before, and in the meantime a new star had appeared: Gaspar Schetz, the eldest son of the now deceased Erasmus. In November Ducci was unable to arrange the funds requested by the central government in time.[299]

A few weeks later, on 24 December 1551, the definitive judgement came in the trial against Ducci. His partners Grimmel and Seiler had already been convicted on 31 July. All three had 'formed a monopoly to constrain and manipulate the Exchange of the city

298 AGR, PEA 1414/4, no. 80, and ROPB, 2nd ser., VI, 179-83.
299 AGR, PEA 1661/1, November 1551.

[of Antwerp], so that the prices of exchanges and loans would be whatever they wanted and desired; this conflicted with the general interest of our *landen van herwaertsover* [the Habsburg Netherlands], was disadvantageous and detrimental to fair trade, and violated our authority and our ordinances and edicts'. The Council of Brabant referred in particular to the imperial ordinance of 4 October 1540 against 'monopolies and improper contracts which many merchants and traders make and use in our land to the detriment of other good and righteous merchants and traders and against the common welfare.' They were fined all three: Ducci fl.20,000 and Grimmel and Seiler fl.60,000 fl.; they also had to share the court costs between them.[300] The judgement undoubtedly raised questions among contemporaries. The mastermind behind the Antwerp-Lyon speculations got off far more lightly than his accomplices; the court provided no justification for this distinction. While fl.20,000 would buy a prestigious residence in Antwerp, the amount is unlikely to have made inroads into the profits that Ducci had made. Considering the circumstances, he was clearly fortunate. Why did he get off so easily? Why did the true instigator of all the manipulations receive preferential treatment? Was the governess protecting the man with whom she had worked so fruitfully for so many years, and was she influencing the course of justice? Or did she intend to make clear to her brother that Ducci was less culpable than initially believed, and that she was therefore not seriously mistaken about 'her' banker? Or did other factors come into play?

Mary of Hungary may have pointed out to Charles V that a major player was going unpunished. Although Neidhart had very clearly engaged in the same speculations as Ducci, Grimmel, and Seiler, the Emperor did not have him prosecuted. The reason was not merely that Neidhart had provided him with huge loans in Spain (as Ducci had too, often together with Neidhart), but also because of his excellent relationship with King Ferdinand, Charles V's brother, whom he had served for many years, especially in finance, as Ferdinand publicly emphasized in 1551.[301] The prosecution of Grimmel and Seiler forced Neidhart to defend himself, because both the accused tried to gain acquittal at the expense of the other participants. Grimmel filed charges against Seiler in the Council of Brabant, accusing him of chicanery, while Seiler argued that he had not operated on his own behalf but as a factor for Neidhart, which Neidhart vehemently denied. Bartholomäus Welser valiantly defended his son-in-law. In 1553 he stated that Neidhart was beyond reproach, because the Lyon exchange operations were in compliance with normal trading practices, which was certainly open to dispute. In 1554 the Augsburg city court ruled that Seiler had indeed served as factor for Neidhart (who died that year), rendering the latter the true guilty party, upon which Neidhart's heirs filed charges with the *Reichskammergericht*.[302] The 'great scandal' did not, however, influence business strategies within the Neidhart family, except that the exchange operations of the firm became even more obscure. Nor was there any impact on Pecori, Ducci's previous front man, who now took up with the

300 'Zeker monopolie te committeren ende die bourse onser voirs. stadt zulcx te benauwen ende forceren dat die materie van ghelde ende finan. loop hebben moeste nae hueren wille ende appetite, tselve grootelick tenderende teghens die gemeyne welvaert van onsen lande van herweertsover, tot grooten achterdeele ende prejudicce van den rechtveerdigen treyn van der commenscap ende verachtinge van onser auctoriteyt, ordinantien ende edicten'. RAB, RB, AG 597, f° 100-102, 165v°-167. On the anti-monopoly ordinance of 1540, see Cowen (2007).

301 Pölnitz (1971), III/1, 177, 208, 230. See also Häberlein (1998b).

302 Bauer (1936), 178-80; Häberlein (1998a), 131-4.

heirs of Neidhart. The Lyon firm continued as Neidhart & Pecori and according to the financial records generated excellent profits for many more years.[303]

A very different course of events awaited Ducci. Even though he had been granted special treatment by the court in the case of the 'monopoly' of the Lyon firm, his conviction for financial manipulations marked the end of his supremacy in Antwerp and in international business circles. In 1553 he arranged a loan for the States of Brabant,[304] but that was his last major transaction on the Antwerp Exchange. Presumably, South-German merchant bankers preferred to keep their distance from him, as many had feared they might be dragged into the judicial prosecution of the Lyon company as well. Gaspar Schetz was moreover a highly intelligent and affluent replacement with an impeccable reputation and good contacts with Spain, which was becoming economically more important for Antwerp. Ducci had most probably lost the support of the Florentines, as from 1551 Cosimo I de' Medici no longer contacted *mercati di Anversa* to obtain loans but instead approached the Fuggers and bankers in Genoa (Centurione, Grimaldi, Spinola) and Milan (Minali).[305] In 1556 he appeared in the ledger of the Affaitadi firm for the last time. This was shortly after the death of Gian Carlo, the business partner who had often covered for him, and it was a final invoice.[306]

For years, Ducci had had an international network of merchant bankers that worked closely with him, and that network fell apart. The consequences were especially serious, since he could not call upon family members to help him. Large South-German and Italian firms had extensive commercial networks based largely on relations between brothers, fathers, sons, sons-in-laws, uncles, ... They operated as 'family consortia'. Such organizational formats had drawbacks but generally offered protection, when an individual member ran into trouble. Ducci could not rely on such a network. He had always stayed in contact with his brothers and uncles in Pescia, but they were not economically active. As an *Einzelgänger*, a loner, he faced all the associated risks from the moment that something went wrong. In high-level politics he had a powerful patroness, but this relationship of trust with Mary of Hungary was strained by the 'great scandal'. On 25 October 1555 – together with the abdication by Charles V – the governess ceded her authority over the Habsburg Netherlands. One year later she settled in Spain permanently.

Ducci therefore had all reason to conclude his turbulent career as a broker and banker. His decision was made easier by the attack on him in the early evening on Friday 23 November 1554. It happened right in front of his palace on Huidevettersstraat, where he and his servant were attacked from behind by two people. Although they were both injured, Ducci and his servant escaped. On Sunday rumours circulated that Lodovico Guicciardini, who in the meantime had disappeared from the city, was one of the perpetrators and had been injured during the attack. It was not surprising that he was a suspect, as he was the brother of Giovan Battista and Lorenzo, who had accused Ducci of cheating them. Giovan Battista had been spotted with Lodovico in Antwerp a few days before the attack. Lodovico had not yet started his career as a writer and was still a merchant. Like

303 Jeannin (2001), 61, 81-2.
304 Denucé (1934b), 35.
305 Parigino (1999), 64.
306 Denucé (1934b), 38.

his brothers, he had traded in Toulouse pastel, with equal lack of success. According to the Florentine merchant in whose home he had his office, his business had been poor in the past two years. The magistrate examined his *kassier*, cashier, and everybody who lived in the house but learned nothing to cast suspicion on Lodovico, nor did he find a trail of evidence relating to the attack. The case quietly ended there. A few years later Lodovico returned to Antwerp, where he wrote his famous *Description*.[307]

Did the attack put an end to the criticism of Ducci? That Guicciardini did not write about him extensively and mentioned the misconduct on the Antwerp Exchange only very generally is understandable. More remarkably, however, not a single chronicler, historian, moralist, or rhetorician in the Low Countries mentioned the great scandal of 1550/1, not even in a handwritten text for family members or other close contacts. The contrast with *literati* from Augsburg, such as Gasser and Mair, is striking. Did people in Antwerp and Brussels still fear Ducci's long arm? Although they knew that he was no longer 'invulnerable' in business the way he had been in the 1540s, the central government clearly continued to value his expertise in financial matters. When the Italian merchant Giovanni Battista Ferrufini proposed that all businessmen involved in marine insurance in Antwerp have their policies drafted and registered by a public broker – i.e. Ferrufini – he encountered opposition, and the Council of Finance formed a commission of four businessmen in the summer of 1558 tasked with formulating carefully considered advice: Gaspar Schetz and Gaspar Ducci as experts, Lazarus Tucher as the representative of the South-German merchants, and Antonio Palos, consul to the Portuguese 'nation'.[308]

This invitation from 'Brussels' to serve on a small, select commission undoubtedly flattered Ducci, but it did not encourage him to pick up where he had left off. He had the good sense to understand that he could never reclaim the position he had had on the Antwerp Exchange in the 1540s. Money was not an incentive, as his fortune enabled him to retire from business. Some authors have inferred from the sale of the Hoboken seigniory in 1559 that he desperately needed money, but in fact he was not in a position to refuse, as fifteen years earlier he had agreed to the right of repurchase, and this right was exercised in 1559. Henceforth, Balthasar Schetz was entitled to be Lord of Hoboken in exchange for fl.20,000.[309] Not even an approximate estimate of Ducci's fortune is possible. We know only that both in Antwerp and outside the city (especially in Schoonsel and Kruibeke), he owned valuable properties, which yielded significant annual returns. He took action to increase the value of these properties, as shown by the large water mill he had built in Kruibeke in 1555. His many lawsuits throughout the 1560s against those who in his view infringed on his seignorial rights attest to the same involvement.[310]

His only son, Lorenzo, died in Brussels on 24 March 1559. He was 21 years old.[311] Whether Elisabeth Stegemans was still alive remains unclear. But the death of his cherished only son

---

307 Prims (1931); Roobaert (1958), 80-1.

308 De Groote (1975), 66, 73, 79; De Ruysscher and Puttevils (2015), 37, 44. On Palos, see Goris (1925).

309 Dierickx (1954), 33; d'Ursel (2004), 108.

310 See esp. SAA, T 927, and AGR, GRM 857, no. 120, GRM 862, no. 59, GRM 864, no. 56, GRM 866, no. 11, GRM 867, no. 133, GRM 868, nos 95-96, GRM 871, nos 81 and 107, and GRM 873, no. 3.

311 In the modest Church of Kruibeke, Ducci built an impressive monument for him; it was demolished in 1592, and replaced by a tombstone in the wall of the choir. Vander Maelen (1834), 39; De Groodt (1933), 46. See the photo in De Cock (1979), 15.

probably led Ducci to spend his time afterwards literally as Lord of Kruibeke, away from the hustle and bustle of Antwerp. He leased his palatial residence on Huidevettersstraat to the city of Antwerp, which used it as banquetting halls for prestigious wedding celebrations and as deluxe accommodation for distinguished guests.[312] He purchased properties in the vicinity of Florence, which in his final will and testament he bequeathed to the two sons of his brother Ludovico. Since he no longer had direct heirs, he focused increasingly on his ties with his family in Pescia. In 1571 he determined that the properties he had by then acquired in Val di Nievole, in the southwest of the province of Pistoia, would also go to the sons of Ludovico after his death, and that his other brother, Antonio, would inherit the Kruibeke seigniory. Upon his death in 1577 – at age 82 – he still owned his city palace, which his heirs sold two years later to the wealthy Antwerp merchant Jacob della Faille, as well as Schoonsel, which his brother Lorenzo inherited and sold soon afterwards at a public auction.[313]

After a long, tumultuous, and largely successful business career, Ducci retired and lived in relative obscurity for about twenty years, as Lord of Kruibeke, a village along the Scheldt – a stone's throw away from the city. Did he still have sources of information, and was he interested in news about the economy in 1559? If he was, he would have noted that the highest political authorities had once again opted for an alum monopoly. Philip II had signed a contract with the Genoese Negrone di Negro to supply 4,000 *last* of Spanish alum at a fixed price in Antwerp for nine years. Negrone di Negro was in fact operating on instructions from Gaspar Schetz, who as the King's factor on the Antwerp Exchange had promised to stop trading… A structure that was obscure to the outside world was set up, in which the Genoese brokers Alberto Pinello and Giovanni Battista Spinola acted as front men for the Schetz brothers, in exchange for shares. At the same time, Negrone di Negro and a few other unspecified partners entered an extended contract with the Italian alum lessees and put Spinola in charge of the shipments to Antwerp. A cartel was formed, in which Gaspar Schetz was pivotal.[314] Ducci had gained a highly competent successor.

---

312 While he sold some of his properties in the city, this does not suggest that he needed the money, as he allowed his loyal servant Antonio Rustici and his wife Marie Van Duyn to continue staying free of charge in the large house next to his city palace and gifted them this residence in 1564, on condition that they would continue to serve him. Denucé (1934b), 40-1; Goldstein (2013a).

313 Brulez (1959), 191, 198-9; Stumpo (1992). Pauwel van Gemert, who owned annuities based on Schoonsel via his marriage, sued Gaspar Ducci, accusing him of defaulting on payment. In 1578 Lorenzo erred on the side of caution and auctioned off Schoonsel. Van Passen (1982), 736.

314 Delumeau (1962), 221; Soly (1974), 827-35; Ruiz Martín (2005), Ch. 4.

Plate 3. Portrait of Gilbert van Schoonbeke by the Master of the 1540s. Antwerp, Museum Maagdenhuis

PART 3

Gilbert van Schoonbeke, 1519-1556

3.1 How to Dominate the Real Estate Market

Little research has been conducted on real estate development projects in pre-industrial European cities. Presumably, in urban centres where private property predominated and real-estate projects were not subject to tight regulations the combination of demographic and commercial growth was conducive to land speculation and speculative residential building.[1] The course taken by such operations, however, the people who initiated them, and what effects these activities had on the physical form and social topography of towns remains unclear. Even with economic centres with very dynamic growth, such as Lyon and Seville in the sixteenth century, or Amsterdam and London in the seventeenth century, the impact of private real-estate development on the urban environment is impossible to determine at this time.[2] Who were the real-estate speculators and project developers, what were their objectives, what leeway did they have, how did they interact with public authorities, how did they finance their projects? All these questions have yet to be answered. In tracing changes in the built environment of early modern economic centres, little more can be done than compare city views from different periods. This is what the French historian and urbanist Pierre Lavedan did for sixteenth-century Antwerp in his reference work on the history of early modern European urbanism in 1941. He lacked sufficient data to elaborate on the achievements of Van Schoonbeke but on the basis of cartographic data described him as an exceptional project developer, as 'one of the most remarkable figures from the sixteenth century'.[3] My archival research confirms his opinion and moreover makes clear how Gilbert van Schoonbeke operated. First, however, I will indicate what opportunities the urban real estate market in Antwerp offered.

In late medieval and early modern European cities real-estate transactions were extremely important in the economy and in finance, as well as in social life. Property rights and relations varied greatly,[4] but in all cities privately owned land and buildings consistently represented far more capital than movable goods. This also held true for commercial centres. The Hundredth Penny levied in 1569 on orders from the Duke of Alba on the value of private property in cities and villages in the Duchy of Brabant confirms this. In

---

1 With the exception of small city states such as Genoa and Venice, where land was scarce and patrician property was dominant. On speculative building, see the general remarks of Baer (2007). Real-estate development projects in sixteenth- and seventeenth-century Paris were subject to powerful constraints: Chartier (1994).

2 On building contractors in London and Amsterdam, see Baer (2012) and Abrahamse et al. (2015). Studies on project developers are wanting.

3 Lavedan (1941), 158-60 (on p. 159).

4 See *inter alia* Keene (1989); Jehel (1994); Harding (2002); Chauvard (2005); Vigneron (2007); Van Bochove, Deneweth & Zuiderduijn (2013).

Antwerp the tax on private wealth yielded fl.160,497, of which fl.122,720 or 75.5 percent was paid for houses and land. Cash, jewels, valuables, and merchandise were undoubtedly undervalued, as nobody could be taxed above fl.1,000 for movable items. Still, investments were mainly in buildings and land. In Antwerp they accounted for an even greater share of private wealth than in Bruges, where they represented a 'mere' 67.5 percent of the total.[5]

The combination of demographic and economic growth, linked to concentration of capital, provided a boost to the Antwerp real estate market. Between 1526 and 1568 the housing stock grew from 8720 to 13,173, i.e. an increase of 4453 units or 106 *per annum* on average.[6] Unfortunately, no figures are available for the interim years, but the abortive siege of the city by Maarten van Rossum in July 1542 is known to have been followed by intense construction activities. In August of that same year Charles V ordered the medieval city walls to be demolished and replaced by a new type of defensive fortifications. Since this construction project was exceptionally expensive and would impede expansion of the city in the future, the local authorities decided to incorporate land located to the north, adding an area of 23 to 25 hectares. This urban expansion – the last of this magnitude before the nineteenth century[7] – was also deemed necessary, because a safety perimeter was introduced.[8] The northern expansion, known as the New Town, did not immediately solve the severe shortage of space, however, as it included marshland that still needed to be reclaimed (see below).

In this period of accelerated economic growth, merchants, transport firms, and industrial entrepreneurs sought good locations for their business operations, and the relentlessly rising value of land and buildings *intra muros* made such investments still more appealing. As the value of a plot of land or a building increased, new *erfrenten* or *erfelijke renten* (hereditary rent-charges) were sold on the property. In such cases the owner (the borrower) sold the buyer (the lender) the right to a periodic – ordinarily annual or semi-annual – remuneration (in effect an annuity) in exchange for a principal sum. Although this financial instrument had all the earmarks of a secured debt, it was conceptualized as a sale (of money) in return for a perpetual rent, secured by the asset owned by the seller (the debtor). Throughout most of the sixteenth century the interest on rent-charges in Antwerp was 6.25 percent ('penny 16'), a modest return, compared with what could be made on the stock exchange, but the risks were minimal and in times of economic growth virtually non-existent.

Sales of rent-charges were a well-established practice, as in 1520 Charles V had proclaimed an ordinance stipulating that in the Duchy of Brabant owners of an *erfrente*

5 Stabel and Vermeylen (1997), 25, 31, 39, 90-2, 186-8. I have not included annuities charged against the City of Antwerp and the States of Brabant, because rental income from privately-owned buildings was not taxed and accounted for the vast majority of all annuities.

6 Soly (1977), 52-3. In the late eighteenth century nearly all houses in Antwerp contained a basement and an attic, but 22 percent had no additional level, and 32 percent consisted of only two rooms on the lower and two on the upper level: De Belder (1977), 376-81.

7 In 1567/8 the city was extended to the south by the Citadel, built on orders from the Duke of Alba.

8 The Emperor ordered that all buildings be demolished within a radius of 2500 feet or 717 meters of the city walls and moreover prohibited building houses or planting trees within an additional radius of 1000 feet or 287 meters. AGR, PEA 1629/3, *Memorie*; SAA, PK 78, f° 176v°-177; ROPB, 2nd ser., IV, 400-401. In 1556 the local athorities stated that about 1500 houses had been demolished *extra muros* in 1542: AGR, PEA 1414/1, 3.

(which was in principle perpetual) were henceforth legally entitled to redeem the annuity, if they wished.[9] The *erfrente* contract was not to be regarded as a loan, as buyers of a perpetual annuity could never demand repayment of the principal sum, as long as the seller continued to pay the annuity as required. Anyone who wished to reclaim part or all of the principal had to find a third party willing to buy the annuity or part of it. This rule did not present a problem in a period of economic growth, as rent-charges were fully negotiable. All redeemable rents secured by real estate were considered to be immovable: they had to stay attached to the land or house involved as a form of security for the creditor. The Antwerp mortgage market was based on two other foundations. All transfers of land or houses located in the city and the *Vrijheid* (Liberty) of the City,[10] as well as all rent-charges associated with such properties had to be recorded in the *schepenregisters* (registers of the aldermen).[11] This made it easy to identify who owned a property, and with which mortgages it was encumbered. Equally importantly, mortgage legislation, though flexible, was rigidly enforced with borrowers who defaulted on their payments.[12]

Quantitative review of all property transactions in the City of Antwerp in 1545 – including the rent-charges – demonstrates that such investments were in great demand at the time: their combined capital value was at least fl. 870,000, of which the various types of houses accounted for nearly 64 percent, annuities 34.2 percent, and vacant plots of land 1.8 percent. The capital value of the houses and land, i.e. fl. 572,501, is comparable to the known proceeds of the *pondgeld* from later years. This *pondgeld* tax was introduced in 1547 for each transaction in which a house, building, or tract of land changed hands, whether through sale, donation, or inheritance. Both the former owner and the new owner paid 5 percent of the capital value. Nobody was exempt, not even members of the clergy. The comparison is somewhat distorted, because *pondgeld* concerned the city *and* the *Vrijheid* of Antwerp, whereas the value calculated for 1545 reflects only properties *intra muros*. Checking the records for 1555, however, reveals that the difference was minimal.[13]

The figures confirm what may be inferred from other sources: until the early 1550s Antwerp thrived economically, as manifested by a very dynamic real-estate market; afterwards serious problems arose from a combination of wars, financial crises, commercial shifts, epidemics, and declining standards of living.[14] Contemporaries observed the disastrous consequences of the Habsburg-Valois War that broke out in September 1551 and except for the fleeting truce of Vaucelles was waged continuously until the Peace of Cateau-Cambrésis (2-3 April 1559). In December 1556 a high-ranking government official stated that the economic recovery in Antwerp would become possible only 'once a good

9 ROPB, 2nd ser., II, 36-9. On the complex history of *erfrente* contracts, see Munro (2008), 981-9, and Howell (2014), 553-8.

10 In the mid-sixteenth century the *Vrijheid* (Liberty) of Antwerp covered about 1,800 hectares, including the area *intra muros* (*c.* 225 hectares). Outside the city walls the *Vrijheid* extended from Dambrugge in the north to Hoboken in the south: De Nave (1978), 59-64.

11 In the 1490s and 1500s some notaries had executed deeds to this effect as well, but in 1515 the city council had strictly prohibited such practices De Longé (1870), I, 194, 198, 200; Oosterbosch (1995), 89.

12 De Ruysscher (2015). See also Van Bochove, Deneweth & Zuiderduijn (2013), 27.

13 Based on the *pondgeld* the amount would have been fl. 249,056, while the capital value of the transactions of land and buildings *intra muros* was approximately fl. 246,152

14 Van der Wee (1963), I, 213-28. Also Soly (1977), 103-7. On the declining standard of living, see Scholliers (1960), 133-5.

Table 6. Capital Value of Land and Buildings Transactions in Antwerp, 1545-60

Year	Capital value in florins	Based on
1545	572,501	Estimate
1550	588,576	*Pondgeld*
1551	690,848	*Pondgeld*
1555a	249,056	*Pondgeld*
1555b	246,152	Estimate
1559	445,056	*Pondgeld*
1560	522,681	*Pondgeld*

Sources: Soly (1977), 94 and 102; Masure (1986), 216.

and enduring peace [is] reached'.[15] The new heyday on the Antwerp real-estate market in 1559 and 1560 proved him right: the end of the war caused trade and industry to flourish, which promptly led demand for houses to soar.

A thriving real-estate market that attracted both businessmen and those of independent means, both speculators and investors, those with modest savings and the wealthy: the context was ideally suited to Gilbert van Schoonbeke. He was a local man. Nearly all his projects were situated in Antwerp, where he operated as a property speculator, project developer, and industrial entrepreneur When he died in 1556 at the age of 37, he had significantly changed the Antwerp cityscape, successfully completed the new city walls (the greatest construction site in Antwerp until the nineteenth century), brought about the first real port quarter in the metropolis, and set up the biggest industrial undertaking that ever came into being in the sixteenth-century Low Countries. His innovative projects enabled him to make a fortune, evoked admiration among the highest public authorities in the Habsburg Netherlands, and also made him many enemies in a wide variety of population groups: among the local elite, the social middle groups, and skilled building workers.

His economic success – or more accurately chain of successes – was attributable to a combination of different factors, as I will demonstrate, but would have been inconceivable without a thorough knowledge of the urban infrastructure and the local institutions and political relations. No foreign businessman could have carried out similar projects. Gilbert van Schoonbeke benefited from his lineage. He was an illegitimate child, born in 1519, but his father, whose name was also Gilbert, supported his request 'to declare him legitimate and pardon the insufficiency of his birth', which the Emperor granted in June 1540.[16] His father moreover ensured that Van Schoonbeke Jr. succeeded him that same year as receiver of the income from the Great Weighing House and the smaller Iron, Butter, and Cheese Weighing House,[17] where goods weighing more than fifty pounds (*c.* 23.5 kgs)

15 SAA, R 1787.

16 'Te legittimerene ende opt gebreck van zijne voirs. geboerte gracie [te] verleenen'. AGR, CC 641, f° 73v°, and CC 20788, f°34. Van Schoonbeke Sr. ('Gilbert de Beaurieu') was most probably from the princebishopric of Liège, and had registered as a citizen of Antwerp in 1507.

17 SAA, T 818, no. 19, and T 1017, no. 52.

had to be weighed each time they changed ownership. The position was both interesting and lucrative in a city where ever more products were appearing on the market, to be consumed locally as well as for the purposes of export and re-export. Weighing house masters obviously interacted with a great many merchants and their factors, which was conducive to networking. Last but not least: in addition to engaging in profitable trade, Van Schoonbeke Sr. made a great amount of money through land speculation, and his widow Anna Stegemans, sister of Elisabeth, the wife of Gaspar Ducci, had her stepson wind up a real-estate project her late husband had started. She sold him properties that represented a capital of fl. 16,168, for which he was expected to pay fl. 4,800 immediately, i.e. over one hundred times the annual wages of a skilled worker. Anna Stegemans, however, gave him four years to pay, without charging any interest. This arrangement reflected her faith in the business acumen and strategic competence of her stepson, whom she also needed to ensure discretion. Her husband had reached agreements with two high-ranking civil servants, first city receiver Michiel van der Heyden and city secretary Willem van der Ryt, who at this point teamed up with Van Schoonbeke Jr. to sell the plots and houses on Koningstraat 'for a shared profit, damages and loss.' Van Schoonbeke and Van der Heyden each took up five twelfths and Van der Ryt two twelfths. The interest-free loan from his stepmother placed Van Schoonbeke at her mercy, thereby ensuring his discretion. And discretion was indispensable, as the city officials involved remained in the background: their names were not to appear in any official documents. Van Schoonbeke Jr. had to enter all transactions in his own name; only after everything was sold, would he square up with his partners, doing so in secret.[18] They must have convinced him that they would always arrange decisions by the municipal administration for his benefit, when he wanted to undertake new projects – just as they are very likely to have done for his father.

The three partners realized earnings of at least fl. 2722 or 17 percent of the capital value of the plots and houses, at the time of their original purchase.[19] This return might seem modest, as the sales occurred over a three-year period. But since Anna Stegemans had agreed to wait four years for payment, the partners did not need to invest any of their own money, until they had to repay Stegemans in 1546.[20] Van Schoonbeke used the money he made to finance other projects. In June 1543, together with the 25 year-old wealthy lawyer Hubrecht de But, originally from Brussels but a citizen of Antwerp for the previous two years, he purchased a site comprising an orchard and a large garden, situated south of the alms house of the Carmelites on Huidevettersstraat. A few days later they signed a contract with the Carmelites, who agreed to pay them fl. 800, to have a street run through the land they had just acquired. That same month, Van Schoonbeke convinced the city to build and pave the new street; the partners had to cede a small piece of land, for which they received fl. 200.[21] The good relations with first city receiver Michiel van der Heyden were already bearing fruit. In July the new street, Vaartstraat (now Jodenstraat), was opened by the city council, according to plans drafted by Van Schoonbeke. The street extended from Huidevettersstraat in the west to the Wapper in the east, at a section of the Herentalse Vaart

18 RAB, RB, OF, Reg. 8, Document dated 9 February 1554, and SAA, T 1319/3, nos 34-35.
19 See the calculations in Soly (1977), 150-2.
20 SAA, SR 220, f° 151.
21 SAA, SR 209, f° 281, 298-300, 304v°, SR 212, f° 98, N 2071 (3 July 1543), and R 12, f° 90.

(canal), where plots and houses belonging to Michiel van der Heyden were situated – little wonder that the city council supported the project! The partners parcelled out the land in July and sold all the plots and buildings within fifteen months. On the sale of the plots alone they earned nearly fl. 1864 or 30 percent on the capital they had invested.[22]

By this time, the talented property developer had married. In January 1544 he came of age, and a few months later he married Elisabeth Hendrickx, age 17 and the only child of a deceased master tailor, who had left his daughter some valuable houses. The newlyweds both had their portraits painted by the so-called Master of the 1540s, who specialized in portraits of men and women from social middle groups.[23] Wives of businessmen were very rarely portrayed individually in the first half of the sixteenth century, while Van Schoonbeke had portraits of his wife painted not only at the time of the marriage but later on as well.[24] Could this have been a token of affection or love?[25] Elisabeth Hendrickx gave birth to five daughters and a son: Susanna in 1547, when she was 20, Gilbert in 1549, Sara in 1551, Maria in 1553, Leonora in 1555, and Elisabeth in 1556.[26]

In 1545/6, Van Schoonbeke had sufficient capital and experience to operate as an independent project developer. Direct contacts with established families whose members served on the city council provided wonderful opportunities. Patrician families were drawn to the real-estate market. Large-scale estates, both within and outside the city, constituted the bulk of their patrimony. They understood that fortunes were being made in wholesale and finance but could not participate in these or at least only indirectly, because they lacked access to the networks of firms specialized in the highly lucrative commodities trade. They must have been aware that nearly all major operators in commerce and finance were foreigners, and that very few of those who hailed from the Low Countries reached the top of the business world. Until the middle of the century international trade was dominated by foreign merchants, most of whom did not intend to settle permanently in the metropolis. This must have complicated their integration among the local elite, as in such circumstances establishing lasting relations with newcomers was risky for patrician families. Real-estate operations were attractive, because using their patrimony, their political decision-making power, or a combination of the two, easily enabled them to make high profits. Members of established families who served on the city council were well positioned: they had the power to influence decisions regarding the sale of city property, expropriations for public use, opening new streets, paving roads, widening or covering waterways, building bridges, and the like. They had to proceed cautiously, however, as such projects were universally visible and could easily give rise to awkward questions.

High-ranking city officials could benefi from outsourcing public works projects to specific entrepreneurs. They could also leverage their decision-making authority on urbanization and public works in other ways to profit from real-estate speculations. Property developers in Antwerp faced few restrictions in terms of urban planning regulations but

22 See the calculations in Soly (1977), 154-5.

23 Friedländer (1936), 84-6, 162.

24 Frans Floris de Vriendt, *Portrait of Elisabeth Hendrickx*, Museum Maagdenhuis Antwerp.

25 Although Elisabeth Hendrickx survived her husband by more than thirty years – she died in 1587 – she never remarried.

26 SAA, IB 3005, f° 202, IB 2174, no. 11/3, IB 3016, no. 41, and CERT 32, f° 47.

did need permission from the city council to open up a new street.[27] This was not merely a formality. It remains unclear whether specific criteria existed, and, if so, what they were, but fragmentary data suggest that approval depended mainly on the social status of the property owner. Another important question for a land speculator was who would pay for the infrastructure. Paving represented a huge expense, which the city did not automatically cover; this was all the more true for bridges and other infrastructure works. Where individuals were to cover such costs, their profit margin would decline accordingly.

By the very nature of the undertaking it is difficult to identify those of the local authorities involved in massive real-estate operations who operated through a front man, teamed up in secret with a private entrepreneur, and/or accepted bribes, and when and how they did so. Sometimes witness statements were recorded by higher authorities. Michiel van der Heyden, who served year after year from 1535 until his death in 1549 in high public offices, seems to have set the record. In 1549-50, when the central government launched a massive investigation into corruption in Antwerp, it became known that Van der Heyden had appropriated properties owned by the city for a pittance or even free of charge. Projects that exclusively benefited his real-estate speculation ventures had been funded by the city. On several loans obtained by the city Van der Heyden had added a half percent to the interest rate for his own benefit. He was not the only one who had appropriated funds from the *Fortificatiekas* (Fortification Fund) earmarked for the construction of the walls, but he had been the greediest of all. He could not have operated without the knowledge of his brother-in-law Lancelot van Ursel, however, who had also unlawfully appropriated large sums from the *Fortificatiekas*. According to the attorney general of Brabant, in the period 1542-47, Van der Heyden and Van Ursel together had embezzled no less than fl. 57,546, i.e. 900 times the annual wage of a skilled worker.[28]

How had this been possible? Had not a single member of the city council or the Broad Council ever grown suspicious?[29] Well-informed witnesses stated that for many years a few members of the city government had been taking all major decisions regarding the sale of city property, public works and financial matters.[30] In Antwerp following the unsuccessful revolt of 1477, guild deans were in any case prohibited from holding office as burgomaster or alderman. They could address the Broad Council and had a say in decisions on proposals from the executive with financial implications, but that was precisely what Van der Heyden and his political cronies had been trying to prevent for years by disclosing as little as possible about the sale of city property and the construction of the city walls, 'leaving the citizens and inhabitants deeply scandalized and causing gossip to reverberate'. Whoever had the courage to raise questions on the Broad Council, however,

---

27 Tys (1993), 62-3, 75.

28 RAB, RB, Reg. 603, no. 51. For more detail, see Soly (forthcoming).

29 In this period, the city government was in the hands of two burgomasters and sixteen aldermen (*schepenen*). The first burgomaster or outer burgomaster handled Antwerp's relations with the outside world; he headed the city's delegations in the States of Brabant. The Broad Council – considered to represent the *corpus* or body of the city – consisted of four branches: the executive, the former aldermen, the *poorterij* (the headmen and wardmasters as representatives of the wealthy citizenry), and the deans of the privileged guilds. See Wells (1982), 80-1, and Marnef (1996), 14, 17-18 (with references to the literature).

30 SAA, T 1317, f° 4, 11v°-15, 18, 19, 21.

had encountered opposition from Van der Heyden in other matters, quickly leading most members to stop their inquiries.[31]

The corruption of prominent members of the magistracy gave Van Schoonbeke opportunities for incremental earnings. Yet, he was not simply a speculator who advanced thanks to devious practices. His enduring and growing success on the Antwerp real-estate market resulted mainly from his keen insight into how best to handle real-estate projects. He differed in several ways from other land speculators, rarely selling existing buildings and constructing few new houses. Instead, he purchased vast vacant sites, ran streets through them, parcelled out the remaining land and sold the plots individually. He was essentially a project developer, not a builder or speculator in houses. Van Schoonbeke understood that success depended on speed. That is clear from the rapid succession and usually even simultaneity of his real-estate operations. Still more importantly, he quickly understood that spatial quality would result in financial benefit. In the burgeoning trade metropolis, this initially meant bringing about new economic infrastructure. Good relations with powerful members of the city council and (other) patrician families enabled him to acquire vast vacant sites situated within the city which thanks to their strategic location were suitable for setting up commercial centres and in many cases bordered on elegant neighbourhoods as well. This made an optimal combination of economic and residential functions possible, soon encouraging prospective buyers from different segments of the social middle groups with different objectives to express an interest. Such a project required a well-considered plan, taking into account the accessibility of the new city district, especially for carts loaded with merchandise, the alignment and width of the connecting roads to be opened, connections to existing residential streets, and the like. The success of any project, however, depended largely on whether the new commercial zone met the needs and expectations of the potential buyers so well that it was quickly regarded as ideal for carrying out the activities planned over the long term. This held true for the two major projects that Van Schoonbeke realized in 1547-48: the Stadswaag and the Friday Market.

As weighing-house master, Van Schoonbeke noted that there was so much incoming merchandise that many merchants had to leave their goods outside the building for two or three days, before they could be weighed, which led to incessant protests and according to Van Schoonbeke increased the already widespread fraud.[32] In early March 1547 he proposed a radical solution: a new weighing house. Where should it be built? No other site was 'so favourable, useful, and suitable' as that of the former city warehouse *Houten Eeckhof*, south of the wide Paardenmarkt (Horse Market).[33] Coincidentally, on 4 March the city council had sold this building to a front man operating for Van Schoonbeke, together with another large warehouse, known as the *Artilleriehuys*, where artillery was stored, as well as some small houses and land with an area of 8587 square metres, for a total sum of fl. 26,333. The project developer had to agree to cover the cost of building the new weighing house at his own expense and to transfer it to the City. In return, the city

---

31 SAA, T 1317, *inter alia* f° 15, 18, 48v° ('waerdeure oyck de burghers ende ingesetenen zeere geschandalizeert zijn ende vele daerop gesproken hebben'), and T 1319/1, no. 4, *inter alia* f° 19, 21v°, 44.

32 SAA, IB 2979, no. 35, T 1017, no. 36. Fraud prevention had already created fierce conflicts with substantial merchants, including his uncle Gaspar Ducci, who had made an attempt on his life. See Chapter 2.6.

33 SAA, IB 2979, no. 32.

council agreed to pay for building materials, to sell the old weighing house, and to give the proceeds to Van Schoonbeke, together with a strategically situated site on Varkensmarkt (Pig Market), close to Paardenmarkt.[34] The deal was very advantageous for the project developer – so advantageous that the accusations of bribery made in 1549 must have had some foundation.[35]

The contract for building the new weighing house was ratified on 7 May 1547 by Charles V, in exchange for an annuity of fl. 200 at 'penny 25' or 4 percent. The building was to be constructed in the middle of a square measuring 57.4 by 40.1 metres, and the square was to be accessed via two new thoroughfares that were 9.2 metres wide, one oriented north-south and the other east-west. The actual weighing house was to measure 28.7 metres by 11.5 metres and would have two large gates and eight doors, as well as a full basement and three stories and an attic.[36] In September Van Schoonbeke proposed some improvements: along the north and south façades of the new weighing house would be a porch 3.15 metres wide with five skylights to enable the packing and unpacking of the merchandise in dry surroundings in rain or snow. In the building a 'suspended room' of 5.7 by 3.0 metres with a chimney and a toilet would be installed, 'providing weighers and other workers with a comfortable shelter in winter.' The two large attics would have floors suitable of storing 1400 to 1500 *viertelen* (*c.* 100,000 hectolitres) of grain. The cellars would also have a proper floor, making them suitable for use as storage areas.[37] As compensation, the city council let the attics and cellars to Van Schoonbeke for twelve years at fl. 300 *per annum* and henceforth paid the fl. 200 annuity that Van Schoonbeke had given the Emperor. All these provisions were rigidly adhered to by the parties concerned. Following their inspection on 7 March 1548, the government commissioners stated that Van Schoonbeke had completed a building of which 'the brickwork was even finer than that envisaged in the plan'. Five days later the first merchandise was weighed in the new weighing house.[38]

The city plan of Virgilius Bononiensis from 1565 gives an impression of the exterior of the new weighing house: a building with three stories and an attic, constructed in a traditional style, i.e. brick walls with alternating stone bands in natural stone and step gables on the east and west sides and as the most striking feature the two-branched scales protruding from the wall along the south side.[39] Visual reconstruction of the premises based on descriptions and ground plans from later dates reveals four or five movable two-armed scales along both the north and the south sides. They could be guided along an iron rail attached to the ceiling. As merchants waited outside, the weigh-house master inside would place the official weights on the other scale outside. This allowed faster processing of large quantities of merchandise. A dedicated weighing house of this size with so many movable scales did not exist anywhere else in Europe.[40] The available documents do not reveal who

34 SAA, R 1783, no. 6, R 1787, no. 11, IB 2979, nos 31, 34, 35; T 1705, no. 287.
35 SAA, T 1317, f° 5v°, 43, 45v°, and T 1319/1, no. 4, f° 28-9.
36 AGR, CC 139, f° 78v°-80; SAA, T 1705, nos 287 and 290.
37 SAA, IB 2979, nos 45 and 47.
38 *Ibidem*, nos 49-50; SBA, B11285, f° 39v°.
39 Antwerp, Museum Plantin-Moretus. See Voet et al. (1978).
40 Kiem (2009), 81-5. See also Ottenheym & De Jonge (2007), 240, and De Vylder (2011), 81.

advised Van Schoonbeke and drew the plans, but he may have retained the services of one of the Italian engineers involved in constructing the city walls in this period.

The new weighing house had been situated at its location following careful consideration. Erecting the building in the middle of the square left a surrounding open area of nearly 14.5 metres for carts loaded with merchandise to circulate as efficiently as possible. The actual square, which was named Stadswaag (meaning Urban Weighing House), could be reached on three sides via new, straight, and wide streets, whose paving was paid for by the city. Van Schoonbeke pursued two aims: first and foremost an optimal connection to existing traffic arteries, while at the same time aligning with residential neighbourhoods. The interests of merchants and carters prevailed, but potential buyers' desire for social prestige was taken into account as well, because the new zone bordered on streets where members of the political elite resided, including the elegant Prinsstraat, site of the prestigious Hof van Liere, which some years later became the headquarters of the Merchant Adventurers.[41]

The Friday Market was designed according to a similar scenario, except that in this case the land belonged to an established family. On 19 November 1547 Van Schoonbeke paid *Ridder* Cornelis van Spangen, who was burgomaster at the time, fl. 16,000 for the gigantic Hof van Spangen. He was clearly to a plan, as he also purchased (parts of) houses in the same neighbourhood, so that he owned a continuous complex of land and buildings, situated in the middle of the city, close to the Scheldt and the important Hoogstraat, where the Cloth Hall was situated, and where many Spanish merchants were based as well.[42] His plan was to set up a permanent marketplace for old clothes dealers (*oudkleerkopers*), and the idea was sound. These merchants, who were organized in a guild, in addition to trading second-hand goods, as their name suggests, were also the only ones authorized to organize auctions of estates (in which they often operated as valuers) and to sell their goods in public at what was known as a 'Friday market'. In addition, they auctioned off to the highest bidder all properties sold by individuals or as instructed by the *amman*.[43] Most of these old clothes dealers were therefore wealthy businessmen. Participating in public sales of properties, Van Schoonbeke noticed that they had a serious problem finding spaces to set up booths. They needed a large, centrally situated open area to carry on their trade optimally, but in Antwerp very few true marketplaces were available.[44]

After purchasing Hof van Spangen and the adjacent buildings, Van Schoonbeke negotiated with the old clothes dealers. They soon reached an agreement, which was approved by the city council on 23 July 1548.[45] Van Schoonbeke benefited once again from his close ties with the city authorities. The contract he signed with the local authority stipulated that the Friday Market and the adjacent streets would be paved at the city's expense within twelve months, and that the city would also cover the cost of building two stone bridges across the moat connecting the Friday Market with the street along Steenhouwersvest; these bridges would be sufficiently wide for two carts to ride across them at the same time without blocking one another. Each bridge cost the city about fl. 2000. Had I known that,

41 Nowadays Hof van Liere houses the City Campus of the University of Antwerp.
42 AGR, CC 29789, f° 6; SAA, SR 225, f° 240-247, SR 229, f° 156, COLL 9, f° 23, 26, T 1705, no. 334.
43 Geudens (1905).
44 SAA, PK 914, f° 100v°-101, 113v°, 114v°, and PK 915, f° 58, 80v°-82.
45 SAA, GA 4276, f° 15v°-19; IB 2979, nos 2, 8, 13; Geudens (1905), 25-7.

stated Cornelis van Spangen in 1549, I would never have sold my property at such a low price. In the end, the local government allowed the buyers of the plots to put up a *loove*, i.e. an overhead shelter that was six feet wide (1.72 metres), instead of the regulation four feet (1.15 metres), and to construct a basement under their houses extending halfway into the street, giving them more display room and storage space, which of course made the plots easier to sell.[46]

Van Schoonbeke never sought to maximize his returns. In 1548 he claimed that most land speculators committed the unforgivable error of trying to sell their plots at the highest price of the moment. If the area of land available was limited, such a strategy might work in a period of economic growth. Where vast vacant sites were available, however, it was rarely or never feasible in the short term: even in years of economic prosperity, little capital was invested in massive construction projects. Speculators therefore rarely managed to sell their land quickly. Van Schoonbeke noted that 'convincing people to lay bricks and do carpentry requires great subtlety, as earnings are modest in this trade, and there is a substantial risk of encountering problems and wasting time and money'. Project developers always had to keep in mind that large and medium-sized plots were impossible to sell quickly, unless the buyers were given the opportunity to profit as well. The most interesting buyers operated as intermediaries: rather than purchasing a plot for their own use, they intended to build houses there to sell or let. If the land was priced too high in relation to the expected return, few speculators would undertake such a venture. Asking less and selling all plots quickly was therefore wiser than holding out for the maximum price and spending many years parcelling them out. This method also offered the invaluable advantage of always having cash available to finance new projects.[47]

He parcelled out the land adjacent to both the Stadswaag and the Friday Market according to these principles, and sold fairly large plots at reasonable prices (averaging fl.9 per square metre), enabling speculators and building entrepreneurs to make a profit. The merchant and speculator Jacob van Hencxthoven, for example, purchased 1913 square metres at Stadswaag and 900 square metres near the Friday Market; he parcelled out and sold some plots, while he had others built up, after which he sold or let the houses. By September 1550 Van Schoonbeke had sold all properties in the two new city districts. Since some data are missing, his profits can be calculated only approximately: he made a return of at least fl.26,828 or 73 percent on the capital invested from urbanizing the Stadswaag and a minimum of 43 to a maximum of 80 percent on the capital invested from urbanizing the Friday Market.[48]

In addition to launching two major real-estate projects *intra muros* in 1547, Van Schoonbeke tried his hand at planning a new residential district outside the city, nearby the walls, but just beyond the zone where construction was prohibited. He conceived the neighbourhood as a garden city *avant la lettre*, intended for wealthy citizens, who were able to afford a comfortable residence but found that the rising cost of land rendered owning a

46 SAA, IB 2979, nos 17, 20, IB 3018, no. 7, T 1705, no. 335/1, R 14, f° 3, PK 2273, f° 188.

47 'De luyden te bringhen tot metsen ende timmeren moet subtylyck toegaen, want in deselve nerringhe selden groot proffyt leyt, maer in contrarye grooten hooftswer, tijt verliesinghe ende veel ghelts quyt te worden'. SAA, IB 2992, no. 51.

48 See the calculations in Soly (1977), 168-9, 175-6, 181-3, 185.

vast garden or orchard in the city a waste of money. The Antwerp elite welcomed the *retour à la nature* that had been apparent in Italy since the fifteenth century, for example in the proliferation of the *villa rustica*.[49] Owning a residence outside the walls (a *villa suburbana*) became more attractive in the 1540s, as the crowds, the noise, and the stench of the city were increasing in direct proportion to its economic and demographic growth. When the merchant Frans De Cater later reflected on the heyday of the metropolis, he mentioned the downside as well: 'Every day the streets were filled with people, carts, and horses and were often blocked for half an hour, making it impossible to pass through and leading people to make a detour of three or four blocks to avoid all the turmoil'.[50] Because building a house was prohibited by law within a radius of 1 kilometre beyond the walls, finding a good location for a summer residence near the city had become difficult since August 1542, while staying within the Liberty of Antwerp was advisable on legal grounds.[51] Both for reasons of safety and to avoid wasting time, sites accessible by cart and/or flat-bottomed barges were moreover preferred. Van Schoonbeke found the ideal spot.

On 18 January 1547 he paid Margrave Willem van de Werve fl. 15,900 for the vast Hof ter Beke, situated one to two kilometres south of the surrounding walls, and covering a total area of *c.* 46 hectares. The entire domain was easily accessible, as it was intersected by roads and waterways leading to the city. On these grounds Van Schoonbeke built Lange Lei or Markgravelei, which served as the main thoroughfare across the new residential district, as well as several avenues whose location can no longer be identified. The distance between the new avenues and Saint George's Gate (the main entrance to the city),[52] varied from 1200 to 2000 metres. To make the new neighbourhood appear both rustic and residential, he sold the plots – according to a late sixteenth-century manuscript – 'on the condition that whoever purchased land to build summer residences on it had to plant trees spaced twenty feet [*c.* 5.7 metres] apart in front of his house'.[53] None of the remaining deeds of purchase specifies such a condition, but it may have been agreed orally. This is in fact highly likely, as on later plans of the new neighbourhood, which was named *Leikwartier*, all avenues appear with trees planted at regular intervals along both sides.[54]

Between 15 March 1547 and 9 May 1551, i.e. within about four years, Van Schoonbeke sold 55 plots with a total area of nearly 20 hectares. Over half the Ter Beke Estate was therefore not offered for sale. Were buyers becoming more difficult to find in a period of increasing commercial difficulties (see below)? In 1550-51 very few plots were sold, these were smaller, and their prices had declined to one and a half stuivers per square metre (compared with two stuivers or more in previous years). The changes seem to suggest such a trend. In any

---

49 Muylle (2009), 188. See also Lis and Soly (2012), 215-16, 423-4.

50 'De straeten daeghelijcx vol van volcke, wagens ende peerden, die dickmael meer dan een halff ure in malcanderen soe verveerdt waeren, datmer niet deur en cost ende om 't groot gewuel te mijden, soe liep men dickmael drij oft vier straten omme'. SAA, IB 3017, p. 64.

51 The city council had jurisdiction in the *Liberty*.

52 On 25 November 1545 Charles V solemnly opened this gate, which afterwards was often mentioned as *Keizerspoort*, Imperial Gate.

53 'Op conditien die van hem erven cochten om huysen ende speelhovens te maecken, dat die elck 20 voeten voor sijn huys ofte hoff eenen boom moest planten'. SAA, IB 3017, p. 126. Also SAA, PK 116, p. 181.

54 SAA, ICON, P 16/18a. In 1570 the value of these linden and oak trees was estimated at fl. 300. SAA, R 2179, f° 36v°. See also Muylle (2020).

case, Van Schoonbeke did not want to sell at bargain prices and was waiting for better times. After all, he had by then made a profit. He had sold 20 hectares at fl. 18,617, in other words fl. 2717 or 17 percent more than what the Ter Beke Estate had cost. The profit may also be calculated differently. He had purchased the 20 hectares at *c.* 0.6 stuivers per square metre, but he sold them on average for three times that amount, yielding gross earnings of about 180 percent. In addition, the remaining grounds increased in value because of the urbanization of the *Leikwartier*, which enabled him to sell three rent-charges on the Ter Beke Estate for a total of fl. 1200 at the 'penny 16', generating fl. 19,200.[55] On 10 October 1556, about two months before his death, he sold the large house, the grounds, the trees, and the annuities to Jacob van Hencxthoven for an undisclosed amount.[56]

3.2 Creating a Port and a New District

As far as the early modern period is concerned, public-private partnerships for realizing infrastructure projects tend to be associated with mercantilism, focused mainly on rulers and central governments.[57] The process of state-building made infrastructure a priority on government agendas in the seventeenth and – especially – the eighteenth century, but in earlier periods public authorities and individuals might also collaborate on building roads, wharfs, bridges, drinking water systems, or other infrastructure works. This was especially likely in cities. In Rome, for example, individuals sponsored semi-public fountains from the 1570s; in return for their contribution to the municipal water supply, they received reduced water rates or were entirely exempt from them.[58] It remains unclear, however, whether city councils entered public/private partnerships in the true sense during the late Middle Ages and/or first half of the sixteenth century. They signed contracts with master artisans or architects to construct specific public works, but no cases are currently known of long-term contracts where the private party guaranteed financing of an infrastructure project in part or entirely, was responsible for its management, and incurred a significant risk. It is therefore all the more remarkable that the two largest urban development projects in Antwerp's Golden Age were realized through public/private partnerships. The city council signed agreements with Van Schoonbeke to urbanize the New Town in the north and the vast Schuttershoven (the training grounds of the militia companies) in the southeast of the (old) city. In both cases the initiative came from the project developer, who agreed to finance the necessary infrastructure, parcel out the expansive land lots, and sell all the plots that belonged to the city in exchange for part of the proceeds. Contemporaries were aware that these projects would drastically alter the Antwerp cityscape because of their massive scale, *and* that by forming a public/private partnership one single project developer would become dominant on the real estate market.

The disastrous state of urban finance and the inability of the local government to levy new taxes enabled Van Schoonbeke to propose these ambitious real-estate projects and

---

55 Soly (1977), 188-91.
56 SAA, SR 258, f° 88v°-89.
57 On infrastructure financing in pre-industrial Europe, see De Luca & Lorenzini (2013), and Lorenzini (2016).
58 Rinne (2019).

to get them approved quickly - with support from Mary of Hungary. Although the new fortifications were far from completed in 1548, the city was deeply in debt. Finances were out of control, and the city authorities had to convene the Broad Council to approve new tax measures. They could not convince the *poorterij* (the wealthy citizenry) and the privileged guilds.[59] Both members formulated an alternative proposal, suggesting that 'superfluous' city property situated in the New Town and Schuttershoven be sold. The local government in desperation appealed to the central government in Brussels. Mary of Hungary was alarmed and travelled to Antwerp on 25 August 1548, accompanied by prominent members of the central government. They convened a general meeting and announced that concrete proposals to benefit the city treasury were to be submitted in writing, enabling Van Schoonbeke to take centre stage: he wrote a letter mentioning that there were simple and efficient ways of raising capital quickly. Mary was interested but wanted to resolve the political impasse in Antwerp first. On 3 September she presented four proposals to the Broad Council: sell 'superfluous' city property, increase specific consumer taxes, have property owners pay a tenth penny on the rental value of houses and land, and sell annuities at 6.25 percent for a total sum of fl. 600,000 backed by the city's income. The proposed measures had no impact on wage workers and lower segments of the social middle groups. Selling city property, moreover, corresponded to the wishes of the representatives of both the *poorterij* and the guilds. Subject to a few minor amendments, the members of the Broad Council approved these measures unanimously on 4 September.[60]

That day marked the start of a new stage in Van Schoonbeke's career: Mary of Hungary summoned him and asked him to elaborate on his plans to help raise money for the City.[61] Van Schoonbeke advised selling the land in the New Town and the Schuttershoven as soon as possible, because the economy was stronger than it had been in a long time. Everybody was looking for investment opportunities, as there was plenty of money to spend. He argued that the sites concerned could be transformed into thriving economic centres with minimal financial investment, thereby increasing their value considerably. To valorize the New Town, proper water management and a systematic allotment procedure were required, explained Van Schoonbeke. His idea was to set up a long-coveted facility, i.e. a proper seaport. Merchants had long been confronted with a serious shortage of good berths. The problem could be solved by digging four canals in the New Town that would serve as inner docks. Each canal could be reserved for ships from a specific area. The many small ships from the Zeeland harbours at Arnemuiden, Middelburg, Veere, and Vlissingen could berth in the first canal. Large quantities of woad could be unloaded there. The second canal could serve French and Spanish ships loaded with oil, syrup, and wine, as well as ships coming from Dordrecht bringing Rhine wine. In the third canal ships carrying bulk goods from Amsterdam, the Baltic countries, England, and Scotland could tie up. Finally, the fourth canal could be used for unloading timber on one side, while the other side would be for entrepreneurs importing large quantities of heavy raw materials (e.g. brewers).

59 On the composition of the Broad Council, see 3.3. note 21.
60 SAA, R 1756, f° 34-41v°.
61 SAA, IB 3000, no. 49.

Merchants might object to the plan for two reasons: the excentric location of the New Town, and the canals would not be accessible to ships of 250 tons or more. Van Schoonbeke acknowledged these points as legitimate concerns but offered solutions. The city should hire transport workers: a large group equipped with eighteen horses and the necessary carts to convey merchandise from the New Town to warehouses in the old city, and twenty-five workers be based on the Wijngaard Bridge in the centre of the old city, to transport goods to the ships. The first group had to be much larger, because 'three times as much merchandise is unloaded from the ships as is loaded'. In addition, six to eight small cranes would be installed in the New Town to ensure rapid loading and unloading. As for the larger ocean-going vessels: the city council should station 75 workers in the New Town and have them use sixteen to eighteen lighters (flat-bottomed barges) to convey goods to and from the ships moored in the Scheldt.[62]

The project conceived by Van Schoonbeke was the first attempt in Antwerp to put in place a port infrastructure that would solve the longstanding problems that traders and shippers faced. By 1548 this was certainly necessary. Only four or five ocean-going vessels could moor at the Wharf, which was the heart of the Scheldt quays, as well as two or three from the north end of the Wharf up to the Great Crane; south of that point to the end of the Fish Market, ships could berth only bow-on and lay alongside one another. Small ships could take advantage of high water to sail further into the city via one of the five inner docks, but these waterways were very narrow. Moreover, the many bridges and houses situated near the water further limited the available berths. During the first quarter of the sixteenth century, the city council had regulated maritime traffic, and in 1547 all kinds of new, rigid restrictions were added. Regulations, though necessary, failed to solve the fundamental problem, which was the shortage of berths.[63]

Until then the only contribution from the city council towards improving the port infrastructure had been the installation of a second crane on the Wharf in 1547.[64] While some of the ships in the Scheldt delta sailed only as far as Middelburg or Arnemuiden, most cargo was destined for Antwerp and was therefore transferred to smaller ships able to berth there. Was the city council uninterested in expanding the port because medium-sized and large ships were relatively few? Or was the political elite interested in commercial facilities in this period only where they benefited the city treasury? Whatever the case, Van Schoonbeke rightly emphasized that the commercial expansion of Antwerp was essentially an expansion of *overseas* trade and consequently of *maritime* traffic. He was right, as maritime activity in the Scheldt delta is estimated to have exceeded 2,500 ships *per annum* in this period.[65] Because ongoing growth would indisputably cause congestion, planning for the future was necessary.

Mary of Hungary and the senior government officials accompanying her obviously welcomed this view. They asked for details about the practicalities of the real-estate

62 'Want men drymale meer ghoets vuyten schepen bringht dan derweerts voert'. SAA, IB 2981, no. 24.

63 The Hanseatic merchants objected in vain that their large ships were allowed to moor at the Wharf for only three working days. From 1549, ships from Holland could remain moored at Boterrui/Suikkerrui for at most three days in the spring and summer. De Smedt (1950-54), II, 304-13; Asaert (1973a), 125-37, and (1986), 99-110.

64 Degryse (1991), 161.

65 Brulez (1975), 122.

project. Would his plan require the city council to purchase plots in the New Town owned by individuals and covering roughly one-third of the total area? How should the price of this land be calculated? And how could all construction sites (covering at least fifteen hectares) be sold at a decent profit within a reasonable time? Van Schoonbeke answered first that the increased value of the land arising from the urbanization of the New Town should not benefit a few individuals but should serve the City of Antwerp (the entire community bearing its cost).[66] He had an answer ready for the second question too. The land should be sold by private contract and in relatively small plots. Public auctions were out of the question, as potential buyers could not be approached, informed, and convinced individually on such occasions. Everything had to be negotiated 'in secret with persons who truly intend to build, so that one person who is unwilling will not dissuade seven who are interested'. He showed no false modesty about his share in the entire operation: 'If I gain possession of all the land, I will do my utmost to make it profitable, and no-one can deny that the proceeds will be half as much again as when the city sells it', because 'over the past six years I have sold more land than anyone else in a hundred years'.[67] He guaranteed that the land in the New Town would sell for a minimum of fl. 300,000. If the whole operation were to be completed within four years of the completion of the planned canals, he would take 16.66 percent commission. So great was his self-confidence that he was willing to pay a fine of fl.10,000, if he did not sell enough land by the deadline set.[68]

Mary of Hungary supported the arguments put forward by Van Schoonbeke and urged the city council to sign a contract with him as quickly as possible. His project seemed ideal for providing the city with cash while boosting trade at the same time: urbanizing the New Town would make it one of the best equipped port cities in the world. The only subject of debate was Van Schoonbeke's earnings. Mary as governor was very astute and drove a hard bargain. Van Schoonbeke reduced his commission on the sale of the land to 10 percent, in exchange for which the penalty clause was deleted.[69] The city council in consultation with Mary of Hungary accepted Van Schoonbeke's terms and signed a definitive contract, which Charles V ratified on 5 February 1549.[70] The decision-making process was remarkable: the city council needed to be convinced by the central government to approve a project to promote Antwerp's commercial growth, and that project was to be carried out by a private developer.

The plan for the New Town included one major change: on 20 May 1549 Van Schoonbeke proposed digging three instead of four canals and received instant approval from the city council.[71] A later copy of a map that the municipal *erfscheider* (surveyor) Peter Frans had drawn on 29 December 1550 on instructions from Van Schoonbeke reveals clearly how

66 AGR, PEA 1191/41, no. 16.

67 'Soo staet te consydereren dat soo wanneer de voors. stadterve in mijne handen is ende ick mijn uterste industrye daertoe besyghde om de voors. erve rendabel te maken, dat de erve alsdan de helft beter is in mijne handen dan in der stadt handen', want 'Gilbert meer erven vercocht heeft binnen ses jaeren dan iemant in hondert jaeren tevoren'. SAA, IB 2992, no. 51.

68 SAA, IB 2981, nos 4, 6, and 8, IB 2992, nos 51 and 55.

69 SAA, IB 2977, no. 2, IB 2978, no. 78, IB 2981, nos 16-17, IB 3000, no. 49; AGR, PEA, 1191/41, no.16.

70 ROPB, 2nd ser., V, 486-91.

71 AGR, PEA 1633/1; SAA, R 1756, f° 32.

the new port quarter was conceived.[72] Three wide canals were to be dug equidistant from each other from west to east and perpendicular to the bank of the Scheldt. The distances were calculated to ensure that between every two canals, two rows of buildings could be constructed, separated by a street, so that each building fronted a quay on one side and a street on the other. The canals were connected by smaller North-South waterways, which were intended to ensure proper drainage. This grid-like structure of waterways and traffic arteries served two purposes: optimal drainage of all land and efficient distribution of the available area in uniform building zones. The cost of each canal – including a lock house, a lock, and a drawbridge – was estimated at *c.* fl. 30,000.[73]

The plan to build a dock quarter in the New Town was original indeed. Nobody had ever launched such an idea. The proposal of using four or three parallel canals as inner docks (each with a specified function) was also original. Nowhere else in Europe was such a maritime infrastructure present. Urbanizing new zones on a grid pattern was not really new in Antwerp, but the scale of the New Town was entirely different: over 20 hectares were divided into regular city blocks. Never before had a chessboard pattern appeared across such a vast area in Antwerp or in other large or medium-sized European cities. In the Central Middle Ages new cities were built according to a chessboard pattern,[74] and from the second half of the fifteenth century the proposed designs of an 'ideal city' appeared in rigid geometric shapes, but they are unlikely to have inspired Van Schoonbeke. Nor was this necessary, as once the decision had been taken to build canals from west (the Scheldt) to east (the new city walls), a chessboard pattern became inevitable on pragmatic grounds. It was the only way to resolve the drainage problem adequately, while ensuring an economically efficient division into building blocks.

In the summer of 1549 local builders started laying the quays of the first two canals. They rushed to get the job done, but problems soon arose. Lack of money, inefficiency, suspicion, and quarrelling greatly slowed the works. In January 1551 (a year and a half after the works began), the canals in the New Town were far from ready. Moreover, half the city walls had yet to be built – and this project had been going on for over eight years. The total cost of all the remaining works was estimated at fl. 472,545, while the debt had grown to fl. 1,168,313.[75] Was the situation hopeless? Not at all, according to Van Schoonbeke, who made Mary of Hungary a spectacular new offer: he could build half the remaining fortifications at only 65 percent per running meter of what the city had hitherto paid. The city council was urged to sign a contract with him immediately. On 17 February Van Schoonbeke agreed to build a stone fortress wall of 4000 rods or 37,600 cubic metres within five years.[76] On 19 March he promised to complete the canals in the New Town before the end of 1552 and to give the Schuttershoven an entirely new economic function that would increase land prices there considerably.[77] On 2 June 1551 he also agreed to

72 SAA, ICON, P 25/1bis.
73 SAA, IB 2990, no. 96, IB 3002, no. 15, R 1770, f° 3.
74 See Boucheron, Menjot and Boone (2003), 410-18.
75 SAA, IB 3002, no. 15, R 1770, no. 161, and R 1782.
76 A *rod* of masonry was 20 feet high or deep, 20 feet long, and 1 foot wide, or *c.* 9.4 cubic metres: SAA, IB 2977, no. 17, and IB 2990, no. 98. One Antwerp foot = 0.2868 metres.
77 See the references in Soly (1977), 220-1.

sell a series of buildings and tracts of land owned by the city. He was gaining control of everything associated with public works and city property.

A chronological account would convey the simultaneity of his different activities and their mutual cohesion but would be too complex to provide insight into the sub-projects. Urbanizing the Schuttershoven and building the city walls will therefore be addressed later. Completion of the canals in the New Town is the main focus here. Van Schoonbeke achieved his aim. Within six months of signing the contract on 19 March, he had completed two canals, i.e. the remaining half of the first canal and nearly three quarters of the second canal, totalling over 3300 cubic metres of quayside.[78] He was unable to start working on the third canal, because the individual landowners refused to sell. The local authorities requested assistance from the Emperor, whose threats failed to convince the owners to change their minds. They filed suit at the Council of Brabant, where the case dragged on for years. Only in 1555/6 was an out-of-court settlement reached, so that the third canal could be dug.[79]

Setting up the new dock quarter solved the problems that Van Schoonbeke had identified in 1549, especially the shortage of good berths and more generally points for loading and unloading the vessels. No exact figures are available regarding the numbers of ships that docked in the canals, and only fragmentary data remain about their load capacity. In any case, all three canals could accommodate ships of 80 to 85 metric tons. In January 1563 a 200-ton caravel berthed in the New Town, most probably in the second canal, named *Middenvliet* (Middle Canal) or *Graanvliet* (Grain Canal), which Van Schoonbeke had intended for larger ships. Guicciardini expressed great praise for this inner dock 'so wide and so long that over one hundred ships could berth there'.[80] The canals in the New Town solved the congestion problem. They were not suitable for Italian, Spanish, or Portuguese ships of 250 tons or more but they did cut the waiting times for large ships to load or unload: space became available on the Scheldt quays, because smaller ships could berth in the canals of the New Town.

Pursuant to his contract on urbanization of the New Town, Van Schoonbeke was also expected to parcel out the Schuttershoven and sell the plots. This operation was sensitive, as militia companies were important organizations. In these elite corps, members were co-opted from among adult citizens of good moral standing, which in practice meant that most hailed from the social middle groups. There were six militia companies,[81] each one having its own structure, deans, coat of arms, and attire. Altogether, they comprised 400 to 500 active members.[82] Their training grounds were situated south of Schuttershofstraat, 100 metres from Jodenstraat, 200 metres from Huidevettersstraat, and 400 metres from Meir. The sites covered an area of 2.5 hectares. It was this proximity to prestigious thoroughfares that made the Schuttershoven so attractive to the city: they were expected to fetch a high

78 SAA, IB 2976 no. 3, and IB 2991, nos 18-21.

79 The rapid progress at that point is featured on the famous copper etching 'A bird's eye view of Antwerp', published by Hieronymus Cock in 1557. See Martens (2017).

80 SAA, T 1710, no. 1361, and CERT 18, f° 33; Guicciardini (1567b), 91.

81 There were two crossbow guilds (*Oude Voetboog* and *Jonge Voetboog*), two archers' guilds (*Oude Handboog* and *Jonge Handboog*), an Arquebusiers' Guild (*Kolveniers*), and a Fencers' Guild (*Schermers*).

82 ROPB, 2nd ser., VI, 139-41; Boumans (1965), 164-7.

price after the urbanization. Still, several problems persisted. First, the city would need to find the militia companies new training grounds on land that was much less valuable than their present sites. The second question was how best to valorize the latter.

Van Schoonbeke once again envisaged the centre of the new district as an economic hub and opted for a *Tapissierspand*, a market hall for weavers of and traders in tapestries. Antwerp was not only an important manufacturing centre.[83] It was also the main international market for selling and exporting tapestries woven elsewhere in the Southern Netherlands: large numbers of *verdures* from Oudenaarde in the County of Flanders, tapestries in which the background and generally the borders consisted entirely of decorative foliage, and the far more luxurious and costlier tapestries from Brussels, Tournai in the County of Hainault, and Sint-Truiden in the Prince Bishopric of Liège. These were intended mainly for France, Spain, and England.[84] By the mid-1550s the estimated total value of tapestry exports was at least fl. 700,000 *per annum*.[85] The strong growth of this export trade enabled a new market hall to be constructed. Since 1517 tapestry weavers and merchants had been using a church property named *Vette Hinne* on Cammerstraat (now Kammenstraat) behind Our Lady's *Pand*.[86] Though fairly large, the building could not store massive quantities of tapestries, let alone exhibit them, especially as the proportion of larger tapestries in total production was increasing. Where would the new building be constructed? Van Schoonbeke opted for the Schuttershoven but understood that such a plan might elicit controversy, and that it should preferably be presented by the authorities. The city council was cautious and recorded in the minutes four suitable sites: the gallery on the second floor of the New Exchange (where since 1540 paintings and sculptures were sold), in the middle of Meir, in the New Town, or on the Schuttershoven. Each option would incur costs. What elements should determine the choice? In February 1550 the local authorities reached a decision and sent a lengthy report to Mary of Hungary. They adopted and elaborated the arguments made by Van Schoonbeke: the Schuttershoven were the best site for the new *pand*, as this was the heart of the city, close to the Meir and the New Exchange. Mary thought the proposal was perfect. On 11 March she prohibited the Antwerp tapestry weavers and merchants, mercers, and jewellers from extending the lease on the *Vette Hinne*. All those involved in selling tapestries would need to move to the new *pand* to be built on the Schuttershoven according to the plan that Van Schoonbeke would submit. The others were to transfer their trade to the second floor of the New Exchange, where shops would open on the basis of instructions that Van Schoonbeke would provide.[87] Fourteen days later she approved the plan for the new Tapestry Hall sent to her by Van Schoonbeke and ordered the Antwerp city council to implement it as quickly as possible.[88]

Construction of the new Tapestry Hall could begin only after the six militia companies had been assigned other training grounds. This proved more difficult than anticipated,

83 Thijs (1987), 115-19. Brosens, Alen and Slegten (2018), 9, argue that the *Tapissierspand* was also intended to 'facilitate and support the development of tapestry *production* in Antwerp.' My italics.

84 Evans (2006), 54- 64; Vanwelden (2006), 207-13; Puttevils (2016), 133-6.

85 Brulez (1970), 41. According to Vermeylen (2003), 88, this figure is underestimated.

86 This *pand* was expressly built by the Church of Our Lady for the marketing of art: Ewing (1990).

87 SAA, T 726, f° 17v°-22, and IB 2979, no. 101.

88 AGR, PEA 1633/3, and PEA 1652/1, Letters dated 26 March 1550.

because a minimum of 1.5 hectares was needed. The guilds agreed to move, on condition that they were granted sites in the Gasthuisbeemden ('Hospital Meadows'), south of the Schuttershoven, and that the city would pay for the infrastructure and redeem the annuities with which their land was encumbered.[89] The authorities agreed but then faced a new problem: Johanna Nuyens, the Mother Superior of Saint Elisabeth Hospital, refused to give up a large section of the Gasthuisbeemden. Admittedly, the area demanded was substantial: 675 rods or 22,200 square metres. The city government notified the Emperor, who sent two commissioners to Antwerp to negotiate with the Mother Superior. They were told that selling the land was out of the question, as so much pasture could not be given up. This was a convincing argument, as every spring Saint Elisabeth Hospital purchased fifteen or sixteen young oxen and ten lean cows, of which some were slaughtered in the autumn after being fattened up to feed the Sisters and the patients, while others were sold at a profit.[90] Second, having militia companies 'come and make a lot of noise with drums and pipes' in direct proximity to a place where the sick were nursed, and a house of prayer was present, was deemed unacceptable. Finally, the price the city was willing to pay (i.e. twelve stuivers per square metre) was equally unacceptable: at public auction the land would sell for two to three times this amount. The commissioners tried to refute these arguments, but the Hospital Sisters stood their ground.[91] The Emperor had to intervene, and the Bishop of Cambrai needed to pressure the Mother Superior, who demanded some concessions. On 30 September 1551 the sale was finally accomplished. Due to 'advanced age and poor health', Nuyens was forced to withdraw.[92]

This course of events instigated a public outcry. The oldest and most reputable hospital in Antwerp was admitting increasing numbers of patients and therefore faced a growing shortage of space. Nursing the sick became an ever greater burden for the seven or eight sisters – their number remained unchanged until 1551/2. Having to sell pastures with a total area of 22,200 square metres that had benefited the infirm and the religious, in order to accommodate associations engaging in military and recreational pursuits hardly exemplified charity.[93] On 23 October (three weeks after Saint Elisabeth Hospital was forced to sell its land), the city gave Van Schoonbeke 154 ½ rods (over 5000 square metres).[94] While he in fact needed this land to open a new connecting road *c.* 11.5 metres wide from the Tapestry Hall (which had yet to be built) to Saint Georges' Gate,[95] he must have seemed to be deriving personal benefit from commercializing the Gasthuisbeemden. This may be inferred from one of the most original paintings produced in sixteenth-century Antwerp: Pieter Aertsen's *Meat Stall*, which the artist dated 10 March 1551 (1552, according to the present calendar).[96]

---

89 SAA, GA 4624, f° 53v°-56.

90 Scholliers (1960), 37-8; De Commer and Soly (1988), 81 and 90.

91 SAA, GA 4621, no. 2.

92 De Commer and Soly (1988), 70-4.

93 SAA, T 1707, nos 666, 676-677, and R 1786, no. 1.

94 SAA, T 16, f° 29.

95 On 29 April 1552 the Mother Superior of Saint Elisabeth Hospital officially agreed to open this street (now Leopoldstraat): SAA, KK 2145.

96 Pieter Aertsen, *A Meat Stall with the Holy Family Giving Alms*, 1551. North Carolina Museum of Art, Raleigh, No. 93.2.

On this large-scale work (measuring 115.6 x 168.9 cm) Aertsen depicted piles of meat from freshly slaughtered animals almost obliterating a very tiny background scene portraying the flight into Egypt. This intriguing scene has led to very different interpretations. The American art historian Charlotte Houghton has emphasized the handwritten and clearly legible message written in Dutch on a placard at the upper right of the painting: 'Behind here are 154 rods of land for sale immediately, either by the rod or all at once, at your convenience',[97] which she interprets as a reference to the 'sale' of the same area of land by the city to Van Schoonbeke on 23 October 1551, in other words as a specifically local scandal. Aertsen was indeed providing a moral commentary. He depicted the announcement of the sale of the tract of land far more prominently than the Virgin Mary, who was giving a small boy alms during the flight into Egypt: 'Poverty and charity are dwarfed by a display of worldly bounty'.[98] The author could have added another two elements to support her interpretation. First, the fact that Saint Elisabeth Hospital had oxen and cows slaughtered every year, as noted, rendering the visualization of large quantities of fresh meat very appropriate, also metaphorically. In this context, moreover, English 'horse trading' is *koehandel* in Dutch (literally 'cattle trading'), always with the connotation of tampering or swindling. Second, the brightly highlighted emblems that Aertsen painted on a wooden post may be attributed a specific significance: the lower-case 'g' and 'b' as abbreviations of *gasthuis* [i.e. hospital in Dutch] *beemden*, while the images of a (cow) bell and a clover leaf between both letters related to grassy pastures.[99]

Given the theme, *Meat Stall* was most likely painted on commission. As the work was large and therefore expensive, it would have been intended for a wealthy patron familiar with the Gasthuisbeemden saga. Aertsen undoubtedly understood that the work would be viewed by various persons and would be interpreted as a satire of current events, and that Van Schoonbeke, the militia companies, and the city council would quickly come to mind as the parties involved. In 1551/2, it was common knowledge that the Hospital Sisters had sold their land under duress, as well as the reasons why. Few observers would have failed to appreciate a satirical representation of the events. Members of the elite and the social middle groups were still being summoned as witnesses in the major corruption investigation in progress from 1549 on, and rumours of shady transactions and financial misconduct reverberated throughout the city. The sale of the Gasthuisbeemden merely confirmed what many citizens already suspected.

Whether Van Schoonbeke ultimately made a huge profit from the complex real-estate transactions he conducted 'on commission from' or 'on behalf of' the city council in the area of the new market hall is impossible to determine. In any case, he committed to constructing half the *Tapissierspand* for a sum of fl. 9000.[100] The structure was as simple as it was efficient: a rectangular building of *c.* 80 by *c.* 37 metres, covering an area of *c.* 2960

97 The Flemish original reads 'hier achter is erve te coope tersto[n]t metter roeye[n] elck syn gerief oft teenemaele 154'.

98 Houghton (2004), 285-90 (the quotation on 287).

99 The capital X with two smaller lines on each side (IIXII), depicted above the 'g' and the 'b', remains enigmatic. Could it be a reference to the date (IIII-X, i.e. 4 October), when the militia companies obtained their new training grounds on the Gasthuisbeemden?

100 He had also agreed to open a new street (Arenbergstraat) south of the *pand*, parallel to Schuttershofstraat, to improve access to the new district, while ensuring an optimal division into plots. The city agreed to pay him fl. 4000 for this project. For more detail, see Soly (1977), 221, 223, 237

square metres, built of brick; the sole ornamentation consisting of the alternation of brick and blue stone, and pointed gables running the length of four or six naves.[101] Along the west and east sides were entrance gates of 2.8 by 2.8 metres opening into the building, which was divided in three aisles: a wide middle aisle and on each side a row of 12 or 13 shops, each with an area of *c.* 40 square metres and 5.7 metres high, allowing hangings to be displayed to full advantage. As the prospective tenants explicitly requested, a common room extending 23 metres in length was provided, where tapestry series could be exhibited. At the start of the works the cost was estimated at fl. 17,300, and this sum does not appear to have been exceeded.[102]

On 8 March 1553 Charles V ordered the tapestry merchants to move to the new market hall.[103] To the amazement of the city council, some affluent weavers and merchants refused. Their salesrooms were on Grote Markt, Hoogstraat, or at other commercially interesting sites. Moving was therefore pointless and even disadvantageous for them. Their fellow merchants were furious. A fierce struggle ensued. On 3 April the Emperor decreed that no tapestry weaver or merchant in Antwerp was allowed have a shop open to the public or place a sign indicating that he sold tapestries; if he traded indoors, he would not be eligible to rent a shop in the Tapestry Hall.[104] This did not settle the matter. In September 1554 the *Fortificatiemeesters* complained that both citizens and outsiders continue to sell tapestries on Grote Markt, Hoogstraat, Reyndersstraat, and elsewhere in houses, basements, and warehouses. Three months later the authorities reminded all merchants that they had to comply with the imperial decree of 3 April or risk severe penalties. Transgressions remained difficult to detect however.[105] Anyway, Van Schoonbeke achieved the general objective: the bulk of all tapestries was henceforth sold from the Tapestry Hall.[106] The results were conducive to selling tracts of land in this neighbourhood, which had been the primary objective of the city council. Ongoing urbanization of the former Schuttershoven was another contributing factor. In 1551/2 Van Schoonbeke opened five streets around the new market hall. At his recommendation, at the end of 1552 the city council moved the weekly grain market to the east of the Tapestry Hall.[107] The aim was twofold: find more potential candidates for plots on the Schuttershoven in the short term and ensure an additional and enduring economic pole of attraction for the district in the long term. Van Schoonbeke opened a square measuring 80 by 50 metres, which after a few decades was consequently named Graanmarkt (Grain Market) and continues to serve as a food market to this day.

Nobody had ever changed the appearance of Antwerp so dramatically. Aside from the New Town, between 1502 and 1600, 85 new streets were opened with a combined total length of 8800 metres, as well as four markets with a total area exceeding 10,000 square metres. This development peaked in 1540-53: 48 new streets, of which half were by Van

---

101 The number of aisles is problematic. See Evans (2006), 84 n. 29. The *Tapissierspand* was built on the site where the Bourla Schouwburg (Theatre) stands today.

102 AA, IB 2979, nos 70-71. Evans (2006), 84-5, interprets some data from the sources incorrectly.

103 SAA, PK 2765, f° 44.

104 SAA, PK 2765, f° 71v°-73.

105 IB 3014, no. 38, IB 211, no. 85, PK 915, f° 191.

106 See the claims for the tapestries stolen during the Spanish Fury of 1576: Evans (2006), Ch. 4.

107 Vande Weghe (1977), 197.

Schoonbeke, who opened the three new markets as well. The streets he opened had a combined length of 2750 metres, over 31 percent of the sixteenth-century total.[108] Even more important than his quantitative output was his exceptional view of project development and urbanization. Van Schoonbeke was highly innovative in organizing urban space. He was the first real-estate speculator in Antwerp – and in Europe – who acted as a project developer *cum* town planner, operating on a huge scale and with systematic approach: he formed spacious, rectangular squares, where wide streets converged at right angles. In addition to applying a geometric grid, enabling economic-rational allotment of the entire site, he added value to the plots by concentrating them around a commercial centre. Each new centre was consistently defined in relation to existing city districts, from the perspective of traffic, economic, and social aspects, enabling optimal alignment of commercial and residential functions. The urbanization of the New Town by Van Schoonbeke was unprecedented in sixteenth-century Europe. He designed a docklands district comprising three parallel canals serving as inner quays and parcelled out the entire area like a chessboard. No other European port city had a comparable maritime infrastructure.

Available studies on urbanism and city planning in early modern Europe indicate that Van Schoonbeke was an exceptional project developer. Unlike Antwerp, real-estate operations in other economic centres experiencing strong demographic growth were rarely part of town-planning projects. In Lyon, for example, where Italian merchant-bankers became dominant, the expansion of urban infrastructure was not systematic. Several streets were straightened, and new ones were opened, but there was no system or consideration for subsequent development of the city districts concerned. Three new squares were built, but their shape was very uneven, and the largest, designed in 1562/3, was in fact a military training ground that was transformed into the present Place Bellecour only much later on.[109] Even in burgeoning London, new districts emerged largely at random and in some cases unconstrained. At the end of the sixteenth century most of the overpopulated city appeared chaotic.[110] Lisbon, which during the reign of King Manuel I (1495-1521) thrived in all respects, was an exception, because the ruler maintained a town-planning policy there. In addition to constructing a new palace and administrative buildings, he developed the city and opened *Rua Nova d'El Rey* (the King's New Street). The new residential quarter *Bairro Alto* (High Quarter) was parcelled out by private landowners in a geometric pattern, but they did so in close consultation with the court of Manuel I.[111] The renowned Strada Nuova (now Via Garibaldi) in Genoa was also built according to plan between 1558 and 1583, but the ruling classes - comprised of the old aristocracy and the *nouveaux riches* - were interested exclusively in building magnificent palaces, far away from the port and the markets. Power and prestige were all that they were interested in.[112] The new thoroughfare was only 250 metres long and 7.5 metres wide, whereas the streets opened around the Antwerp Urban Weighing House averaged 9 metres in width.

108 For more detail, see Soly (1977), 372-9.
109 Lavedan (1941), 153-155; Estier (2009); Rau (2014), 128-143.
110 Porter (1994), 43-46, 63-64, and (Baer) 2012.
111 Barreiros (2008), 207-210.
112 Doria (1995).

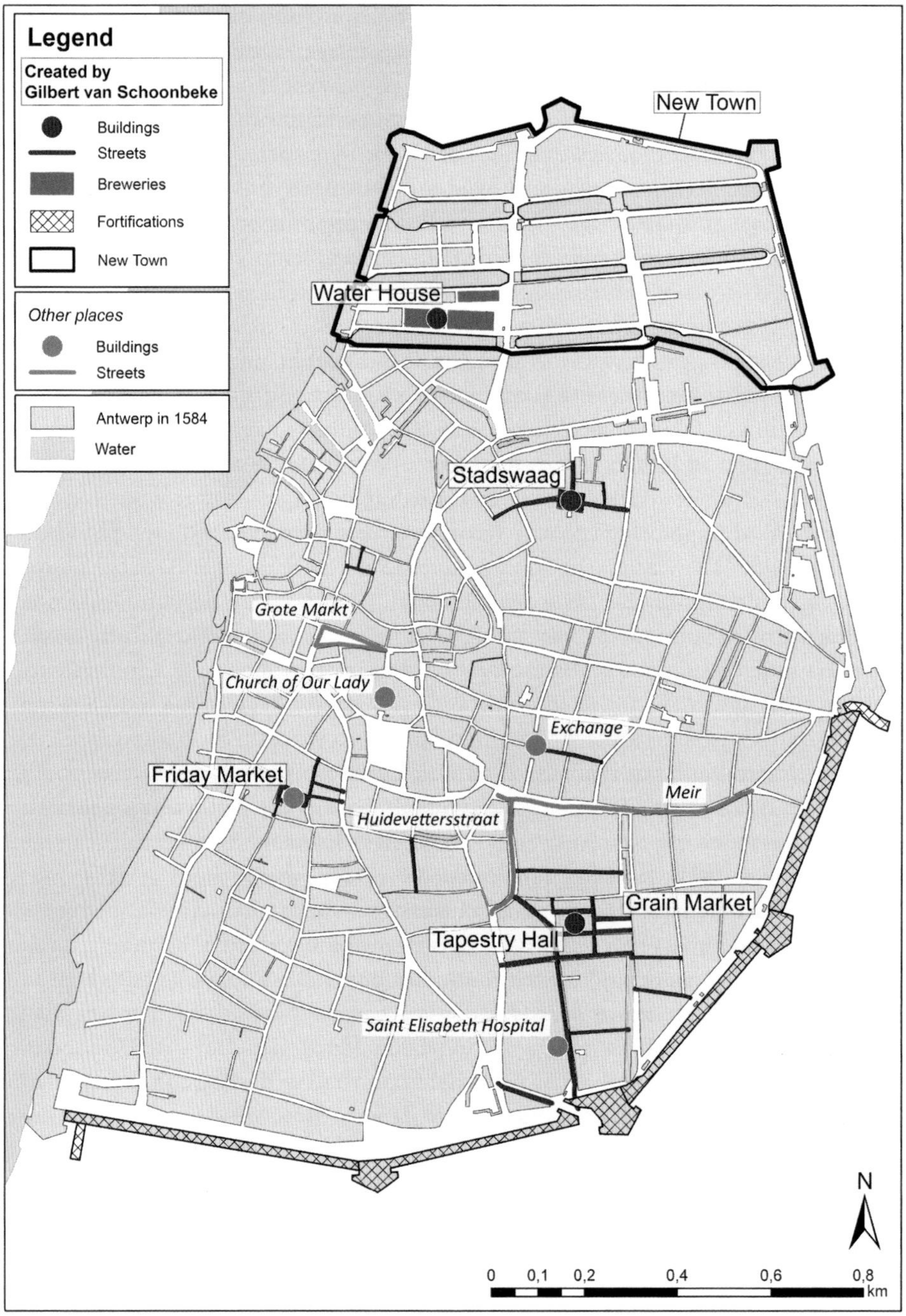

Map 2. Streets and Buildings Created by Gilbert van Schoonbeke

Political rulers in some other European cities launched town-planning initiatives as well. Except in the new fortress cities designed according to a radial-concentric pattern, such as Mariembourg and Philippeville in the county of Namur, or Vitry-le-François and Villefranche-sur-Meuse in Northern France,[113] political and ideological considerations nearly always prevailed. Nowhere were the new urban planning principles propagated by Renaissance theoreticians applied as consistently or as impressively as in Rome during the second half of the sixteenth century. In urbanizing two new districts and opening over thirty new streets, the popes (especially Sixtus V) and the architects advising them (including Domenico Fontana) kept in mind that a programme and comprehensive plan were expected to be based on the organic link between the different city districts and their subordination to a religious centre, which entailed a monumental perspective.[114] The urban planning and the architecture adapted to this practice made it clear that the Pope was the major force and Rome the spiritual and cultural centre of Christianity. In Italian city states run by autocratic rulers, urban projects serving essentially political-ideological objectives were realized as well. In the radically different context of a trading metropolis such as Antwerp, this type of urbanism was inconceivable. Here economic considerations nearly always prevailed. Van Schoonbeke had a keen sense of how to optimize urban spaces as commercial hubs: this was what made him so unique as a project developer-town planner.

3.3 Monopolizing the Greatest Public Works

Until the mid-nineteenth century the building industry in Europe did not experience fundamental changes with respect to construction materials and methods. Nor did lasting organizational changes take place in the long run. On major construction projects lasting many years or even decades Church and Crown generally appointed a central coordinator to recruit, supervise, and pay master artisans and journeymen, but this did not make for different relations of production. Housing construction was too dependent on economic trends and fluctuations for large companies to operate profitably for long. In many cities guilds were important forces as well, and the statutes prohibited contractors from working on more than one construction project at a time or subjected them to other restrictions. Still, trends towards concentration appeared in some cities in certain periods. In late medieval Bruges a few substantial master artisans gained control of a large share of the public works.[115] In Antwerp the increased scale of residential construction during the second quarter of the sixteenth century benefited entrepreneurs with enough capital and credit to pay the wages of large numbers of workers and advance the costs of raw materials. At the time, twenty master masons were responsible for over half of all new residential construction.[116] The contracts that Gilbert van Schoonbeke entered into with the city council to build the new city walls made unprecedented concentration possible. He set up a vertically integrated building trust and, with the support of the public authorities,

113 Berckmans (1977-1979); Chartier (1981), 110-11.
114 Delumeau (1957-1959), I, 223-339. See also Long (2018).
115 Sosson (1977).
116 Daems (1976), 134.

was able to circumvent guild-based regulations and therefore succeeded in monopolizing the public works in Antwerp. He was a new-style entrepreneur in the building industry: a capitalist contractor.

The construction of up-to-date fortifications in the 1540s was an exceptional project, the cost of which was appalling. Never before had a European city been fully surrounded by a ring of bastions and ramparts. In Northern Italy, where the new defence system arose and was appropriately named *trace italienne*, some cities added bastions to their existing fortifications during the first half of the sixteenth century, but none underwent complete transformation.[117] The Habsburg-Valois wars, which entailed almost continuous fighting and destruction in the border region of the Netherlands and sometimes endangered the Duchy of Brabant, encouraged the application of Italian methods. The defence works in Antwerp outdid all others: eight curtain walls and nine bastions covering *c.* 4,500 metres in length, equipped with five monumental gates accessible via stone bridges across a wide moat. Praising the new Antwerp *enceinte*, Guicciardini wrote in 1567 that 'its cost had been exorbitant', but that it was 'a beauty to behold' and made the city 'virtually impossible to take', 'so strong and so secure that many from the surroundings and from other provinces seek shelter there'.[118]

The cost of the new Antwerp fortifications was exorbitant, not only because they were so long, but also because the eight curtain walls were made entirely of brickwork, faced with bluestone. The protruding sections of the nine bastions (the external faces) were also built solidly of brick to ensure that they were strong enough to withstand canon fire from a besieger. Consequently, a lot of brickwork was needed. All the walls were 10 metres high and topped by a parapet of *c.* 1.30 metres. They were 2.85 metres wide at the base and 2.10 metres at the top. Additional supporting and retaining walls were built with a length of 2.30 metres.[119] Based on calculations by the *erfscheiders* relating to the construction of 50 running rods or *c.* 287 metres of rampart, not including the foundations, raw materials appear to have accounted for 80 percent of the total cost, estimated at nearly fl. 20,000, with bricks accounting for the greatest single expense at approximately 50 percent.[120]

The combination of massive public works and a rapid increase in housebuilding led to soaring brick prices in the 1540s. This was aggravated by the city council's prohibition in 1546 of new wooden façades *intra muros* and the requirement that contractors build partitions exclusively in masonry.[121] According to the Antwerp authorities, the owners of the brick kilns in Hemiksem, on the right bank of the Scheldt about ten kilometres south of Antwerp, seized on the enormous demand for bricks to set up 'conspiracies, secret deals, and monopolies' that caused prices to rise: by 1548 the price of 25,000 bricks

117 See the classic article by Hale (1965).

118 Guicciardini (1567b), 89-90, 114.

119 Soly (1977), 199; Lombaerde (2009), 28, 35-7. All sections of the new-style fortifications corresponded to the blueprints by the Italian military architect Donato de Boni, the Emperor's chief engineer in the Netherlands. He authorized all decisions, including the construction materials selected, but the chief city *erfscheider* (surveyor) Peter Frans was entrusted by the city authorities with technical management and execution. SAA, PK 2242, no. 1, and T 1319/1, no. 4, f° 33v°. On Donato de Boni, see Van den Heuvel (1991), 25-6; Roosens (2005), 328-41, 344-57; Geerts (2009), 69-70; Martens (2009), 60-1.

120 See the calculations in Soly (1977), 244-6.

121 SAA, PK 915, f° 70v°-71.

(a shipload) of the best quality had increased to fl. 32-33.[122] This probably resulted less from price-fixing than from the shortage of new brick kilns, but the city council feared that the resumption of the public works after halting them in 1548 would drive brick prices higher still. Rather than open new brick kilns as other cities had done in the past, the city council encouraged entrepreneurs to take the initiative. In June 1548 Jacob van Hencxthoven agreed to purchase clayfields in Hemiksem and construct brick kilns there, provided the city would purchase 400 shiploads *per annum* at fl. 24 each for three years. The proposal was accepted and approved by Charles V, after which a formal contract was signed with Van Hencxthoven on 12 September 1548.[123]

Van Schoonbeke saw a missed opportunity. Not satisfied merely to build canals in the New Town, which required large quantities of bricks, it soon became clear that he was planning ahead. He therefore proposed to Mary of Hungary in September 1548 – shortly after Van Hencxthoven had signed his contract – that in addition to building the canals in the New Town at his own expense, he would construct four times as many brick kilns as Van Hencxthoven, while charging only fl. 23 per shipload of bricks. Under such attractive conditions Charles V allowed him on 5 February 1549 to purchase *c.* 21 hectares of clayfields from St. Bernard's Abbey in Hemiksem and to set up brick kilns there. He had to agree to supply the *Fortificatiemeesters* with the bricks they needed annually at fl. 23 per shipload, but they were required to advance one quarter of the total due. To avert any risk, Van Schoonbeke insisted that if the *Fortificatiemeesters* refused the goods supplied for any reason, the city authorities had to grant him a monopoly on the brick trade in Antwerp until he had sold his entire stock. This could create problems, as Van Schoonbeke was not a member of the masons' guild. To avoid these, Charles V granted the City of Antwerp a patent enabling anyone to supply construction materials from that point onward without being subject to guild regulations.[124] Van Hencxthoven obviously felt betrayed and objected strenuously to the preferential treatment granted to Van Schoonbeke. When he threatened to bring the case to the Council of Brabant, which might have culminated in a loss for both parties, Van Schoonbeke offered to team up with his competitor and purchase a share in his firm, which is indeed what happened: Van Hencxthoven acquired a one-third share in brick production and trade.[125]

In 1549/50 they together constructed fifteen permanent brick kilns, several storage sites and sixty homes for workers in Hemiksem. Capitalist organization was now solidly introduced in the Scheldt-Rupel area.[126] By June 1549 five or six of the new kilns were already in use. They must have been operating at full capacity soon afterwards, because between August 1549 and late December 1551 the partners supplied an average of 450 shiploads annually, an output of *c.* 11,250,000 bricks. This figure becomes still more remarkable when we consider that a brick kiln could operate only four or five times a year at best. Assuming

122 SAA, IB 2177, no. 57. In Lier in the second half of the 1540s the prices per shipload fluctuated between fl. 25 and fl. 28, but these were first, second, and third-class bricks. Van der Wee (1963), I, 257 and 261.

123 AGR, R 20789, f° 40; SAA, PK 1434, no. 9, and R 1756, f° 42.

124 SAA, IB 2981, no. 52, IB 2177, nos 58 and 65; ROPB, 2nd ser., V, 486-91, 508-9.

125 SAA, IB 2977, no. 151.

126 Along the Scheldt and the Rupel, several other brick kilns were situated, producing what were known as 'Callebekers', but these outfits tended to be small, see De Schepper (1953), 15-25; Hollestelle (1961), 26-127; Limberger (2008), 132-6.

a maximum output from the fifteen kilns each one would have contained 150,000 bricks on average – an immense volume.[127] The Van Schoonbeke and Van Hencxthoven partnership was so dominant that it neutralized all competition.

According to Van Schoonbeke, 400 to 500 workers were employed at the partners' brickworks, which seems plausible, considering the high production and large number of homes for workers. Sixty new dwellings were necessary for two reasons: the area north of Saint Bernard's Abbey was sparsely populated (migrant labour was therefore indispensable), and brickmaking was a seasonal industry. Freezing weather made it impossible to work clay, and night frosts in spring or autumn could ruin bricks that still had to be fired. To encourage workers to stay with the company, the partners offered them free shelter when the season was over and even gave them an 'earnest penny' to purchase a modest food supply to help them through the winter.[128]

How much did the two partners invest in this undertaking? In their correspondence with the city council they listed the start-up capital as fl. 23,000, and considering the prices for small kilns, this does not seem excessive. In October 1551 the firm was split up. The reason remains unclear. There was no dispute between the two partners, who continued to work together on other ventures. Perhaps they wished to avoid misunderstandings and disagreements. Previously, Van Schoonbeke had been the only one with council contracts to build sections of the new walls (see below), but at this point Van Hencxthoven started to contract for himself on a smaller scale, giving cause to separate the brick shipments. At any rate, Van Schoonbeke retained fifteen *bunder* of clayfields, eleven brick kilns, 47 homes for workers, and several storage sites, while Van Hencxthoven kept the remaining clayfields, four brick kilns, and thirteen dwellings.[129]

Brickmaking required a large amount of fuel. Since fuel cost far more than wage labour,[130] Van Schoonbeke needed to obtain a more inexpensive source of fuel than those available to the other entrepreneurs in the Scheldt-Rupel region. Only then would he be able to reduce the cost of making bricks. When he presented Mary of Hungary in September 1548 with his idea of building the canals in the New Town at his own expense and constructing the brick kilns required, he had plans to organize his own peat extraction as well. This was characteristic of Van Schoonbeke: competitive pricing while at the same time maximizing earnings by controlling all parts of the production cycle. The capital-intensive nature of peat extraction entailed risks, but in the 1540s peat was a very attractive product. In addition to supplying brickworks operations, commercial opportunities were continuously expanding, as the combination of demographic growth and industrial expansion led demand for fuel to rise exponentially, driving up the cost of firewood and peat.[131] Well aware of what was going on, Van Schoonbeke seized his opportunity in 1549, with an eye to exploiting the imperial peatlands in the Gelderse Vallei (partially in the province of Gelderland and partially in that of Utrecht). The advisors sent by Charles V to inspect the area reported

127 SAA, IB 2977, no. 151, and IB 2992, nos 18-23.

128 SAA, IB 2992, no. 52. Nothing is known about the wages, but data from the second half of the century clearly show that most brick makers relied on poor relief in the winter. Limberger (2008), 136.

129 SAA, R 1758, f° 86, PS 1634, IB 2988, nos 19, 20, 29, and PK 2242, no. 30.

130 Hollestelle (1961), 41-2, 44, 184-5.

131 Scholliers (1960), 44-5.

that while the land had huge potential, given the high cost of peat, operating it profitably would be possible only once the transport problem was resolved. Peat was a bulk product and its value relative to its volume was modest; it therefore had to be transported along waterways. The Eem River connected Amersfoort with the Zuiderzee, but the advisors wondered how peat could be conveyed from the Gelderse Vallei to Amersfoort.[132]

Van Schoonbeke provided the solution: he offered to cover the cost of digging a *grift*, a shallow canal over sixteen kilometres to connect the northern section of the imperial peatlands with Amersfoort. He had prepared the project well and was confident, as was clear from his purchase of several tracts of peat in the Gelderse Vallei throughout 1549.[133] The government welcomed his plan, acknowledged that Van Schoonbeke was the only one who had approached the problem rationally, and praised him as the 'inventor and first man to think of the new canal'. The *grift* was to be *c.* 6 metres wide and *c.* 5 metres deep. Digging was to start in the summer of 1550, and the canal was to be completed within six years. Van Schoonbeke also had to agree to widen and dredge out part of the Eem river. He had to invest a total of fl. 12,000. The returns were commensurate: he was allowed to purchase 600 *morgen* of peat bog and was issued a lease on 200 *morgen* for 36 years at fl. 1100 *per annum*, with payments starting only on 1 May 1553. He would have the exclusive right to transport peat along the new canal for 24 years, but he had to pay the Emperor one stuiver per fifty barrels shipped via the *grift* as a 'recognition fee'.[134] This clause gave Van Schoonbeke a monopoly on the peat trade in the northern section of the Gelderse Vallei for a quarter of a century. The extended lease periods reveal that fuel for his brick kilns was not his only consideration. Was he already considering setting up beer breweries in the New Town in 1550? This is conceivable: Van Schoonbeke was an entrepreneur who always made long-term plans. Given the rising fuel prices, he could in any case expect to sell the peat easily and profitably in Antwerp. In June 1551, i.e. one year after the works began, the *Schonebeker grift* was virtually complete along its entire length of sixteen kilometres, an impressive achievement, even considering the intensive use of existing waterways.[135]

After recently investing a lot of money in brick kilns, tying up yet more capital in peat digging would have been too great a risk. Van Schoonbeke did not intend to purchase any peat bog, but building a canal and digging peat on 270 *morgen* of leased land itself required a considerable investment. Soon after signing the contract with the Emperor, he contacted some prominent businessmen and quickly convinced them that peat extraction could be enormously profitable, especially because in what is now Veenendaal the layers of peat were metres thick.[136] In April they agreed to participate in the venture, and on 20 June 1550 they signed the charter founding the *Compagnie van de Moeren* (Peat Company) for 36 years, commencing retroactively on 1 May 1550. Van Schoonbeke contributed all the peat bog that he had on lease. The area was divided into 32 'shares'. In exchange for eight shares, Van

132 HUA, FI 37/ 2, f° 16v°-17.

133 Génard (1880), 190 no. 53, and 217 no. 208.

134 HUA, FI 37, no. 2, f° 22-24v°, no. 30, f° 42, no. 31, f° 44, and no. 32, f° 46; Stol (1992), 61-4. In the Gelderse Vallei, 1 *morgen* = 8571 square metres.

135 AGR, PEA 135, no. 70, and PEA 1634/1, Letter dated 16 May 1551; SAA, PK 2764, f° 86; HUA, FI 37/2, f° 29v°-31; Stol (1992), 68-70.

136 Over five metres in the area now known as Veenendaal: Smolders and Grootheest (2005), 95.

Table 7. Capital structure and governance of the peat digging company founded by Gilbert van Schoonbeke in 1550

Partners	Shares	Capital investment (in fl.)	Voices
Gilbert van Schoonbeke	8/32	?	3/13
Schetz brothers	8	10,125.0	3
Joris de Veselaer & Co.	5	6,328.1	2
Jacob Rehlinger	4	5,062.5	2
Jan Calvo	3	3,796.9	1
Conrad Sleycher	2	2,531.5	1
Wouter Moermans	2	2,531.5	1
Total	24/32	30,375.0	10/13

Source: AGR, FU, L 226.

Schoonbeke agreed to pay the Emperor the annual lease fee of fl. 1100. His shares entitled him to three of the thirteen votes. The other partners purchased shares corresponding to a given area of land and entitling them to a number of votes in the company. Fl. 150 was payable to Van Schoonbeke for each *morgen* of land. In addition, they contributed towards building the new canal according to their number of shares. Each partner was responsible for his share in the company and received a proportionate share of the annual earnings. Shares were transferable to others, but only after three months, and the other partners had the right of first refusal. All shareholders were entitled to associate third parties in their package of shares, but such second-tier participants had no voting rights.[137]

The Peat Company may be regarded as a precursor to stock companies. Partnerships were not new and became increasingly commonplace in the sixteenth century, but the *Compagnie* was distinctive in several respects. It was an industrial enterprise, whereas merchants nearly always formed associations to carry out commercial or financial ventures. The few exceptions recorded for Antwerp were nothing like the massive, capital-intensive peat operations: the other industrial companies were artisanal undertakings, mainly in the textile industry. The Peat Company was equally exceptional in that there were seven partners, including two firms (Schetz and Veselaer), each with several associates. The majority of the existing partnerships examined in Antwerp comprised two partners, and the largest six merchants. The most distinctive feature of the Peat Company was its extended duration: 36 years. Most partnerships in sixteenth-century Europe lasted from two to ten years; the longest lasted twenty years.[138]

The partners were an impressive group. The Schetz brothers Gaspar, Melchior, and Balthasar, whose father Erasmus had died only recently, were by far the most successful businessmen in Antwerp. They took up eight shares and held three of the thirteen votes. The other partners were all international merchants. Joris de Veselaer (or Vezeleer) traded with France, mainly in luxury goods, and served as Mint Master General for the Duchy of

137 AGR, FU, L 226.
138 On partnership contracts in sixteenth-century Antwerp, see Puttevils (2015), ch. 3, and Van Hofstraeten (2016).

Brabant. He participated in the peat digging company together with six other merchants.[139] They bought five shares, which entitled them to two votes. The South-German merchant-financier Jacob Rehlinger, who traded luxury goods between Antwerp and Venice, had invested in embankments and reclaimed land in Zeeland in the 1530s and 40s.[140] He took up four shares with two votes. Young Jan Calvo was the scion of a Genoese merchant family and was in business in Antwerp from 1545 on.[141] He bought three shares and held one vote. He was appointed director of the *Compagnie*. The financier Conrad Sleycher or Schleicher from Ulm, who in the 1540s provided several loans to the City of Antwerp, took up two shares (one vote), as did the merchant Wouter Moermans, who hailed from Bergen op Zoom.[142]

Together, the partners paid Van Schoonbeke fl. 30,375.[143] All were convinced that the investment would be very profitable, as in April 1553, when peat digging was in progress, Sleycher sold the two shares he had purchased at fl. 2531 to Van Schoonbeke for fl. 4200.[144] The capital went first of all toward digging the new canal, of which the cost had been estimated at fl. 12,000. Next, 76 *aken* were purchased, flat-bottomed barges averaging fl. 28 each, as well as an unknown number of *samoureuzen*, which were large flat cargo vessels that transported peat by river and by sea. As with brickmaking, labour needed to be recruited for peat digging, as few people lived in the area of the imperial peatland. Five spacious buildings were constructed and sparsely furnished. Where the partners found workers to cut and transport peat remains unclear. The only information is the brief announcement from Jan Calvo in the spring of 1551 that 'our people have been sent on three journeys to Amersfoort, costing fl. 400'.[145] All elements suggest well-organized, long-distance migration by large numbers of workers: the high cost, the destination, and the three different groups.

From June 1551 on, peat was conveyed in barges via the *Schonebeker grift* to Amersfoort. Ten gangs were already at work by then, each gang comprising 5 to 6 workers, who were assigned specific tasks.[146] In other words, Van Schoonbeke had commercialized peat digging within the space of a year. This was a feat in itself but also absolutely necessary, as on 17 February 1551 he had signed a contract with the City of Antwerp, in which he agreed to build 4000 rods or 37,600 cubic metres of new walls at fl. 26 per rod within five years,[147] including all the materials: bricks, hardstone, and lime. Old bricks could be used in half the inner walls, but the other half had to be made of top-quality new bricks. The contract was very advantageous to the local government, as in the past contractors had charged the City of Antwerp fl. 36 to fl. 40 per rod.[148] To build the city walls at such an incredibly

139 Coornaert (1961), I, 343-4, and II, 228-9, 257; Wijnroks (2003), 93; Puttevils (2015), 65-6.

140 Kellenbenz (1965); Dekker and Baetens (2010), 288.

141 AGR, FU, L 241, no. 28; SAA, CERT 10, f° 134v°, and CERT 14, f° 164.

142 In June 1552 Sleycher, together with Matthäus Ortel, factor of the Fuggers, and Thomas Balbani from Lucca, lent the City of Antwerp fl. 36,000 at 9 percent: SAA, IB 2999, no. 127. See also IB 2991, nos 88 and 92.

143 AGR, FU, L 226. Calculation based on 200 *morgen*, because the lease of the 70 *morgen* did not materialize.

144 Génard (1880), 211 nos 52 and 168. Van Schoonbeke consequently owned 10 of the 32 shares and became the main partner, holding 4 of the 13 votes from that point onward.

145 'Daernaer heeft de rentmeester ons volck tot Amersfort gesonden in drye reysen. In als 400 ghulden'. SAA, IB 2991, no. 6, and IB 3005, f° 521.

146 SAA, IB 3005, f° 518v°.

147 A rod of masonry measured 20 x 20 x 1 feet, which based on 1 foot = 0.2868 cm, yields a total of 9.4 cubic metres.

148 SAA, IB 2968, IB 2977, no. 27, IB 2992, no. 26, R 1758, f° 175.

low price while turning a profit as well, Van Schoonbeke needed to find inexpensive fuel for his brickworks. To this end, he successfully shipped vast quantities of peat from the Gelderse Valley to the Rupel region. In 1553 he wished to expand operations. He had signed contracts with the vast majority of beer brewers in Antwerp to provide them with a constant fuel supply (see below), necessitating yet more extensive peat digging. Despite initial objections by local landowners, on 9 February 1554 Charles V granted permission to transport the peat situated in the southern section via the Rhine, in fact via the Lek River, to Antwerp.[149]

Obtaining inexpensive fuel for the brick kilns was crucial to keeping down the tender price per cubic metre of brickwork. Other construction materials made a difference as well, especially lime, which accounted for 16 to 19 percent of the total cost of the brickwork in around 1550.[150] Van Schoonbeke therefore arranged his own lime kilns. Charles V let him use two dilapidated houses on the Meuse River near Namur to burn lime and trass (volcanic tuff), and also gave him the run-down Saeftinghe Castle on the Scheldt.[151] Output from the kilns must have been substantial, as within a year he managed to supply his contractors with lime at 8 or 9 stuivers a cargo, where it had previously cost master masons 10 to 12 stuivers.[152]

One indispensable construction material was still missing: the bluestone used to face the new walls. Van Schoonbeke did not, however, start operating stone quarries, which were situated mainly around Vilvoorde near Brussels and in Écaussines in the County of Hainault. One reason was that once the walls in Antwerp were completed, demand for bluestone would wither away. Another was that the highly specialized production process necessitated skilled workers who were available only in the area of the stone quarries. Pre-processing the stones while they were still in the quarries had become customary to reduce their weight and cut transport costs.[153] In this case such action went without saying, as only standard components were used in the new walls. Van Schoonbeke contacted the owners of stone quarries at Brussels, where transport via water did not present a problem. He signed a contract with the master stonemason and merchant Jan de Pelsmaker, who had been operating seven stone quarries in the area of Vilvoorde since 1549 and agreed to supply twenty rods of bluestone with specified measurements and four shiploads of 'perpends' each week for thirty weeks. The total cost was fl. 26,700. De Pelsmaker agreed not to sell bluestone to others for the duration of this contract and pledged goods valued at one thousand guilders as security.[154]

Building the walls required setting up wooden scaffolding. Moreover, large solid wooden beams and a great many boards were needed to construct the Tapestry Hall and somewhat later the breweries in the New Town. Hoping to cut the cost of such materials, Van Schoonbeke asked the Emperor for permission to cut down oaks in the Buggenhout forest he owned at Dendermonde. Obtaining timber from the nearby forest had the additional

---

149 GAV, VGSV 83 and 86; HUA, FI 37/2, f° 55v°-58v°; Stol (1992), 74-7, and (2000), 155.
150 See the calculations in Soly (1977), 244-6.
151 SAA, IB 2996, IB 3008, p. 127, PK 116, p. 182.
152 SAA, IB 2991, no. 52, IB 2992, no. 69/8, R 1773, R 1785, PK 2213.
153 Hurx (2013), 135-6.
154 SAA, IB 3006, File II, passim.

advantage of facilitating transport via the Scheldt to Antwerp, about forty kilometres away. What was expected from Van Schoonbeke in return remains a mystery. In any case, a great many trees were felled, as the receiver of Baasrode, Buggenhout, and Sint-Amands reported that the entrepreneur received timber valued at fl. 5072 in 1554 and 1555.[155]

In 24 to 30 months Van Schoonbeke set up a vertical building trust: he had brickworks and lime kilns and peat and forestry operations, and he was able to supply great quantities of bluestone. This was unprecedented in the Low Countries and probably throughout Europe. His connections in the highest political echelons were indispensable, and he obtained this support on the one hand by convincing the authorities that his system made it possible to build the walls at a far lower cost than the city had paid previously, and on the other hand because the arrangements benefited the Emperor, who owned peatland and forests. These savings were considerable. Following the contract of 17 February 1551 regarding construction of the walls (see above), Van Schoonbeke signed three related contracts with the city council, on 16 July 1551 and on 23 June and 2 July 1552, respectively. Altogether, he built 8439 rods or over 79,000 cubic metres of fortifications, i.e. more than half of the entire defence system, at an average price of fl. 23 per rod, i.e. 40 percent less than what the city had previously paid contractors. In each contract he had assured the city council that in 'normal conditions', not including the winter, within a fixed period 200 rods would be completed weekly on average; the available data indicate that he always delivered the agreed output.[156]

According to guild regulations, carrying out more than two *taswerken* (construction projects) simultaneously or outsourcing construction to others was prohibited. To circumvent these regulations, the city officers would keep signing new contracts with Van Schoonbeke to build a very large part of the walls, and Van Schoonbeke entrusted this *taswerk* to a single affluent master mason. Six to seven contractors took on 96 percent of all the works contracted to Van Schoonbeke; some set up temporary partnerships to raise the necessary capital and spread the risk. The building trust enabled Van Schoonbeke to negotiate a very low contract price. Moreover, he boosted his profits considerably by requiring contractors to accept partial payment in land, consistently assessing each square metre well above what he had paid.[157]

Lack of account books makes the profit that Van Schoonbeke made on his building contracts impossible to calculate. He mentioned an average of fl. 6 per rod. This figure, however, was underestimated, as the remaining agreements he signed with his subcontractors reveal that his earnings averaged fl. 8 per rod, suggesting that his total profit from building the city walls was *c.* fl. 67,500. Were these gross earnings? Van Schoonbeke argued that they were, emphasizing that the necessary construction materials had been very costly. His argument is disputable, as he must have factored in setting up the brick kilns in pricing his bricks and moreover profited finally from selling the kilns in 1554 (see below). At any rate, he was aware that nobody doubted that he made a handsome profit from building the walls and wisely justified this by insisting that nobody should begrudge him his profit,

155 SAA, IB 2989, f° 176v°, IB 2996, IB 3005, f° 529, IB 3013, File II, no. 14; Génard (1880), 196 nos 86-87, and 203 no. 126.

156 See the calculations in Soly (1977), 225, 227-8, 242.

157 SAA, IB 2977, and IB 2999, no. 13.

'as it is thanks to Gilbert that masonry is now available to the city at such a low price', he explained with pride.[158] Moreover, all these contracts 'had already brought him many enemies and caused others to harbour ill intentions toward him, as in building the walls at such a low price, he had put an end to the previous monopolies and deception as regards the prices of construction materials'.[159]

Although Van Schoonbeke indisputably achieved reductions in the cost of construction materials and contracted works, he was by no means averse to 'monopolies.' He had set up new companies and brought about a capitalist organizational structure that enabled him to increase brick production substantially, while reducing its cost. In the years 1551-53 no entrepreneur in the Scheldt-Rupel region could compete with Van Schoonbeke. Thanks to the support of the central government and the city authorities he obtained, moreover, an effective monopoly on public works in Antwerp: starting the New Town, building the Tapestry Hall, and constructing more than half the new walls, the 'building site of the century.' While he admitted that he made a great many enemies, he refused to acknowledge that he was stigmatized as the great monopolist, whose activities had negative social consequences. Yet, by working with only six or seven contractors, he deprived small master masons of opportunities, hurting them all the more as residential construction declined rapidly in the early 1550s. Social divisions in the construction industry were already vast, but the contracts that Van Schoonbeke signed to build the city walls reinforced this inequality, because the small contractors were left empty-handed at a time when far fewer private homes were being built.

His effective monopoly of public works caused problems for wage workers as well. When signing his contract regarding urbanization of the New Town and the Schuttershoven, Van Schoonbeke had convinced the central government to lift restrictions on the Antwerp labour market. On 21 February 1549 an imperial decree proclaimed that masons and carpenters were allowed to come work in Antwerp, regardless of whether they were citizens or had served an apprenticeship with a guild. These 'unfree' workers were required to pay the relevant guild a single registration fee of four stuivers and two stuivers weekly *kaarsgeld* ('candle dues').[160] As a result of the subsequent immigration of skilled and mainly unskilled workers, nominal wages no longer kept pace with the rising cost of living. The decline in purchasing power soon gave rise to discontent, as was clear from the repressive measures that the local authorities took in August and September. This discontent deepened, when wages remained at the old level upon the resumption of work on the defence system in February-March 1551. Thanks to his exclusive agreements with a few contractors, Van Schoonbeke neutralized all competition between the master masons, eliminating any possible incentive to offer better terms of employment. In the end, the steep rise in grain prices in 1552 necessitated adjusting the wages of skilled workers but brought no change for the 'unfree' workers. They responded by trying to impede the

---

158 'Want dat men nu tertyt de metselrye van der stadt tot soo cleynen prijse can besteden, soe is Gilbert daeraff de cause ende occasie geweest'. SAA, IB 3008, no. 21.

159 'Que par ces mesmes contracts icelluy a aussi acquis beaucoup d'ennemys et malveullans, car pour faire la susd. muraille a si bas pris luy a esté besoing de mettre ordre a tous monopoles et larchins qu'on avoit auparavant usé au faict des materiaulx'. SAA, IB 2968.

160 ROPB, 2nd ser., V, 508-9

works on the fortifications in July openly hurling verbal abuse at the city authorities, at the *Fortificatiemeesters*, and especially 'at those who took on the public works'. Clandestine meetings were held and processions with drums and brass instruments organized.[161] In September, when the city council proposed having some works put out to tender to other entrepreneurs, Van Schoonbeke objected vehemently: 'Entrusting masonry to several individuals is likely to drive up the prices of construction materials and wages'. Agreeing with him, Mary of Hungary prevented the city council from involving other entrepreneurs in building the walls.[162]

3.4 The Beer Production Monopoly

Urbanizing the New Town and constructing the city walls, however profitable they might have been, were by nature short-term projects. Van Schoonbeke understood this and soon sought other ways to make money. In 1551, however, such opportunities were not easily found. The resumption of the Habsburg-Valois War complicated economic prospects, because it was feared that hostilities would drag on and would greatly affect international trade in Antwerp. On 1 September, word reached Antwerp that the French had captured a fleet of twenty-eight ships, forcing many merchants to request an extension on payments.[163] In November, Nicolaes Jonghelinck, receiver of the great toll of Zeeland, reported that revenues in September-October were nearly 40 percent lower than for the same period the previous year.[164] In December the *flotte d'Espagne* (Spanish fleet) was captured by the French *en route* from the Iberian Peninsula to Antwerp. This resulted in huge losses. Government officials declared that rumours of bankruptcies abounded on the Antwerp Exchange, and that no-one dared any longer to talk about trade: 'Hundreds of merchants have toiled their entire life for what they have lost in a single day'.[165] The economic outlook did not improve in 1552. On the contrary, the Emperor had a miserable year, the most disastrous of his reign, as he suffered crushing military defeats on all fronts.[166] In Antwerp everyone deplored the heavy losses of merchants and master artisans alike: the former as a result of piracy and disruption of international trade and the latter because of delays in English cloth imports, which greatly affected cloth shearers and cloth dyers.[167]

Still, everyone in this populous city needed to eat and drink. In a capital-intensive industry such as brewing, the decline in demand during an economic slump affected only expensive beer varieties. After all, the masses had to stick to beer. Wine was too expensive and the water in most parts of Antwerp sub-standard. Not even patients at Saint Elisabeth Hospital were given water to drink. The available data suggest that around the middle

161 SAA, PK 915, f° 99v°-101, 149v°-150, 151v°, 165v°; Scholliers (1960), 133.

162 'Qu'en donnant lesd. heuvres de massonnerie es mains de particuliers personnes, qu'il estoit a craindre que les materiaulx et salaires des travailleurs viendroient grandement a monter'. SAA, IB 3000, no. 27.

163 AGR, PEA 1634/2, Letter dated 1 September 1551, and SAA, IB 3002, no. 5.

164 SAA, COLL 8, f° 196v°-197. See also Coornaert (1961), I, 99.

165 'Il y a cent et cent marchans qui ont travaillé toute leur vye pour gaigner ce que pour ceste foiz en ung jour ilz ont perdu'. AGR, PEA 1634/2, *Information*.

166 Parker (2019), 435-9.

167 SAA, IB 2976, no. 6; De Smedt (1950-1952), I, 186, 193-4, 205-7, and II, 432-3.

of the century annual beer consumption in the city averaged 350 to 360 litres per capita, keeping in mind that much of the consumption consisted of *cleyn bier* (small beer), with an alcohol content less than 0.7 percent, comparable to 'heated water', as a contemporary stated. Even a middle-category beer, such as *koyte* or *kuit*, had an alcohol content of only 1.9 percent.[168] When Van Schoonbeke proposed his plan for urbanizing the New Town in September 1548, he had already mentioned briefly that breweries might be built there. He was captivated by the idea, which first took form in 1551. He wanted to become thoroughly familiar with the industry first however. The best means to this end was by collecting the excise duties on beer. Since many innkeepers sold both beer and wine, leading to overlap between the excise revenues, Van Schoonbeke opted to lease the right to collect the wine excise duties as well.[169]

Receiving excise duties on beer did not benefit Van Schoonbeke financially but was nonetheless of immense value, as he could learn exactly what was going wrong in the Antwerp brewing industry and why. Local production was far from sufficient: 40 to 50 percent of the beer consumed in the city was imported. Most came from places in the immediate vicinity: Berchem, Borgerhout, Deurne, Merksem, and Wilrijk. In addition, large quantities were imported from Hoegaarden and Zoutleeuw, the two most important export centres in Brabant, as well as from Mechelen and (in smaller quantities) Leuven. Upmarket varieties from abroad accounted for only a small proportion of all imports.[170] The main competitors of the Antwerp brewers were therefore the 'outside brewers', operating 3 to 6 kilometres outside the city walls. Better soil conditions or the availability of clean running water (the River Schijn in Borgerhout, Deurne, and Merksem) enabled them to produce much better beer there.[171] In Antwerp only the few brewers in relatively close proximity to the Herentalse Vaart had access to clean water. Most of their fellow brewers used well water, which because of the neighbouring Scheldt often ruined the taste of the beer. Moreover, according to contemporaries the briny water required a higher grain content per barrel of beer.[172] As in the surrounding villages no excise duties were payable or were only half of those levied in Antwerp, beer there could be priced much lower. Many citizens therefore often drank their beer outside the city.

Van Schoonbeke quickly understood that the local brewing industry had massive growth potential. The crucial need was to improve the quality of beer brewed, which depended primarily on whether the majority of the brewers could be provided with clean water. In addition, competition from the 'outside brewers' would either need to be countered, for example by granting the Antwerp brewers excise privileges, or neutralized by prohibiting imports into the city. Since the brewers had no guild,[173] any drastic and extensive reorganization of the industry could be carried out without regulations on company size, output, and the like needing to be taken into account. Negotiations were possible with each individual brewer, and a group contract could be entered into without

168 Soly (1968), 342, 349-50; Aerts (2011b), 35-7.
169 For more detail, see Soly (1977), 285-7.
170 Soly (1968), 346-9.
171 Nooyens (1981), I, 377-81, 490, 581-2.; Patroons (2009), 21-5.
172 SAA, IB 3017.
173 Only in 1581 did the Antwerp brewers unite in a *Natie*, a guild-like organization.

everyone necessarily agreeing. A collective agreement was necessary, because solving the water problem efficiently required a concentration of breweries, which would yield other economies of scale. Relocations, however, were costly undertakings. It was important therefore to assure potential participants that they would receive exceptional privileges, enabling them to obtain far greater earnings than those who were reluctant to make the change. Without assistance from the public authorities, these relocations would not have come about.

First, Van Schoonbeke dealt with the competition from the 'outside brewers', achieving agreement between the local and central authorities. On 8 April 1552 Charles V prohibited the inhabitants of Antwerp from drinking beer within one league (i.e. 5.5 kilometres) of the city. Brewers and innkeepers operating in this zone who had the temerity to sell or serve beer to Antwerp residents were fined ten guilders and were expelled upon repeat offences. The only exceptions were made for weddings, fairs, and pilgrimages.[174] This prohibition – the first of many – is unlikely to have achieved the desired effect, but that did not matter. Van Schoonbeke had demonstrated that as receiver of the excise duties on beer he took the interests of the Antwerp brewers seriously, *and* that he was sufficiently influential to turn a drastic fiscal measure to their advantage.

His negotiations with the city council paralleled those with the local brewers, as each party had to convince the other. He offered to build several breweries at his own expense in the New Town between the first and the second canals. In addition to increasing land values in the area and making land easier to sell, these operations would increase beer production, and therefore revenues from excise duties for the city. In the intensive negotiations that followed, the city authorities wanted to be certain that most brewers would settle in the New Town, which was indeed what happened: by September Van Schoonbeke had thirteen of the twenty brewers on board. On 2 December 1552 he signed a contract with them. By then, however, he had already reached an agreement with the City of Antwerp – post-dated to 22 December.[175] Since Van Schoonbeke's new project was unlikely to please everybody, the burgomasters and aldermen notified the Broad Council only two weeks later, in vague terms and without the name of the pivotal operator. They conveyed the impression that 'a few good men, from outside and inside the city alike, wish to set up some breweries' and easily obtained approval from the Council. When central government officials saw the contract, they understood it would have sweeping ramifications and asked whether the representatives of the Antwerp city council or the Broad Council had indeed approved all clauses. The elusive reply was that the *gist* or general intent had been explained and accepted, and that all details of an agreement were not ordinarily discussed in public.[176]

To convince over half the brewers of Antwerp to move to the New Town, the benefits for them had to be very enticing, especially considering that they had to pledge in the contract never again to produce beer other than in Van Schoonbeke's breweries. If they sold or leased their old brewery, they had to prohibit the new owner or tenant from ever again using the building as a brewery. Why did most brewers agree to join Van Schoonbeke in his plan? The entrepreneur promised to build a large brewery for each of them in the New

174 SAA, T 199.
175 SAA, IB 2973, no. 9, and IB 2976, no. 6.
176 SAA, T 726, f° 69-72, and IB 3002, no. 67.

Town. These breweries would include a full basement, offices, stables, and a paved attic but would not be equipped with kettles or other equipment. He promised that he would guarantee a continual supply of enough clean water. 'His' brewers would get permission to replicate the superior beer from Hoegaarden Zoutleeuw, Mechelen, and other centres in the Netherlands, and to sell it for the same price as the importers of these products.[177] They would receive exceptional tax benefits moreover: exemption from export taxes on beer transported to places where the city did not levy excise duties,[178] and exemption from all conceivable taxes levied in Antwerp at the time or introduced later on. Van Schoonbeke guaranteed them that for 25 years these benefits would apply exclusively to those setting up business in his breweries. Storage sites for foreign beer and excise offices would be transferred to the New Town, to avert any lost time in settling accounts.

Not all brewers accepted the proposal, however. Small entrepreneurs are likely to have objected to the prohibition in the New Town against launching any additional economic sidelines besides brewing beer. Some may have been deterred at the prospect of having to arrange for their own equipment, as they would probably need to purchase a new kettle upon moving to much larger premises.[179] Statements made later on indicate that they also feared losing *clandise*, custom. Since they ran small businesses in poor neighbourhoods and therefore had to sell on credit, moving to the New Town complicated direct contact and consequently debt collection as well.[180] As with his effective monopoly of the public works, the effort by Van Schoonbeke to concentrate beer production in a single brewery complex led to polarization between large and small entrepreneurs.

Why did the city council grant Van Schoonbeke's brewers so many privileges, thereby promoting his drive towards monopoly? The main reason was that this project increased the value of the vast tracts in the New Town owned by the City of Antwerp. The same held true for the smaller projects that Van Schoonbeke aimed to carry out at the same time, especially building large cellars/storage areas and installing cranes, which would encourage commercial activity. Prospective tax revenues were at least as important. The city authorities expected Van Schoonbeke's project to boost local beer production, creating a surge in income from excise duties, which were the main source of city finance. Excise duties on alcoholic beverages accounted for 70 to 80 percent of the annual income of the city, with 50 to 60 percent of such income coming from excise duties on beer. Few first-rate brewery centres in the Netherlands derived such a substantial share of their income from this source.[181] The proportions reveal that the Antwerp city council relied almost exclusively on indirect taxes, and that beer consumption was the main focus in taxation, meaning that the least affluent population groups contributed disproportionately. Van Schoonbeke proved that excise duties on beer could be collected far more efficiently and convinced the Emperor to prohibit 'drinking outside the city walls'. From the perspective of city finances, he showed himself once again as the ideal entrepreneur: in addition to the savings achieved, he offered prospects for additional income.

177 Van Schoonbeke had urged the city council to allow this practice: SAA, T 199, *Remonstrantie*.

178 Exports were taxed at three stuivers per barrel (*c.* 150 litres). SAA, IB 3002, no. 11.

179 In 1580 Gerard Gramaye estimated the value of equipment at a large brewery at *c.* fl. 700. SAA, IB 768, f° 12v°.

180 See SAA, GA 4416.

181 Soly (1968), 339; Masure (1986), Table IV; Unger (2004), 196-8.

Soon afterwards, however, the city authorities faced a major dilemma, since Van Schoonbeke offered to purchase a vast area in the New Town but insisted on very low prices: 400 rods or 13,160 square metres between the first and the second canal at fl. 160 per rod, which was less than fl. 5 per square metre, payable on 1 October 1553, and 1100 rods or 36,910 square metres at only fl. 56 per rod or fl. 1.7 per square metre.The price for the second lot was so ridiculously low that the city council members changed their minds a few months later and voided the purchase. Van Schoonbeke planned to build twenty breweries on the first lot, plus eight more later on, at the discretion of the city council. Along the first canal he would pay to provide eighty to one hundred cellars, each one measuring *c.* 6.3 by *c.* 11 metres, as space for the wholesale trade. Van Schoonbeke insisted that this was absolutely necessary, as many shipmasters importing Spanish wine, oil, and 'solid fruit' lacked suitable storage areas and therefore often unloaded their ships in Middelburg. He was authorized to entrust all construction of industrial sites to masons and carpenters who did not belong to the guilds in the city and obtained permission to set up four cranes along both canals to load and unload the ships, provided that he give the city one third of the proceeds. Last but not least, the local authorities agreed to shut down the city brewery Backersveer on the Scheldt, once the lease expired. It is little wonder that government officials asked whether the Broad Council had been notified! The 'details' of the contract proved that Van Schoonbeke had his own way on all counts.[182]

Brewers who set up operations in the New Town henceforth had to pay Van Schoonbeke two stuivers for each *aam* of beer (*c.* 150 litres) they produced: the 'two-stuiver dues'. These dues were halved for the *koyte*, as well as for beer exported to places where the city did not charge excise duties. Averse to taking risks, Van Schoonbeke stipulated that every brewer had to pay at least ten guilders a week, even if the minimum output of one hundred *amen* had not been reached. Only those whose annual output exceeded 10,000 *amen*, i.e. nearly 200 *amen* weekly, were permitted to engage in other economic activities. Brewers were allowed to use only firewood or peat as fuel. Once again, the Peat Company proved immensely important: since firewood was very expensive indeed, brewers could afford only peat, which they had to buy from Van Schoonbeke at three guilders per *last*.[183] Although they had six months to repay their debts, immediate cash payment entitled them to a discount of 8.3 percent. The brewers also had to allow Van Schoonbeke to use two-thirds of the cellars and three grain lofts for his own use at each firm. Finally, they agreed to use the transport service he would organize,[184] as well as to have their grain processed in the watermills he intended to set up in the New Town.

In a stroke of genius, Van Schoonbeke involved the highest authority in his brewery site. On 18 February 1553 Charles V ratified his contract with the city council; all the benefits the brewers in the New Town had been granted were thus sanctioned by the Emperor. Van Schoonbeke wanted to have the two-stuiver dues guaranteed by law as well. He convinced the central government that these dues would not affect consumers. On 20 February 1554 Charles V officially authorized him to collect these 'duties'. In exchange for the favour, Van

182 SAA, IB 2976, no. 6, and IB 3002, no. 34.

183 In the contract, one *last* equalled forty large barrels, with one barrel comprising 150 pieces. According to the brewers, peat accounted for ten percent of the cost of producing an *aam* of quality beer: SAA, IB 3014, no. 49.

184 They paid him the *biersteker* duties, i.e. for beer transport in the city, ¼ stuiver per *aam*.

Schoonbeke offered the Emperor five sixteenths of the two-stuiver dues. Charles V in turn stipulated that if his share exceeded fl. 2,000 *per annum*, he would pay Van Schoonbeke a year fee of fl. 800. While this may still be regarded as customary, the willingness of the Emperor to invest in Van Schoonbeke's new enterprise was most unusual: he purchased an annuity of fl. 6250 in the brewery site, for which he paid fl. 125,000.[185] Based on the available data, Charles V did not form such close ties with any other industrial or commercial enterprise in the Netherlands or elsewhere. How Van Schoonbeke achieved this remains unclear, except that he was supported by Gaspar Schetz, who participated in the Peat Company and served as financial advisor to the central government. This is revealed by the fact that Charles V transferred one sixteenth of the two-stuiver dues and a fifth of the annuity in the brewery complex (i.e. fl. 1250) to Schetz. This share in the two-stuiver dues was given to him as the result of a request by Van Schoonbeke, making clear that Schetz had been the intermediary, but the fl. 1250 annuity was paid for by him.[186] Still, a recommendation by Schetz does not explain why the Emperor entered into this commitment personally. Did he do so at the urging of Mary of Hungary, who trusted Van Schoonbeke and Schetz blindly? One important motive may have been that a considerable increase in local beer production would drive up income from excise duties for the City of Antwerp, making it harder for the local authority to argue that insufficient financial means were available to provide the Emperor with new funds. In 1553/4 the central government was constantly being told this (see below). Few people in Antwerp would have been aware in 1553 and 1554 that the Emperor was directly and personally involved in the brewery complex in the New Town, but hardly anyone would have doubted that Van Schoonbeke had a great deal and probably everything to do with it. The population of Antwerp kept a close watch on the course of events. Chroniclers carefully recorded the date on which the first stone was placed: 11 April 1553.[187] They also noted that less than one year later, specifically by Holy Week (i.e. before 25 March 1554), ten breweries had opened in the New Town.[188]

Van Schoonbeke's brewery complex was unique in the sixteenth century, both in the Netherlands and throughout Northwest and Central Europe. Nowhere else did one individual manage to concentrate the bulk of local beer production in his own undertaking. Breweries by definition required a substantial capital investment. In this case, there were sixteen breweries, ten of which were situated on the north side of the first canal (now Brouwersvliet), and each covered nearly 800 square metres; in 1560 their estimated value averaged fl. 10,000. The six others were along the south side of the second canal, and each covered 510 square metres; their value averaged out at fl. 8000.[189] Whether the differences in surface area and price reflect two different types of brewery is impossible to determine, for lack of a basis of comparison. Van Schoonbeke also incurred additional costs as well. To organise transport of the beer, he purchased fourteen large drays and eleven carts, as well as seventeen horses kept in a spacious new stable. According to the city authorities,

185 SAA, IB 2978, nos 25 and 29. Charles V paid a large share in *rentmeestersbrieven*, which Van Schoonbeke had the Schetz brothers disburse: AGR, FU, L 237; SAA, T 1707, nos 723-728.

186 SAA, IB 2978, no. 28, IB 2981, no. 60, T 1325.

187 De Weert (1879), 133.

188 U[llens] (1743), 50; *Chronycke* (1843), 48.

189 SAA, IB 3002, *Estimatie*.

concentration of brewing justified building inspection facilities for the city along the first canal: two excise duties offices, one building for the beer carriers and another for the *segeleers*, the city officials who recorded how many barrels of beer were produced and exported every day. The buildings of these official institutions were constructed at the expense of the city.

The guarantee that they would have continuous access to fresh, pure water was initially the main incentive for the brewers. When for obscure reasons the system he had designed was not yet ready for use in 1553/4, Van Schoonbeke purchased four *waterschepen* to convey water from the Rupel to the New Town. The arrangement was expensive,[190] but the makeshift supply was to be replaced by a permanent and central water supply system: a *Waterhuis* (Water House). The solution was both ingenious and simple. Van Schoonbeke diverted a tributary from the small Schijn River to a closed section of the moat at the city wall, whence it continued 932 metres via an underground brick conduit from the Rode Poort (Red Gate) to the *Waterhuis*, where a horse-powered scoop wheel transferred the water to an elevated reservoir. From there the water flowed through lead pipes to the different breweries.[191] The mechanism was not technologically sophisticated and in fact dated back centuries. Water distribution systems moreover had already been developed in several medieval cities. In Bruges there was a Water House, whence water was pumped to several fountains in the city, where inhabitants could collect it. In Ypres water was brought from a remote pond via lead pipes to the city.[192] In the fourteenth century in the Hanse cities Lübeck, Hamburg, and Bremen, water distribution systems were set up for the brewing industry that was so essential there, and in Braunschweig during the first half of the sixteenth century a great many breweries were connected to a central water supply.[193] The Antwerp Water House was distinctive, however, in that in addition to providing the breweries in the immediate surroundings with water, it was equipped to supply other industrial buildings and individual residences in the New Town and in fact did so in the centuries that followed. The innovative quality of the brewery complex that Van Schoonbeke created derived from its organizational structure. He brought everything necessary to brew and distribute beer within and around a single geographically concentrated undertaking: unloading facilities and storage sites for grain and hops, breweries, the water distribution system, means of transport, a large stable, urban control of production and exports, and management of excise duties on beer. Nowhere else in sixteenth-century Europe was there anything comparable.

The brewery complex became pivotal to Van Schoonbeke's business interests at this point. All other economic activities were rendered subordinate. Peat operations had become far more important than in previous years and therefore continued, but the brick kilns rapidly lost significance, as by the end of 1553 work on the city walls had mostly been finished. Therefore he sold his eleven kilns in Hemiksem.[194] Excise duties on beer

190 See SAA, SR 250, f° 152, and IB 3012, no. 1.

191 SAA, IB 3012/1, *Extract*, and IB 2170, *Verbael*; Van Craenenbroeck (2019a), 100-10.

192 Van Craenenbroeck (1988), 65 (with references to the literature).

193 Hoffmann (2000), 114-16.

194 On the contract, see SAA, IB 2999, no. 176, and IB 3005, f° 504-7; Schepper (1953), 116. Van Hencxthoven retained his brick kilns. See Limberger (2008), 135.

now became more important than ever. Van Schoonbeke, having learned from his lease experience, stated that he was willing to serve only as receiver in the future. From 12 April 1553 he was commissioned for the duration of the war against France to collect excise duties on beer in exchange for 1 percent of the annual proceeds.[195] Since the wine trade in Antwerp seemed to be recovering at the end of that year, leasing the excise duties on wine no longer seemed as risky, and on 10 January 1554 Van Schoonbeke signed a two-year contract with Van Hencxthoven, Nicolaes Maes, and two other businessmen at fl. 75,000 *per annum*. They also paid fl. 1000 *per annum* to lease the crane excise duties.[196]

At this time, the city finances appeared to revolve entirely around Van Schoonbeke. Most of the expenditure from the *Fortificatiekas* went toward paying for his work on the city walls. In addition, he controlled nearly all essential municipal excise duties, including the excise duties on beer, i.e. more than half the municipal income. Together with a few other businessmen he held a lease on the excise duties on wine and cranes, which accounted for an additional 25 to 30 percent of the annual city revenues. Never before had an individual entrepreneur become so dominant in city finance. As he also concentrated 80 to 90 percent of local beer production in his breweries, his activities had an enormous impact on the daily consumer habits of Antwerp's citizens.

3.5 An Anti-Monopoly Revolt

Henri Pirenne stressed that during the rule of Charles V 'no revolts or riots' occurred in Antwerp, substantiating his view of a successful mercantile-monarchical alliance. He argued that the prosperity of Antwerp was attributable to the dissolution of commercial privileges by the city council with the approval of the Emperor.[197] Pirenne presented no evidence for this assertion, but that still does not explain why he ignored the dramatic events of 11-12 July 1554, which is all the more remarkable, because this was the only collective action in the sixteenth-century metropolis in which political and religious motives had no role whatsoever. Precisely for this reason, the revolt gave rise to such an outcry in the Netherlands. Later, i.e. after it was suppressed, the awareness that businessmen had been the targets, and that the political elite had immediately granted the demands of the insurgents had raised questions that led to very different interpretations. Pirenne had read Guicciardini's 'Description', in which the insurgency – this *tragédie* according to the Italian author – was depicted as one of the three most important events in the recent history of Antwerp.[198] He was also familiar with the voluminous study by Alexandre Henne about the rule of Charles V, which dealt at length with the events of 11-12 July, and the

195 SAA, IB 2976, no. 6.

196 The duties payable for unloading or loading barrels of wine and other goods using one of the two cranes on the banks of the Scheldt: SAA, T 532; Masure (1986), 124-5. A rotating wooden crane that had stood on the wharf since the thirteenth century was dismantled around 1550. Shortly before, the city had paid to set up two new wooden cranes, one on the wharf and the other near Sint-Jansvliet. See Degryse (1991), 153-66.

197 Pirenne (1923; first edition 1912), 268-72 (here 269).

198 The other major events were: the abortive siege of the city by Maarten van Rossum in 1542 and the Joyous Entry of Prince Philip in 1549. Guicciardini (1567b), 118-20.

sources edited by Charles Piot on the topic.[199] Was he unable to contextualize the revolt and therefore also unable to interpret it properly? Or did he regard too many elements as incompatible with his view of Antwerp's Golden Age, namely a new alliance between a 'progressive' city council opposed to economic privileges and a monarchy opposed to political privileges? He was mistaken about Antwerp's political elite, which was certainly not known for its commercial initiatives.[200] Relations between city and state were moreover far more complex and conflictual than he believed.[201] Other historians did mention the revolt, and some even discussed it extensively, noting the resistance to Van Schoonbeke's new breweries.[202] Because they failed to consult the main archival sources, however, they misinterpreted crucial aspects and, moreover, did not manage to make clear which groups instigated the unrest and why.

Undoubtedly, the revolt was anti-monopolist. While widespread discontent about Van Schoonbeke's 'cunning practices' was longstanding, his concentration of beer production in the New Town was a turning point. Beer was above all the drink of the masses, and attempts to monopolize vital foodstuffs had been harshly condemned for centuries. The edict *De monopoliis* proclaimed by Emperor Zeno in 483 and later included in the *Codex Justinianus* stated that no one was 'to exercise a monopoly' in food or clothing or any other useful thing, and that merchants or other persons were not allowed to 'combine or agree' concerning a minimum price for merchandise.[203] In medieval Europe the edict inspired theologians and moralists,[204] as well as scholars of law, as is clear from the statutes of Italian cities, the *Polizeiverordnungen* proclaimed in large German cities, several ordinances of French kings, and English Common Law. The prohibitions mainly or even exclusively targeted forestallers of victuals, known in German as *Fürkauf*; sometimes maximum prices were set for bread and ale or wine to preclude such practices.[205]

In the Habsburg Netherlands legal scholars debated the monopoly issue from the early sixteenth century onward. Between 1510 and 1516 the Flemish-born legal scholar Filip(s) Wielant composed a manual on criminal offences, in which he devoted a chapter to monopolist practices. The work was never published, but manuscripts are very likely to have circulated. In 1531 and 1540 imperial ordinances were issued prohibiting merchants from entering 'contracts, pacts or agreements smacking of monopoly or prejudicial to the common good, such as to buy all the commodities of any sort to keep them amongst themselves and afterwards to sell at excessive prices, or other similar practice'. In practice, however, nothing changed, as the legal scholar Joos de Damhouder noted ten years later. He had copied the bulk of Wielant's treatise, added bits here and there, and translated it all into Latin. The complete work was published as *Praxis Rerum Criminalium*. This immensely influential manual was reprinted 36 times between 1554 and 1660 and was translated into Dutch, French, and German. He qualified monopolies and price fixing as 'detestable

199 Henne (1860), X, 177-81; Piot (1879), 148-72.
200 Goris (1925), 6, already noted correctly that 'the city council manifested a more than slight interest in commercial initiative.'
201 See the critical remarks by Wells (1982), 16-18.
202 See, e.g., the extensive discussions by Wegg (1916), 266-70, and Prims (1938b).
203 *Corpus Iuris Civilis*, Codex, Book IV, Title LIX.2.
204 See esp. Langholm (2003).
205 Piotrowski (1933), 111-17, 138-52; Isenmann (2014), 957-60.

crimes', contrary to both Christian doctrine and the Common Good. He regarded the placards issued by Charles V in 1531 and 1540 as exemplary laws but added that although monopoly is often committed, 'it goes almost unpunished'.[206] In Antwerp this even held true for grain speculation. In 1511 the city council explicitly prohibited purchasing grain before it had been reaped and threshed and offered for sale on the city market by the farmer-producer. The ordinance was repeatedly proclaimed afterwards, but in each case the penal provisions were of so little significance that few speculators would have been deterred. Only in times of extreme scarcity and consequently very high prices were more serious sanctions proclaimed, but whether they were actually imposed is doubtful.[207]

Basically, efforts to monopolize essential victuals could be condemned on theological, moral, and legal grounds, but effective actions were not traditionally taken against those who violated legislation or regulations. The local authorities did not expect Van Schoonbeke's concentration of beer production and collection of excise duties to cause a scandal and therefore took no precautionary measures. They did not realize how ubiquitous and deep-seated the discontent was. Van Schoonbekes's new initiative soon proved a fertile breeding ground for a wave of rumours that caused still greater damage to his reputation. Shortly after several breweries opened in the New Town, rumours of doubtful water quality proliferated. Van Schoonbeke had a fountain built, where people could drink the water brought in from the Rupel.[208] He knew, however, that he was also blamed for the flawed execution of some of the work on the city walls and for questionable sales of city property. He therefore urged Mary of Hungary to announce in Antwerp that all his contracts had been approved by the central government.[209] The malicious gossip persisted. On 3 July 1554 the rumour spread throughout Antwerp that beer brewed in the New Town 'from semi-putrid water led it to be infested by a species of maggots'.[210] City council delegates investigated the matter and demonstrated that the brewer who had produced the beer was located on Paardenmarkt and had no contract with Van Schoonbeke, but refuting rumours did not engender goodwill. Some members of the political elite had long mistrusted Van Schoonbeke and used the hint of scandal to target the entrepreneur in other ways. In early June 1554 rumour had it that Margrave Willem van de Werve had welcomed both brewers from the old city and brewers from Borgerhout and Deurne to his castle in Schilde and had assured them that they had his full support, which clearly suggested that he disapproved of the reorganization in the brewery industry.[211]

The rising tensions in Antwerp worsened because of the considerable subsidies requested by the Emperor and the responses from the clergy and the aristocracy in the States of Brabant.[212] When in 1554 a new grant of fl. 400,000 was requested, the clergy – with reluctant agreement from the aristocracy – stated that the amount could not be raised solely by increasing excise duties on beer, wine, wheat, and meat but would also

206 Wielant (1995), 263-5; De Damhouder (1981), 244-8. Quotations from: Cowen (2007), 39-40.
207 Scholliers (1960), 52-4.
208 SAA, IB 3011, no. 1.
209 AGR, PEA 1634/1, Letter of 12 April 1554.
210 'Van een water dat halff stanck, waerdoor datter een specie van maeyen in 't bier quamp'. U[llens] (1743), 50.
211 SAA, V 279, 4-6 July 1554, V 1095, f° 241v°.
212 Prims (1938a).

necessitate taxing commercial commodities, such as cloth and silks. Representatives from the cities of Antwerp, Brussels, Leuven, and 's-Hertogenbosch, who together made up the third estate, objected vehemently. Especially the deans of the three main guilds in Antwerp – the Cloth Dressers, the Mercers, and the Shipmen – fought tooth and nail, causing a serious problem, because as long as they resisted, the City of Antwerp could not approve the subsidy. The automatic consequence was that the third estate persisted in its refusal, and the States had no choice but to turn down the request from the imperial government. The representatives of Antwerp were pressured without success and the guild deans persisted in their objections. They argued that a tax on trade commodities in these economically difficult times would lead to the general downfall and ruin of the city and community, because the international merchants would then relocate to other centres. This was all the more likely, because 'malicious foreign cities and individuals' would take advantage of the situation to offer attractive conditions. They mentioned Hamburg, the port city that had been evolving into a formidable competitor since the 1540s,[213] and which from 1550 onward started to benefit from the shift of the commercial epicentre from Central Europe to the North-German coast.[214] They feared the possible revival of the cloth market in Bergen op Zoom, which the city was aiming at, and in which the wealthy London members of the Merchant Adventurers were immensely interested as an alternative to Antwerp, in case of possible problems there.[215] The guild deans made equally clear that new taxes on beer, wine, wheat, and meat were out of the question, as 'all food products and beverages in the city are already so heavily taxed and assessed that increasing that burden is truly impossible.' Moreover, most master craftsmen were already facing serious reductions in income, and the number of paupers was rising. 'It seems fair to us', the deans continued, 'that this contribution should respect *equaliteyt* (equality), without taxing the urban population more heavily than the prelates and noblemen or this city more than another'. The clergy was unaffected by a tax on trade commodities or by new taxes on food products and beverages. The cities were expected to bear the entire burden, with Antwerp contributing at least half, 'which did not provide equality'.[216]

The discourse revealed widespread and deeply-rooted discontent. Broad population groups in Antwerp were fed up with having to make huge financial contributions, especially because several members of the local government had been involved in mismanagement and corruption in previous years, while the aldermen had done little to protect the commercial or industrial interests of the urban community, let alone encourage them, and instead had signed contracts with 'monopolists'. Mary of Hungary was not fully aware of the tensions at play but understood that concessions were needed. She informed the representatives of the City of Antwerp that the tax on merchandise would be abolished, and that small beers would not be taxed.[217] They would, however, have to accept a tax on the higher-priced beer varieties, on wine, on wheat and on meat, as the Emperor desperately needed the

213 Brulez (1962), 178-9.

214 Van der Wee (1963), II, 216-17.

215 Sutton (2005), 422-3. See also De Smedt (1950-1954), I, 192-3.

216 'Dat in dese contributie equaliteyt zoude betamen geobserveert te worden zonder meer de gemeynte dan de prelaten ende edelen te bezwaren'. SAA, PK 2393, 'Corte verthooninghe'.

217 Defined by the central government as beers costing less than 1/8 stuiver for a jar of *c.* 1.4 litres.

new income. After some haggling on 1 July 1554 the Antwerp delegation finally submitted and returned to the metropolis with its tail between its legs, well aware of the adverse reactions this would elicit.[218] The extent of tension is clear from the two urgent letters that the city sent to Brussels on 3 and 4 July, reporting in the first letter that the order from the governor to arm all men of fighting age presented serious risks and in the second advising against consulting the Broad Council to avert 'perplexing the population still more and making still clearer how dire prospects appear.'[219] Discontent peaked in Antwerp, when on 7 July Mary of Hungary ordered that four detachments of foot soldiers be raised at the city's expense.[220] Little more was necessary for an uproar to ensue – which was what happened a few days later.

During the inspection of the armed citizens on Sunday 8 July, rebellious talk was already audible, but serious incidents did not yet occur. The mass gathering, however, was a catalyst, as many realized only then how widespread the discontent and embitterment were. Three days later, on Wednesday 11 July at around seven 'o clock in the evening, the situation exploded. Pensionary Jacob Maes had obliged men of military age from several neighbourhoods to assemble again on Grote Markt in front of the city hall.[221] Witnesses later stated unanimously that he had called them *canaille* and *rapaille* (scoundrels and scum) and to make matters worse had told those from Kronenburgwijk that they were *pyonniers*, navvies, and folk for digging canals, but not real men.[222] When a scornful city messenger loudly proclaimed that a regiment of Spanish soldiers would march into the city that night and might ravish the wives of the inhabitants,[223] two to three thousand irate men shouted that they were fed up. There was an avalanche of reproaches and accusations. Van Schoonbeke's brewery complex was a disgrace, the receivers of the excise duties were dishonest, pensionary Maes was to be dismissed immediately, and no money should be wasted on recruiting troops... Burgomaster Hendrik van Berchem, alderman Jacob Hertsen, and treasurer general Antoon van Stralen tried to calm the angry mob, explaining that the city messenger had been talking nonsense, but they were pelted with stones.[224] The officeholders no longer wielded any moral authority. The revelations of corruption on the part of Van der Heyden, Van Ursel, and other members of the municipal government in the late 1540s and the early 1550s had already undermined public trust, compounded by the recent accusations by the *Fortificatiemeesters*, that in the construction of the city walls the sole concern of burgomaster Van Berchem and several aldermen had been to 'profit and benefit personally from them'.[225] Since the crowd continued to swell and became more threatening, militia companies were called in. They were attacked, and Herman Coninckx, who had recently been proclaimed King of the Marksmen for the Old Crossbow Guild, was beaten so severely that he died of his injuries a few days later. The militia companies

218 SAA, PK 2514, f° 278-280v°, 288.

219 SAA, PK 2401, nos 75-76. See also Prims (1938b), 251-3.

220 SAA, PK 2393.

221 The medieval city hall was on the south side of Grote Markt, along Suikerrui.

222 RAB, RB, OF 510, no. 24.

223 Spanish soldiers were widely known for lewd and lascivious behaviour. In 1553 Charles V had to remove them from Brussels to avert unrest. Henne (1858-60), X, 171.

224 SAA, IB 2979, no. 29.

225 SAA, R 1757, *Copie*, Introduction.

ultimately charged the crowd and managed to clear the area around the city hall, after which they cordoned off the streets leading there with chains and set up arquebusses in the adjacent houses. The wardmasters were instructed to arm their hundredth men and tenth men and set up defences in the streets of their wards.[226]

In the night of 11 to 12 July the revolt spread throughout the city. Some wardmasters later reported that residents of Kronenburgwijk and Kauwenberg (both poor neighbourhoods) were starting to speak of *metten rijcken te deylen*, sharing with the rich.[227] In vain, the authorities tried to have arms transferred from the city warehouse to Grote Markt. Early in the morning alderman Dierick van de Werve went to the House of Aachen with an armed bodyguard, where he met with Cornelis de Schepper (member of the Council of State) who was staying with Gaspar Schetz. He was told that the unrest would have to stop one way or another, because the risk of attack and pillage of the homes of wealthy citizens was unacceptable. The sense of panic at city hall became palpable. When the deans of the militia companies, the wardmasters, and the guild officials indicated that they could not vouch for anyone's safety in the event of a citywide revolt, the authorities decided to grant the demands of the insurgents. On 12 July at noon a municipal decree was proclaimed in each individual district stipulating that (1) the offices for excise duties on beer were to be transferred to the old city immediately, and foreign beer was to be unloaded once again at the Bierhoofd on the Wharf, (2) everyone in the entire city was allowed to brew beer, and beer brewed outside the city would not be subject to higher excise duties, (3) Van Schoonbeke, Van Hencxthoven, and Nicolaes Maes 'with their associates' were to be dismissed from city service, including receiving the excise duties on wine and meat,[228] and (4) all those who had paid for raising four detachments of foot soldiers would have their money refunded.[229] According to the wardmasters, the Kronenburgwijk inhabitants were not satisfied with these measures and demanded that pensionary Jacob Maes resign as well. The authorities relented. Van Schoonbeke did not wait and fled the city by boat.[230] Maes hid out at the city hall for the next few days, but his house was kept under siege, and Mary of Hungary thought it would be safer to have him secretly transferred to Brussels. She wanted above all to avert new riots in Antwerp, with the attendant risk that events might give rise to discontent elsewhere, especially in Brussels, as no troops could be withdrawn from the border with France.[231] When Antwerp seemed to have calmed down, Jan Scheyfve and Charles Tisnacq (members of the Privy Council) and De Schepper went there to assess the situation on 18 July. They noted that for the time being the decree of 12 July, though promulgated under duress, did not need to be revoked, and they requested the members of the Broad Council to compile a written record of the grievances expressed by large numbers of citizens.[232] They tried to buy time, as the central government certainly did not want social unrest in its backyard, not only because of the military threat along

226 In 1554 there were twelve districts. The New Town would count as the thirteenth district only from around 1560.

227 RAB, RB, OF 510, nos 12, 17, 20, 24; SAA, GA 4626, *Copye*, GA 4811, IB 2979, no. 29.

228 Van Hencxthoven received the meat excise duties from 1551: SAA, PK 915, f° 137; R 1770, no. 161.

229 SAA, IB 2979, no. 28.

230 RAB, RB, OF 510, no. 18; Piot (1879), 148-55.

231 Piot (1879), 156-64. See also AGR, PEA 109, f° 357

232 AGR, MD 165, f° 23, and SAA, PK 1520, *Advertissement*.

the southern border, but also because of the international reputation of the Emperor and his son: on 25 July Philip married Queen Mary I of England in Winchester Cathedral.

Antwerp guild deans and wardmasters were free to convene meetings, the most important of which was on 18 August and was held at the Swane inn in Koepoortstraat, where the late Herman Coninckx had been the innkeeper.[233] This meeting was crucial, as it became clear that while objections to Van Schoonbeke's monopolistic ambitions were widespread, opinions varied as to how best to express them. Social divisions proved decisive. The dean of the small guild of rope makers turned out to be the most radical spokesman. Several witnesses later quoted him as stating 'even on a Sunday, I would twist a rope or tie a knot to hang or strangle Gilbert'. He had also offered to confirm in writing that 'Gilbert had said that if he made one thousand guilders, he would be happy for the Lords to make four thousand guilders', which was tantamount to accusing the city fathers of corruption. Deans from the other guilds had been less outspoken, although some – mainly small masters – had demanded that the municipal decree proclaimed on 12 July remain in effect and to this end had drafted a document for the governor, which they asked those present at the meeting to sign. Deans of the larger and wealthier guilds and most wardmasters had shied away from adopting such a stand, fearing possible consequences. They had argued that Van Schoonbeke's contracts concerning the breweries in the New Town had been ratified by the Emperor, and that challenging them might therefore be regarded as *lèse Majesté*. When the representatives of the *poorterij* and the deans of the militia companies saw the document, they also refused to sign it. In the end, they agreed only on a text that deplored Van Schoonbeke's move towards monopoly in very general terms. This *doleantie* was unanimously approved in the Broad Council and sent to Brussels.[234]

In the months that followed more riots erupted. In September a commotion came about at the Exchange, where a crowd screamed that 'the receivers of the excise duties want the skin off our backs and will suck every last drop of our blood; [...] they are rogues and bloodsuckers', in an attack directed at Van Hencxthoven, who continued to collect meat excise duties via an intermediary. In October turmoil ensued on the Wharf, where those present demanded that the excise duties on beer be abolished. Several individuals threatened that 'the first who has the temerity to pay or collect any more excise duties on beer will be stabbed to death or thrown from the quayside'. On 19 November the Margrave informed the local authority that 'malicious persons', mainly wage workers, had vehemently objected to the collection of excise duties on wheat and meat, which in Antwerp were much higher than in Leuven and 's-Hertogenbosch.[235] Assisted by the wardmasters and the militia companies, the city authorities consistently managed to prevent the riots from spiralling out of control. The central government, which in July and August had been unable

233 On this inn, see Verhuyck and Kisling (1987), 78-9.

234 'Al waert op eenen sondach dat hij wel een zeel drayen oft knoop maken zoude daermede men Gillebert hangen oft verworghen zoude', and 'dat Gillebert geseeght zoude hebben: als hij duysent guldens won dat hij wel lijden mochte dat d'ander heeren wonnen vier duysent guldens'. RAB, RB, OF 510, no. 13, and SAA, PK 1520, *Advertissement*.

235 'Dat de pachters hen vleesch van den beenen wilden cnagen ende hun bloet suypen; [...] dat zij pachters schelmen ende bloetsuypers waeren', and 'dat d'ierste die den selven impost [op bier] zouden betalen [...] dat zij hen zouden dootsteken ende van der caeyen worpen'. RAB, RB, OF 510, no. 16, and PPG 2367, nos 55-64, *Informatie* (Jan van Schoonhoven); SAA, PK 313, Letter dated 19 November 1554, and PK 2765, f° 84v°.

to intervene in the riots because of the military campaign in the south of the Netherlands, could therefore afford to wait a bit longer to take countermeasures.

On 6 February 1555 about 3000 *Landsknechte*, led by the Austrian military commander Lazarus von Schwendi, marched into Antwerp. A few days later, Mary of Hungary, the influential politician Antoine Perrenot de Granvelle, chancellor of Brabant Engelbrecht van den Dale, and several members of the Council of Brabant journeyed to the city.[236] After a great many witnesses had been questioned, the 'insurgents' were arrested. There were two distinct categories. On the one hand there were wage workers and journeymen who had openly engaged in acts of violence and were automatically regarded as rioters. The large numbers of temporary migrant manual labourers were regarded as a problem in this respect. The other category consisted of about twenty wardmasters, deans of militia companies, and guild officials, who stood their ground in a court of law. The central government soon released these suspects on probation but instructed the attorney general of Brabant to investigate their actual involvement in the events of 11-12 July 1554, as well as their motives. The first category of insurgents received little consideration. How the court sentences were arrived at is impossible to trace, but on Monday 1 April on Grote Markt four of the insurgents were executed. A man named Adriaen was sentenced to death as well, but he turned out to be so insane that carrying out the sentence seemed ill-advised in his case, as it might create a wave of protests. Before each beheading, he was whipped and was then banned. A false witness was not only whipped but also had a hole drilled in his tongue, his ears cut off, and was then banned forever from the Netherlands. An unknown number of fugitives was sentenced *in absentia* to permanent exile as well.[237]

The central government did not stop at exemplary punishments.[238] On 2 April 1555 all former and current officeholders and a great many prominent citizens were required to attend, when in the presence of Mary of Hungary the municipal decree of 12 July 1554 was publicly torn to shreds and the imperial revocation read out of all the measures decried as unlawful.[239] Wardmasters were instructed to report the revocations to their respective wards, which at first they refused to do, arguing that their duties did not include public announcement of court decisions and complying only after receiving a threatening letter from the governor. Aiming to reinforce social-political control, Charles V issued an extensive 'police' decree in the City of Antwerp on 17 May 1555. Half the wardmasters were to be replaced immediately, as only the most prominent citizens were still allowed to hold this office, all hundredth and tenth men were required to be home owners, and guild deans were ordered to report the names of all foreign journeymen.[240]

Lack of cooperation from the wardmasters strengthened the conviction of the attorney general of Brabant that the revolt could not be regarded as a simple 'mutiny' by

236 Charles V remained in Brussels, as his debilitating arthritis left him unable to travel.

237 SAB, B11285, f° 46; RAB, RB 603, no. 51, and OF, PPG 2367, Executions; U[llens] (1743), 52.

238 Exemplary punishments were deemed necessary because of the ongoing unrest, despite the presence of troops and dignitaries. In March the city authorities threatened severe recriminations against 'malicious individuals' who insulted and even attacked soldiers. SAA, PK 915, f° 193.

239 AGR, PEA 1191/3, no. 182, and RAB, RB 604, no. 19. The imperial revocation, dated 29 March 1555, has been edited: ROPB, 2nd ser., VI, 427-9.

240 SAA, GA 4811, *Pro Memoria*, and PK 915, f° 194; ROPB, 2nd ser., VI, 457-61. For more detail, see Soly (1970b), 527-8, and Wells (1982), 62-3.

the 'populace'.[241] His approach was very thorough. All wardmasters, headmen of militia companies, and guild officials identified as suspects had to submit a meticulous written report of their actions on 11-12 July 1554, and over one hundred witnesses were summoned. The seventeen suspects included eleven merchants, all serving as wardmaster and/or headman of a militia company,[242] which attests to social standing but also shows that they did not belong to the top of the business world, as members of the economic elite avoided such commitments.[243] In addition, there were three substantial master artisans – including Jan Vos, dean of the masons' guild, and Everard van Royenborch, dean of the tanners' guild – and a lawyer. The occupations of the brothers Hendrik and Christiaen van den Broecke, who were labelled as the 'worst rogues', are not known but they are likely to have been entrepreneurs, as they employed five or six persons. That the suspects were from the middling sort is also clear from the fact that nine of the ten whose identities have been established contributed fl. 100 to fl. 200 toward the zero-interest loan of 1552 and one of them fl. 300.[244] Likewise, the witnesses for the defence summoned by the suspects were active in commerce or industry, employed staff, and had financial assets.[245] Basically, the suspects did not belong to the economic elite but were all members of the intermediate layer. The attorney general of Brabant was positive that they had been the driving forces behind the uprising. They had formed a 'league and gang' and had set up a conspiracy. He was not impressed by the arguments presented to prove their innocence, namely that they had rescued the city government on 11 July 1554 by driving the hostile mob away from Grote Markt and the next day had urged that the revoked decree be proclaimed to stop the situation from becoming far worse. The counterarguments from the attorney general were as follows: on 11 July they had intervened only when the uprising took a dangerous course, i.e. when wealthy citizens were in danger of becoming targets of the enraged masses, and on 12 July they could easily have prevented the municipal decree from being proclaimed, because as headmen of militia companies and civil guards they could have used their arms to suppress outbursts of violence.[246]

In the months preceding the uprising, economically active members of the middling sort had indisputably been instigators, and they had channelled the discontent and embitterment among the lower social groups during and after the insurgence. They encountered no significant resistance, because the political elite lacked any moral legitimacy, and moreover the city council was rife with divisions and rivalries, rendering restoration of the public peace dependent on what the wardmasters and the headmen of the militia companies proposed as necessary measures. The municipal decree proclaimed on 12 July conveyed

241 KB, Ms. 13558-67, f° 11; Piot (1879), 171-3.

242 Dierick de Hane (Old Crossbow Guild: official), Matheeus De(s)pommereaux (master of ward IX, and dean of the Old Crossbow Guild), Claes de Vocht (dean of the Fencers' Guild), Peter de Wint, Steven Sneeuwater (master of ward IX), Jacob van Hulten (Old Crossbow Guild: official), Bartholomeus van Lippeloo (master of ward IV), Hendrik van Olmen (master of ward III), Jan van Oproyen (master of ward V), Hendrik van Thielt (master of ward III), and Willem van Trier (master of ward VI). On the grain merchant Claes de Vocht and the cloth merchant Willem van Trier, see Strieder (1930).

243 In this connection, see the pertinent remarks of Brulez (1959), 211-15, 224-5.

244 Papebrochius (1845), 384-94.

245 RAB, RB, OF 510, no. 2, and KB, Ms. 13558-67, f° 11. For the occupational data, see esp. SAA, T 1317.

246 RAB, RB, OF, PPG 2367, '*Dit zijn die feyten*', and passim.

the frustrations and the aspirations of the intermediate social layer, numbers of whom had strong reasons to oppose Van Schoonbeke, Van Hencxthoven, and Nicolaes Maes. Van Schoonbeke had made enemies of many small contractors, as he was well aware. It was no coincidence that eight deans and former deans from the building trades attended the meeting in the Swane. Van Schoonbeke had also made many enemies in commercial circles. Building and operating the new weighing house and his negotiations with the old clothes dealers had enabled him to identify misconduct in weighing goods and at public auctions and to report such cases to the city council. Moreover, he had started to receive all kinds of commercial duties as well. Urbanization of the New Town will therefore have elicited mixed feelings among those involved in trade and shipping. Everybody was in principle in favour of establishing a port area. What raised general suspicion was that Van Schoonbeke once again appeared to be obtaining full control: in addition to organizing the sale of land owned by the city, he installed cranes for loading and unloading goods along the first canal, while at the same time he was joint receiver of the crane excise duties, built large storage facilities, set up a new transport service, and offered to provide one or two watermills. He would clearly become pivotal in the commercial development of the New Town. If the city decided to carry out Van Schoonbeke's original plan and designate fixed sites for loading and unloading, he was likely to derive the greatest benefit from them. Understandably, officials from the two main guilds in Antwerp for trade and shipping dominated the discussion in the Swane: Jacob Peters, dean of the Mercers, the politically powerful guild that comprised those from the middling sort involved in trade,[247] and Pieter Welser, dean of the equally powerful Shipmen's guild. They had in common their disapproval of monopoly practices. We regret, stated Peters and Welser, together with wardmaster Charles van Berghen later on, that the decree of 12 July arose in the commotion, but they added that its content still 'cannot be qualified as strange and improper', and that 'nobody is forbidden to ask but is in fact legally entitled to ask questions and make requests that displease the ruler or the *fiscus* [treasury], even if they are not customarily granted'.[248]

Wage workers and small master artisans had been hurt by Van Schoonbeke's monopolist practices as well, but the list of demands that the authorities had approved on 12 July 1554 did not essentially accommodate *their* grievances. They had not benefited from the uprising, as they did not drink wine, and they had not needed to contribute to the tax levied to pay for raising four detachments of foot soldiers.[249] Nor had they found support for demands that served their own material interests, especially abolishing or reducing the excise duties on beer. The only concession that they had managed to negotiate, at least so it seemed, was the dismissal of pensionary Maes. Why did they target the pensionary? What the manual workers demanded was respect, which the pensionary would not show them, as his statements had demonstrated when viewing the men of military age on 11 July. He was especially hard on the poor Kronenburgwijk, which got even with him by demanding his dismissal the next day. Yet he did not feel superior to the lower social

---

247 Geudens (1891-1904), II, 16-162; Van Aert (2007), 166-77.

248 'Dat nyemanden verboden en es, maer nae alle rechten toegelaten, te suppleren ende te bidden, oyck om saecken die den Prince oft fisco tegengaen, hoewel dat men die nyet lichtelycken gewoenlycken es t'accorderen'. SAA, PK 1520, *Advertissement*. See also RAB, RB, OF 510, no. 21.

249 RAB, RB, OF 510, passim.

groups, as he expressed comparable contempt of members of the economic and political elites. The unflinching pensionary had dealt with corrupt burgomasters and aldermen for years and had at times openly rebuked them. In the 1540s he had had the courage to lock horns with a powerful businessman such as Ducci, and more recently he had seriously questioned Van Schoonbeke's projects. Maes had never joined the business undertakings of his brother Nicolaes, a fellow receiver of wine excise duties. He was a civil servant with an impeccable reputation, and he of all people was thrown out by the Antwerp citizens, not because of misconduct or deceitful practices but because of what everybody regarded as a lack of respect, as arrogance.

The question is whether members of the political elite and wardmasters might have incited the public against Maes or even have channelled sentiment against him. In other words, did they instrumentalize the chaos and anger among the masses to sideline the pensionary? On 18 July 1554 alderman Van der Meeren, who despised the pensionary, wrote in a confidential letter to Gerard Veltwyck, Lord of Boechout (near Antwerp) and councillor in the Privy Council: Maes is now getting what he deserves 'for the extended and excessive verbal abuse he has so arrogantly directed at his masters [the aldermen], the merchants, and the entire people, because he considers himself superior to everybody else, to the severe detriment of the city'. His colleague Dierick van de Werve agreed with him.[250] They knew that the pensionary could not actually be charged but tried to have him removed, because this 'dogged and defamatory' civil servant, as they described him, was too familiar with the internal mechanisms of the city council. 'All books, papers, privileges, and other documents concerning the matters of this city located in his house were [to be] seized and entrusted to those in charge of law and order in this city'.[251] It was clearly feared that papers compromising the local government would fall into the wrong hands.

Eventually the suspects were not prosecuted. Did the attorney general lack sufficient solid evidence to have them convicted of conspiracy? He based his actions on statements from witnesses for the prosecution, indicating that those who on 11 July 1554 had been chased from Grote Markt had called out to the deans of the militia companies and the wardmasters: 'Now we see that the archers are with the Lords, although they *had said that they were on our side, but now they are against us*, the scoundrels and villains'.[252] Such statements could easily be turned to the advantage of the suspects: they had tried at first to mediate and, when that failed, had resorted to violence to drive the crowd away from Grote Markt. The criminal charges therefore lacked a strong foundation. Presumably, the central government took the dire economic situation into account as well. In October 1554 Mary of Hungary had to allow merchants in Antwerp to pay or charge more than the standard 12 percent interest on loans (taking the form of a *don gratuit*, a free gift), and in May 1555 the wardmasters had informed her that trade and industry were steadily declining,

---

250 'Pour ses longues et excessives invectives avecq une grande superbeté par luy usees contre ses maistres, tous les marchans et tout le populaire, au grant defaulx de la ville'. AGR, PEA, 109, f° 361. See also AGR, MD 165, f° 23. On Veltwyck, see Baelde (1965a), 322-3.

251 'Ont requis et veullent que tous livres, papiers, privilegez et autres enseignemens concernans le lieu et affaires de ceste ville soubz luy et en sa maison reposans soient de luy ostez, prins et confereez es mains des seigneurs de la justice et loy de ceste dicte ville'. AGR, PEA, 109, f° 354.

252 'Nu sien wij wel dat de schutters metten heeren zijn, *sij hadden geseeght dat sij met ons waeren, nu zijn zij tegen ons* die schelmen ende bueswichten'. RAB, RB, OF 510, no. 17 (my italics).

especially the wine and grain trade on the one hand and cloth dyeing works and tanneries on the other.[253] This was the year, moreover, of the change in Habsburg control: on 25 October 1555 Charles V entrusted the Netherlands to Philip; it would be unfortunate for the new sovereign to start with social-political unrest in his economic capital, as it would harm the image of the metropolis and his own reputation.

The revolt of 11-12 July 1554 and the executions on 1 April 1555 caused a stir. Van Schoonbeke and Maes were targeted in local derisory ditties and rhymes.[254] Chronicles focused on Antwerp or Brabant in general gave ample attention to the events. The authors concerned avoided the term 'insurgents' and wrote about the 'community' that had turned against Van Schoonbeke because of the breweries in the New Town and against Maes because of his 'pride'.[255] Some emphasized that the wardmasters and other 'upstanding citizens', who had been arrested and charged following insinuations by the aldermen, were ultimately released for lack of evidence against them, to the shame of the aldermen.[256] The English diplomat (and spy) Sir John Mason described the Antwerp officeholders far less charitably. In a letter to Sir William Petre, Secretary of State, he wrote on 21 May 1555 that Mary of Hungary had removed from office several Antwerp aldermen 'of whom the people had complained for their corrupt administration of justice'.[257] Such interpretations of the events persisted in the Netherlands as well over the years that followed. In 1557 the Antwerp government learned that the Ghent printer and publisher Gerard van Salenson intended to publish a chronicle mentioning that in 1554 'there had been great commotion and rage on the part of the community against the Lords', and that the city authorities had subsequently had to pay 'a large sum of money as a penalty and atonement for their crime'. The city government voiced strong objections and demanded that their Ghent counterparts force the printer to delete this 'mendacious passage' or withdraw the book from commercial circulation. This was apparently done, as the remaining copies of Salenson's chronicle do not contain the incriminating passage.[258]

Pieter Bruegel the Elder, who lived and worked in Antwerp from 1554/5 to 1562/3, is unlikely to have experienced the uprising personally, but he was undoubtedly well-informed, as his patron Nicolaes Jonghelinck did business with Van Hencxthoven. In 1563 he painted the Tower of Babel for Jonghelinck, depicting construction of a building and a city on an unprecedented scale, featuring multiple visual associations with Antwerp. Bruegel did not refer to actual figures but evoked the issue of individual ambition versus collective exertion, which could be interpreted 'as a reminder that the model of entrepreneurship adopted by Van Schoonbeke was an ambivalent one and could have potentially led to the destruction of an otherwise prosperous community', as Barbara Kaminska has observed.[259] Four years later Guicciardini in his 'Description' included an account of the facts that directly contradicted the interpretation by the attorney general of Brabant. He noted that

253 AGR, PEA 143, Letter dated 17 October 1554; SAA, PK 1396, f° 34-43.
254 KB, Ms II.119, f° 182, and SBA, B11285, f° 45-46.
255 See U[llens] (1743), 50-2, and *Chronycke* (1843), 48-51.
256 De Weert (1879), 134-5.
257 CSPF, Mary, no. 360. See also nos 323 and 329.
258 *Chronijcke* (1557). Quotations in Prims (1929), my translation.
259 Kaminska (2014), 10. She discusses the 'Great' Tower of Babel in the Kunsthistorisches Museum in Vienna, to be distinguished from the 'Little' Tower of Babel in the Museum Boijmans Van Beuningen in Rotterdam.

the *sédition* was set off by a regulation stipulating that henceforth beer was to be brewed exclusively in the New Town, but he did not name Van Schoonbeke. He emphasized that the city authorities had been highly unpopular and even 'hated by the people', while the *bourgeois de condition* (the wealthy citizens), who had kept calm and had wielded arms to restore the public peace, had shown exemplary conduct. Thanks to their action, the *tumulte* had subsided. Who was guilty? Thorough investigation had revealed that in fact 'a minor error had been committed by a very small group from the populace, of whom three or four were sentenced'.[260]

Punishment of the insurgents obviously did not settle the matter in 1555. Maes and Van Schoonbeke demanded that their reputation be restored and insisted on compensation for damages. The Antwerp authorities awarded Maes compensation of fl. 9600 for his 'loyal services' to the city, and the government of the Habsburg Netherlands wished to make clear to everybody that he was a very highly respected civil servant. On 4 May 1555 he was appointed by the Emperor as counsellor in the Council of Brabant. Great tribute was paid to him again on 25 October of that year, when Charles V abdicated in the great hall of the Coudenberg palace in Brussels. After the speech by the Emperor, Maes, on behalf of the States-General, pledged the loyalty of the subjects toward the Emperor and his son Philip, who was then given authority over the Netherlands.[261]

Van Schoonbeke had suffered heavy financial losses. After the uprising, seven of the ten brewers that had settled in the New Town had returned to their old breweries, while the three remaining brewers had suffered a considerable fall in revenue. Only in March-April 1555 did the situation recover somewhat. This meant not only that for ten months hardly any two-stuiver dues were received, but also that peat sales collapsed.[262] Van Schoonbeke demanded considerable compensation for damages and had the support of Mary of Hungary, who set the example and gave the entrepreneur 18 months' extension on paying interest to the Emperor. Not wishing to provoke conflict unnecessarily, she asked the Antwerp wardmasters to express their opinion of the entire matter. They acknowledged that setting up breweries in the New Town would cause land values there to soar, and that the efficiency with which Van Schoonbeke had solved the water problem there would boost local beer production, which would benefit the city income. Nonetheless, they recommended that the entrepreneur give the city part of the proceeds, in exchange for the privileges granted to his brewers, as 'this would end the continuous complaint that private persons should not be allowed to control profits and business, unless the ruler or the city benefited as well'.[263] Van Schoonbeke obviously disagreed. He reversed the line of argument: his brewery complex helped prevent new price increases. Mary of Hungary continued to work on the compensation plan, and in early October – a few days before

260 Guicciardini (1567b), 118-20.

261 SAA, R 15, f° 247v°; Gachard (1830), 91-7; Prims (1938c), who notes that Maes spared no effort to safeguard the Antwerp privileges, when Charles V proclaimed a new decree against the 'heretics' in 1550. See also Goossens (1997), 63-8.

262 SAA, IB 2978, no. 39.

263 'Alsoo doende selen comen te cesseren alle murmuratien van dat men dusdanige proffyten ende saecken nyet en soude behoeven te laten in haden van private persoonen sonder eenich proffyt van den Prince oft de stadt'. SAA, IB 3005, f° 94dv°-94jv°.

she stepped down as governor at the same time that Charles V abdicated – she convinced the two parties to accept a compromise, which Philip II confirmed on 15 November.[264]

Both parties made financial concessions. The city paid the entrepreneur damages of fl. 12,000, in addition to granting him a loan of fl. 48,000 which was mortgaged on the breweries, together with a previous loan of fl. 24,000 at 6.25 percent. In other words: the city had now taken out annuities valued at fl. 4500. In return, the entrepreneur agreed to sell annuities for a total amount of fl. 400,000 backed by the city's revenue, which could not be taken for granted during an economic slump, but no payment deadlines were set, nor even a target date.[265] The agreement of course revolved around the monopoly issue. Henceforth, Van Schoonbeke would pay the city one quarter of the proceeds from his entire undertaking, i.e. the two-stuiver duties, the beer transport, and the future watermill, with the peat supply as the sole exception. In addition, he agreed to open only sixteen, instead of twenty breweries in the New Town, and to establish four in the old city, two at Kronenburgpoort – the poor neighbourhood where inhabitants had objected the most strenuously to his monopoly – and two on the old training grounds, along the Graanmarkt recently created by him, nearby Herentalse Vaart. The objective was to avert 'any scandal among the populace', which also led to the regular inspections of the water in the New Town breweries.[266] This mindset caused Van Schoonbeke to be dismissed from the collection of excise duties on beer. In return, however, he was granted the legal monopoly on producing and transporting beer in Antwerp. Brewers who still lived there or in places where Antwerp levied full or half excise duties – primarily the villages of Berchem, Borgerhout, and Deurne – had to operate either in Van Schoonbeke's breweries or abandon their occupation. All the privileges granted to his brewers in 1552 remained in effect.[267] In addition, the import of beer brewed within a distance of 16.5 km around Antwerp was prohibited. The exceptional importance of both stipulations became clear from the fact that Philip II not only confirmed them as part of the new contract between city and entrepreneur but had already affirmed them two days before, on 13 November 1555, in a special charter.[268] On 5 December all new regulations and royal approvals were proclaimed to the citizens of Antwerp.[269] Nobody protested.

The uprising of 11-12 July 1554 cost Van Schoonbeke a considerable sum. The immediate loss of income mattered less to him than the arrangement that required him from that point on to pass on one quarter of the proceeds of his undertaking to the City of Antwerp. Since four sixteenths were already due to Philip II and one sixteenth to Gaspar Schetz, he retained only seven sixteenths; his profit margin was therefore considerably reduced. On the other hand, he had acquired a legal monopoly, and the beer production that was likely

---

264 SAA, IB 2968, IB 2978, nos 2-15, IB 3005, f° 111-115, T 199.

265 For more detail, see Soly (1968), 388.

266 The first inspection was in June 1556. Brewers from Ghent, Gouda, and Menen stated at the time that the water used in the New Town had not been contaminated and could not contain any impurities either. SAA, IB 3012, no. 7.

267 The four brewers in the old city were granted the same rights but were allowed to produce only three types of beer. Nor were they exempt from the taxes on beer exported to places where the City of Antwerp did not levy excise duties.

268 SAA, IB 2975, no. 1.

269 SAA, PK 915, f° 199.

to develop in the city in a period of strong growth thanks to his organizational innovations augured ample opportunities for compensation. At the end of 1555 he was in any case unique: nobody in a large or medium-sized city had ever cornered beer production. Nor would anyone after him succeed in doing so in early modern Europe.

3.6 Supplying the Army

At first sight the uprising left Van Schoonbeke with dismal economic prospects. He knew that the Emperor could not send troops to Antwerp for the time being, and that several brewers no longer dared to remain in the New Town. This situation would greatly affect beer production and reduce his income. It was impossible to predict how long these conditions would last, but Van Schoonbeke realized that even the abrogation of the city decree of 12 July 1554 – which he expected – would not solve all his problems. He anticipated that in the end he would have to pay at least part of the two-stuiver dues to the City of Antwerp. Nor was the real estate market profitable, as the economic difficulties caused by the Habsburg-Valois War led to a collapse in demand for land, houses, and annuities. Van Schoonbeke understood that he had to find new ways to make money quickly. During his forced sojourn in Brussels in the second half of 1554, he explored new prospects and saw the combination of large-scale warfare and rising financial needs as an opportunity to serve the central government, while making a handsome profit.

The Emperor had gathered an enormous body of troops. In 1552, his advisors calculated that in the Low Countries and Germany 22,200 cavalry and 87,000 infantry were ready at all times.[270] Figures for 1554 and 1555 are not available, but it may be assumed that the bulk of the troops had to remain ready for battle in the southern part of the Netherlands at the time, as the war was fought along the border with France. In the autumn of 1554, the situation became critical. Insufficient funds were available to pay the imperial troops. The problem was exacerbated by the fact that soldiers were expected to provide for all their own needs (food and clothes) and in many cases even their arms. There was no central, permanent commissary service to stockpile supplies. Army commanders signed agreements with local authorities or traders to supply bread and other essential food for the troops stationed in the garrison cities or had them 'live off the country', whenever they were on the move.[271] In the early 1550 the government proclaimed decrees prohibiting the export of all kinds of foods from the Habsburg Netherlands, justified primarily by the need to supply the troops along the border with France.[272] Such measures, however, failed to solve the problem of victualling the troops. Clothing was another major problem. There were no uniforms in the true sense. Soldiers within the same regiment and bearing the same arms might wear different clothes. The Habsburg armies were identifiable by the

---

270 Parker (1988), 45.

271 See the comments of Hale (1985), 181-9. On the victualling of the armies of Henry VIII, see the classic article of Davies (1964/5). In France, 'practically every campaign of the Habsburg-Valois wars saw bodies of troops short of cash and supplies'. Potter (2008), 248.

272 Separate prohibitions applied in the areas with the greatest troop concentrations, i.e. the Duchy of Luxembourg and the County of Chiny. ROPB, 2nd ser., VI, 286-7, 317-8, 334, 341-2, 357-8, 380, 387-8.

red tokens they wore, while the French wore blue ones.[273] Worn-out or damaged clothes still had to be replaced, and this was not easy when demand soared in a region where large forces were stationed for a long time. In early December 1552, the Antwerp merchant Joost van de Steene signed a contract with the central government to supply textile goods that were suitable for various military ranks. Their total cost was fl. 75,000, and they had to be transported to Thionville. Van de Steene delivered the goods in January and was paid in early March. He did not have a chance of a new contract, as he died soon afterwards.[274] Since Van Schoonbeke collected the excise duties on beer together with him, he probably figured out that supplying the army could be highly lucrative. He wanted to be guaranteed enough textiles at good prices and at short notice and contacted the silk cloth merchants Lenaert Chalet and Erasmus Pesteau, both distant relatives, and the cloth merchant Wouter Seroye, brother-in-law of Van Hencxthoven.[275] They promised him large and regular deliveries on attractive terms from the autumn of 1554, after which he signed a contract with them and in October suggested to the central government that the troops no longer be paid in cash.

Paying the troops in kind whenever possible was an innovative proposal. Never before had the idea occurred to anyone in the Low Countries or elsewhere in Europe. The practice would yield countless benefits, argued Van Schoonbeke. It enabled the government to solve the credit problem temporarily. Purchasing massive quantities of textiles and food products from wholesalers made it possible to arrange to pay them the amounts due after six or twelve months, eliminating the need to obtain new loans. The government also benefited from the difference between wholesale and retail prices. In addition, they could take market price fluctuations into account, which entailed waiting for the best moment to supply certain commodities to the troops. Food products, for example, were best purchased immediately after the harvest and provided to the military in the winter or spring, when prices rose. By assigning a few wholesalers contractual responsibility for ensuring a regular and adequate supply, the government relieved itself of the burden of resolving complex problems, needing only to provide enough storage areas for the army commanders and/or local authorities. The troops were unlikely to object, as they would finally be able to obtain good food and decent fabric for appropriate clothing at 'reasonable' prices. Since a small group of suppliers was easy to track, abuse could almost be ruled out, according to Van Schoonbeke.

The Council of Finance was jubilant. On 8 November 1554, the first large contract was signed. Van Schoonbeke agreed to supply textile goods valued at fl. 156,500 to Cambrai within a month, mainly English cloth (56,000 ells at 30 stuivers per el) and Flemish cloth (40,000 ells at 18 to 24 stuivers per ell). Differences in quality and price might have been based on the military hierarchy, but other reasons might underlie the prevalence of expensive English cloth: soldiers cared very much about their appearance, and they could use valuable commodities as currency. Van Schoonbeke had to cover the transport costs but was allowed to requisition the necessary carts and horses and was exempt from

273 Parker (1988), 71.

274 AGR, PEA 1635/1, 10 December 1551; SAA, IB 2999, no. 37, and SR 246, f° 155.

275 Lenaert Chalet was a grandson of Dierick Moens, father of Anna, the first wife of Van Schoonbeke Sr., and Erasmus Pesteau was married to Johanna Chalet, sister of Lenaert. See Soly (1977), 132 and 328.

tolls. Moreover, the government covered all risks associated with the transport, especially plundering and destruction. He observed the contract to the letter. By 22 November soldiers in the William of Orange regiment were paid in textiles, which they accepted without any objection.[276] Five other contracts followed, the last one dated 27 April 1556. Their total value was fl.438,000, of which textile goods accounted for 70 percent. Van Schoonbeke associated with both affluent textile merchants and Van Hencxthoven and the Schetz brothers, but he took on the organization of transports to border towns and garrisons.[277] Even considering that he was allowed to requisition transport vehicles, rapid deliveries (in some cases within a week) required strong organizational skills. He once again demonstrated his skill in planning.[278]

Mary of Hungary was so delighted with the advantageous payment system that Van Schoonbeke had devised and his efficient execution of it that she advised her brother to appoint the entrepreneur *commis* (clerk) in the Council of Finance. This office was far more important than the humble title suggests. These civil servants were economic and/or financial experts, and their advice was taken as seriously as that of regular councillors. They often had to investigate a given complex problem thoroughly, submit a report to the Council, and formulate a reasoned proposal. In addition, they were charged with many confidential missions.[279] The appointment opened new prospects for Van Schoonbeke. First, he was aware of all economic decisions that the central government intended to take. Second, thanks to the many secret missions assigned to him, he was an important liaison between the central government and the Schetzes, which in turn improved his leverage with the central government. In November 1555 Philip II even instructed him to convince Gaspar Schetz to serve as royal factor to His Majesty on the Antwerp Exchange.[280] Schetz was probably easy to convince, but the fact that Van Schoonbeke was asked to convey the message/request indicates that he had earned the trust of the highest authorities. This is also clear from other sensitive missions that he was given. On 2 March 1556, for example, Mary of Hungary wrote to the Antwerp city authorities that she was sending Van Schoonbeke there to speak with the aldermen regarding matters that were of importance to the King. The aldermen were instructed to listen to him, to trust him blindly, and to provide him with every conceivable assistance, as she had always done.[281] His office offered direct material benefits as well. He received an annual salary of *c.* fl. 880 and was entitled to an annual 'pension' of fl. 400.[282] More importantly, he was exempt from all taxes, which obviously made his breweries and peat operations more profitable.

Since paying the troops in kind benefited the suppliers and the government alike, the system remained in use. Philip II acknowledged that it yielded substantial savings. In 1560 the ruler, who was not known for being particularly generous, gave Elisabeth Hendrickx fl. 3000 as a token of appreciation for the many services her late husband had

276 AGR, PEA 143, f° 225-227, 264; SAA, PK 2764, f° 228.
277 Soly (1977), 329-32.
278 AGR, PEA 144, f° 13, and PEA 1652/2, Letter dated 17 January 1555.
279 Baelde (1965a), 125.
280 Génard (1880), 196 no. 89. See also AGR, PEA 147, f° 197.
281 AGR, PEA 1674/1.
282 SAA, IB 2989, f° 135-137, 214v°-215v°.

rendered, noting that 'Gilbert van Schoonbeke was the first to come up with the system of supplying the soldiers [...] with cloth, silk fabrics, and other items they need [...], which has so greatly benefited the late Emperor, Charles V, My Lord and Father, and ourselves'.[283] Whether the system was similarly advantageous to the men-at-arms depends on the point of view. They received supplies more regularly, which they undoubtedly appreciated. The data also indicate that they were able to purchase on credit, which they must have appreciated as well. Their purchasing power as such, however, did not increase. They received the food when prices were highest. Whether they had sufficient business acumen to assess the value of textile goods is doubtful, and they were probably not able to sell cloth or silk for the price they were charged in lieu of cash payment. The profits of the suppliers and savings by the government were therefore realized in part by eroding the purchasing power of the soldiers.

Would Van Schoonbeke henceforth have aligned his activities still more with the needs of the central government, i.e. by continuing to supply the armed forces and broker financial transactions? This seems plausible, as the economic outlook remained dismal in Antwerp in the 1550s, but we will never be certain. In September 1556, he came down with a fever, and three months later, on 16 December 1556 at around eleven o'clock in the evening, he died, only 37 years old, in the house De Keyser on Minderbroedersrui in Antwerp.[284] He was buried in the Church of the Brothers Minor, in front of the pulpit – nearby the Stadswaag, his first major real-estate project.[285]

Four days before he passed away, he had appointed his wife Elisabeth Hendrickx estate executor and guardian of their six underage children, and his brother-in-law Sebastiaen van Utrecht co-guardian. Since the many businesses of her husband were so complicated that nobody could assess the charges and debts of the succession, his widow asked Philip II for permission to accept the estate with the benefit of inventory. Her request was granted on 22 December. The King instructed the secretary to the Council of Brabant to compile a complete inventory and summon all creditors and debtors. Since he owned shares in the brewery complex, he ordered high-ranking government officials to audit this enterprise.[286]

The estate soon turned out to be a gargantuan maze. The accounts of the construction contracts had never been finalized. The uprising of July 1554 and its aftermath had impeded not only payment and collection of the two-stuiver dues but had made a mess of peat supplies and sales as well. Neither the central government nor the partners had paid Van Schoonbeke for the items supplied to the armed forces. The list of pending matters in effect included all economic activities and businesses that the deceased had launched since the late 1540s. The absence of central accounts made them still more obscure. Van

---

283 'A esté le principal et premier qui auroit entremis et trouvé le moyen de contenter les gendarmes, souldars et aultres gens de guerre [...] avec drapz de layne, de soye, vivres et aultres choses a eulx necessaires [...] dont feu de tres haulte memoire l'Empereur, Charles Quint, Mon Seigneur et Pere, et nous avons receu somme bien prouffitable'. AGR, PEA 2536. See also SAA, IB 2989, f° 214v°.

284 He had rented the house since 1546. Tying up as little capital as possible for personal needs was typical of Van Schoonbeke. De Keyser, however, was a large and elegant house, as the high rent indicates: fl. 380 *per annum*. SAA, R 2387.

285 Soly (1977), 142-3. This church stood on the present site of the Koninklijke Academie voor Schone Kunsten (Royal Academy of Fine Arts).

286 SAA, IB 3007, passim, and IB 3008, nos 8 and 18.

Schoonbeke had practised an extreme distribution of tasks, assigning the administration of each project to a specific employee, so that no-one was aware of the total picture. Real-estate transactions were not registered systematically. The management of the brewery complex was divided into separate parts, each audited by different employees, none of whom had comprehensive insight. Van Schoonbeke was in charge of all strategic and operational decisions. This typically unitary structure had the advantage of optimizing control of capital in the various sub-structures, but the serious disadvantage was that the entire system was left rudderless, once Van Schoonbeke was no longer there to operate it.

On 24 April 1557 Melchior Schetz, who two years before had been appointed treasurer general of Antwerp, presented the widow with a claim amounting to fl. 212,097.[287] The claim later turned out to have been systematically forged, but Elisabeth Hendrickx was unaware or at least insufficiently aware of the business affairs of her late husband to refute it, and the same held true for Sebastiaen van Utrecht. They were also presented with a – bona fide and accurate – claim from the ruler amounting to fl. 51,000 and faced the refusal of the brewers to pay the two-stuiver dues, as long as the city failed to comply with various contractual obligations.[288] On 21 December 1557, they waived their claim to the estate, provided that the widow could retain the goods she had brought into the marriage and assert her right as creditor, while the children retained their rights to the estate, regardless of this 'repudiation', should the balance later turn out to be positive.[289] The balance of the estate was indeed positive, but this came to light only many decades later, and even then Van Schoonbeke's possessions were grossly undervalued. Historical research has revealed that after all debts were subtracted, his fortune was *c.* fl. 112,000, of which 95 percent consisted of shares in industrial and commercial undertakings.[290] Considering that Van Schoonbeke was economically active for only fifteen years, he was extraordinarily successful.[291]

Fearing that the high claim from Melchior Schetz would jeopardize his shares in the brewery complex, Philip II appointed two trustees to conduct a thorough investigation and to manage and/or sell the possessions of the deceased as profitably as possible. They were unable to sort out the complex affairs of the deceased. This was due primarily to the absence of central accounts, but there were two additional factors: they were severely pressed for time, because the interest on the exorbitant claims was mounting rapidly, and they soon became aware that powerful members of the local elite did not expect them to protect the interests of the heirs, and that they would benefit, if they 'took the superior interests into account'. The brewery complex was by far the most valuable component. In addition to its capital value, it had a huge profit potential, even if it was divided into separate parts. Nobody understood this better than Melchior Schetz, and nobody was more aptly positioned to benefit from an arrangement, as in this period the offices of receiver and treasurer, were alternately held by him, by his partner Christoffel Pruynen, or by his friend the financier Gerard Gramaye. He went very strategically to work. As (co)manager of municipal finance, he appeared to represent the public interest. In 1560/1 on behalf of the

287 SAA, IB 3005, f° 218-248.
288 For more detail, see Soly (1977), 338-41.
289 SAA, IB 3009, nos 1-2.
290 See the calculations in Soly (1977), 428-9.
291 His assets represented over 1250 times the annual wages of a skilled worker. Calculated from Scholliers (1960), 90.

Table 8. The brewery-complex formed by Gilbert van Schoonbeke: estimated value in 1560

Different parts of the undertaking	Estimated value (in florins)
Complex situated in New Town:	
– Land	*64,000*
– Ten breweries	*100,000*
– Six breweries	*48,000*
– Water House and small stable	*4,800*
– Large stable	*2,200*
– Watermill	*4,000*
Subtotal	223,000
Two breweries near Kronenburgpoort	13,000
Two breweries on Schuttershoven	12,000
Miscellaneous	23,300
Total	271,300

Sources: Soly (1968), 375, and (1977), 296-7, 310.

city, he bought up the shares of Philip II and his brother Gaspar in the brewery complex. After that, the trustees did what was expected of them by the established powers: they sold the entire complex to the City of Antwerp for fl. 240,000.[292] In the interests of avoiding future problems with the brewers concerned, the city government signed a contract with them on 10 February 1561, stipulating that they would retain all privileges they had been granted during the period when Van Schoonbeke was in charge. They were henceforth required to pay the two-stuiver dues to the City. The local authorities reserved the right to grant the same privileges to other entrepreneurs who might wish to start a brewery in Antwerp in the future, however, thereby ending the monopoly that Van Schoonbeke had achieved.[293]

The city kept the Water House, which for centuries remained an important water distribution centre in the New Town,[294] but sold the breweries: six to individual brewers, six to Melchior Schetz and his partners, and four to Gerard Gramaye. Both businessmen very quickly resold the breweries. The corruption of prominent city council members enabled them to make huge profits.[295] Dismantling the brewery complex did not have a negative impact on beer production in Antwerp. Whereas in the 1540s beer production in the metropolis had averaged only 135,000 hl per annum, by 1560 it had increased to *c.* 255,000 hl and in the early 1570s fluctuated between 300,000 and 330,000 hl, with peaks at 370,000 and even 390,000 hl. An increasing share was brewed in the New Town: about 60 percent around 1560, over 70 percent ten years later, and more than 80 percent after 1585. The success of Van Schoonbeke's reorganization of beer production was reflected not only in the increased total output but also in the sharp rise in exports: while in the

292 Including the land that Van Schoonbeke owned between the first and the second canal and the large watermill he built.

293 SAA, IB 2989, f° 84-90, IB 2159, f° 64v°-67v°, T 1710, nos 1285-1287; Soly (1968), 1173, 1194-5.

294 Van Craenenbroeck (2019a) and (2019b).

295 For more detail, see Cuypers (1948), 56-9, 177-81; Soly (1968), 1194-5, and (1977), 347-8.

first half of the century the Antwerp brewers had produced almost exclusively for the local market, by 1560 they sold an average of 10 percent of their beer outside the city, and after 1570 the share of exports exceeded a quarter. Conversely, beer imports from other Brabant towns and from Holland, Germany, and England plummeted to less than 1 percent of local consumption in the 1570s and were negligible after 1585.[296]

In addition to being the driving force behind, and main beneficiary of, winding up the brewery complex, Melchior Schetz acquired Van Schoonbeke's shares in the Peat Company – 10 of the 32 shares – at a bargain price. In 1561 he formed a new partnership that for 22 years was dedicated to leasing royal peat bog with an area of 217 morgen or *c.* 190 hectares. Together with Jan Vleminck Jr. (son-in-law of Gaspar Schetz) and Jan Calvo, he owned half the shares, while Gerard Gramaye and his brother Thomas held the other half of the capital.[297] Meanwhile Van Schoonbekes previous partners Schot, Seroye, Van Hencxthoven, and Van Nispen had formed a new company charged with victualling eleven garrison cities on the border of the Southern Netherlands with France for six years.[298]

Elisabeth Hendrickx and Sebastiaen van Utrecht never asked the trustees to clarify dubious transactions, and they never challenged the claims by Melchior Schetz and members of the city council. The highly disputable winding-up of the businesses owned by the husband/father remained a source of dissatisfaction, however, as became clear when the only son, whose name was also Gilbert, went to study law in Leuven, Douai, and Padua. On returning from Italy, he tried to sort out the complex affairs of his father. He encountered so much opposition from the city council and the former trustees that he gave up after a few years and enlisted in the army of the Estates, which was deployed against the Spanish forces. He is believed to have perished in the battle at Gembloux on 1 January 1578; he was 28 or 29 years old.[299] One year later the husband of his sister Sara, the merchant Frans de Cater, sued the former trustees, and in 1583 he also sued the City of Antwerp, arguing that the estate had been wound up on the basis of forged claims, identifying Melchior Schetz as the main culprit.[300] The huge court case was endless. No judgement was forthcoming. In the final round on 21 March 1634, however, the city council agreed to grant each of the two surviving heirs, Catharina and Susanna de Cater, daughters of Frans, an annuity of fl. 600, provided that they entrusted all the rights they could claim from the City deriving from the estate of the late Gilbert van Schoonbeke to the *Kamer van de Huisarmen* (the municipal organization for poor relief). It was an implicit admission of guilt.[301]

296 Soly (1968), 1197-1200.
297 Gerard Gramaye owned four sixteenths in the partnership.
298 SAA, IB 2998, f° 8-9, 34v°-36; Soly (1972).
299 SAA, CERT 32, f° 47v°, IB 3005, *Proëmium*, IB 3021, f° 68.
300 See esp. SAA, IB 3017, p. 8.
301 For more detail, see Soly (1977), 355-8.

Conclusion

In 1527 the Antwerp humanist Cornelis de Schrijver, alias Grapheus, a close friend of Erasmus and Thomas More, published a Latin poem, in which he sang the praises of his city:

> *Do you seek Paradise here on Earth? You will find it in Antwerp.*
> *Are you looking for fun? Go to Antwerp.*
> *Do you need a lot of money? Antwerp can provide it.*
> *Do you seek all kinds of merchandise? You will find it in Antwerp.*
> *[...]*
> *Antwerp, the Wealthy, conquers the entire world.*
> *Whatever the Earth has on offer, Antwerp has an exclusive supply.*
> *Antwerp is such a jewel and an honour for the fatherland.*
> *All by itself the whole world: that is Antwerp!*[1]

Erasmus Schetz would certainly have agreed with him, as would other capitalists, provided they understood Latin. For everybody who participated in big business, Antwerp was the place to be. From 1490 to 1550 not a single European city was Antwerp's equal in terms of the economic advantages arising from the convergence of a rapidly expanding intercontinental trade and the revival of transcontinental trade on the one hand, and the changing geopolitical balance of forces on the other. Shifts in international trade had a significant impact, but without the decisions taken by Emperor Maximilian I and King Manuel I of Portugal the rise of Antwerp as 'metropolis of the west' would have been unthinkable. Up until the 1490s, the Portuguese saw no reason to desert Bruges, which was their most important market for malagueta pepper, Madeira sugar, ivory and other 'exotic' merchandise. This was also true of those foreign merchants supplying essential materials for the textile industry - wool, alum and dyes - and exporting Flemish cloth. It was the changing geopolitical balance of power that gave rise to an irreversible shift in the commercial hub - just as in the 1580s political-military events would put an end to Antwerp's economic supremacy, enabling Amsterdam to assume the lead.

Antwerp by 1550 had become the largest permanent market in Europe. The city's commercial predominance was then overwhelming. No other city could boast such a concentration of merchants from so many countries and regions. Furthermore, the city had become Europe's most important money and capital market, reflecting its stategic position at the epicentre of a political-military superpower. The key role of the Antwerp Exchange in European finance put Emperor Charles V at an advantage, as the concentration of capital in the metropolis made it easier to finance his wars and achieve military supremacy over

1 Latin text and Dutch translation edited by De Schepper (1994), 196-7 (my English translation).

his adversaries. Foreign rulers, the Antwerp city government, and many individuals also turned to the Exchange in the 1540s. Public finance was proving a magnetic attraction to bankers and brokers, investors and speculators. Nowhere else could businessmen hope to make so much profit so quickly by investing in trade or finance.

It is for this reason that Antwerp in the first half of the sixteenth century provides an ideal vantage point from which to observe 'capital at work' in close-up and in practical detail, with as central question: what were these early capitalists really up to, and how did they achieve their objectives? Three exceptional figures have led us through the maze of economic and political opportunities and challenges: Schetz, Ducci and Van Schoonbeke. Inventiveness and organizational skills were necessary – but not sufficient - to exploit Antwerp's unique position as the economic capital of the Habsburg Netherlands and the Empire of Charles V and the primary commercial and financial centre of Europe. This is precisely what the careers of the three moneymakers presented in this book demonstrate. They were not only economically versatile but were also eager to launch new initiatives, to venture down new paths. They were highly innovative. Schetz, Ducci, and Van Schoonbeke introduced changes in very different economic sectors that were highly profitable for them, forged closer ties between political authorities and capitalists, and made the matter of common good versus private profit not only an ideological and legal theme but also a bone of social contention.

Dynamic entrepreneurs nearly always had to accommodate radical uncertainty. Fortunes were made, but heavy losses were suffered as well. The expectation of high profits in the future entailed serious risks, including those associated with increased competition. Since potential profits were highest in international trade and finance, competition there was the most intense. Capitalists were in favour of free trade insofar as it served their own commercial interests. Where such was not the case, their support for the cause was often purely rhetorical. In practice, they tried as much as possible to avoid competition. Their aim was to find a profitable niche market and to differentiate themselves from competitors or, even better, to occupy a market segment where other important players were absent, since – as the French saying has it – '*Les loups ne se mangent pas entre eux*' (wolves don't eat each other).

Schetz & Co. took an original approach to the spice trade. By concentrating on brassware and African (later also Asian) pepper in their Antwerp-Lisbon trade, they could make a profit without confronting the Fuggers, who were specialised in copper and other commodities. The extended commercial success of their import/export network was largely determined by the capitalist commodity chain they formed and controlled: they could supply brass manufacturers in Aachen with both calamine from the Altenberg mine and the finest quality copper, giving them direct control over production of manilas and other brassware intended for West Africa. This was an important innovation. Bruges firms such as Despars had also exported brassware to Portugal in the fifteenth century, but they had never set up commodity chains. For several decades the capacity to supply raw materials for the manufacture of products highly suited to trade with the Gold Coast and adjacent areas was the mainstay of Schetz & Co. Only in 1548 did the Fuggers also start to export brassware, but they were not involved in production, and the most profitable period was over by then, as became clear when they ceased trading with West Africa shortly after the middle of the century.

Several historians have pointed out that the importance of the spice trade should not be overestimated, since the grain trade was larger in volume and represented a much greater total capital.[2] Braudel countered this with the argument that capitalists were more interested in large and easy profits, such as were to be made in the spice trade at the early stage of globalisation.[3] In my opinion, it should also be emphasized that firms wishing in the early half of the sixteenth century to participate in the spice trade via Portugal would have been well advised to supply cereals to Lisbon as well, especially in years of rising prices, since Portuguese agriculture was underdeveloped. This is precisely what Schetz did, which also explains why he invested large sums in the reclamation and protection of low-lying land north of Antwerp, rather than in Zealand, where numerous other (mainly German and Italian) merchants were active.

Ducci was similarly creative as a merchant-banker. To collect the 6-percent tax on trade with France and the 1-percent tax on the value of exports from the Habsburg Netherlands to all other countries, he opened a great many customs offices in 1542/3 and designed a complex administration system. Although the operation was by no means flawless, setting up an entirely new customs system certainly qualifies as an achievement. The issue of large numbers of *rentmeestersbrieven*, bonds of the provincial Receivers-General, was still more important. This was Ducci's master stroke, as such bonds could raise small capital directly, reducing the dependence of the central government on the South-German bankers. By systematically offering future provincial tax revenues as financial backing, bond-secured loans were easily obtained. They circulated increasingly on the Exchange and were even used to pay commercial debts. Lacking financial records – Ducci destroyed them deliberately – very few complex financial transactions can be reconstructed, particularly his exchange-arbitrations between Antwerp and Lyon. Still, such operations were undoubtedly well-organized and highly profitable for many years.

As a property speculator, Van Schoonbeke faced stiff competition, because from 1542 on prices of land and real estate soared in Antwerp. His success as a project developer derived primarily from his understanding of urban planning. The corruption of city officials put him in a position to acquire and parcel up extensive vacant lots advantageously, but the combination of new economic centres, traffic efficiency, and residential functions enabled him to become dominant on Antwerp's real-estate market. Also, he set up two industrial undertakings founded on circulating/financial capital and qualifying as unique examples of organizational innovation in sixteenth-century Europe. He started a vertical construction building trust that supplied all the raw materials necessary to build 79,000 cubic metres of city walls: bricks, lime, beams, and bluestone. Constructing fifteen permanent brick kilns south of Antwerp, led him to set up a large peat extraction works in the provinces of Gelderland and Utrecht, where he had a canal dug in record time over sixteen kilometres for transporting the heavy raw material. Likewise, by concentrating nearly all the beer production of Antwerp in the New Town that he developed, he achieved economies of scale and vertical integration. The Water House (now Museum Brouwershuis), which he had constructed amid his new breweries and which supplied these (and later on also

2 Jacques Heers reviewing Delumeau (1962) in *Revue du Nord*, 46, 1964, 105-7. For a similar point of view, see Brulez (1968) and (1969).

3 Braudel (1966), I, 403.

other) enterprises with clean water, was not a technological innovation. By concentrating everything related to brewing in one place, however, Van Schoonbeke solved the water problem and achieved economies of scale that increased the brewers' earnings considerably and in turn boosted beer production. His brewery complex was unique in early modern Europe not only because of the massive capital investment but also because its organisationally innovative quality preserved the favourable effects after his decease. Finally, he presented a highly innovative proposal for paying the imperial troops partially in kind, taking on the organization of deliveries in the garrison cities along the border with France. Following his death, this system long remained in use by some of his partners (including the Schetz brothers).

During the first half of the sixteenth century distribution and production of manufactures were becoming more closely linked, and, consequently, the rise of commercial capitalism accelerated. Merchant capitalists did not readily engage in industrial production directly, particularly where fixed capital assets were required, since circulation was almost always more profitable than manufacturing. Sometimes, however, industrial enterprise was the clearest or even the only way to achieve or maintain a dominant position in a given market. In the second half of the fifteenth century merchants had interfered increasingly with production, if only by coordinating it, but from the 1500s this trend accelerated. Decisions made by businessmen with regard to investment flows had an increasing influence on the growth or otherwise of local and even regional industries. This was the case with Ducci, since control of the distribution of raw materials such as woad (in the Low Countries) or alum (in Northwest and Central Europe) allowed him to develop strategies that would greatly affect numerous textile manufacturers and merchants. He continued, however, to operate as a typical merchant and did not engage in production directly. Schetz and Van Schoonbeke, on the other hand, did not hesitate to control manufacturing themselves and to dominate it partially or even entirely, enabling capitalist relations of production to arise.

Schetz & Co. invested not only in operating the Altenberg mine but also and especially in manufacturing brassware in Aachen. Ascertaining how they organized production is not possible. Presumably, they had their own smelting works, but they must have resorted to subcontracting and putting out as well. In any case, from the 1520s they controlled the bulk of local production – and Aachen by then was the main centre of the brassware industry in Western Europe. Other initiatives by Schetz & Co. also attest to efforts to dominate the production of industrial commodities directly or indirectly. These decisions dated to the 1530s and reflected changes throughout the international economic landscape making it difficult or impossible to achieve dominance in some markets without control of the production. After pepper, English cloth was the company's main export product to Germany. To be able to buy in on favourable terms and supply customers abroad on time, they consistently placed their orders with the same Antwerp master cloth dressers, making those entrepreneurs heavily dependent on merchant capital. Ties between commercial capital and production were even closer in the sugar trade. Schetz imported large quantities and had the raw sugar refined at his own Antwerp plant. In addition, he invested in a sugar plantation and a sugar mill in Brazil, where free black males operated the technical facilities and a great many enslaved Native Americans performed the heavy unskilled work.

Van Schoonbeke went furthest in subordinating production to capital. During the busy season at the huge brick kilns he set up with Van Hencxthoven south of the metropolis,

400 to 500 workers were active, and sixty spacious homes were constructed for them. After completing the new fortifications, he sold the brick kilns he owned, but in the provinces of Gelderland and Utrecht his peat operations were continued long after his death by the Schetz brothers and other shareholders. The number of peat cutters cannot even be estimated approximately, but soon after the new canal he had dug was completed, Van Schoonbeke already had several 'gangs' sent to the sparsely populated region; all data suggest well-organized, long-distance migration by large numbers of workers.

The role of Antwerp's financial market in the Emperor's political and military ambitions was of the greatest importance for moneymakers for two reasons. First, the Antwerp capital market offered unprecedented opportunities to invest *and* speculate. From the 1520s a steadily declining number of merchant-bankers backed the financial dealings with the Emperor and his representatives, and in the 1540s ever fewer financiers/brokers were able to provide the increasingly large loans that Charles V and other monarchs were trying to raise on the Antwerp Exchange. Second, Antwerp capitalists who provided financial services to the Emperor by granting him loans and/or supplying new sources of income were generally protected and even actively supported by him – also in setting up or continuing lucrative but questionable economic operations. Van Schoonbeke was not active on the Exchange, but he let the Emperor participate directly or indirectly in his industrial ventures which yielded recurring income, which was greatly appreciated. Schetz and Ducci granted Charles V many substantial loans. They did not compete with the southern German and Genuese bankers in Antwerp, but they did commit themselves repeatedly to considerable sums when the Emperor's needs were greatest and other creditors were unable to comply for various reasons. Schetz was a strategic, risk-averse investor. The loans he arranged for Charles V and the government in the Habsburg Netherlands brought him large profits, but they were not intended exclusively or even primarily to amass capital faster than through commercial activities. Rather, he regarded such loans as investments: in exchange for financial services, he obtained vital economic benefits. Only towards the end of his life did he become far more active on the Antwerp money market and extend huge loans to the Emperor, probably encouraged by his eldest son, Gaspar, who, unlike his father, focused far more on finance than on the commodities trade. Ducci, on the other hand, was a financial capitalist willing to take great risks. Like Schetz, he obtained economic advantages in exchange for the financial services he provided for the Emperor and the government in the Habsburg Netherlands, but he wanted much more. Nobody in the 1540s drove the speculation frenzy on the Antwerp Exchange more or benefited as much from it as he did. He managed to become the main broker for both the Emperor and the King of England. Issuing loans to rival rulers or their allies was not unusual for bankers but did entail serious political risks, as Ducci learned. He had long worked with foreign partners on money and exchange arbitrage between Antwerp and Lyon, but by 1550 such transactions began to involve huge sums. The great danger was that the loans to the King of France and especially the efforts to create an artificial money shortage might seriously harm the Emperor.

Yet in the early half of the sixteenth century the Antwerp economy did not become overly financial. Short-term loans on the Exchange in the 1540s and the early 1550s earned the greatest and easiest profits, but the main aim of capitalists remained obtaining and retaining monopolist advantages. This was the real 'crock of gold'. Schetz, Ducci, and Van

Schoonbeke were highly innovative, had strong organizational skills, and were immensely talented at adapting to changing circumstances, but they had to cope with a context of economic, political, and ideological uncertainties, confusion, and even chaos. Long-term business success depended on having a competitive advantage and often involved efforts to obtain exceptional leverage via privileged or exclusive access to a specific commodity on a given market. Such a position could not be achieved simply by following the 'rules of the game' on a 'free market'. Support from public authorities was indispensable, a discrete rather than invisible hand, to achieve a decisive competitive edge. The growing need for liquidities in the context of state building and warfare provided more opportunities than ever to obtain commercial or financial monopolies. Commercial 'monopoly' or 'oligopoly' meant that small numbers of great merchants systematically organised distribution of a product to their advantage on certain markets, rather than trying to dominate the entire European market. Financial monopolies also arose, where merchant-bankers were given the exclusive right in certain areas to levy a given tax or duty. Competition was especially problematical for businessmen launching new initiatives, as investing in new ventures could be very risky. Ideally, they wanted a market sector without competition or with as little competition as possible. That was why they tried to obtain a monopoly, which meant that they had to address the 'visible hand': in most cases this was the State, in exceptional cases municipal authorities.

Schetz, Ducci and Van Schoonbeke were all monopolists and it was mainly on the basis of exclusive economic rights that they were able to make their fortunes. As leaseholder of the Altenberg mine, Schetz had no monopoly in the legal sense. In practice, however, he did have a monopoly, as no competitors were ever considered. When other capitalists tried to take over the lease and offered to pay a higher price, the central government ignored them. Henceforth, the contract of the Antwerp firm was extended without a call for tenders and in all cases for a modest fee. That was immensely important, as without mining Altenberg calamine combined with brass manufacturing in Aachen, Schetz would have been unable to create a highly lucrative commodity chain and to amass so much capital so rapidly. He was always looking for new opportunities to gain full control of a market. In 1525/6 he used the war with France to convince the Emperor to grant him a *de facto* monopoly on woad imports in the Low Countries and succeeded briefly in this effort. In the mid-1540s he offered to pay the English government for large amounts of lead from the dissolved monasteries insisting in return that he be granted the exclusive right to sell these stocks on the continent, but the Privy Council rejected this offer.

Wars offered opportunities to dominate imports or exports of certain commodities, as the government was in such dire financial straits at the time that it was inclined to grant exceptions to the general ban on 'trading with the enemy' in return for payment. War to a large extent 'made' Ducci. During the Habsburg-Valois War of 1542-44 he in effect obtained a monopoly on the import of Toulouse pastel in the Netherlands. Thanks to the ongoing financial difficulties of the Emperor, Ducci also obtained a monopoly in the alum trade for ten years in 1544, not only in the Low Countries but in the rest of Northwest Europe as well, for which Antwerp was the distribution centre. Never before had any individual businessman gained such firm control of the international alum trade. The imperial decision sent shudders throughout Europe, as it upset delicate political balances and harmed established economic interests. The Pope felt he had been bypassed, powerful Italian bankers were no longer price setters in Northwest Europe, and public authorities feared the reactions of textile manufacturers. Geopolitical changes led the Pope and other key international operators to accept Ducci's monopoly in 1547 and in turn led to its being declared null and void two years later. A fixed contractual maximum selling price in Antwerp could have been to the advantage of the textile manufacturers and merchants, but Ducci was too greedy. Rather than market his alum directly, he made secret agreements with wholesalers who resold their stock at much higher prices. Only in the 1560s did the government of the Habsburg Netherlands provide for a regular control on whether alum was being sold at more than the maximum price.[4]

During the period examined in this study, commercial monopolies nearly always involved commodities intended for international markets, but some monopolies arose that had a strong local impact, as Van Schoonbeke's ventures demonstrate. Completing the new city walls proceeded so swiftly and yielded such a handsome profit only because Van Schoonbeke had acquired the *de facto* monopoly on public works in Antwerp. This was formally the responsibility of the city government (which concluded the contracts with the entrepreneur), but it consistently resulted from urging by Mary of Hungary. The governor never explained her motives, but they are likely to have been twofold: military strengthening of the economic capital of the Habsburg Netherlands as quickly and as inexpensively as possible, while at the same time supporting an entrepreneur whose peat extraction in the provinces of Gelderland and Utrecht represented a vast source of income for her brother. The prospect of financial gain also explains why the Emperor was willing to purchase a share in the brewery complex. This step had major consequences, as it enabled the revolt of 11-12 July 1554 to be labelled as a type of *lèse majesté*, after which the Emperor compensated Van Schoonbeke for damages by granting him a legal monopoly on beer production and transport in Antwerp. As far as can be determined, nowhere else in the empire did so many private monopolies come about in so many different economic sectors. In Augsburg, for example, where the Fuggers and other powerful South-German trading companies were based, monopolies existed 'only' in mining and the metal industry.

It was in capitalists' interest to allow as little insight as possible into their affairs and this was doubly so where they held exclusive economic rights. This was the main reason why Schetz took as partners only close relatives. Like the Fuggers, the Welsers, the Imhoffs, and other large South-German merchant houses, Schetz & Co. was a family-based firm, as trust between the partners was considered essential, especially in view of the Altenberg-Aachen connection: all dealings connected with calamine extraction, distribution and processing were kept secret. For many years, Schetz could rely on two members of related families, with whom strong reciprocal relations existed; after they died, his three eldest sons took their place. Family members (especially younger ones) were also preferred as permanent representatives in crucial places abroad. It is extremely doubtful whether Schetz the businessman was 'above all suspicion', as suggested by prominent contemporaries, but no evidence of unlawful practice can be found.

Keenly aware of the risks he was taking, Ducci made sure that nobody was ever given full insight into his commercial and financial transactions. Secrecy was his trademark, as

4 Soly (1974), 829-34, 844.

contemporaries noted repeatedly. He had no family members at his disposal in Antwerp, but he managed to form a small international network of experienced merchant bankers. He teamed up with the wealthy and powerful Gian Carlo Affaitadi, who ran the Antwerp branch of a family business that extended throughout western and southern Europe. In any commercial disputes with third parties, Ducci could count on Affaitadi's unconditional support, since they each needed the other for business purposes: Ducci could help Affaitadi in the jewellery trade and even more so in the profitable trade in woad, where shady deals were being made, so that Affaitadi had good reason to protect Ducci. Affaitadi is worthy of serious study, since there are indications that he played a pivotal role in many mysterious commercial and financial networks in Antwerp in the 1530s and 1540s. Getting to the bottom of such networks requires very much archive research, since obfuscation was intentional on the part of the participants. It is in any case striking that in cases of conflict Italian merchants, irrespective of their origins, almost invariably turned to Affaitadi to adjudicate. Was he a sort of godfather? From the mid-1530s Ducci also entered into partnerships with South-German and Swiss financiers with whom he issued loans to the Emperor and became increasingly active on the Lyon money market. All parties involved in exchange-arbitrage between Antwerp and Lyon and loans to the French monarchy understood that secrecy was essential. Grimmel, Neidhart and Seiler accused each other - and Ducci - only when they were imprisoned. In brief, relations between Ducci and his most important partners were based primarily on calculation. They relied on each other's cooperation and loyalty because they were all very much at risk, not only economically, but politically and judicially as well.

Calculation was also a characteristic of Van Schoonbeke's partnerships and networks. He was unable to take on family members as partners but he did involve young businessmen with more capital than he had in his property speculations and construction companies. His good connections with corrupt city officials, who leveraged their political authority in his favour beyond what was permitted by law, were a major asset. Interdependence greatly benefited all parties concerned, and high profits soon opened many doors. When he needed considerable capital to start his own peat extraction operation, substantial businessmen – including the Schetz brothers – were willing to become partners. Gaspar Schetz convinced Charles V to invest in Van Schoonbeke's brewery complex, for which Schetz was amply rewarded. Like Ducci, Van Schoonbeke allowed no-one complete insight into his businesses. He maintained an extreme division of labour and had everybody who worked for him solemnly swear never to disclose anything that he saw or heard.

It would be wrong to regard state intervention as mere interference in local government. The city authorities were simply lacking in economic intiative. Antwerp was governed by a landholding and *rentier* elite that had no direct personal connections with the new and growing world of business and whose fortune consisted largely of immovable items. Their preoccupation 'capital at work' translated into a need to activate 'dormant' real estate by endowing it with a new purpose, thereby converting existing hereditary rent charges (*erfrenten*) into instruments of credit. As to the other sectors of the urban economy, they considered their top priorities to be taxation and industrial activities involving large numbers of well-organized craftsmen that might have an impact on the socio-political order. That was why they did not object to Van Schoonbeke concentrating the breweries in the New Town: excises on beer accounted for 50 to 60 percent of the total annual income of the city. This was also why they protested vociferously (but in vain), when the practices of Ducci led to unemployment among the cloth dressers, who were a large and powerful craft guild. And that was why the Merchant Adventurers, who imported large quantities of unfinished cloth, were granted substantial commercial and tax benefits by the city council. The other 'nations' could only dream of such preferential treatment. The Antwerp authorities were of course happy to welcome foreign merchants, but they made no concessions to the other 'nations' other than what was already current in Bruges and other European centres. No attempt was made to encourage international trade. With the exception of the installation of one new quayside crane and the establishment of the New Exchange - essentially an immense real-estate operation - nothing was undertaken to improve commercial infrastructure, although by 1540 the need for anchorages, roofed markets, open markets and warehouses had become urgent, as the merchants repeatedly pointed out. It fell to a private entrepreneur, Van Schoonbeke, to draft and carry out solutions. The local authorities adapted some of their litigation procedures to the businessmen's needs, but failed during the Golden Age to create any body of commercial law.[5] In sum, there are no indications to support the thesis that Antwerp's success may be largely attributed to the local authorities' efforts to change or adapt institutional arrangements in order to create efficient markets.[6] International merchants well understood from the beginning that they need expect no special 'privileges' from the Antwerp authorities. All the 'nations' of foreign merchants were established by the imperial authorities and, as far as can be ascertained, without prior consultation with the local authorities. Major businessmen would ask Schetz to request the central government to introduce new commercial or financial regulations or to propose amendments to current legislation. Nearly all his negotiations with the highest authorities were successful, i.e. he achieved the result envisaged by his fellow businessmen, without involving the Antwerp city government. It would appear that Schetz played his part as go-between to everyone's satisfaction, but this was certainly not the case with Ducci, who often adopted and imposed standpoints in monetary, financial and commercial matters that would damage large numbers of those concerned. The lack of commitment by the local political elite with regard to such matters certainly did not encourage the city's economic development and left at the same time a wide opening for sharp capitalists.

Capitalists and rulers needed each other more than ever before. Political-military conflict on a large scale and a ballooning public debt among all the rival European factions created fertile ground for the mutual dependence of state and capital. All possible sources of income were explored, involving greater interaction between state interests and private interests, as shown by the introduction and organisation of new taxes and customs duties and the granting of all kinds of monopolies. Forms of collusion between rulers and capitalists were not new, but the extent and nature of the entanglement assumed much greater proportions in the early half of the sixteenth century. The strong tendency towards monopoly is a reflection of this. Businessmen in the most economically advanced part of the Spanish-Habsburg Empire were in the best position to leverage the new capitalist

5 De Ruysscher (2009) and (2020).
6 As argued by Gelderblom (2013).

dynamic and at the same time shape it, as the concentration of political power facilitated forms of government intervention that benefited big business. That the changes were the most pronounced in Antwerp is not purely coincidental, as for a few decades the city was the crucial nexus of capital accumulation. No other European city benefited so much from the emerging world economy, and nowhere else did big business and the state have so much to offer one another. Inventiveness and organizational skills were necessary, however, to exploit to the full Antwerp's unique position as the economic capital of the Habsburg Netherlands and primary commercial and financial centre of Europe. This is precisely what the careers of Schetz, Ducci, and Van Schoonbeke demonstrate.

Were their monopolies economically efficient? Did they serve the common good in the short or long term?[7] Such questions cannot be answered unconditionally. Some historians and economists have done so for later periods. Peter Klein, for example, has emphasized that trade in Amsterdam during the Dutch Golden Age derived largely from monopolies and based on his masterful study of the Trip firm, which made a fortune from the arms trade, he argues that monopolization was an essential condition for economic progress.[8] He supports the theory of Joseph Schumpeter, who asserts that capitalists prefer to launch new products on the market, because this gives them a better chance of maintaining full control over a niche and making higher profits for an extended period. In his view, the dynamics of capitalism therefore imply monopolist practices: 'The introduction of new methods of production and new commodities is hardly conceivable with perfect – and perfectly prompt – competition from the start. And this means that the bulk of what we call economic progress is incompatible with it'.[9] Did this also hold true for the monopolist practices of the three capitalists examined in this book? In some cases it did, but not in others. Beyond question, the calamine monopoly was highly profitable, even long after the Schetz brothers were no longer directly involved in brassware manufacturing in Aachen. The interest of the Schetzes, however, can hardly be equated with the common good of Aachen or Antwerp. Nor were the war-time woad monopolies of Erasmus Schetz and Ducci intended to promote the economies of Antwerp or the Netherlands. Ducci's alum monopoly could have served such a purpose, as setting a reasonable maximum price by imperial decree for twelve years basically provided a hitherto unprecedented guaranteed supply and cost alike for the textile dyers and their clients. But Ducci corrupted the new system by charging this price only to wholesalers; all other buyers had to pay far more. Van Schoonbeke's monopoly of public works enabled the entrepreneur to make large profits. He had to invest in fixed capital, but he could rely on affluent partners, and peat extraction operations were an efficient investment over the long term as well. On the other hand, the City of Antwerp greatly benefited from Van Schoonbeke's monopoly of the public works. That held true in still greater measure for his concentration of beer production. Without exclusive privileges, this highly capital-intensive venture would probably not have come about, but a legal monopoly proved unnecessary to increase beer production, and consequently beer excises, following the death of the initiator.

7 In this connection, see the interesting remarks of Ogilvie (2007).
8 Klein (1965).
9 Schumpeter (1976), 105. See the comment of Vries (2013), 113-14.

The expansion of capitalist organizations reflected the economic and political transformations that occurred in Europe in the period 1450-1550. Globalization and state formation entailed scale expansion, as well as concentration of economic and political power in the hands of a few individuals. For capitalists, monopolization and cartelization were strategies to avoid, limit, or, wherever possible, eliminate the rise of competition in highly profitable commercial sectors, as well as to curtail the risks associated with investing large amounts of capital in new ventures. Sometimes such strategies failed[10] or succeeded only briefly. But that is not the point. Monopolies and cartels were not always established everywhere, but they were likely to come about in upcoming trade centres, and they continued to increase. Much research is still needed on monopolist practices to establish Europe-wide comparisons, but by the mid-sixteenth century the foundations were indisputably in place for what Adam Smith would later describe as the 'mercantile system'. In his opinion, such a system was imbued with 'the wretched spirit of monopoly', permanently on the lookout for ways of neutralizing competition: 'Monopoly of one kind or another, indeed, seems to be the sole engine of the mercantile system'.[11] Other authors would later qualify the 'mercantile system' as 'commercial capitalism'. At any rate, from the late fifteenth century, monopolies started to become increasingly significant in various economic sectors, and the rise of capitalism accelerated.

Monopolist practices that were fairly easily perceptible – which was not the case for Schetz's calamine mine – had an impact on public social life as well. This is clear from the *Monopolstreit* in the Holy Roman Empire between 1510 and 1530. The critics of the large German trading houses were a heterogeneous group, but representatives from nearly all substantial economic centres accused 'monopolists' of dominating the market. In the 1540s, violent interpersonal conflicts ensued in Antwerp. The surge of speculations in both the financial and the real-estate markets in the 1540s, the growing rumours about exchange-arbitrage between Antwerp and Lyon, the leaks with regard to Van Schoonbeke's secret deals with members of the political élite, the bankruptcies of respected merchants that were put down to Ducci's malpractices and last but not least the unashamedly monopolistic manoeuvring of the two moneymakers, all created an explosive mixture that weighed heavily on both personal relations and the tissue of society. Stephen Vaughan was not exactly an expert in financial matters and it only dawned on him that he had made a bad deal when it was already too late, but he did not exaggerate in depicting the Antwerp Exchange as a sort of hellhole where the 'wolves' were forever waiting to pounce. Chief amongst his wolves was Ducci, who was described by other contemporaries as the terror of the Antwerp Exchange, as an unscrupulous speculator, a swindler, and moreover a dangerous bully, who instructed those he employed to beat up or even murder anyone who stood in his path. This was a lopsided view, since Ducci was also an innovative banker, as demonstrated by his successful introduction of *rentmeestersbrieven* on a large scale, though this is not to deny that he was indeed unscrupulous. In the 1540s he was without doubt the most hated banker-broker in Antwerp, but the numerous murderous conflicts in and round the Exchange prove that other businessmen - particularly Italians - were quick to draw their weapons. The Exchange was a financially *and* physically dangerous place.

---

10 See, e.g., Ambrosius Höchstetter's unsuccessful attempt to establish a quicksilver monopoly: Safley (2008), 47-50.

11 Adam Smith, *The Wealth of Nations*, Books IV and V. See Salvadori & Signorino (2013), and Kurz (2016).

There were not only the spectacular personal conflicts in the business world. More alarming were the growing numbers of complaints from both wage workers and members of the socially intermediate groups with regard to Van Schoonbeke's *de facto* monopoly of public works, his complete control of the municipal duties on beer and wine, and his concentration of beer brewing, all of which were very visible, large-scale operations that were regarded by broad segments of the population as morally unacceptable, particularly since these monopolistic practices were widely regarded as causing a direct and indirect lowering of the standard of living. The revolt of 11-12 July 1554 was in many respects a milestone. It was the only collective action in sixteenth-century Antwerp in which religious motives did not play a part, and the first anti-monopoly revolt in European history. It was a movement borne and most probably set off by the socially intermediate groups. The subsequent repression made it clear once and for all that the city government had little latitude whenever 'higher interests' were at stake: when the economic or financial interests of the Emperor were directly or indirectly involved, the central government had the final say. This was not new, but up until then such interventions had always concentrated on Ducci. The city council had to accept that Mary of Hungary reversed the decision to ban Ducci from the Exchange for three years, that she disregarded all protests against Ducci's arbitrage transactions at the Lyon fairs (despite the harm they had caused many Antwerp merchants), that Charles V cared more about claims by Ducci for compensation from Henry VIII than about the activities of the Merchant Adventurers and employment in Antwerp, that Ducci could not be prosecuted in a court of law (not even after an attempted assassination on his orders), and that resisting his alum monopoly was futile (as long as the central government supported it).

From 1548/9 on, Mary of Hungary put intense pressure on the Antwerp local authorities to sign contracts with Van Schoonbeke, largely on the basis of military and financial considerations. Van Schoonbeke, as she saw it, was capable of doing what the city council could not: establishing a port that would generate income and finishing the new fortifications rapidly and at a low cost. Van Schoonbeke's successful monopoly of public works would not have been possible without the Emperor's supportive measures: the suspension of corporative privileges, the opening-up of the labour market and the grant of a monopoly of trade in Gelderland peat. All possible material, institutional and social obstacles were cleared away and the local authorities' arms twisted where necessary. The state's interests and the personal interests of Charles V were perfectly attuned: Antwerp's defences were a maximum priority in the early fifties and the exploitation of the imperial peatlands represented a new source of income. These motives underlay Charles V's steps to support Van Schoonbeke's concentration of brewing in Antwerp: breweries required large quantities of peat and Van Schoonbeke moreover offered the emperor a share in the new company.

An Emperor who follows up a serious revolt in the economic capital of his realm by granting the capitalist in question a public and formal monopoly, moreover via a company in which the Emperor himself has a share, represents a considerable ideological development. In the 1540s imperial officials had increasingly advocated the Emperor's granting of exclusive economic rights to private individuals in the public interest, as evidenced by the debates on Ducci's alum monopoly. Theologians and moralists from the School of Salamanca supported this view, which aligned closely with their own political position.

In his enormously influential *Manual de confesores y penitentes* ('Handbook for Confessors and Penitents'), written in 1549 and published in 1553, Martín de Azpilcueta, alias Doctor Navarrus, acknowledged the legitimacy of a monopoly granted for political reasons: a ruler was entitled to decree in the public interest that a subject could purchase and sell certain merchandise. The same position was defended by the Dominican Domingo de Soto, the confessor of Charles V and a very active participant in the Council of Trent.[12] The social and ideological consequences of the accelerated rise of capitalism did not escape the attention of contemporary artists, as Aertsen's *Meat Stall* (1552) indicates. Far more strikingly, in 1557 Pieter van der Heyden published an etching in Antwerp based on a drawing made by Bruegel the previous year, with the title 'Big Fish Eat Little Fish' – an old Latin adage that became more current than ever and at the same time acquired new connotations.[13]

12 Rosolino (2013), 799-802.

13 Pieter van der Heyden (engraver) and Pieter Bruegel the Elder (designer), *Big Fish Eat Little Fish*, 1557. Antwerp, Museum Plantin-Moretus, Prentenkabinet, PK.OP.13802.

Bibliography

Manuscript sources

Stadsarchief, Antwerp (SAA), Belgium

Insolvente Boedelskamer

IB 766: Gerard Grameye, Journaal, 1561-65
IB 2968-3021: Fonds Gilbert van schoonbeke

Schepenkamer

CERT 5-15: Certicificatieboeken, 1542-59 (samples)
COLL 8-10: Collectanea, 1550-55
SR 97-281: Schepenregisters, 1490-1560 (samples)
CC 2-13: Coopers en comparanten, 1490-1566 (samples)

Privilegekamer

PK 78: *Secundum Volumen Privilegiorum*, 1249-1650
PK 116: Louis van Caucercken, *Cronycke der stad Antwerpen*
PK 149: H. De Moy, *Tractaet der officieren*
PK 313-316: Secretary A. Grapheus
PK 318: Secretary H. De Moy
PK 481: Pensionary J. Gillis
PK 914-916: Gebodboeken, 1489-1576
PK 1012: Handel en Scheepvaart ('Trade and Shipping'), 1464-1610
PK 1347: Wethoudersboek,1200-1601
PK 1396: Stadskeurmeesters
PK 1434: Stadsbestuur ('Town government')
PK 2213-2216: Nieuwstad, 1549-51
PK 2242-2245: Fortifications1542-80
PK 2393: Staten van Brabant (Accounts)
PK 2438: Staten van Brabant (Correspondence)
PK 2764-2765: Plakkaten van den Hove, 1500-67
PK 3479: Nota's Henry L.V. De Groote

Tresorij

T 1: Adolf van der Noot, *Recueil*, 1539
T 16: Collegiaal Actenboek, 1551-52.
T 55: Gaspar Ducci, 6-percent tax
T 199: Beer excises
T 532-533: Wine excises
T 622-629: Alum
T 818: Tolls
T 927: Kruibeke and Backersveer
T 1017-1019: Waag ('Weigh House')
T 1242-1244: Lancelot van Ursel
T 1257: Debt
T 1317-1319: Michiel van der Heyden
T 1705-1710: Stadsprotocollen, 1517-80

Rekenkamer

R 11-15: Stadsrekeningen ('Town accounts'), 1541-43, 1549-51, 1554-55
R 1756-1759: Peter van Wesenbeke, Memorialen, 1549-52
R 1770, 1783-1787: Fortifications, 1542-52
R 2179: Hundredth Penny, 1570
R 2387: Tenth Penny, 1553

Gilden en Ambachten

GA 4001: Ambachten Boeck, 1430-1561
GA 4029: Lakenbereiders ('Cloth dressers')
GA 4276: Oudkleerkopers ('Old Clothes Dealers')
GA 4416, 4475: Brewers, 1500-60
GA 4426, 4626: Oude Voetboog
GA 4579: Sint-Niklaasgilde
GA 4621: Schuttershoven, 1548-55
GA 4811: Burgerwacht

Vierschaar

V 176: Poortersboek, 1463-1550
V 279: Gerechtszaken
V 322-349: Schetz-Pruynen
V 1095: Collegiaal gedingboek, 1552-54
V 1233: Vonnisboek, 1542-52

Notariaat

N 547: Stephanus Claeys, 1568
N 2071-2074: Zeger 's Hertoghen Sr., 1540-51
N 3638: Dierick vanden Bossche, 1576

Kerken en Kloosters

KK 2141-2145: Saint Elisabeth Hospital, 1549-51
Genealogisch Fonds
GF 50: Families

Museum Plantin-Moretus, Antwerp (MPMA), Belgium

No. 318: Willem van Lare, *Regula Transporti.*

Stadsbibliotheek, Antwerp (SBA), Belgium

B11285: *Rijmkronijk van Antwerpen*, 1472-1556

Archives générales du Royaume (AGR), Brussels, Belgium

Chambres des Comptes

CC 138-139: Registres aux chartes, 1529-55
CC 294: Actes et appointements, 1520-42
CC 637-641: Registres des chartes, 1516-21
CC 2453-2458: Comptes des recettes générales: Limbourg, 1514-60
CC 4977-4979: Comptes particuliers des domaines: Anvers, 1513-25
CC 20786-20788: Comptes des droits des seaux: Brabant, 1515-45
CC 23357-23364, 50245-50249: Gaspar Ducci: droit d'un pour cent, 1543-45
CC 23497-23508, 49871-49873: Gaspar Ducci: droit de six pour cent, 1542-44

Papiers d'État et l'Audience

PEA 109, 128-132: Correspondance de Marie de Hongrie, 1536-48
PEA 135, 139, 143-147: Correspondance en matière de finances, 1550-57
PEA 819: Registre aux actes, 1538-44
PEA 872: Compte de Jean Micault, 1522
PEA 879: Lettres patentes de noblesse 1515-96
PEA 1191/41-45: Anvers, 1540-65
PEA 1414: Alun, 1536-59
PEA 1417/8: Correspondance de l'Empereur avec Marie de Hongrie, 1551-12
PEA 1627-1637: Lettres missives: généralités, 1531-55

PEA 1638: Lettres missives: requêtes, 1531-48
PEA 1641: Lettres missives: correspondance de l'Empereur avec Marie de Hongrie
PEA 1652: Lettres missives: Anvers, 1536-55
PEA 1661/1-2: Lettres missives: Gaspar Ducci, 1542-52
PEA 1666/1: Lettres missives: Schetz, 1547-54
PEA 1674: Lettres missives: généralités, 1555-56

Chancellerie de Marie de Hongrie

CMH 33-35: Prêts, 1542
CMH 63: Lettres d'obligations, 1549

Grote Raad van Mechelen

GRM 820- 874: Geëxtendeerde sententiën, 1522-72

Fonds d'Ursel

FU, L 182: Érasme Schetz
FU, L 191: Anvers, 1544-71
FU, L 192: Nouvelles brasseries à Anvers, 1552-84
FU, L 199: Brésil, 1548-1615
FU, L 226: Moeres, 1550-1610
FU, L 237: Vieille Cie Érasme Schetz et fils, 1555-56
FU, L 241: Wouter Seroye et Cie, 1558-79

Manuscrits divers

MD 165: Collection de documents historiques
MD 809: Écrit contre Gaspar Schetz, 1575

Rijksarchief Brussel (RAB), Belgium

Raad van Brabant

RB, Archief van de Griffies (AG), nos 594-604: Vonnisboeken, 1547-56
RB, Officie Fiscaal (OF), Klein nummer 510: Proces Van den Broecke, 1555
RB, OF, Processen Procureur-Generaal (PPG) 223: Grimmel-Seiler, 1551
RB, OF, Processen Procureur-Generaal (PPG) 326: Francisco Francesqui, 1544
RB, OF, Processen Procureur-generaal (PPG) 2367: Joachim Gooris et al.

Koninklijke Bibliotheek (KB), Brussels, Belgium

KB 13558-67: Documents relatifs à l'histoire d'Anvers

Het Utrechts Archief (HUA), Netherlands

FI 37/2: Register van akten, 1547-72
FI 37/26a-29: Rentmeester-generaal, Rekeningen, 1551-54

Gemeentearchief Veenendaal (GAV), Netherlands

VGSV 83: Octrooien, 1550-51
VGSV 86: Grift, 1553

West-Brabants Archief (WBA), Netherlands

BoZ, Heerlijkheidsarchieven (HA) 441: Erasmus Schetz, 1541
BoZ, Register van Procuraties en Certificaten (RPC) 5270 (inv. 392), 1506-20

Regionaal Historisch Centrum Maastricht (RHCM), Netherlands

Brabants Hooggerecht Maastricht (BHM), Gichtregister 713, 1528-40

Archives départementales du Nord (ADN), Lille, France

Série B: Recette générale des finances: 2229, 2309, 2327, 2363, 2430, 2436, 2442, 2448, 2454, 2460 (microfilms in AGR)

Arquivo nacional da Torre do Tombo (ANTT), Lisbon, Portugal

Chanc. de Don Manuel [I], livro 25
Corpo Chronológico (CC), Parte II, maço 15, doc. 25 (2/15/25), and maço 22, doc. 91 (2/22/9)

Archivo General de Simancas (AGS), Spain

SE Negociación de Flandes: Legajo 502: 1546-48
SE Sueltos de Estado: Legajo 8336

Archivo de la Real Chancillería de Valladolid (ARCHV), Spain

Pergaminos, Carpeta 147: Strozzi-Ducci, 1547-48

Haus-, Hof- und Staatsarchiv (HHS), Vienna, Austria

Belgien-PA 31-75: Korrespondenzen, 1540-1552 (Microfilms in AGR)

Printed sources

Baelde, Michel (1965b). 'Onuitgegeven dokumenten betreffende de zestiende-eeuwse Collaterale Raden (1533-1577)', *Handelingen van de Koninklijke Commissie voor Geschiedenis*, **131**, 129-229.

Bandello, Matteo (1895). *Twelve Stories*, transl. and ed. by Percy Pinkerton (London: John C. Nimmo).

Beer, Rudolf (1891). 'Acten, Regesten und Inventare aus dem Archivo General zu Simancas', *Jahrbuch der kunsthistorischen Sammlungen des Allerhöchsten Kaiserhauses*, **12**, XCI-CCIV.

Braancamp Freire, Anselmo (1920). *Noticias da Feitoria de Flandres Precedidas dos Brandões Poetas do Cancioneiro Estudos* (Lisbon: Arquivo Historico Portugues).

Bréard, Charles, and Philippe Barrey (1906). 'Documents relatifs à la marine normande aux XVe et XVIe siècles', *Mélanges de la Société de l'Histoire de Normandie*, **6**, 203-90.

Butkens, Christopher (1726). *Supplément aux trophées tant sacrés que profanes du duché de Brabant* (2 vols; The Hague: Chretien van Lom).

Calvete de Estrella, Juan Christoval (1552). *El Felicissimo viaie d'el muy alto e muy poderoso Principe Don Phelippe, Hijo d'el Emperador Don Carlos Quinto Maximo' desde España à sus tierra dela baxa Alemaña* (Antwerp: M. Nucio).

Calvete de Estrella, Juan Christoval 1883). *Le très-heureux voyage fait par très-haut et très puissant Prince Don Philippe fils du grand empereur Charles-Quint depuis l'Espagne jusqu'à ses domaines de la Basse-Allemagne*, transl. by Jules Petit, (Brussels: Fr.-J. Olivier).

Chronijcke (1557). *De Chronijcke van Vlaenderen in tcorte, metsgaeders van Brabant, Arthois, Henegauwe, Hollant, Zeelant, Vrieslant ende andere omligghenden landen* (Ghent: Gheeraert van Salenson).

Chroniques (1879). *Chroniques de Brabant et de Flandre*, ed. Charles Piot (Brussels: F. Hayez).

Correspondance (1979-82): *La correspondance d'Érasme*, Vols VII-XI: *1527-1536*, transl. and ed. by Aloïs Gerlo (Brussels: University Press; *Institut Interuniversitaire pour l'Étude de la Renaissance et de l'Humanisme*).

Correspondence (2003): *The Correspondence of Erasmus*, Vol. 12: *Letters 1658 to 1817, January 1526-March 1527*, transl. by Alexander Dalzell and annot. by Charles G. Nauert (Toronto: University of Toronto Press).

Correspondence (2016): *The Correspondence of Erasmus*, Vol. 17: *Letters 2357 to 2471, August 1530-March 1531*, transl. by Charles Fantazzi and annot. by James Martin Estes (Toronto: University of Toronto Press).

De Damhouder, Joos (1981). *Practycke ende handbouck in criminele zaeken*, ed. Jozef Dauwe and Jos Monballyu (Roeselare: Den Wijngaert).

De Longé, Guillaume (1870). *Coutumes de la ville d'Anvers*, Vol. 1 (Brussels: F. Gobbaerts; Coutumes du pays et duché de Babant: Quartier d'Anvers, 1).

Denucé, Jan (1934a). *Inventaire des Affaitadi, banquiers italiens à Anvers de l'année 1568* (Antwerp: De Sikkel).

De Poerck, Guy (1951). *La draperie médiévale en Flandre et en Artois. Technique et terminologie* (3 vols; Bruges: De Tempel).

De Weert, Josse (1879). 'Chronijcke van Nederlant, besonderlijck der stadt Antwerpen, sedert den jaere 1097 tot den jaere 1565', in *Chroniques de Brabant et de Flandre*, ed. Charles Piot (Brussels: F. Hayez), 71-172.

Dokumenten (1959): *Dokumenten voor de geschiedenis van prijzen en lonen in Vlaanderen en Brabant, XVe-XVIIIe eeuw*, ed. by Charles Verlinden and Jan Craeybeckx (Bruges: De Tempel).

Drost, M.A. (1984). *Documents pour servir à l'histoire du commerce des Pays-Bas avec la France jusqu'à 1585*, Vol. I: *Actes notariés de La Rochelle, 1423-1585* (The Hague: Martinus Nijhoff; Rijks Geschiedkundige Publicatiën, Grote Serie, 190).

Duerloo, Luc, and Paul Janssens (1992). *Wapenboek van de Belgische adel, van de 15de tot de 20ste eeuw* (4 vols; Brussels: Gemeentekrediet).

Dürer, Albrecht (1978). *Tagebuch der Reise in die Niederlande: mit Illustrationen aus seinen Skizzenbüchern*, ed. Fedja Anzelewsky (Zürich: Seefeld).

Geffcken, Peter, and Mark Häberlein (2014). *Rechnungsfragmente der Augsburger-Gesellschaft (1496-1551). Oberdeutsche Fernhandel am Beginn der neuzeitlichen Weltwirtschaft* (Stuttgart: Franz Steiner Verlag; Deutsche Handelsakten des Mittelalters und der Neuzeit, XXII).

Génard, Pierre (1880). 'De inventaris van het sterfhuis van Gilbert van Schoonbeke', *Antwerpsch Archievenblad*, **17**, 175-249.

Génard, Pierre (1882). 'Un acte de société commerciale au XVIe siècle. La Maison Schetz Frères d'Anvers', *Bulletin de la Société de Géographie d'Anvers*', **VII**, 475-87.

Génard, Pierre (1888). 'Un procès célèbre au XVIe siècle: Gilbert van Schoonbeke contre Gaspar Dozzi', *Bulletin de la Commission royale d'Histoire de Belgique*, 4th ser., **15**, 307-45.

Geudens, Edmond (1905). *Dit raect het oude cleercoopersambacht binnen der stede van Antwerpen* (Brecht: Braeckmans).

Gorter-Van Royen, Laetitia V.G., and Jean-Paul Hoyois (2009). *Correspondance de Marie de Hongrie avec Charles Quint et Nicolas de Granvelle* (Turnhout: Brepols).

Guicciardini, Lodovico (1567a). *Descrittione di tutti i Paesi Bassi altrimenti detti Germania inferiore* (Antwerp: Silvius).

Guicciardini, Lodovico (1567b). *Description de tout le Païs-Bas ou autrement dict Germanie inférieure ou Basse-Allemaigne* (Antwerp: Silvius).

Häpke, Rudolf (1913). *Niederländische Akten und Urkunden zur Geschichte der Hanse und zur deutschen Geschichte*, Vol. 1: *1531-1557* (Munich and Leipzig: Duncker & Humblot).

Jasparus, Jacob (1548). *Honestissimae matronae, Dominae Idae, uxoris Erasmi Scheti, Antverpiae, Epitaphium* (Antwerp: Gillis Coppens van Diest).

Lanz, Karl (1844-46). *Correspondenz des Kaisers Karl V.* (3 vols; Leipzig: F.A. Brockhaus).

Lettere (1950). *Lettere di Giovan Battista Guicciardini a Cosimo e Francesco de' Medici scritte dal Belgio dal 1559 al 1577*, ed. Mario Battistini (Brussels and Rome: Academia Belgica; Bibliothèque historique belge de Rome, II).

Luther, Martin (1524). *On Commerce and Usury*, ed. with introd. and notes by Philipp Robinson Rössner (London: Anthem Press, 2014).

Mair, Paul Hektor (1917). 'Zwei Chroniken des Augsburger Ratsdieners Paul Hektor Mair von 1548 bezw. 1547-1565 bezw. 1564', in *Die Chroniken der Schwäbischen Städte: Augsburg*, Vol. 7, *Die Chroniken der deutschen Städte vom 14. bis ins 16. Jahrhundert*, Vol. 32 (Leipzig: Historische Kommission bei der Königlichen Akademie der Wissenschaften).

Müller, Heidi A. (2002). 'Tand und Nürnberger Waren', in *Quasi Centrum Europeae: Europa kauft in Nürnberg, 1400-1800*, ed. Hermann Maué et al. (Nuremberg: Germanisches Museum), 73-95.

Müller, Karl Otto (1962). *Welthandelsbräuche, 1480-1540* (Wiesbaden: Franz Steiner Verlag).

Papebrochius, Daniel (1845). *Annales Antverpienses ab Urbe Condita ad Annum MDCC*, ed. F.H. Mertens and Ern. Buschmann, Vol. II (Antwerp: J.E. Buschmann).
Piot, Charles, ed. (1879). *Chroniques de Brabant et de Flandre* (Brussels: F. Hayez).
Regesten (2006): *Regesten des Archivs der Grafen von Henneberg-Römhild*, Vol. 1, ed. Johannes Mötsch (Cologne: Böhlau).
'Relazione' (1839): 'Relazione di Borgogna da Vincenzo Quirini', in *Le Relazioni degli ambasciatori veneti al Senato*, ed. Eugenio Albèri, Ser. I, Vol. 1 (Florence: Società editrice fiorentina), pp. 1-30.
'Relazione' (1840a): 'Relazione di Gaspare Contarini', in *Le Relazioni degli ambasciatori veneti al Senato*, ed. Eugenio Albèri, Ser. I, Vol. 2 (Florence: Società editrice fiorentina, 1840), pp. 9-74.
'Relazione (1840b): 'Relazione di Marino Cavalli', in *Le Relazioni degli ambasciatori veneti al Senato*, ed. Eugenio Albèri, Ser. I, Vol. 2 (Florence: Società editrice fiorentina, 1840), pp. 193-223.
'Relazione' (1853): 'Relazione di Federico Badoaro', in *Le Relazioni degli ambasciatori veneti al Senato*, ed. Eugenio Albèri, Ser. I, Vol. 3 (Florence: Società editrice fiorentina), pp. 175-330.
'Relazione' (2005). 'Relazione di Bernardo Navagero, 1546'. Roma: Bibiotheca Italiana - Online: http://www.bibliotecaitaliana.it/indice/visualizza_testo_html/bibit001314 (accessed December 2020).
Servilius, Johannes (1544). *Geldro-Gallica coniuratio in totius Belgicae clarissimam civitatem Belgicam, duce Martino Rosheymio* (Augsburg: Henricus Steyner).
Simson, Paul (1913). *Danziger Inventar, 1531-1591, mit einem Akten-Anhang* (Munich and Leipzig: Duncker & Humblot; Inventare Hansischer Archive des sechzehnten Jahrhunderts, III).
Sneller, Zeger Willem, and Willem Sybrand Unger (1930). *Bronnen tot de geschiedenis van de handel met Frankrijk* (2 vols; The Hague: Martinus Nijhoff).
Sousa, Pero Lopes de (1839). *Diario da navegação da armada que foi á terra do Brasil em 1530 sob a Capitania-Mor de Martin Affonso de Sousa*, ed. Francisco Adolfo de Varnhagen (Lisbon: Typopraphia da Sociedade propagadora dos conhecimentos uteis).
Stols, Eddy (1968). 'Um dos primeiros documentos sobre o engenho dos Schetz em São Vicente', *Revista de História*, no. **76**, 407-19.
Strieder, Jakob (1930). *Aus Antwerpener Notariatsarchiven. Quellen zur deutschen Wirtschaftsgeschichte des 16. Jahrhunderts* (Stuttgart: Deutsche Verlags-Anstalt).
U[llens], F.G. (1743). *Antwerpsch Chronykje* (Leiden: Pieter vander Eyck).
Unger, W.S. (1939). *De tol van Iersekeroord. Documenten en rekeningen, 1321-1572* (The Hague: Martinus Nijhoff; Rijks Geschiedkundige Publicatiën, Kleine Serie 29).
Urkundenbuch (1915): *Urkundenbuch zur Geschichte des Mansfeldischen Saigerhandels im 16. Jahrhundert*, ed. by Walter Möllenberg (Halle an der Saale: Otto Hendel).
Vandenesse, Jean de (1874). 'Journal des voyages de Charles-Quint, de 1514 à 1551', in *Collection des voyages des souverains des Pays-Bas*, Vol. II, ed. Louis-Prosper Gachard, (Brussels: F. Hayez, 1874).
Verzameling (1856): *Verzameling der graf- en gedenkschriften van de provincie Antwerpen*, Vol. 1, *Antwerpen: Cathedrale Kerk* (Antwerp: Buschmann).
Voyage (1992). *Voyage d'Eustache Delafosse sur la côte de Guinée, au Portugal et en Espagne (1479-1481)*, trans. and ed. by Denis Escudier (Paris: Éditions Chandeigne).

Wackernagel, Hans Georg (1951). *Die Matrikel der Universität Basel*, Vol. 1: *1460-1529* (Basel: Verlag der Universitätsbibliothek).

Westermann, Ekkehard, and Markus A. Denzel (2011). *Das Kaufmannsnotizbuch des Matthäus Schwarz aus Augsburg von 1548* (Stuttgart: Franz Steiner Verlag); Vierteljahrschrift für Sozial- und Wirtschaftsgeschichte, Beiheft 215).

Wielant, Filips (1995). *Corte instructie in materie criminele*, ed. Jos Monballyu (Brussels: Paleis der Academiën).

Ympyn, Jan (1979). *Nieuwe instructie ende bewijs der looffelijcker consten des rekenboecks* (London: Scholar; reprint of the 1543-edition).

Literature

Abel, Wilhelm (1974). *Massenarmut und Hungerkrisen im vorindustriellen Europa. Versuch einer Synopsis* (Hamburg and Berlin: Paul Parey).

Abrahamse, Jaap Evert, et al. (2015). 'Gouden kansen? Vastgoedstrategieën van bouwondernemers in de stadsuitleg van Amsterdam in de Gouden Eeuw', *Bulletin van de Koninklijke Nederlandse Oudheidkundige Bond*, **114**, 229-57.

Acidini, Cristina (2011). 'Cosimo, Piero and Lorenzo. From Money to Maestri', in *Money and Beauty: Bankers, Botticelli and the Bonfire of the Vanities*, ed. Ludovica Sebregondi and Tim Parks (Florence: Fondazione Palazzo Strozzi), 103-17.

Aerts, Erik (2011a). 'The Absence of Public Exchange Banks in Medieval and Early Modern Flanders and Brabant (1400-1800): A Historical Anomaly to Be Explained', *Financial History Review*, **18**, 91-117.

Aerts, Erik (2011b). 'Zwaar superbier of opgewarmd water? De alcoholsterkte van Antwerpse biersoorten (zestiende-zeventiende eeuw)', in *Antwerpen bierstad. Acht eeuwen biercultuur*, ed. Ivan Derycke (Brasschaat: Pandora), 29-39.

Aerts, Erik, and Herman van der Wee (2016). *Geschiedenis van Lier. Welvaart en samenleving, van het ontstaan van de stad tot de Eerste Wereldoorlog* (Lier: Gilde Heren van Lier).

Almeida, A.A. Marques de (1993). *Capitais e capitalistas no comércio da especiaria: o eixo Lisboa-Antuérpia, 1501-1549. Aproximação a um estudo de geofinança* (Lisbon: Cosmos).

Andreatta, Margarida Davina (1999). 'Engenho São Jorge dos Erasmos: Prospecção arqueológica, histórica e industrial', *Revista USP*, no. **41**, 28-47.

Anievas, Alexander, and Kerem Nişancioğlu (2015). *How the West Came to Rule: The Geopolitical Origins of Capitalism* (London: PlutoPress).

Antunes, Cátia, and Amélia Polónia, eds ((2016). *Beyond Empires: Global, Self-Organized, Cross-Imperial Networks, 1500-1800* (Leiden and Boston: Brill).

Arbelo García, Adolfo (2005). 'De Amberes a la isla de La Palma: El protagonismo socioeconómico y político de los Van Dale en la sociedad canaria de los siglos XVI-XVIII', in *Flandes y Canarias: nuestros orígenes nórdicos*, ed. Manuel de Paz Sánchez, Vol. 2 (Tenerife: Centro de la Cultura Popular Canaria), 53-93.

Arrighi, Giovanni (1994). *The Long Twentieth Century: Money, Power, and the Origins of Our Times* (London: Verso).

Aristodemo, Dina (2004). 'Guicciardini, Giovan Battista', in *Dizionario Biografico degli Italiani*, **61**.

Asaert, Gustaaf (1973a). *De Antwerpse scheepvaart in de XVe eeuw (1394-1480). Bijdrage tot de ekonomische geschiedenis van de stad Antwerpen* (Brussels: Paleis der Academiën).

Asaert, Gustaaf (1973b). 'Handel in kleurstoffen op de Antwerpse markt tijdens de XVe eeuw', *Bijdragen en Mededelingen betreffende de Geschiedenis der Nederlanden*, **88**, 377-402.

Asaert, Gustaaf (1986). 'From Wharf to Commercial Metropolis', in *Antwerp: A Port for All Seasons*, ed. Fernand Suykens (Antwerp: Ortelius), 17-164.

Asaert, Gustaaf (2019). *Onder de vlag met de hand*, Vol. I: *Antwerpens scheepvaart van de zestiende eeuw* (Antwerp: Self-Published).

Baelde, Michel (1963). 'Financiële politiek en domaniale evolutie in de Nederlanden onder Karel V en Filips II, 1530-1560', *Tijdschrift voor Geschiedenis*,**76**, 14-33.

Baelde, Michel (1965a). *De Collaterale Raden onder Karel V en Filips II (1531-1578). Bijdrage tot de geschiedenis van de centrale instellingen in de zestiende eeuw* (Brussels: Paleis der Academiën).

Baer, William C. (2007). 'Is Speculative Building Underappreciated in Urban History?', *Urban History*, **34**, 296-316.

Baer, William C. (2012). 'The House-Building Sector of London's Economy, 1550-1650', *Urban History*, **39**, 409-30.

Baetens, Roland (1985). 'La *villa rustica*, phénomène italien dans le paysage brabançon au 16e siècle', in *Aspetti della vita economica medievale. Atti del Convegno di Studi nel X Anniversario della morte di Federigo Melis, Firenze-Pisa-Prato, 10-14 marzo 1984* (Florence: Università degli studi di Firenze, Istituto di storia economica), 171-91.

Ballong-Wen-Mewuda, Joseph Bato'ora (1993). *São Jorge da Mina, 1482-1637. La vie d'un comptoir portugais en Afrique occidentale* (Lisbon and Paris: Fondation Calouste Gulbenkian).

Banaji, Jairus (2010). *Theory as History: Essays on Modes of Production and Exploitation* Chicago, Ill.: Haymarket Books).

Banaji, Jairus (2018). 'Globalising the History of Capital: Ways Forward', *Historical Materialism*, **26**, 143-66.

Banaji, Jairus (2020). *A Short History of Commercial Capitalism* (Chicago, IL: Haywood Press).

Barreiros, Maria Helena (2008). 'Urban Landscapes: Houses, Streets and Squares of 18th Century Lisbon', *Journal of Early Modern History*, **12**, 205-32.

Bartolomé, Bennassar, and Jean Jacquart (1972). *Le XVIe siècle* (Paris: Armand Colin).

Basso, Enrico (2014). 'Prima di Tolfa: i mercanti genovesi e l'allume orientale', *Mélanges de l'École française de Rome*, 126, 1; online: http://mefrm.revues.org/1578 (accessed January 2021).

Bataillon, Marcel (1974). 'Érasme et la Cour de Portugal', in Idem, *Études sur le Portugal au temps de l'humanisme* (Paris: Fundação Caluste Gulbenkian), 49-100.

Bauer, Clemens (1936). *Unternehmung und Unternehmungsformen im Spätmittelalter und in der beginnenden Neuzeit* (Jena: Gustav Fischer).

Bauernfeind, Walter (2011). 'Marktinformationen und Personalentwicklung einer Nürnberger Handelsgesellschaft im 16. Jahrhundert - Das Briefarchiv von Anthoni und Linhart Tucher in der Zeit von 1508 bis 1566', in *Beschaffungs- und Absatzmärkte oberdeutscher Firmen im Zeitalter der Welser und Fugger*, ed. Angelika Westermann and Stefanie von Welser (Husum: Matthiesen Verlag), 23-60.

Beck, Colette (1989). 'Éléments économiques et sociaux de la vie des marchands génois à Anvers entre 1528 et 1555', *Revue du Nord*, **64**, 759-84.

Berckmans, Olivier (1977-1979). 'Mariembourg et Philippeville, villes neuves et fortes de la Renaissance', *Bulletin de la Commission royale des Monuments et des Sites*, **6**, 62-85, and **8**, 106-38.

Bernstein, Eckhard (1985-6). 'Erasmus' Money Connection: The Antwerp Banker Erasmus Schetz and Erasmus of Rotterdam, 1525-36', *Erasmus in English*, **14**, 2-7.

Bihr, Alain (2019). *Le premier âge du capitalisme, 1415-1763*, Vol. 2: *La marche de l'Europe occidentale vers le capitalisme* (Paris: Syllepse).

Bisson, Douglas Ronald (1989). *The Merchant Adventurers and the Tudor Commonwealth: The Formulation of a Trade Policy, 1485-1565* (Ann Arbor, MI: UMI).

Blaich, Fritz (1967). *Die Reichsmonopolgesetzgebung im Zeitalter Karls V. Ihre ordnungspolitische Problematik* (Stuttgart: Gustav Fischer).

Blanchard, Ian (1995). *International Lead Production and Trade in the 'Age of the Saigerprozess'* (Stuttgart: Franz Steiner Verlag; *Zeitschrift für Unternehmensgeschichte*, Vol. 85), 44-72.

Blanchard, Ian (1996). 'English Royal Borrowing at Antwerp, 1544-1564', in *Public and Private Finances in the Late Middle Ages*, ed. Marc Boone and Walter Prevenier (Leuven and Apeldoorn: Garant), 57-73.

Blanchard, Ian (2005). *Mining, Metallurgy and Minting in the Middle Ages*, Vol. 3: *Continuing Afro-European Supremacy, 1250-1450* (Stuttgart: Franz Steiner Verlag).

Blanchard, Ian (2009). *The International Economy in the 'Age of Discoveries', 1470-1570: Antwerp and the English Merchants' World* (Stuttgart: Franz Steiner Verlag; *Studien zur Gewerbe- und Handelsgeschichte*, 29).

Blockmans, Wim (1978). *De volksvertegenwoordiging in Vlaanderen in de overgang van Middeleeuwen naar Nieuwe Tijden, 1384-1506* (Brussels: Paleis der Academiën).

Blockmans, Wim (1985). 'Financiers italiens et flamands aux XIIIe-XIVe siècles', in *Aspetti della vita economica medievale. Atti del Convegno di Studi nel X Anniversario della morte di Federigo Melis. Firenze-Pisa-Prato, 10-14 marzo 1984* (Florence: Università degli Studi di Firenze), 192-214.

Blockmans, Wim (2010). *Metropolen aan de Noordzee. De geschiedenis van Nederland, 1100-1560* (Amterdam: Bert Bakker).

Blockmans, Wim, and Nicolette Mout, eds (2004). *The World of Emperor Charles V* (Amsterdam: Royal Netherlands Academy of Arts and Sciences).

Blondé, Bruno, and Jeroen Puttevils, eds (2020). *Antwerp in the Renaissance* (Turnhout: Brepols).

Boisseuil, Didier (2005). 'L'alun en Toscane à la fin du Moyen Âge', in Borgard et al., *L'alun*, 105-18.

Boisseuil, Didier, and Ivana Ait (2014). 'Le monopole de l'alun pontifical à la fin du Moyen Âge: Introduction', *Mélanges de l'École française de Rome*, 126, 1; online: http://mefrm.revues.org/1578_(accessed January 2021).

Boisseuil, Didier, and Pascal Chareille (2014). 'Le salariat en Toscane à la fin du Moyen Âge: les ouvriers de l'alunière de Monterotondo Marittimo', in *Rémunérer le travail au Moyen Âge. Pour une histoire sociale du salariat*, ed. Patrice Beck, Philippe Bernardi and Laurent Feller (Paris: Picard), 424-60.

Boone, Marc (1999). 'Apologie d'un banquier médiéval: Tommaso Portinari et l'État bourguignon', *Le Moyen Âge*, **105**, 31-54.

Borgard, Philippe, et al., eds (2003). *L'alun de Méditerranée. Colloque intenational, Naples, 4-5-6 juin 2003, Lipari, 7-8 juin 2003* (Naples and Aix-en-Provence, Centre Jean Bérard).

Bottin, Jacques (2014). 'Commerce, finances et pouvoir: la redistribution des aluns méditerranéens dans l'Europe du Nord-Ouest et en France au XVIe siècle', *Mélanges de l'École française de Rome*, 126, 1; online: http://mefrm.revues.org/1578 (accessed January 2021).

Boucheron, Patrick, Denis Menjot, and Marc Boone (2003), 'La ville médiévale', in *Histoire de l'Europe urbaine*, Vol. I: *De l'Antiquité au XVIIIe siècle. Genèse des villes européennes*, ed. Patrick Boucheron et al. (Paris: Seuil), 285-592.

Boumans, René (1965). *Het Antwerps stadsbestuur voor en tijdens de Franse overheersing. Bijdrage tot de ontwikkelingsgeschiedenis van de stedelijke bestuursinstellingen in de Zuidelijke Nederlanden* (Bruges: De Tempel).

Brady, Thomas A, Jr. (1997). 'The Rise of Merchant Empires, 1400-1700: A European Counterpoint', in *The Political Economy of Merchant Empires: State Power and World Trade, 1350-1750*, ed. James M. Tracy (Cambridge: Cambridge University Press), 117-60.

Brandi, Karl (1964). *Kaiser Karl V. Werden und Schicksal einer Persönlichkeit und eines Weltreiches* (Munich: Bruckmann, 7th edn).

Braudel, Fernand (1959). 'Les emprunts de Charles-Quint sur la place d'Anvers', in *Charles-Quint et son temps* (Paris: C.N.R.S.), 191-201.

Braudel, Fernand (1966). *La Méditerranée et le monde méditerranéen à l'époque de Pilippe II* (2 vols; Paris: Armand Colin).

Braudel, Fernand (1979). *Civilisation matérielle, économie et capitalisme, XVe-XVIIIe siècle* (3 vols; Paris: Armand Colin).

Braudel, Fernand (1992). *Civilization and Capitalism, 15th-18th Century*, transl. by Siân Reynolds (3 vols; Berkeley and Los Angeles, CA: University of California Press).

Bril, Louis (1962). 'De handel tussen de Nederlanden en het Iberisch Schiereiland, midden XVIe eeuw. Een kwantitatieve benadering' (Unpublished 'Licentiate' Thesis: Ghent University).

Brosens, Koenraad, Klara Alen and Astrid Slegten (2018). 'Claiming Commerce, Quality and Credit: *Raisons d'être* of the Antwerp and Brussels *Tapissierspanden* (Sixteenth-Eighteenth Centuries)', *Textile History*, **49**, 5-21.

Brown, Andrew, and Jan Dumolyn, eds (2018). *Medieval Bruges, c. 850-1850* (Cambridge: Cambridge University Press).

Brübach, Nils (1994). *Die Reichsmessen von Frankfurt am Main, Leipzig und Braunschweig, 14.-18. Jahrhundert* (Stuttgart: Franz Steiner Verlag).

Bruckner, Clemens (1967). *Zur Wirtschaftsgeschichte des Regierungsbezirk Aachen* (Cologne: Rheinisch-Westfälisches Wirtschaftsarchiv).

Brulez, Wilfrid (1959a). *De firma della Faille en de internationale handel van Vlaamse firma's in de 16e eeuw* (Brussels: Paleis der Academiën).

Brulez, Wilfrid (1959b). 'L'exportation des Pays-Bas vers l'Italie par voie de terre au milieu du XVIe siècle', *Annales. Économies. Sociétés. Civilisations*, **14**, 461-91.

Brulez, Wilfrid (1962). 'Les routes commerciales d'Angleterre en Italie au XVIe siècle', in *Studi in Onore di Amintore Fanfani*, Vol. IV: *Evo moderno* (Milan: Giuffrè), 123-83.

Brulez, Wilfrid (1968). 'Le commerce international des Pays-Bas au XVIe siècle: essai d'appréciation quantitative', *Revue Belge de Philologie et d'Histoire*, **46**, 1205-21.

Brulez, Wilfrid (1969). 'Der Kolonialhandel und die Handelsblüte der Niederlande in der Mitte des 16. Jahrhunderts', *Kölner Vorträge zur Sozial- und Wirtschaftsgeschichte*, **3**, 3-20.

Brulez, Wilfrid (1970). 'The Balance of Trade of the Netherlands in the Middle of the 16th Century', *Acta Historiae Neerlandica*, **IV**, 20-48.

Brulez, Wilfrid (1973). 'Bruges and Antwerp in the 15th and 16th Centuries: An Antithesis?', *Acta Historiae Neerlandicae*, **VI**, 1-26.

Brulez, Wilfrid (1975). 'De handel', in *Antwerpen in de XVIde eeuw* (Antwerp: Mercurius), 109-42.

Brumont, Francis (2002), 'Pierre Assézat, un marchand dans son siècle', in *L'Hôtel d'Assézat*, ed. Louis Peyrusse and Bruno Tollon (Toulouse: Association des Amis de l'Hôtel d'Assézat), 37-76.

Brumont, Francis (2009). 'Cinquante ans après: le pastel de Gilles Caster et sa postérité', in *Toulouse, unc métropole méridionale: vingt siècles de vie urbaine*, ed. Bernadette Suau, Jean-Pierre Amalric and Jean-Marc Olivier (Toulouse: Fédération Historique de Midi-Pyrénées), 415-27.

Brumont, Francis (2015). 'De Burdeos a Amberes, Londres, Ruán y Bilbao: el commercio del pastel: índice de la conyuntura económica Europea en el siglo XVI?' in *Comercio y cultura en la edad moderna. Communicaciones de la XIII Reuníon científica de la Fundacíon española de historia moderna*, ed. Juan José Iglesias Rodríguez, Rafael M. Pérez García and Manuel F. Fernández Chaves (Sevilla: Editorial Universidad de Sevilla), 849-61.

Brumont, Francis (2016). 'Rouen, la voide et le pastel (vers 1500-vers 1560)', *Annales de Normandie*, **66**, 47-63.

Buchanan, Iain (1992). 'Designers, Weavers and Entrepreneurs: Sixteenth-Century Flemish Tapestries in the Patrimonio Nacional', *The Burlington Magazine*, **134**, 380-4.

Burke, Peter (2000). 'Presenting and Re-presenting Charles V', in Soly, *Charles V*, 393-477.

Buylaert, Frederik, Wim De Clercq and Jan Dumolyn (2011). 'Sumptuary Legislation, Material Culture and the Semiotics of '*vivre noblement*' in the County of Flanders (14th-16th Centuries)', *Social History*, **36**, 393-417.

Caillé, Alain (1986). 'Comment on écrit l'histoire du marché', in *Splendeurs et misères des sciences sociales. Esquisses d'une mythologie*, ed. Alain Caillé (Geneva: Droz), 151-99.

Campbell, Thomas P. (2002). *Tapestries in the Renaissance: Art and Magnificence* (New York: The Metropolitan Museum of Art).

Caracausi, Andrea, and Christof Jeggle, eds (2014). *Commercial networks and European Cities, 1400-1800* (London: Pickering & Chatto).

Carande, Ramón (1960). 'María de Hungría en el mercado de Amberes', in *Karl V, der Kaiser und seine Zeit. Kölner Colloquium 26.-29. November 1958*, ed. Peter Rassow and Fritz Schalk (Cologne and Graz: Böhlau), 38-50.

Carande, Ramón (1967). *Carlos V y sus banqueros*, Vol. 3: *Los caminos del oro y de la plata, deuda exterior y tesoros ultramarinos* (Madrid: Sociedad de Estudios y Publicaciones).

Carroll, Stuart (2016). 'Revenge and Reconciliation in Early Modern Italy', *Past and Present*, **233**, 101-42.

Casado Alonso, Hilario (1990). 'El comercio del pastel. Datos para una geografia de la industria pañera española en el siglo XVI', *Revista de Historia Económica - Journal of Iberian and Latin American Economic History*, **8**, 523-48.

Casado Alonso, Hilario (1997). 'De la Juderia a la Grandeza de España: la trayectoria de la familia de mercaderes de los Bernuy (siglos XIV-XIX)', *Society for Spanish and Portuguese Historical Studies*, **22**, 9-27.

Casado Alonso, Hilario (2011). 'La colonie des marchands castillans de Bruges au milieu du XVe siècle', *Publication du Centre européen d'Études bourguignonnes (XIVe-XVIe siècles)*, **51**, 233-51.

Caster, Gilles (1962). *Le commerce du pastel et de l'épicerie à Toulouse de 1450 environ à 1561* (Toulouse: Privat).

Chartier, Roger (1981). 'La ville-chantier', in *Histoire de la France urbaine*, Vol. 3: *La ville classique de la Renaissance aux Révolutions*, ed. Emmanuel Le Roy Ladurie (Paris: Seuil), 109-55.

Chartier, Roger (1994). 'Power, Space, and Investments in Paris', in *Edo and Paris: Urban Life and the State in the Early Modern Era*, ed. James L. McCain, John M. Merriman and Ugawa Kaoru (Ithaca, NY: Cornell University Press), 132-52.

Chauvard, Jean-François (2005). *La circulation des biens à Venise. Stratégies patrimoniales et marché immobilier, 1600-1750* (Rome: École française de Rome).

Coenen, Daniel (1990). 'Une vaine tentative de stabilisation monétaire dans les Pays-Bas, 1541-1555', *Revue Belge de Philologie et d'Histoire*, **68**, 817-49.

Concato, Francis (1975). 'La technique drapière en Normandie à la fin du Moyen Âge (XIVe-XVe siècles', *Annales de Normandie*, **25**, 75-98.

Coornaert, Émile (1952). 'L'État et les villes à la fin du Moyen Âge: la politique d'Anvers', *Revue Historique*, **207**, 185-210.

Coornaert, Émile (1961). *Les Français et le commerce international à Anvers, fin du XVe-XVIe siècle* (2 vols; Paris: Marcel Rivière).

Coornaert, Kevin (2000). 'De Vlaamse Natie op de Canarische eilanden in de 16de eeuw' (Unpublished 'Licentiate' Thesis: Ghent University).

Córdoba de la Llave, Ricardo, Alfonso Franco Silva and Germán Navarro Espinach (2005). 'L'alun de la Péninsule Ibérique durant la période médiévale (Royaumes de Castille et d'Aragon)', in Borgard et al., *L'alun*, 125-38.

Correns, Raymond, Hugo Rau and Marc van de Cruys (2014). *Het leven en de tijd van Jan Vleminck, Heer van Wijnegem, 1526-1568* (Wijnegem: Homunculus).

Coulon, Damien, ed. (2010). *Réseaux marchands et réseaux de commerce. Concepts récents, réalités historiques, du Moyen Âge au XIXe siècle* (Strasbourg: Presses universitaires de Strasbourg).

Cowen, Denis V. (2007). 'Ancient Origins of Competition Law', *Advocate*, **20/2**, 38-41.

Cracco, Giorgio (1967). *Società e stato nel medioevo Veneziano, secoli XII-XIV* (Florence: Leo S. Olschki).

Craeybeckx, Jan (1952). 'De eerste jaren van Karel V, 1515-1530', in *Algemene Geschiedenis der Nederlanden*, Vol. IV, ed. Jan Albert Van Houtte et al. (Utrecht: De Haan), 51-71.

Craeybeckx, Jan (1958). *Un grand commerce d'importation: les vins de France aux anciens Pays-Bas, XIIIe-XVIe siècle* (Paris: S.E.V.P.E.N.).

Craeybeckx, Jan (1984). 'Prijsstijging, "monopolisme" en pre-mercantilisme: de regering der Nederlanden en de groothandelaars-importeurs van Franse wijn (1541-1549)', *Handelingen van de Koninklijke Commissie voor Geschiedenis*, **CL**, 380-407.

Cuypers, John (1948). 'Geeraard Gramaye. Sociaal-ekonomische studie van een Antwerpse persoonlijkheid, ca. 1525-ca. 1582' (Unpublished 'Licentiate' Thesis: Ghent University).

Daems, Paul (1986). 'Private huizenbouw te Antwerpen, 1526-1550' (Unpublished 'Licentiate' Thesis, Ghent University).

Dambruyne, Johan, Johan Decavele, and Paul Van Peteghem (1990). 'De Gentse opstand', in *Keizer tussen stroppendragers: Karel V, 1500-1558*, ed. Johan Decavele (Leuven: Davidsfonds), 121-90.

Davies, C.S.L. (1964/5). 'Provisions for Armies, 1509-1550. A Study in the Effectiveness of Early Tudor Government', *Economic History Review*, **17**, 234-48.

De Belder, Jos (1974). 'De behuizing te Antwerpen op het einde van de XVIIIe eeuw', *Belgisch Tijdschrift voor Nieuwste Geschiedenis*, **8**, 367-443.

De Cock, Siegfried (1979). *Gaspar Ducci, bankier van Keizer Karel. Heer van Schoonsel en Kruibeke* (Borgerhout: Drukkerij Cools).

De Commer, Paul, and Hugo Soly (1988). 'Harde tijden voor zusters en zieken, 1490-1585', in *Het St.-Elisabetziekenhuis te Antwerpen: 750 jaar Gasthuis op 't Elzenveld, 1238-1988* (Brussels: Gemeentekrediet), 65-98.

De Groodt, Raymond (1933). *Geschiedenis van Kruibeke* (Sint-Niklaas: Van Haver).

De Groote, Henry L.V. (1968). 'Een handschrift over rekenkunde van Michiel Coignet. Hoe berekende de Brusselse Rekenkamer een annuïteit in 1538?', *Scientiarum Historia*, **10**, 199-207.

De Groote, Henry L.V. (1972). 'De vermogensbalans van Melchior Schetz en zijn vrouw Anna Van Stralen, met hun testament van 1 juli 1569', *Bijdragen tot de Geschiedenis*, **55**, 226-63.

De Groote, Henry L.V. (1975). *De zeeassurantie te Antwerpen en te Brugge in de zestiende eeuw* (Antwerp: Marine Academie).

Degryse, Roger (1991). 'De oudste houten kranen in de Vlaamse en andere havens (13de-16de eeuw)', *Handelingen van het Genootschap voor Geschiedenis*, **128**, 5-46, 153-87.

Dekker, Cornelis, and Roland Baetens (2010). *Geld in het water. Antwerps en Mechels kapitaal in Zuid-Beveland na de stormvloeden in de 16e eeuw* (Hilversum: Verloren).

De Luca, Giuseppe, and Marcella Lorenzini (2013). 'A Taxonomy of Infrastructure Financing in Europe on the Long Run (12th-18th Century)', *Entreprises et Histoire*, **70**, 10-36.

Delumeau, Jean (1957). *Vie économique et sociale de Rome dans la seconde moitié du XVIe siècle* (2 vols; Paris: De Boccard).

Delumeau, Jean (1962). *L'alun de Rome, XVe-XIXe siècle* (Paris: S.E.V.P.E.N.).

De Nave, Francine (1978). 'De vrijheid van Antwerpen, vanaf de Middeleeuwen tot de tijd van Rubens', in Voet et al., *De stad Antwerpen*, 59-93.

Denk, Rolf (2017). *Das Manillen-Geld Westafrikas. Spurensuche und Spurensicherung, 1439-2016* (Berlin: Pro Business).

Denucé, Jan (1909). 'Privilèges commerciaux accordés par les rois de Portugal aux Flamands et aux Allemands', *Archivo Historico Portuguez*, **7**, 310-19.

Denucé, Jan (1931). 'De Beurs van Antwerpen. Oorsprong en eerste ontwikkeling, 15de en 16de eeuwen', *Antwerpsch Archievenblad*, 2nd ser., **VI**, 82-145.

Denucé, Jan (1934b). *Italiaansche koopmansgeslachten te Atwerpen in de XVIe-XVIIIe eeuwen* (Mechelen: Kompas).

Denucé, Jan (1936). *Antwerpsche tapijtkunst en handel* (Antwerp: De Sikkel).

De Roover, Raymond (1949). *Gresham on Foreign Exchange: An Essay on Early English Mercantilism* (Cambridge, Mas.: Harvard University Press).

De Roover, Raymond (1963). *The Rise and Decline of the Medici Bank* (Cambridge, Mass.: Harvard University Press).

De Ruysscher, Dave (2008). 'Designing the Limits of Creditworthiness: Insolvency in Antwerp Bankruptcy Legislation and Practice (16th-17th Centuries)', *The Legal History Review*, **76**, 307-27.

De Ruysscher, Dave (2009). *'Naer het Romeinsch recht alsmede den stiel mercantiel': handel en recht in de Antwerpse rechtbank, 16de-17de eeuw* (Leuven: UGA).

De Ruysscher, Dave (2010). 'Over Themis en Mercurius. Handelsgebruiken en –recht in Antwerpen (vijftiende-zeventiende eeuw)', *Belgisch Tijdschrift voor Filologie en Geschiedenis*, **88**, 1105-34.

De Ruysscher, Dave (2012). 'Lobbyen, vleien en herinneren: vergeefs onderhandelen om privileges bij de Blijde Inkomst van Filips in Antwerpen (1549)', *Noordbrabants Historisch Jaarboek*, **29**, 65-76.

De Ruysscher, Dave (2013). 'Bankruptcy, Insolvency and Debt Collection among Merchants in Antwerp (*c.* 1490-*c.* 1540)', in *The History of Bankruptcy: Economic, Social and Cultural Implications in Early Modern Europe*, ed. Thomas M. Safley (New York: Routledge), 185-99.

De Ruysscher, Dave (2015). 'Antwerp, 1490-1590: Insurance and Speculation', in *Marine Insurance: Origins and Institutions*, ed. A.B. Leonard (Basingstoke: Palgrave Macmillan), 78-105.

De Ruysscher, Dave (2020). 'Antwerp Commercial Law in the Sixteenth Century: A Product of the Renaissance? The Legal Facilitating, Appropriating and Improving of Mercantile Practices', in Blondé and Puttevils, *Antwerp in the Renaissance*, 55-88.

De Ruysscher, Dave, and Jeroen Puttevils (2015). 'The Art of Compromise: Legislative Deliberations on Marine Insurance Institutions in Antwerp (*c.* 1550-*c.* 1570)', *Bijdragen en Mededelingen betreffende de Geschiedenis der Nederlanden*, **130**, 25-49.

De Schepper, Marcus (1994). 'Sola una totus mundus est Antverpia: humanisme en humanisten te Antwerpen (1470-1648)', *Colloquium Neerlandicum*, **12**, 181-200.

De Smedt, Oskar (1928). 'Stephen Vaughan, agent van de Engelsche Kroon, en de Antwerpsche geldmarkt in de jaren 1544-1545', *Antwerpsch Archievenblad*, Second Ser., **3**, 229-56.

De Smedt, Oskar (1950-54). *De Engelse Natie te Antwerpen in de 16e eeuw, 1496-1582* (2 vols; Antwerp: De Sikkel).

De Vylder, Jochen (2011). 'The Grid and the Existing City, or How New Civic Buildings and Interventions on Confiscated Grounds Transformed the Medieval City in Early Modern Times: A Focus on Antwerp (1531-84)', in *Early Modern Urbanism and the Grid: Town Planning in the Low Countries in International Context. Exchanges in Theory and Practice, 1550-1800*, ed. Piet Lombaerde and Charles van den Heuvel (Turnhout: Brepols), 77-93.

Dias, Manuel Nunes (1964). *O capitalismo monárquico português (1415-1549). Contribuição para o estudo das origens do capitalismo moderno* (2 vols; Coïmbra: Instituto de Estudos Históricos).

Dierickx, Hendrik (1954). *Geschiedenis van Hoboken. Evolutie van plattelandsgemeente tot industrieel centrum, 1100-1950* (Antwerpen: De Sikkel).

Dietrich, Richard (1991). *Untersuchungen zum Frühkapitalismus im mitteldeutschen Erzbergbau und Metallhandel* (Hildesheim: Georg Olms).

Dietz, Alexander (1910). *Frankfurter Handelsgeschichte* (2 vols; Frankfurt: Hermann Minjon).

Doehaerd, Renée (1963). *Études anversoises. Documents sur le commerce international à Anvers, 1488-1514* (3 vols; Paris: S.E.V.P.E.N.).

Donnet, Fernand (1895-96). 'Les Anversois aux Canaries, un voyage mouvementé au XVIe siècle', *Bulletin de la Société de Géographie d'Anvers*, **18**, 276-311, and **19**, 202-365.

Doria, Giorgio (1995). *Nobiltà e investimenti a Genova in età moderna* (Genoa: Istituto di Storia Economica).

Dröge, Philip (2016). *Moresnet: opkomst en ondergang van een vergeten buurlandje* (Houten & Antwerp: Spectrum).

Druwé, Wouter (2020). *Loans and Credit in Consilia and Decisiones in the Low Countries, c. 1500-1680* (Leiden: Brill & Nijhoff).

Dumolyn, Jan, and Bart Lambert (2018). 'A Chemical Compound in a Capitalist Commodity Chain: The Production, Distribution and Industrial Use of Alum in the Mediterranean and the Textile Centers of the Low Countries (Thirteenth-Sixteenth Centuries)', *Journal of Early Modern History*, **22**, 238-58.

Dumolyn, Jan, et al. (2018). 'Social Groups, Political Power and Institutions II, *c.* 1300-*c.* 1500', in Brown and Dumolyn, *Medieval Bruges*, 268-328.

d'Ursel, Baudouin (1984). 'Grobbendonk. Morphologie d'une seigneurie du XVIe au XVIIIe siècle', *Le Parchemin. Recueil de l'Office généalogique et héraldique de Belgique*, **34**, 41-114.

d'Ursel, Baudouin (2004). *Les Schetz: La Maison de Grobbendonk* (Brussels: Office généalogique et héraldique de Belgique).

Ebert, Christopher (2008). 'European Competition and Cooperation in Pre-Modern Globalization: "Portuguese" West and Central Africa, 1500-1600', *African Economic History*, **36**, 53-78.

Edler, Florence (1937). 'The Effects of the Financial Measures of Charles V on the Commerce of Antwerp, 1539-42', *Revue Belge de Philologie et d'Histoire*, **16**, 665-73.

Edler, Florence (1938). 'The Van der Molen, Commission Merchants of Antwerp: Trade with Italy, 1538-44', in *Medieval and Historiographical Essays in Honour of James Westfall Thompson*, ed. J. Lea Cate and E.N. Anderson (Chicago, IL.: Chicago University Press), 78-145.

Edler-De Roover, Florence (1938). 'The Market for Spices in Antwerp, 1538-1544', *Revue Belge de Philologie et d'Histoire*, **17**, 212-21.

Ehrenberg, Richard (1896). *Das Zeitalter der Fugger. Geldkapital und Creditverkehr im 16. Jahrhundert* (2 vols; Jena: Fischer).

Eiden, Herbert (2002). 'Die Hanse, die Leipziger Messen', *Hansische Geschichtsblätter*, **120**, 73-95.

Elbl, Ivana (2007). 'The King's Business in Africa: Decisions and Strategies of the Portuguese Crown', in *Money, Markets and Trade in Late Medieval Europe. Essays in Honour of John H.A. Munro*, ed. Lawrin Armstrong, Ivana Elbl and Martin M. Elbl (Leiden and Boston: Brill), 89-118.

Engelen, F.H.G. (1976). 'Delfstoffen en hun invloed op politieke beslissingen; het ontstaan van het neutrale gebied Moresnet en de geschiedenis van de mijnbouw in dit gebied', *Grondboor en Hamer*, **30**, 20-31.

Estier, Delphine (2009). 'Paysages urbains de Lyon aux XVIe-XVIIe siècles. Le regard des artistes forains et étrangers', in *Lyon vu/e d'ailleurs (1245-1800). Échanges, compétitions et perceptions*, ed. Jean-Louis Gaulin and Susanne Rau (Lyon: Presses Universitaires de Lyon), 161-80.

Evans, Allison Celia (2012). '*Het Tapissierspand*: Interpreting the Success of the Antwerp Tapestry Market in the 1500s' (Unpublished PhD Thesis: Duke University).

Everaert, John (1986). 'Marchands flamands à Lisbonne et l'exportation du sucre de Madère (1480-1530', *Actas do I Colóquio international de História da Madeira* (Funchal: Governo Regional da Madeira), 442-77.

Everaert, John (1991). 'Les barons flamands du sucre à Madeire (vers 1480-1620)', in *Flandre et Portugal. Au confluent de deux cultures*, ed. John Everaert and Eddy Stols (Antwerp: Mercatorfonds), 99-117.

Everaert, John (2002). 'Les marchés de sucre en Flandre: Bruges et Anvers, centres de distribution (1470-1570)', in *História do açúcar: rotas e mercados*, ed. Alberto Vieira (Funchal: Centro de Estudos de História Atlântico), 193-202.

Everaert, John (2008). 'Dulces del Atlántico el comercio Flamenco en busca de nuevos azúcares (ca 1480-ca 1580)', in *Azúcar. Los ingenios en la colonización canaria, 1487-1525* (Tenerife: Museo de Historia y Antropología), 133-40.

Everaert, John (2009a). 'De lokroep van de suiker. Vlaamse planters en handelaars op het Canarische eiland La Palma, 1508-ca. 1635)', *Mededelingen van de Zittingen van de Koninklijke Academie voor Overzeese Wetenschappen*, **55**, 135-62.

Everaert, John (2009b). 'Una "Pesadilla Dulce": Problemas de gestion y de Rendimiento de un ingenio Flamenco en el Brasil (ca 1548-1615)', in *O Açúcar Antes e Depois de Colombo. Seminário Internacional de História do Açúcar* (Funchal: Centro de Estudos de História Atlântico), 127-33.

Everaert, John (2020). 'Een zoete nachtmerrie. De suikerplantage der Schetzen (ca. 1540-1615)', *Historiant*, **8**, 11-26.

Ewing, Dan (1990). 'Marketing Art in Antwerp, 1460-1560: Our Lady's Pand', *The Art Bulletin*, **72**, 558-84.

Ewing, Dan (2004/5). 'Magi and Merchants: The Force Behind the Antwerp Mannerists' Adoration Pictures', *Antwerp Royal Museum Annual*, 275-99.

Ezra, Kate (1992). *Royal Art of Benin: The Perls Collection* (New York: Metropolitan Museum of Art).

Fabra, Paul (1986). 'Économie politique et histoire économique', in *Une leçon d'histoire de Fernand Braudel. Châteauvallon. Journées Fernand Braudel, 18, 19 et 20 octobre 1985* (Paris: Arthaud-Flammarion), 87-95.

Fagel, Raymond (1996). *De Hispano-Vlaamse wereld. De contacten tussen Spanjaarden en Nederlanders, 1496-1555* (Brussels: Archief- en Bibliotheekwezen in België).

Fagel, Raymond (2005). 'Guerra y comercio en los Países Bajos: el control del comercio en tiempos de guerra a travès de las ordenanzas (1506-1559)', *Studia historica. Historia moderna*, **27**, 25-55.

Favier, Jean (2013). *De l'or et des épices. Naissance de l'homme d'affaires au Moyen Âge* (Paris: Pluriel).

Feniello, Amedeo (2005). 'L'allume di Napoli nel XV secolo', in Borgard, et al., *L'alun*, 97-104.

Finot, Jules (1902). 'Le commerce de l'alun dans les Pays-bas et la bulle encyclique du Pape Jules II en 1506', *Bulletin Historique et Philologique* [du] *Comité des Travaux Historiques et Scientifiques*, nos 1-2, 418-31.

Fischer, Gerhard (1929). *Aus zwei Jahrhunderten Leipziger Handelsgeschichte, 1470-1650. Die kaufmännische Einwanderung und ihre Auswirkungen* (Leipzig: Meiner).

Franceschi, Franco (2011). 'The Merchant-Bankers of 15th-Century Florence', in *Money and Beauty: Bankers, Botticelli and the Bonfire of the Vanities*, ed. Ludovica Sebregondi and Tim Parks (Florence: Fondazione Palazzo Strozzi), 37-45.

Friedländer, Max J. (1936). *Die altniederländische Malerei*, Vol. 13: *Anthonis Mor und seine Zeitgenossen* (Leiden: A.W. Sijthoff).

Gachard, Louis Prosper (1830). 'Abdication de Charles-Quint', *Analectes Belgiques*, **II**, 70-106.

Gascon, Richard (1971). *Grand commerce et vie urbaine au XVIe siècle: Lyon et ses marchands (environs de 1520 – environs de 1580)* (2 vols; Paris: S.E.V.P.E.N.).

Geerts, Katelijne (2009). 'Fortificatiebouwers in Antwerpen in de zestiende eeuw', in *Antwerpen versterkt. De Spaanse omwalling vanaf haar bouw in 1542 tot haar afbraak in 1870*, ed. Piet Lombaerde (Antwerp: University Press Antwerp and Stadsarchief Antwerpen), 62-91.

Gelderblom, Oscar (2013). *Cities of Commerce: The Institutional Foundations of International Trade in the Low Countries, 1250-1650* (Princeton and Oxford: Princeton University Press).

Génard, Pierre (1874). 'L'Hôtel des monnaies d'Anvers', *Annales de l'Académie d'Archéologie de Belgique*, **30**, 5-170.

Geudens, Edmond (1891-1904). *Het hoofdambacht der meerseniers* (4 vols; Antwerp: Dela Montagne).

Geudens, Edmond (1895), *Het Antwerpsch Knechtjeshuis sedert zijn voorhistorisch tijdperk tot op onze dagen* (Antwerpen: Dela Montagne).

Godin, Alain (1987). 'Érasme et son banquier', *Revue d'Histoire Moderne et Contemporaine*, **34**, 529-52.

Goldstein, Claudia (2013a). 'A Fool Goes to a Wedding: The Social, Visual, and Performative Functions of the Wedding Banquet in Early Modern Antwerp', *Predella, Journal of Visual Arts*, **33**, 133-43.

Goldstein, Claudia (2013b). *Pieter Bruegel and the Culture of the Early Modern Dinner Party* (Farnham: Ashgate).

Goldthwaite, Richard A. (1968). *Private Wealth in Renaissance Florence: A Study of Four Families* (Princeton, NJ: Princeton University Press).

Goldthwaite, Richard A. (2009). *The Economy of Renaissance Florence* (Baltimore, MA: The Johns Hopkins UniversityPress).

Goris, Jan Albert (1925). *Étude sur les colonies marchandes méridionales (Portugais, Espagnols, Italiens) à Anvers de 1488 à 1567* (Louvain: Uystpruyst).

Gorter-Van Royen, Laetitia V.G. (1993). 'Het bedreigde Brabant en de verdedigingsinspanning door Maria van Hongarije in 1541-1542', *Noordbrabants Historisch Jaarboek*, **10**, 60-98.

Gorter-Van Royen, Laetitia V.G. (1995). *Maria van Hongarije, regentes der Nederlanden. Een politieke analyse op basis van haar regentschapsordonnanties en haar correspondentie met Karel V* (Hilversum: Verloren).

Gramula, Gertrud Susanna (1972). *Handelsbeziehungen Kölner Kaufleute zwischen 1500 und 1650* (Cologne and Vienna: Böhlau; *Forschungen zur internationalen Sozial- und Wirtschaftsgeschichte*, 4).

Graulau, Jeannette (2008). 'Finance, Industry, and Globalisation in the Early Modern Period: The Example of the Metallic Business of the House of Fugger', *Rivista di Studi Politici Internazionali*, **300**, 554-98.

Guidi Bruscoli, Francesco (2007). *Papal Banking in Renaissance Rome: Benvenuto Olivieri and Paul III, 1534-1549* (Aldershot: Ashgate).

Gunn, Steven, David Grummitt, and Hans Cools (2007). *War, State and Society in England and the Netherlands, 1477-1559* (Oxford: Oxford University Press).

Günster, Andrea, and Stephen Martin (2015). 'A Holy Alliance: Collusion in the Renaissance Alum Market', *Review of Industrial Organization*, **47**, 1-23.

Guy, John (2019). *Gresham's Law. The Life and World of Queen Elizabeth I's Banker* (London: Profile Books).

Häberlein, Mark (1996). 'Die Tag und Nacht auff Fürkauff trachten. Ausburger Grosskaufleute des 16. und beginnenden 17. Jahrhunderts in der Beurteilung ihrer Zeitgenossen und

Mitbürger', in *Augsburger Handelshäuser im Wandel des historischen Urteils*, ed. Johannes Burkhardt (Berlin: Akademie Verlag), 46-68.

Häberlein, Mark (1998a). *Brüder, Freunde und Betrüger: Soziale Beziehungen, Normen und Konflikte in der Augsburger Kaufmannschaft um die Mitte des 16. Jahrhunderts* (Berlin: Akademie Verlag).

Häberlein, Mark (1998b). 'Neidhart, Sebastian von', in *Neue Deutsche Biographie*, Vol. 19, 45-6; online: https://www.deutsche-biographie.de/gnd137224435.html#ndbcontent (accessed January 2021).

Häberlein, Mark (2005). 'Sailer, Hieronymus', in *Neue Deutsche Biographie*, Vol. 22, 355-6; online: https://www.deutsche-biographie.de/gnd137224435.html#ndbcontent_(accessed January 2021).

Häberlein, Mark (2012). *The Fuggers of Augsburg: Pursuing Wealth and Honor in Renaissance Germany* (Charlottesville, VA: University of Virginia Press).

Häberlein, Mark (2013). 'Lins: Kolonialunternehmer', in *Augsburger Stadtlexikon Online* (Augsburg: Wissner-Verlag).

Häberlein, Mark (2016a). 'Kaufleute, Höflinge und Humanisten. Die Augsburger Welser-Gesellschaft und die Eliten des Habsburgerreiches in der ersten Hälfte des 16. Jahrhunderts', *Zeitschrift für Historische Forschung*, **43**, 667-702.

Häberlein, Mark (2016b). *Aufbruch ins globale Zeitalter. Die Handelswelt der Fugger und Welser* (Darmstadt: Wissenschaftliche Buchgesellschaft).

Hachenberg, Karl (1992). 'Brass in Central European Instrument-making from the 16th through the 18th Centuries', *Historic Brass Society Journal*, **4**, 229-52.

Hale, John R. (1965). 'The Development of the Bastion: An Italian Chronology', in *Europe in the Late Middle Ages*, ed. John R. Hale, John R.L. Highfield and Beryl Smalley (Evanston, IL: Nothwestern University Press), 466-94.

Hale, John R. (1985). *War and Society in Renaissance Europe, 1450-1620* (London: Fontana).

Halikowski-Smith, Stefan (2002). 'A Question of Quality. The commercial Contest between Portuguese Atlantic Spices and their Venetian Levantine Equivalents during the Sixteenth Century', *Itinerario*, **26**, 45-63.

Halleux, Robert (2015). 'Les métaux non ferreux', in *Histoire des techniques en Belgique*, Vol. 2: *La période préindustrielle*, ed. Robert Halleux and Jan Vandersmissen (Liège: Éditions de la Province de Liège), 315-34.

Hamon, Philippe (1994). *L'argent du roi. Les finances sous François Ier* (Paris: Comité pour l'Histoire économique et financière de la France).

Hamon, Philippe (2009). *Les Renaissances, 1453-1559* (Paris: Belin).

Häpke, Rudolf (1914). *Die Regierung Karl V. und der europäische Norden* (Lübeck: Schmidt).

Harding, Vanessa (2002). 'Space, Property and Propriety in Urban England', *Journal of Interdisciplinary History*, **32**, 549-69.

Harreld, Donald J. (2002). 'Antwerp Sugar Prices from the Hundredth Penny Tax Records, 1543-45', *Journal of European Economic History*, **31**, 611-17.

Harreld, Donald J. (2003). 'Atlantic Sugar and Antwerp's Trade with Germany in the Sixteenth Century', *Journal of Early Modern History*, **7**, 148-63.

Harreld, Donald J. (2004a). *High Germans in the Low Countries: German Merchants and Commerce in Golden Age Antwerp* (Leiden and Boston: Brill).

Harreld, Donald J. (2010). 'Foreign Merchants and International Trade Networks in the Sixteenth-Century Low Countries', *Journal of European Economic History*, **39**, 11-31.

Hayward, Maria (2015). 'Dressed in Blue: The Impact of Woad on English Clothing, *c.* 1350-*c.* 1670', *Costume*, **49**, 168-85.

Heal, Felicity (2014). *The Power of Gifts: Gift-Exchange in Early Modern England* (Oxford: Oxford University Press).

Heers, Jacques (1966). *L'Occident aux XIVe et XVe siècles. Aspects économiques et sociaux* (Paris: Presses Universitaires de France).

Heers, Jacques (2014). *La naissance du capitalisme au Moyen Âge. Changeurs, usuriers et grands financiers* (Paris: Perrin-Tempus).

Heers, Marie-Louise (1954); 'Les Génois et le commerce de l'alun à la fin du Moyen Âge', *Revue d'Histoire économique et sociale*, **32**, 31-53.

Heller, Henry (2011). *The Birth of Capitalism: A twenry-First-Century Perspective* (London: Pluto Press).

Henne, Alexandre (1858-60). *Histoire du règne de Charles-Quint en Belgique* (10 vols; Brussels and Leipzig: Émile Flatau).

Henri, Alfred (1904). 'Les batteurs en cuivre de Bouvignes', *Annales de la Fédération archéologique et historique de Belgique: XVIIe Congrès de Dinant* (Namur: Société archéologique), 821-56.

Herbert, Eugenia W. (1984). *Red Gold of Africa: Copper in Precolonial History and Culture* (Madison, WI: University of Wisconsin Press).

Herborn, Wolfgang (1983/84). 'Der Antwerpener Markt und die Kauf- und Furhmannschaft der Reichsstadt Aachen (1490-1513)', *Zeitschrift des Aachener Geschichtsvereins*, **90/91**, 97-147.

Hocquet, Jean-Claude (1978). *Le sel et la fortune de Venise*, Vol. 1: *Production et monopole* (Villeneuve d'Ascq: Publications de l'Université de Lille III).

Hodgkin, Thomas (1960). *Nigerian Perspectives: An Historical Anthology* (Oxford: Oxford University Press).

Hoffmann, Albrecht (2000). 'Zum Stand der städtischen Wasserversorgung in Mitteleuropa vor dem Dreissigjährigen Krieg', in *Die Wasserversorgung in der Renaissancezeit*, ed. Albrecht Hoffmann (Mainz: Verlag Philipp von Zabern; Geschichte der Wasserversorgung 5), 101-44.

Hofmeister, Adolf (1886). 'Eine Hansische Seeversicherung aus dem Jahre 1531', *Hansische Geschichtsblätter*, **5**, 169-77.

Holbach, Rudolf (1994). *Frühformen von Verlag und Grossbetrieb in der gewerblichen Produktion, 13.-16. Jahrhundert* (Stuttgart: Franz Steiner Verlag).

Hollestelle, Johanna (1961). *De steenbakkerij in de Nederlanden tot omstreeks 1560* (Assen: Van Gorcum).

Houghton, Charlotte (2004). 'This Was Tomorrow: Pieter Aertsen's *Meat Stall* as Contemporary Art', *The Art Bulletin*, **86**, 277-300.

Howell, Martha C. (2010). *Commerce before Capitalism in Europe, 1300-1600* (Cambridge: Cambridge University Press).

Howell, Martha C. (2014). 'Movable/Immovable, what's in a Name? The Case of Late Medieval Ghent', in *Money, Markets and Trade in Late Medieval Europe. Essays in Honour of John H.A. Munro*, ed. Lawrin Armstrong, Ivana Elbl and Martin M. Elbl (Leiden and Boston: Brill), 538-71.

Hurx, Merlijn (2013). *Architect en aannemer. De opkomst van de bouwmarkt in de Nederlanden, 1350-1530* (Nijmegen: Vantilt).

Inalcik, Halil (1977). 'An Outline of Ottoman-Venetian Relations', in *Venezia centro di mediazione tra Oriente e Occidente, secoli XV-XVI: aspetti e* problemi, ed. Hans-Georg Beck, Manoussos Mannoussacas and Agostino Petruzi (2 vols; Florence: Olschki), I, 83-9.

Irsigler, Franz (1979a) 'Hansischer Kupferhandel im 15. und in der ersten Hälfte des 16. Jahrhunderts', *Hansische Geschichtsblätter*, **97**, 15-35.

Irsigler, Franz (1979b). *Die wirtschaftliche Stellung der Stadt Köln im 14. und 15. Jahrhundert. Strukturanalyse einer spätmittelalterlichen Exportgewerbe- und Fernhandelsstadt* (Stuttgart: Franz Steiner Verlag; Vierteljahrschrift für Sozial- und Wirtschaftsgeschichte, Beiheft 65).

Isenmann, Eberhard (2014). *Die deutsche Stadt im Mittelalter, 1150-1550* (Cologne: Böhlau).

Jacqmain, Monique (1977). 'Guicciardini, Giovan Battista', *Nationaal Biografisch Woordenboek*, **7**, 301-4.

Jeannin, Pierre (1955). 'Le cuivre, les Fugger et la Hanse', *Annales. Économies. Sociétés. Civilisations*, **10**, 229-36.

Jeannin, Pierre (1956). 'Les relations économiques des villes de la Baltique avec Anvers au XVIe siècle', *Vierteljahrschrift für Sozial- und Wirtschaftsgeschichte*, **43**, 195-217.

Jeannin, Pierre (1978). 'Armements et commerce international dans la seconde moitié du XVIe siècle', in *Wirtschaftskräfte und Wirtschaftswege: Festschrift für Hermann Kellenbenz*, ed. Jürgen Schneider (Stuttgart, 1978; *Beiträge zur Wirtschaftsgeschichte*, Vol. 5), 101-22.

Jeannin, Pierre (2001). *Change, crédit et circulation monétaire à Augsbourg au milieu du 16e siècle* (Paris: E.H.E.S.S.).

Jehel, Georges (1994). 'Le marché immobilier génois, XIIIe-XIVe siècles', in *Villes et sociétés au Moyen Âge. Hommage à M. le Professeur Jacques Heers* (Paris: Presses de l'Université Paris-Sorbonne), 45-56.

Johnson, Christine R. (2008). *The German Discovery of the World: Renaissance Encounters with the Strange and Marvelous* (Charlottesville and London: University of Virginia Press).

Jones, Evan T. (2001). 'Illicit Business: Accounting for Smuggling in Mid-Sixteenth-Century Bristol', *Economic History Review*, **54**, 17-38.

Jones, Evan T. (2017). *Inside the Illicit Economy: Reconstructing the Smugglers' Trade of Sixteenth Century Bristol* (London: Routledge, Taylor and Francis Group).

Kamen, Henry (2000). *Early Modern European Society* (London and New York: Routledge).

Kaminska, Brabara A. (2014). 'Come, let us make a city and a tower': Pieter Bruegel the Elder's *Tower of Babel* and the Creation of a Harmonious Community in Antwerp', *Journal of Historians of Netherlandish Art*, **6:2**, DOI: 10.5092/jhna.2014.6.2.3

Keene, Derek (1989). 'The Property Market in English Towns, A.D. 1100-1600', in *D'une ville à l'autre. Structures matérielles et organisation de l'espace dans les villes européennes, XIIIe-XVIe siécle* (Rome: École française de Rome), 201-26.

Kellenbenz, Hermann (1959). 'Karl V. und die Messen in Lyon', *Spanische Forschungen der Görresgesellschaft*, 1st ser., *Gesammelte Aufsätze zur Kulturgeschichte Spaniens*, **14**, 194-202.

Kellenbenz, Hermann (1960). 'Nürnberger Handel um 1540', *Mitteilungen des Vereins für Geschichte der Stadt Nürnberg*, **50**, 299-324.

Kellenbenz, Hermann (1965). 'Jakob Rehlinger: ein Augsburger Kaufmann in Venedig', in *Beiträge zur Wirtschafts- und Sozialgeschichte*, ed. Hermann Aubin et al. (Wiesbaden: Steiner), 362-79.

Kellenbenz, Hermann (1970a). 'Die Aachener Kupfermeister', *Zeitschrift des Aachener Geschichtsvereins*, **80**, 99-125.

Kellenbenz, Hermann (1970b). *Fremde Kaufleute auf der iberischen Halbinsel* (Cologne and Vienna: Böhlau).

Kellenbenz, Hermann (1974). 'Briefe über Pfeffer und Kupfer', in *Geschichte, Wirtschaft, Gesellschaft. Festschrift für Clemens Bauer*, ed. Erich Hassinger (Berlin: Duncker & Humblot), 205-28.

Kellenbenz, Hermann (1976/7). 'Die Brüder Diego und Cristóbal de Haro', *Portugiesische Forschungen der Görresgesellschaftt, Erste Reihe, Aufsätze zur Kulturgeschichte*, **14**, 303-15.

Kellenbenz, Hermann (1987). 'Sächsisches und böhmisches Zinn', in *Historia Socialis et Oeconomica. Festschrift für Wolfgang Zorn zum 65. Geburtstag*, ed. Hermann Kellenbenz and Hans Pohl (Stuttgart: Franz Steiner Verlag).

Kellenbenz, Hermann (1990). *Die Fugger in Spanien und Portugal bis 1560. Ein Grossunternehmen des 16. Jahrhunderts* (2 vols; Munich: Ernst Vögel).

Kellenbenz, Hermann (1993). 'Hieronymus Sailer, 1495-1559, Faktor der Welser', *Lebensbilder aus dem Bayerischen Schwaben*, **14**, 33-5.

Kellenbenz, Hermann, and Rolf Walter (2001). *Oberdeutsche Kaufleute in Sevilla und Cadiz, 1525-1560. Eine Edition von Notarisakten aus den dortigen Archiven* (Stuttgart: Franz Steiner Verlag; Deutsche Handelsakten des Mittelalters und der Neuzeit, 21).

Kiem, Karl (2009). *Die Waage. Ein Bautyp des Goldenen Jahrhunderts in Holland* (Berlin: Mann).

Kint, An (1996). 'The Community of Commerce: Social Relations in Sixteenth-Century Antwerp' (Unpublished PhD Thesis: Columbia University).

Klein, Peter Wolfgang (1965). *De Trippen in de zeventiende eeuw. Een studie over het ondernemersgedrag op de Hollandse stapelmarkt* (Assen: Van Gorcum).

Knecht, Robert J. (1994). *Renaissance Warrior and Patron: The Reign of Francis I* (Cambridge: Cambridge University Press).

Kocka, Jürgen (2016). *Capitalism: A Short History* (Princeton, NJ: Princeton University Press).

Kohler, Alfred (1999). *Karl V., 1500-1558. Eine Biographie* (Munich: C.H. Beck Verlag).

Kurz, Heinz D. (2016). 'Adam Smith on Markets, Competition and Violations of Natural Liberty', *Cambridge Journal of Economics*, **40**, 615-38.

Laga, Carl (1963). 'O engenho dos Erasmos em São Vicente; resultado de pesquisas em arquivos belgas', *Revista Estudos Historicos*, **1**, 13-43.

Lambert, Bart (2006). *The City, the Duke and Their Banker. The Rapondi Family and the Formation of the Burgundian State, 1384-1430* (Tutnhout: Brepols).

Lang, Heinrich (2012). 'Herrscherfinanzen un Bankiers unter Franz I. Die Rolle der Florentiner Salviati im französischen Finanzsystem des frühen 16. Jahrhunderts', in *Das "Blut des Staatskörpers": Forschungen zur Finanzgeschichte der Frühen Neuzeit*, ed. Peter Rauscher, Andrea Serles, and Thomas Winkelbauer (Munich: Oldenbourg; Historische Zeitschrift, Beihefte, 56), 459-510.

Lang, Heinrich (2014). 'Networks and Merchant Diasporas: Florentine Bankers in Lyon and Antwerp in the Sixteenth century', in Caracausi and Jeggle, *Commercial Networks*, 107-120.

Langholm, Odd (2003). *The Merchant in the Confessional: Trade and Price in the Pre-Reformation Penitential Handbooks* (Leiden and Boston: Brill).

Lapeyre, Henri (1955). *Une famille de marchands: les Ruiz* (Paris: S.E.V.P.E.N.).

Lavedan, Pierre (1941). *Histoire de l'urbanisme*, Vol. II: *Renaissance et Temps Modernes* (Paris: Laurens).

Lejeune, Jean (1939). *La formation du capitalisme moderne dans la Principauté de Liège au XVIe siècle* (Liège and Paris: Faculté de Philosophie et Lettres).

Leone Leoni, Aron di (2005). *The Hebrew Portuguese Nations in Antwerp and London at the Time of Charles V and Henry VIII. New Documents and Interpretations* (Jersey City, NJ: KTAV Publishing House).

Le Roy Ladurie, Emmanuel (1962). *Histoire du Languedoc* (Paris: Presses Universitaires de France).

Lesger, Clé (2001). *Handel in Amsterdam ten tijde van de Opstand. Kooplieden, commerciële expansie en verandering in de ruimtelijke economie van de Nederlanden, ca. 1550-ca. 1630* (Hilversum: Verloren).

Levy, Jonathan (2017). 'Capital as Process and the History of Capitalism', *Business History Review*, **91**, 483-510.

l'Héritier, Maxime, and Florian Tereygeol (2010). 'From Copper to Silver: Understanding the Saigerprocess through Experimental Liquation and Drying', *Historical Metallurgy*, **44**, 136-52.

Li, Ling-Fan (2015). 'Information Asymmetry and the Speed of Adjustment: Debasements in the Mid-Sixteenth Century', *Economic History Review*, **68**, 1203-25.

Liagre, Léone (1955). 'Le commerce de l'alun en Flandre au Moyen Âge', *Le Moyen Âge*, **61**, 177-206.

Limberger, Michael (2008). *Sixteenth-Century Antwerp and its Rural Surroundings: Social and Economic Changes in the Hinterland of a Commercial Metropolis, ca. 1450-ca. 1570* (Turnhout: Brepols).

Lipartito, Kenneth (2016). 'Reassembling the Economic: New Departures in Historical Materialism', *American Historical Review*, **121**, 101-39.

Lis, Catharina, and Hugo Soly (2006). 'Craft Guilds in Comparative Perspective: The Northern and Southern Netherlands, a Survey', in *Craft Guilds in the Early Modern Low Countries: Work, Power, and Representation*, ed. Maarten Prak et al. (Aldershot: Ashgate), 1-31.

Lis, Catharina, and Hugo Soly (2012). *Worthy Efforts: Attitudes to Work and Workers in Pre-Industrial Europe* (Leiden and Boston: Brill).

Lombaerde, Piet (2009). 'De vroege versterkingswerken van Antwerpen en de Spaanse omwalling, vanaf ca. 1507 tot het einde van de Spaanse Successieoorlog in 1713', in *Antwerpen versterkt. De Spaanse omwalling vanaf haar bouw in 1542 tot haar afbraak in 1870*, ed. Piet Lombaerde (Antwerp: University Press Antwerp and Stadsarchief Antwerpen), 14-61.

Lonchay, Henri (1907). 'Études sur les emprunts des souverains belges aux XVIe et XVII siècles', *Académie royale de Belgique, Bulletin de la Classe des Lettres*, **12**, 923-1013.

Long, Pamela (2018). *Engineering the Eternal City: Infrastructure, Topography, and the Culture of Knowledge in Late Sixteenth-Century Rome* (Chicago, IL: University of Chicago Press).

Lopez, Robert S. (1971). *The Commercial Revolution of the Middle Ages, 950-1350* (Englewood Cliffs, NJ: Prentice-Hall).

Lorenzini, Marcella (2016). 'Infrastructure Financing in the Early Modern Age. The Beginning of a Little Divergence', in *Infrastructure Finance in Europe. Insights into the History of Water, Transport and Telecommunications*, ed. Youssef Cassis (Oxford: Oxford University Press), 61-80.

Maclot, Petra, and Stefaan Grieten (2002). 'Het renaissance-interieur van palazzo Ducci: flirt van een Italiaans bankier met keizer Karel', in *Vreemd gebouwd: westerse en niet-westerse elementen in onze architectuur*, ed. Stefaan Grieten (Antwerpen: Brepols), 61-90.

Maddens, Nicolaas (1979). 'De invoering van de "nieuwe middelen" in het graafschap Vlaanderen tijdens de regering van Keizer Karel', *Belgisch Tijdschrift voor Filologie en Geschiedenis*, **57**, 342-63, 861-98.

Magalhães Godinho, Vitorino (1969). *L'Économie de l'empire portugais aux XVe et XVIe siècles* (Paris: S.E.V.P.E.N.).
Mallett, M.E. (1962). 'Anglo-Florentine Commercial Relations, 1465-1491', *Economic History Review*, **15**, 250-65.
Marcocci, Giuseppe (2014). 'Trading with the Muslim World: Religious Limits and Proscriptions in the Portuguese Empire (ca. 1480-1570)', in *Religion and Trade: Cross-Cultural Exchanges in World History, 1000-1900*, ed. Francesca Trivellato, Leor Halevi and Cátia Antunes (Oxford: Oxford University Press), 91-106.
Maréchal, Joseph (1951). 'Le départ de Bruges des marchands étrangers (XVe-XVIe siècles)', *Handelingen van het Genootschap voor Geschiedenis te Brugge*, **88**, 26-74.
Marnef, Guido (1996). *Antwerp in the Age of Reformation: Underground Protestantism in a Commercial Metropolis, 1550-1557* (Baltimore, MD: Johns Hopkins University Press).
Martens, Pieter (2009). 'Militaire architectuur en vestingoorlog in de Nederlanden tijdens het regentschap van Mariavan Hongarije, 1531-1555' (Unpublished PhD Thesis: KULeuven).
Martens, Pieter (2017). 'Hieronymus Cock's View of Antwerp (1557): Its Genesis and Offspring, from Antwerp to Italy', *Simiolus*, **39**, 171-96.
Maschke, Erich (1980). 'Deutsche Kartelle des 15. Jahrhunderts', in *Städte und Menschen. Beiträge zur Geschichte der Stadt, der Wirtschaft und Gesellschaft, 1959-1977*, ed. Erich Maschke (Wiesbaden: Franz Steiner Verlag; Vierteljahrschrift für Sozial- und Wirtschaftsgeschichte, Beiheft 68), 447-60.
Masure, Thierry (1986). 'De stadsfinanciën van Antwerpen, 1531-1571. Een poging tot rekonstruktie' (Unpublished 'Licentiate' Thesis: Ghent University).
Materné, Jan (1992a). 'L'heure d'Anvers, marché des épices portugaises', in *Saveurs de paradis. Les routes des épices* (Brussels: CGER), 168-81.
Materné, Jan (1992b). '*Schoon ende bequaem tot versamelinghe der cooplieden*: Antwerpens beurswereld tijdens de Gouden Zestiende Eeuw', in *Ter Beurze. Geschiedenis van de aandelenhandel in België, 1300-1990*, ed. Geert De Clercq (Bruges and Antwerp: Marc van de Wiele and Uitgeversbedrijf Tijd), 51-85.
Materné, Jan (1993). 'Antwerpen als verdeel- en veredelingscentrum van specerijen en suiker van de late 15de eeuw tot de 17de eeuw', in *Europa aan tafel. Een verkenning van onze eet- en tafelcultuur* (Deurne-Antwerp: MIM), 49-73.
Mathers, Constance Jones (1988). 'Family Partnerships and International Trade in Early Modern Europe: Merchants from Burgos in England and France, 1470-1570', *Business History Review*, **62**, 367-97.
Matringe, Nadia (2016). *La Banque en Renaissance. Les Salviati et la place de Lyon au milieu du XVIe siècle* (Rennes: Presses Universitaires de Rennes).
Meilink, P.A. (1923). 'Rapporten en betoogen nopens het congégeld op de granen, 1530-1541', *Bijdragen en Mededeelingen van het Historisch Genootschap*, **44**, 1-124.
Mertens, Bernd (1995). *Im Kampf gegen die Monopole. Reichstagsverhandlungen und Monopolprozesse im frühen 16. Jahrhundert* (Tübingen: Mohr Siebeck).
Mertens, Frans Hendrik, and Karel Lodewijk Torfs (1847). *Geschiedenis van Antwerpen sedert de stichting der stad tot onze tijden*, Vol. III (Antwerp: Van Dieren).
Mertens Frans Hendrik, and Karel Lodewijk Torfs (1848). *Geschiedenis van Antwerpen sedert de stichting der stad tot onze tijden*, Vol. IV (Antwerp: Van Dieren).

Meskens, Ad (2013). *Practical Mathematics in a Commercial Metropolis: Mathematical Life in Late 16th Century Antwerp* (Dordrecht: Springer; Archimedes, 31).
Meulleners, J.L. (1890). 'De Antwerpsche bankier Erasmus Schetz en zijne geassocieerden Jan Vleminck en Arnold Proenen in hunne betrekking tot Maastricht en Aken', *Publications de la Société historique et archéologique dans le Duché de Limbourg*, XXVII, new ser., **VII**, 307-33.
Meurs, Paul (2006). 'Engenho São Jorge dos Erasmos, the Remains of an Early Multinational', *Arquitextos*, **6**, no. 070.03.
Mielants, Eric H. (2007). *The Origins of Capitalism and the Rise of the West* (Philadelphia, PA: Temple University Press).
Miranda, Flávio (2013). 'Before the Empire: Portugal and the Atlantic Trade in the Late Middle Ages', *Journal of Medieval Iberian Studies*, **5**, 69-85.
Miranda, Flávio (2015). 'Die Saga der portugiesischen Feigen. Der Handel mit dem Nord- und Ostseeraum im Mittelalter', *Hansische Geschichtsblätter*, **113**, 77-97.
Molho, Anthony, and Diogo Ramada Curto (2003). 'Les réseaux marchands à l'époque moderne', *Annales. Histoire, Sciences sociales*, **58**, 569-79.
Möllenberg, Walter (1911). *Die Eroberung des Weltmarkts durch das mansfeldische Kupfer* (Gotha: Perthes).
Möllering, Guido (2014). 'Trust, Calculativeness, and Relationships: A Special Issue 20 Years after Williamson's Warning', *Journal of Trust Research*, **4**, 1-21.
Mollwo, Carl (1899). 'Kölner Kaufleute im 16. Jahrhundert auf den kanarischen Inseln', *Mitteilungen aus dem Stadtarchiv von Köln*, **28**, 134-40.
Moore, Jason W. (2009). 'Madeira, Sugar, and the Conquest of Nature in the "First" Sixteenth Century, Part I: From "Island of Timber" to Sugar Revolution, 1420-1506', *Review*, **32**, 345-90.
Moore, Jason W. (2010). 'Madeira, Sugar, and the Conquest of Nature in the "First" Sixteenth Century, Part II: From Regional Crisis to Commodity Frontier, 1506-1530', *Review*, **33**, 1-24.
Müller, Heidi A. (2002). 'Tand und Nürnberger Waren', in *Quasi Centrum Europeae: Europa kauft in Nürnberg, 1400-1800*, ed. Hermann Maué et al. (Nuremberg: Germanisches Museum), 73-95.
Müller, Karl Otto (1962). *Welthandelsbräuche, 1480-1540* (Wiesbaden: Franz Steiner Verlag).
Munro, John H. (2001). 'Money, Wages, and Real Incomes in the Age of Erasmus: The Purchasing Power of Coins and of Building Craftmen's Wages in England and the Low Countries, 1500-1540', University of Toronto, Department of Economics, Working Paper no. 1.
Munro, John H. (2003). 'Medieval Woollens: Textiles, Textile Technology, and Industrial Organisation, *c.* 800-1500', in *The Cambridge History of Western Textiles*, ed. David Jenkins (2 vols; Cambridge: Cambridge University Press), I, 228-324.
Munro, John H. (2008). 'The Usury Doctrine and Urban Public Finances in Late Medieval Flanders (1220-1550): Rentes (Annuities), Excise Taxes, and Income Transfers from the Poor to the Rich', in *La Fiscalità nell'economia europea, secc. XIII-XVIII. Istituto Internazionale di Storia Economica F. Datini. Atti della Trentanovesima Settimana di Studi, 22-26 Aprile 2007*, ed. Simonetta Cavaciocchi (Florence: Firenze University Press), 973-1026.
Munro, John H. (2011). 'The Coinages and Monetary Policies of Henry VIII (r. 1509-47)', in *The Collected Works of Erasmus: The Correspondence of Erasmus*, Vol. 14: *Letters 1926 to 2081, A.D. 1528*, transl. Charles Fantazzi and ed. James Estes (Toronto: University of Toronto Press), 423-76.

Munro, John H. (2012). 'Usury, Calvinism and Credit in Protestant England, from the Sixteenth Century to the Industrial Revolution', in *Religione e istituzioni religiose nell'economia europea, 1000-1800. Istituto Internazionale di Storia Economica F. Datini. Atti della Quarantatreesima Settimana di Studi, 8-12 Maggio 2012*, ed. Francesco Ammannati (Florence: Firenze University Press), 155-84.

Murray, James M. (2005). *Bruges, Cradle of Capitalism* (Cambridge: Cambridge University Press).

Mus, Octaaf (1964). 'De Brugse compagnie Despars op het einde van de 15de eeuw', *Handelingen van het Genootschap Société d'Émulation te Brugge*, **101**, 5-118.

Muylle, Jan (2009). 'Het genot van de *locus amoenus*. De *villa rustica* rondom Antwerpen en het topografisch landschap circa 1545-1585', *Stadsgeschiedenis*, **4**, 115-34.

Muylle, Jan (2020). 'Het aangename buitenleven in speelhoven rond Antwerpen, bijzonder in het Leikwartier (1526/27-1569)', *Historiant*, **8**, 27-46.

Nehlsen-von Stryck, Karen (1988). 'Die Monopolgutachten des rechtsgelehrten Humanisten Conrad Peutinger aus dem frühen 16. Jahrhundert. Ein Beitrag zum frühneuzeitlichen Wirtschaftsrecht', *Zeitschrift für neuere Rechtsgeschichte*, **10**, 1-18.

Niedermayr, Hans (1980). 'Ein Leumundszeugnis für Ambrosius Hoechstetter Jun. (1501-1550)', *Zeitschrift des historischen Vereins für Schwaben und Neuburg*, **74**, 120-30.

Noordam-Croes, M.L.J.C. (1968). *Anton van Lalaing, 1480-1540: kamerheer en chevalier d'honneur van Margareta van Oostenrijk, hoofd van financiën in de Nederlanden, 1514/15-1530* (Hoogstraten: Haseldonckx).

Nooyens, Frans (1981-1982). *Geschiedenis van Deurne* (2 vols; Deurne: Gemeentebestuur).

North, Michael (2014). *Kommunikation, Handel, Geld und Banken in der Frühen Neuzeit* (Oldenbourg: De Gruyter; *Enzyklopädie deutscher Geschichte*, Vol. 59).

Nunes, Naidea (2002). 'Terminologia histórica dos produtos e subprodutos açucareiros. Do Mediterrâneo ao Atlântico', in *História do açúcar: rotas e mercados*, ed. Alberto Vieira (Funchal: Centro de Estudos de História Atlântico), 633-63.

Obermeier, Franz (2005). 'Zeitgenössische Dokumente zu Hans Stadens Aufenthalt in Südbrasilien und im brasilianischen São Vicente', *Jahrbuch Martius-Staden*, no. **52**, 107-33.

Ogilvie, Sheilagh (2007). 'Whatever is, is Right? Economic Institutions in Pre-industrial Europe', *Economic History Review*, **60**, 649-84.

Ogilvie, Sheilagh (2011). *Institutions and European Trade: Merchant Guilds, 1000-1800* (Cambridge: Cambridge University Press).

Ogilvie, Sheilagh (2019). *The European Guilds. An Economic Analysis* (Princeton, NJ: Princeton University Press).

Oldland, John (2019). *The English Woollen Industry, c. 1200-c. 1560* (London and New York: Routledge).

O'Malley, Michelle (2010). 'Finding Fame: Painting and the Making of Careers in Renaissance Italy', *Renaissance Studies*, **24**, 9-32.

Onuf, Alexandra (2012). 'Local Terrains: Imaging the Vernacular Landscape in Sixteenth-Century Antwerp', in *The Transformation of Vernacular Experience in Early Modern Arts*, ed. Joost Keizer and Todd M. Richardson (Leiden and Boston: Brill), 229-70.

Oosterbosch, Michel (1995). '*Van groote abuysen ende ongeregeltheden*'. Overheidsbemoeiingen met het Antwerpse notariaat tijdens de XVIde eeuw', *Tijdschrift voor Rechtsgeschiedenis*, **63**, 83-102.

Op de Beeck, Roland A.E. (1978). *De Gilde van Onze-Lieve-Vrouwe-Lof in de Kathedraal van Antwerpen* (Antwerp: Gilde van Onze-Lieve-Vrouwe-Lof).

O'Rourke, Kevin H., and Jeffrey G. Williamson (2009). 'Did Vasco da Gama Matter for European Markets?', *Economic History Review*, **62**, 655-84.

Ottenheym, Konrad, and Krista de Jonge (2007). 'Civic Prestige: Building the City, 1580-1700', in *Unity and Discontinuity: Architectural Relations between the Southern and Northern Low Countries, 1530-1700*, ed. Krista de Jonge and Konrad Ottenheym (Turnhout: Brepols), 209-50.

Outhwaite, R.B. (1966). 'The Trials of Foreign Borrowing: The English Crown and the Antwerp Money Market in the Mid-Sixteenth Centrury', *Economic History Review*, **19**, 289-305.

Pacini, Arturo (2004). 'Genoa and Charles V', in Blockmans and Mout, *The World*, 161-99.

Parigino, Giuseppe Vittorio (1999). *Il tesoro del principe. Fundazione pubblica e privata del patrimonio della famiglia Medici nel Cinquecento* (Florence: Leo S. Olschki).

Parker, Geoffrey (1988). *The Military Revolution: Military Innovation and the Rise of the West, 1500-1800* (Cambridge: Cambridge University Press).

Parker, Geoffrey (2000). 'The Political World of Charles V', in Soly, *Charles V*, 113-225.

Parker, Geoffrey (2019). *Emperor: A New Life of Charles V* (New Haven and London: Yale University Press).

Pastoureau, Michel (2001). *Blue: The History of a Color* (Princeton, NJ: Princeton University Press).

Patroons, Wilfried (2009). *Van 't Schijn tot 't Scheld: de geschiedenis van de Herentalse Vaart. De vergeten en verdwenen levensader van Antwerpen gedurende 400 jaar* (Malle: MjPublishing).

Peacock, David (2006). 'Dyeing Winchcombe Kersies and Other Kersey Cloth in Sixteenth-Century Newbury', *Textile History*, **37**, 187-202.

Peltzer, Rudolf Arthur (1908). 'Geschichte der Messingindustrie und der künstlerischen Arbeiten in Messing (Dinanderies) in Aachen und den Ländern zwischen Maas und Rhein von der Römerzeit bis zur Gegenwart', *Zeitschrift des Aachener Geschichtsvereins*, **30**, 235-463.

Peltzer, Rudolf Arthur (1925). 'Geschichte der Aachener-Stolberger Messingindustrie', *Beiträge zur Geschichte der Technik und Industrie*, **15**, 196-210.

Pereira, Fernando Jasmins (1969). *O açúcar madeirense de 1500 a 1537: produção e preços* (Lisbon: Instituto Superior de Sciências Sociais).

Pfeiffer, Gerhard (1967). 'Die Bemühungen der oberdeutschen Kaufleute um die Privilegierung ihres Handels in Lyon', in *Beiträge zur Wirtschaftsgeschichte Nürnbergs*, Vol. I (Neuremberg: Stadtarchiv), 407-55.

Phillips, William D. (2000). 'Merchants of the Fleece: Castilians in Bruges and the Wool trade', in *International trade in the Low Countries, 14th-16th Centuries. Merchants, Organisation, Infrastructure. Proceedings of the International Conference, Ghent-Antwerp, 12th-13th January 1997* (Leuven and Apeldoorn: Garant), 87-104.

Piotrowski, Roman (1933). *Cartels and Trusts: Their Origin and Historical Development from the Economic and Legal Aspects* (London: George Allen & Unwin).

Pirenne, Henri (1915). 'The Stages in the Social History of Capitalism', *American Historical Review*, **19**, 494-515.

Pirenne, Henri (1923). *Histoire de Belgique*, Vol. III: *De la mort de Charles le Téméraire à l'arrivée du duc d'Albe dans les Pays-Bas, 1567* (Brussels: Maurice Lamertin).

Pirenne, Henri (1963). *Histoire économique et sociale du Moyen Âge*, ed. by Hans Van Werveke (Paris: Presses Universitaires de France).

Pitz, Ernst (1966). 'Kapitalausstattung und Unternehmensformen in Antwerpen, 1488-1514', *Vierteljahrschrift für Sozial- und Wirtschaftsgeschichte*, **53**, 53-91.

Pohl, Hans (1967). 'Die Zuckereinfuhr nach Antwerpen durch Portugiesische Kaufleute während des 80jährigen Krieges', *Jahrbuch für Geschichte von Staat, Wirtschaft und Gesellschaft Lateinamerikas*, **4**, 348-74.

Pohl, Hans (1971). 'Köln und Antwerpen um 1500', in *Köln, das Reich und Europa. Abhandlungen über weiträumige Verflechtungen der Stadt Köln in Politik, Recht und Wirtschaft im Mittelalter*, ed. Hugo Stehkamper (Cologne: Paul Neubner), 469-598.

Pohl, Hans (1977). 'Kupfergewinnung, Kupververarbeitung und Kupferhandel im Aachen-Stolberger Raum von 1500 bis 1650', in *Schwerpunkte der Kupferproduktion und des Kupferhandels in Europa, 1500-1650*, ed. Hermann Kellenbenz (Cologne and Vienna: Böhlau), 225-40.

Pohle, Jürgen (2000). *Deutschland und die überseeische Expansion Portugals im 15. und 16. Jahrhundert* (Münster: LIT).

Pohle, Jürgen (2007). 'As relações luso-alemãs no reinado de D. Manuel I (1495-1521)', in *Portugal-Alemanha: Memórias e Imaginários*, Vol. I: *Da Idade Média ao Século XVIII*, ed. Maria Manuela Gouveia Delille (Coimbra: Centro Interuniversitário de Estudos Germanísticos), 61-74.

Pölnitz, Götz Freiherr von (1949). *Jakob Fugger. Quellen und Erläuterungen* (2 vols; Tübingen: J.C.B. Mohr).

Pölnitz, Götz Freiherr von (1958). *Anton Fugger*, Vol. 1: *1453-1535* (Tübingen: Mohr, 1958).

Pölnitz, Götz Freiherr von (1963-1967). *Anton Fugger*, Vol. 2: *1536-1548* (2 vols; Tübingen: Mohr).

Pölnitz, Götz Freiherr von (1971-1986). *Anton Fugger*, Vol. 3: *1548-1560* (2 vols; Tübingen: Mohr).

Pölnitz, Götz Freiherr von (1964). 'Die Anfänge der Weissenhorner Barchentweberei unter Jakob dem Reichen', in *Festschrift für Hans Liermann zum 70. Geburtstag*, ed. Klaus Obermayer and Hans-Rudolf Hagemann (Erlangen: Universitätsbund), 196-220.

Poncelet, Alfred (1927-28). *Histoire de la Compagnie de Jésus dans les anciens Pays-Bas* (2 vols; Brussels: Hayez).

Porter, Roy (1994). *London: A Social History* (London: Hamish Hamilton).

Posthumus, N.W. (1971). *De uitvoer van Amsterdam, 1543-1545* (Leiden: E.J. Brill).

Potter, David (2008). *Renaissance France at War: Armies, Culture, and Society, c. 1480-1560* (Woodbridge: Boydell & Brewer).

Prak, Maarten (2006). 'Corporate Politics in the Low Countries: Guilds as Institutions, 14th to 18th Centuries', in *Craft Guilds in the Early Modern Low Countries: Wotk, Power, and Representation*, ed. Maarten Prak et al. (Aldershot: Ashgate), 74-106.

Prims, Floris (1923). *Het Antwerpsche turfdragersambacht, 1447-1863* (Antwerp: Veritas).

Prims, Floris (1929). 'Antwerpen in 1554 en de Cronijke van Vlaenderen van Gheeraert van Salenson, 1557', *De Gulden Passer*, **7**, 146-51.

Prims, Floris (1931). 'De vlucht van Guicciardini (1554)', *De Gulden Passer*, **9**, 91-100.

Prims, Floris (1938a). 'Antwerpen en de oorlogsbeden van 1553', *Antwerpiensia*, **12**, 242-7.

Prims, Floris (1938b). 'De beroerte van juli 1554', *Antwerpiensia*, **12**, 248-53.

Prims, Floris (1938c). 'Jacob Maes, de stadspensionaris (1505-1569)', *Antwerpiensia*, **12**, 218-24.

Prims, Floris, and Rik Dierckx (1933). *Atlas der Antwerpsche stadsbuitenijen van 1698* (Antwerp: Sikkel).

Priotti, Jean-Philippe (2018). 'Governing and Getting Rich Overseas. Public and Private Contractors in Woad Cultivation Europe and America, Early Sixteenth Century)', *Revue Historique*, **686**, 347-76.

Puttevils, Jeroen (2009). 'Klein gewin brengt rijkdom in. De Zuid-Nederlandse handelaars in de export naar Italië in de jaren 1540', *Tijdschrift voor Sociale en Economische Geschiedenis*, **6**, pp. 26-52.

Puttevils, Jeroen (2015a). *Merchants and Trading in the Sixteenth Century: The Golden Age of Antwerp* (London: Pickering & Chatto).

Puttevils, Jeroen (2015b). 'Eating the Bread of Their Mouth: Antwerp's Export Trade and Generalized Institutions, 1544-1545', *Economic History Review*, **68**, 1339-64.

Puttevils, Jeroen (2016). 'Trading Silks and Tapestries in Sixteenth-Century Antwerp', in *Europe's Rich Fabric: The Consumption, Commercialisation and Production of Luxury Textiles in Italy, the Low Countries and Neighbouring Territories, Fourteent-Sixteenth Centuries*, ed. Bart Lambert and Katherine Anne Wilson (Farnham: Ashgate), 131-55.

Puttevils, Jeroen (2020), 'Sixteenth-Century Antwerp, a Hyper-Market for All? The Case of Low Countries Merchants', in Blondé and Puttevils, *Antwerp in the Renaissance*, 29-53.

Quadflieg, Eberhard (1962-3). 'Aachener als Poorter von Antwerpen im 16. Jahrhundert', *Zeitschrift des Aachener Geschichtsvereins*, **74/75**, 393-428.

Ramsay, George D. (1975). *The City of London in International Politics at the Accession of Elizabeth (Manchester: Manchester University Press).*

Rau, Susanne (2014). *Räume der Stadt. Eine Geschichte Lyon, 1300-1800* (Frankfurt and New York: Campus Verlag).

Reinhard, Wolfgang (1996). *Augsburger Eliten des 16. Jahrhunderts. Prosopographie wirtschaftlicher und politischer Führungsgruppen, 1500-1620* (Berlin: Akademie Verlag).

Renouard, Yves (1968). *Les hommes d'affaires italiens du Moyen Âge* (Paris: Armand Colin).

Ribeiro, Ana Sofia (2016). *Early Modern Trading Networks in Europe: Cooperation and the Case of Simon Ruiz* (London and New York: Routledge).

Richardson, W.C. (1953). *Stephen Vaughan: Financial Agent of Henry VIII. A Study of Financial Relations with the Low Countries* (Baton Rouge, LA: Louisiana State University Press).

Richardson, W.C. (1954). 'Some Financial Expedients of Henry VIII', *Economic History Review*, New. Ser., **7**, 33-48.

Rinne, Katherine W. (2019). 'Water in Counter-Reformation Rome', in *Art and Reformation in the Late Renaissance: After Trent*, ed. Jesse M. Locker (Abingdon: Routledge), 222-39.

Rodríguez-Salgado, Mia J. (2000). 'Charles V and the Dynasty', in Soly, *Charles V*, 27-111.

Rodríguez-Salgado, Mia J. (2004). 'Obeying the Ten Commandments: The First War between Charles V and Francis I, 1520-1529', in Blockmans and Mout, *The World*, 15-67.

Roobaert, E.J. (1958). 'Nieuwe gegevens over makerde Estrella en L. Guicciardini uit de rekeningen van de Antwerpse magistraat', *Bijdragen tot de Geschiedenis*, **41**, 68-94.

Roosens, Ben (1977). 'Het arsenaal van Mechelen en de wapenhandel, 1551-1567', *Bijdragen tot de Geschiedenis*, **60**, 175-247.

Roosens, Ben (2005). 'Habsburgse defensiepolitiek en vestingbouw in de Nederlanden, 1520-1560' (2 vols; Unpublished PhD Thesis: Leiden University).

Roper, Lyndal (2016). *Martin Luther: Renegade and Prophet* (London: The Bodley Head).

Rosolino, Riccardo (2013). 'Vices tyranniques. Résistance au monopole, idéologie et marché à l'aube de la modernité', *Annales. Histoire, Sciences Sociales*, **68**, 793-819.

Rössner, Philipp Robinson (2012). *Deflation – Devaluation – Rebellion. Geld im Zeitalter der Reformation* (Stuttgart: Franz Steiner Verlag; Vierteljahrschrift für Sozial- und Wirtschaftsgeschichte, Beiheft 219).

Rössner, Philipp Robinson (2014). 'Critical Introduction', in Martin Luther, *On Commerce and Usury (1524)*, ed. Philipp Robinson Rössner (London and New York: Anthem Press, 2014), 1-166.

Ruiz Albi, Irene (2018). 'El pleito entre Gaspar Ducci, Reinaldo Strozzi y unos armadores de Castro Urdiales por el pastel apresado al la compañía de Juan Bautista y Lorenzo Guicciardini en Aguas Franceses (1543-1552)', in *Comercio, finanzas y fiscalidad en Castilla, siglos XV y XVI*, ed. Hilario Casado Alonso (Madrid: Dykinson), 241-65.

Ruiz Martín, Felipe (2005). *Los Alumbres Españoles: un indice de la conyuntura económica Europea en el siglo XVI* (Madrid: Fundación Española de Historia Moderna).

Sabbatini, Renzo (1985). *'Cerca esca': Mercanti lucchesi ad Anversa nel Cinquecento* (Florence: Salimbeni).

Safley, Thomas Max (2008). 'Staatsmacht und geschäftliches Scheitern. Der Bankrott der Handelsgesellschaft Ambrosius und Hans, Gebrüder Höchstetter, und Mitverwandte im Jahr 1529', *Österreichische Zeitschrift für Geschichtswissenschaften*, **19**, 36-53.

Safley, Thomas Max (2014). 'Institutions and Their Discontents', *Tijdschrift voor Sociale en Economische Geschiedenis*, **11**, 61-73.

Safley, Thomas Max (2020). *Family Firms and Merchant Capitalism in Early Modern Europe. The Business, Bankruptcy and Resilience of the Höchstetters of Augsburg* (London and New York: Routledge).

Salvadori, Neri, and Rodolfo Signorino (2014). 'Adam Smith on Monopoly Theory. Making Good a Lacuna', *Scottish Journal of Political Economy*, **61**, 178-95.

Sánchez, Manuel Herrero, and Klemens Kaps, eds (2017). *Merchants and Trade Networks in the Atlantic and the Mediterranean, 1550-1800: Connectors of Commercial Maritime Systems* (London: Routledge).

Schick, Léon (1957). *Un grand homme d'affaires au début du XVIe siècle: Jacob Fugger* (Paris: S.E.V.P.E.N.).

Schirmer, Uwe (2006). *Kursächsische Staatsfinanzen (1456-1656): Strukturen, Verfassung, Funktionseliten* (Stuttgart: Franz Steiner Verlag; *Quellen und Forschungen zur sächsischen Geschichte*, 28).

Schmidt-Händel, Astrid (2004). *Der Erfurter Waidhandel an der Schwelle zur Neuzeit* (Frankfurt am Main: Peter Lang).

Schmitt, Eberhard (2000). 'Die Ritter vom Güldenen Sporn: eine Leistungselite der Zeit Kaiser Karls V.', in *Kaiser Karl V. und seine Zeit*, ed. Stephan Diller (Bamberg: Universitäts-Verlag), 136-41.

Schmitz, Yves, and Alfons Bousse (1988). *Les van de Werve: 800 ans d'histoire* (2 vols; Brussels: Association familiale van de Werve).

Scholliers, Etienne (1960). *Loonarbeid en honger. De levensstandaard in de XVe en XVIe eeuw te Antwerpen* (Antwerp: De Sikkel).

Scholliers, Etienne (1962). 'Un indice du loyer: les loyers anversois de 1500 à 1873', in *Studi in Onore di Amintore Fanfani*, Vol. V: *Evi moderno e contemporaneo* (Milan: Giuffrè), 593-617.

Schumpeter, Joseph (1976). *Capitalism, Socialism and Democracy* (London: George Allen & Unwin; first edition: 1942).

Schwartz, Stuart B. (1985). *Sugar Plantations in the Formation of Brazilian Society: Bahia, 1550-1835* (Cambridge: Cambridge University Press).

Schwartz, Stuart B. (2004). *Tropical Babylons: Sugar and the Making of the Atlantic World, 1450-1680* (Chapel Hill, NC: University of North Carolina Press).

Schwartz, Stuart B. (2010). *Early Brazil: A Documentary Collection to 1700* (Cambridge: Cambridge University Press).

Servantie, Alain (2006). 'Enquêtes sur les nouveaux chrétiens d'Anvers et leurs relations avec la Turquie (1530-1548)', in *A Bridge between cultures. Studies on Ottoman and Republican Turkey in Memory of Ali Ihsan Bagis*, ed. Sinan Küneralp (Istanbul: The Isis Press), 23-52.

Setton, Kenneth M. (1984). *The Papacy and the Levant, 1204-1571*, Vol. III: *The Sixteenth Century* (Philadelphia: The American Philosophical Society).

Sicking, Louis (1998). *Zeemacht en onmacht. Maritieme politiek in de Nederlanden, 1488-1558* (Amsterdam: De Bataafsche Leeuw).

Sicking, Louis (2015). *La naissance d'une thalassocratie. Les Pays-Bas et la mer à l'aube du Siècle d'Or* (Paris: Presses de l'Université Paris-Sorbonne).

Slootmans, Cornelis J.F. (1985). *Paas- en Koudemarkten te Bergen op Zoom, 1365-1565* (3 vols; Tilburg: Stichting Zuidelijk Historisch Contact; *Bijdragen tot de Geschiedenis van het Zuiden van Nederland*, Tweede reeks, 64-66).

Smolders, Leo W.G., and Adrianus C. van Grootheest (2005). 'De groei van Veenendaal', in *Geschiedenis van Veenendaal*, Vol. 2, ed. Adrianus C. van Grootheest, Roelof Bisschop and Gert C. Groenleer (Veenendaal: Historische Vereniging Oud Veenendaal), 95-105.

Soly, Hugo (1968). 'De brouwerijenonderneming van Gilbert van Schoonbeke (1552-1562)', *Belgisch Tijdschrift voor Filologie en Geschiedenis*, **46**, 337-92, 1166-1204.

Soly, Hugo (1969). 'De Antwerpse onderneemster Anna Janssens en de economische boom na de vrede van Cateau-Cambrésis (1559)', *Bijdragen tot de Geschiedenis*, **52**, 139-64.

Soly, Hugo (1971). 'Een Antwerpse Compagnie voor de levensmiddelenbevoorrading van het leger in de Nederlanden in de 16e eeuw', *Bijdragen en Mededelingen betreffende de Geschiedenis der Nederlanden*, **86**, 350-62.

Soly, Hugo (1974a). 'De schepenregisters als bron voor de conjunctuurgeschiedenis van Zuid- en Noordnederlandse steden in het Ancien Régime. Een concreet voorbeeld: de Antwerpse immobiliënmarkt in de 16de eeuw', *Tijdschrift voor Geschiedenis*, **87**, 521-44.

Soly, Hugo (1974b). 'De aluinhandel in de Nederlanden in de 16e eeuw', *Belgisch Tijdschrift voor Filologie en Geschiedenis*, **52**, 800-57.

Soly, Hugo (1976a). 'The "Betrayal" of the Sixteenth-Century Bourgeoisie: A Myth? Some Considerations on the Behaviour Pattern of the Merchants of Antwerp', *Acta Historiae Neerlandicae. Studies on the History of the Netherlands*, **8**, 31-49.

Soly, Hugo (1976b). 'De bouw van de Antwerpse citadel (1567-1571). Sociaal-economische aspecten', *Belgisch Tijdschrift voor Militaire Geschiedenis*, **21**, 549-78.

Soly, Hugo (1977). *Urbanisme en kapitalisme te Antwerpen in de 16de eeuw. De stedebouwkundige en industriële ondernemingen van Gilbert van Schoonbeke* (Brussels: Gemeentekrediet van België).

Soly, Hugo, ed. (2000). *Charles V, 1500-1558, and His Time* (Antwerp: Mercatorfonds).

Soly, Hugo (2016) 'Social Relations, Political Balances of Power, and Perceptions of Big Business: Contrasting Images of Merchants in Northern Italy, the Low Countries, and Southern Germany, 14th-17th Century', *The Medieval Low Countries: An Annual Review*, **3**, 175-217.

Soly, Hugo, and Alfons K.L. Thijs (1979). 'De nijverheid in de Zuidelijke Nederlanden, 1490-1585', in *Algemene Geschiedenis der Nederlanden*, Vol. VI (Haarlem: Fibula-Van Dishoeck), 27-57.

Sosson, Jean-Pierre (1977). *Les travaux publics de la ville de Bruges, XIVe-XVe siècles* (Brussels: Gemeentekrediet van België).

Spooner, Frank C. (1956). *L'Économie mondiale et les frappes monétaires en France, 1493-1680* (Paris: Armand Colin).

Stabel, Peter (1997). '*Dmeeste, oirboirlixste ende proffitelixste let ende neringhe:* een kwantitatieve benadering van de lakenproductie in het laatmiddeleeuwse en vroegmoderne Vlaanderen', *Handelingen der Maatschappij voor Geschiedenis en Oudheidkunde te Gent*, **51**, 113-53.

Stabel, Peter (2002). 'Kooplieden in de stad', in *Hanzekooplui en Medicibankiers: Brugge, wisselmarkt van Europese culturen*, ed. André Vande walle (Oostkamp: Stichtig Kunstboek), 85-96.

Stabel, Peter, and Jelle Haemers (2006). 'From Bruges to Antwerp: International Commercial Firms and Government's Credit in the Late 15th and Early 16th Century', in *Banca, Crédito y Capital. La Monarquía Hispánica y los antiguos Países Bajos, 1505-1700*, ed. Carmen Sanz Ayán and Bernardo J. Garciá Garciá (Madrid: Fundación Carlos Amberes), 21-38.

Stabel, Peter, et al. (2018). 'Production, Markets and Socio-economic Structures II: *c.* 1320-*c.* 1500', in Brown and Dumolyn, *Medieval Bruges*, 196-267.

Stahlschmidt, Rainer (1970). 'Das Messinggewerbe im spätmittelalterlichen Nürnberg', *Mitteilungen des Vereins für Geschichte der Stadt Nürnberg*, **57**, 124-49.

Stasavage, David (2011). *States of Credit: Size, Power, and the Development of European Polities* (Princeton: NJ: Princeton University Press).

Steegen, Erwin (2006). *Kleinhandel en stedelijke ontwikkeling: het kramersambacht te Maastricht in de vroegmoderne tijd* (Hilversum: Verloren).

Steegen, Erwin (2015). 'Economische transformaties van Maastricht: handelsnetwerken en stedelijke ontwikkeling in de Middeleeuwen en Vroegmoderne Tijd', in *Limburg. Een geschiedenis, 1500-1800*, ed. Paul Tummers et al. (Maastricht: Koninklijk Limburgs Geschied- en Oudheidkundig Genootschap), 285-323.

Stol, Taeke (1992). *De veenkolonie Veenendaal. Turfwinning en waterstaat in het zuiden van de Gelderse Vallei, 1546-1653* (Zutphen: De Walburg Pers).

Stol, Taeke (2000). 'Turfwinning van de vijftiende tot de twintigste eeuw', in *Geschiedenis van Veenendaal*, Vol. 1, ed. Adrianus C. van Grootheest and Roelof Bisschop (Veenendaal: Historische Vereniging Oud Veenendaal), 151-65.

Stols, Eddy (1973). 'Os mercadores flamengas em Portugal e no Brasil antes das conquistas hollandesas', *Anais de História*, **5**, 9-54.

Stols, Eddy (2004). 'The Expansion of the Sugar Market in Western Europe', in Schwartz, *Tropical Babylons*, 237-88.

Straube, Manfred (1979). 'Zur Stellung der Leipziger Messen im überregionalen Warenverkehr zu Beginn des 16. Jahrhunderts', *Jahrbuch für Wirtschaftsgeschichte*, **20**, 185-206.

Straube, Manfred (2012). 'Über die Anfänge der Grossen Märkte in Leipzig', in *Leipzigs Wirtschaft in Vergangenheit und Gegenwart: Akteure, Handlungsspielräume, Wirkungen, 1400-2011* (Leipzig: Universitätverlag), 51-71.

Streeck, Wolfgang (2016). *How Will Capitalism End? Essays on a Failing System* (London and New Yok: Verso).

Strieder, Jakob (1914). *Studien zur Geschichte kapitalistischer Organisationsformen: Monopole, Kartelle und Aktiengesellschaften im Mittelalter und zu Beginn der Neuzeit* (Munich: Dunkler and Humblot).

Strieder, Jakob (1938). 'Deutsche Metallwarenexport nach Westafrika im 16. Jahrhundrt', in *Das reiche Augsburg. Ausgewählte Aufsätze Jakob Strieders zur Augsburger und süddeutschen Wirtschaftsgeschichte des 15. Und 16. Jahrhunderts*, ed. Heinz Friedrich Deininger (Munich: Duncker & Humblot), 155-67.

Struckmeier, Sabine (2011). *Die Textilfärberei vom Spätmittelalter bis zur Frühen Neuzeit (14.-16. Jahrhundert). Eine naturwissenschaftlich-technische Analyse deutschsprachiger Quellen* (Münster: Waxmann).

Studnicki-Gizbert, Daviken (2003). 'La "nation" portugaise. Réseaux marchands dans l'espace atlantique à l'époque moderne', *Annales. Histoire, Sciences sociales*, **58**, 627-48.

Stumpo, Enrico (1992). 'Ducci, Gaspare', *Dizionario Biografico degli Italiani*, **41**.

Suhling, Lothar (1976). *Der Seigerhüttenprozess. Die technologie des Kupferseigerns nach den frühen metallurgischen Schriften* (Stuttgart: Riederer).

Suhling, Lothar (1994). 'Die Technologie des Kupferseigerns in Zentraleuropa im 15. und 16. Jahrhundert – technische, ökonomische und politische Aspekte', in *Mines et métallurgie*, ed. Paul Benoit and Alain Bideau (Villeurbanne: Programme Rhône-Alpes Recherches en Sciences humaines; *Les Chemins de la Recherche*, 21).

Supple, Barry (1977). 'The Nature of Enterprise', in *The Cambridge Economic History of Europe*, Vol. V: *The Economic Organization of Early Modern Europe*, ed. Edwin E. Rich and Charles H. Wilson (Cambridge: Cambridge University Press), 393-461.

Sutton, Anne F. (2005). *The Mercery of London: Trade, Goods and People, 1130-1578* (Farnham: Ashgate).

Teixeira, Paulo (2011). 'Primeiros engenhos do Brasil colonial e o engenho São Jorge dos Erasmos: preliminares de uma doce energia', *História/e-história*, 26 July.

Thijs, Alfons K.L. (1974). 'Weemoes, weemoesputten en weemoesvelden: kanttekeningen betreffende de invloed der stedelijke lakenververij op de ontwikkeling van de landbouw in het Antwerpse', *Bijdragen tot de Geschiedenis*, **57**, 189-202.

Thijs, Alfons K.L. (1975a). 'Van 'werkwinkel' tot 'fabriek': de textielnijverheid te Antwerpen van het einde der vijftiende tot het begin der negentiende eeuw' (Unpublished PhD Thesis: Ghent University).

Thijs, Alfons K.L. (1975b). 'Een gilde van Breslause kooplieden te Antwerpen (einde van de 15de – eerste helft van de 16de eeuw)', in *Album Charles Verlinden* (Ghent: Universa), 353-67.

Thijs, Alfons K.L. (1979). 'De geschiedenis van de suikernijverheid te Antwerpen (16de-19de eeuw): een terreinverkenning', *Bijdragen tot de Geschiedenis*, **62**, 23-50.

Thijs, Alfons K.L. (1987). *Van 'werkwinkel' tot 'fabriek': de textielnijverheid te Antwerpen, einde 15de-begin 19de eeuw* (Brussels: Gemeentekrediet van België).

Thijs, Alfons K.L. (1993). 'Antwerp's Luxury Industries: The Pursuit of Profit and Artistic Sensitivity', in *Antwerp: Story of a Metropolis, 16th-17th Century*, ed. Jan van der Stock (Ghent: Snoeck-Ducaju), 105-13.

Thomas, Nicolas, and David Bourgarit (2018). 'Is the Benefit Worth the Effort? The Production of Brass by Cementation in the Middle Ages through an Economic Perspective', in *History, Archaeology and Archaeometry of the Production of Brass, Bronze and Other Copper Alloy*

Objects in Medieval Europe, 12th-16th Centuries, ed. Nicolas Thomas and Pete Dandridge (Namur: Agence wallonne du Patrimoine; *Études et Documents*, Ser. *Archéologie*), 71-88.

Thornton, John (1992). *Africa and Africans in the Making of the Atlantic World, 1400-1680* (Cambridge: Cambridge University Press).

Thornton, John (2009). 'Portuguese-African Relations, 1500-1750', in *Encompassing the Globe: Portugal and the World in the 16th and 17th Centuries*, ed. Paulo Henriques (Lisbon: Museu Nacional), 104-13.

Thys, Augustin (1882). 'La Maison d'Aix', *Recueil des Bulletins de la Propriété*, **14**, 122-7.

Thys, Augustin (1893). *Historiek der straten en openbare plaatsen van Antwerpen* (Antwerp: Kennes).

Tracy, James D. (1985). *A Financial Revolution in the Habsburg Netherlands:* Renten *and* Renteniers *in the County of Holland, 1515-1565* (Berkeley: University of California Press).

Tracy, James D. (1993). 'Herring Wars: The Habsburg Netherlands and the Struggle for Control of the North Sea, ca. 1520-1560', *The Sixteenth Century Journal*, **24**, 249-72.

Tracy, James D. (2002). *Emperor Charles V, Impresario of War: Campaign Strategy, International Finance, and Domestic politics* (Cambridge: Cambridge University Press).

Tracy, James D. (2004). 'War Finance and Fiscal Devolution in Charles V's Realms', in Blockmans and Mout, *The World*, 69-81.

Trivellato, Francesca (2003). 'Juifs de Livourne, Italiens de Lisbonne, hindous de Goa. Réseaux marchands et échanges interculturels à l'époque moderne', *Annales. Histoire, Sciences sociales*, **58**, 581-603.

Trivellato, Francesca (2009). *The Familiarity of Strangers: The Sephardic Diaspora, Livorno, and Cross-Cultural Trade in the Early Modern Period* (New Haven and London: Yale University Press).

Trocmé, Étienne, and Marcel Delafosse (1952). *Le commerce rochelais de la fin du 15e siècle au début du 17e siècle* (Paris: S.E.V.P.E.N.).

Trusen, Winfried (1971). '*De contractibus mercatorum*: Wirtschaftsethik und gelehrtes Recht im Traktat Johannes Niders', in *Ius et Commercium. Festschrift für Franz Laufke zum 70. Geburtstag* (Würzburg: Holzner Verlag), 51-71.

Tucci, Ugo (1973). 'The Psychology of the Venetian Merchant in the Sixteenth Century', in *Renaissance Venice*, ed. John R. Hale (Totowa, NJ: Rowman & Littlefield), 346-78.

Tys, Rutger (1993). *Tot Cieraet deser Stadt: Bouwtrant en bouwbeleid te Antwerpen van de Middeleeuwen tot heden. Een cultuurhistorische studie over de bouwtrant en de ontwikkeling van het stedebouwkundig beleid van de 13de tot de 20ste eeuw* (Antwerp: Mercatorfonds).

Unger, Manfred (1963).'Die Leipziger Messe und die Niederlande im 16. und 18. Jahrhundert', *Hansische Gechichtsblätter*, **81**, 20-38.

Unger, Richard (2004). *Beer in the Middle Ages and the Renaissance* (Philadelphia, PA: University of Pennsylvania Press).

Van Aert, Laura (2007). 'Tot leven of overleven? Winkelhouden in crisistijd: de Antwerpse meerseniers, ca. 1648-ca. 1748' (Unpublished PhD Thesis: University of Antwerp).

Van Answaarden, Robert (1991). *Les Portugais devant le Grand Conseil des Pays-Bas, 1460-1580* (Paris: Fondation Calouste Gulbenkian).

Van Bavel, Bas (2010). 'The Medieval Origins of Capitalism in the Netherlands', *Bijdragen en Mededelingen betreffende de Geschiedenis der Nederlanden/ The Low Countries Historical Review*, **125**, 45-79.

Van Bavel, Bas (2016). *The Invisible Hand? How Market Economies have Emerged and Declined since AD 500* (Oxford: Oxford University Press).

Van Bochove, Christiaan, Heidi Deneweth and Jaco Zuiderduijn (2013). 'Real Estate and Mortgage Finance in England and the Low Countries, 1300-1800', *Continuity and Change*, **30**, 9-38.

Van Cauwenberghe, Eddy (1982). *Het vorstelijk domein en de overheidsfinanciën in de Nederlanden (15de en 16de eeuw). Een kwantitatieve analyse van Vlaamse en Brabantse domeinrekeningen* (Brussels: Gemeentekrediet van België).

Van Craenenbroeck, Wim (1988). 'Oorsprong en uitbouw van de watervoorziening in het Antwerpse Brouwerskwartier', in *'n Propere tijd!? Onleefbaar Antwerpen thuis en op straat, 1500-1800*, ed. Petra Maclot and Werner Pottier (Antwerp: Antwerpse Vereniging voor Bodem- & Grotonderzoek), 65-92.

Van Craenenbroeck, Wim (2019a). 'Water voor de brouwers: een waterbedrijf in de zestiende eeuw', in *Gilbert van Schoonbeke: Visionair ondernemer in Antwerpens Gouden Eeuw*, ed. Hugo Soly (Antwerp: Pandora), 98-141.

Van Craenenbroeck, Wim (2019b). 'De brouwerswaterleiding van Gilbert van Schoonbeke', *HistoriANT*, **7**, 147-69.

Van den Boogert, Bob (1993). 'Macht en pracht. Het mecenaat van Maria van Hongarije', in *Maria van Hongarije, Koningin tussen keizers en kunstenaars, 1505-1558* (Zwolle: Waanders), 269-301.

Van den Brink, Peter, Maximiliaan P.J. Martens, and Nico Van Hout (2005). *Extravagant. A Forgotten Chapter of Antwerp Painting, 1500-1530* (Schoten: BAI).

Van den Heuvel, Charles (1991). *'Papiere Bolwercken'. De introductie van de Italiaanse stede- en vestingbouw in de Nederlanden (1540-1609) en het gebruik van tekeningen* (Alphen aan den Rijn: Canaletto).

Van der Linden, Marcel (2016). 'Final Thoughts', in *Capitalism. The Reemergence of a Historical Concept*, ed. Jürgen Kocka and Marcel van der Linden (London and New York: Bloombury), 251-66.

Van der Wee, Herman (1963). *The Growth of the Antwerp Market and the European Economy, Fourteenth-Sixteen Centuries* (3 vols; The Hague: Martinus Nijhoff).

Van der Wee, Herman (1967). 'Anvers et les innovations de la technique financière aux XVIe et XVIIe siècles', *Annales. Économies. Sociétés. Civilisations*, **22**, 1067-89.

Van der Wee, Herman (1993). *The Low Countries in the Early Modern World* (Aldershot: Ashgate).

Van der Wee, Herman (2000). 'European Banking in the Middle Ages and Early Modern Period (476-1789)', in *A History of European Banking*, ed. Herman der Wee and Ginette Kurgan-Van Hentenryk (Antwerp: Mercatorfonds), 71-265.

Van der Wee, Herman, and Ian Blanchard (1992). 'The Habsburgs and the Antwerp Money Market: The Exchange Crises of 1521 and 1522-3', in *Industry and Finance in Early Modern History. Essays Presented to George Hammersley to the Occasion of His 74th Birthday*, ed. Ian Blanchard, Anthony Goodman and Jennifer Newman (Stuttgart: Franz Steiner Verlag), 27-56.

Van der Wee, Herman, and Theo Peeters (1970). 'Un modèle dynamique de croissance interséculaire du commerce mondial (XIIe-XVIIIe siècles)', *Annales. Économies. Sociétés. Civilisations*, **25**, 100-26.

Vandewalle, André (1994). 'El Consulado de Burgos en los Países Bajos, in *Actas del V Centenario del Consulado de Burgos, 1494-1994* (Burgos: Diputación Provincial de Burgos), Vol. 1, 283-300.

Vandewalle, André (2002). 'De vreemde naties in Brugge', in *Hanzekooplui en Medicibankiers: Brugge, wisselmarkt van Europese culturen*, ed. André Vande walle (Oostkamp: Stichtig Kunstboek), 27-42.

Vande Weghe, Robert (1977). *Geschiedenis van de Antwerpse straatnamen* (Antwerp: Mercurius).

Van Dijck, Maarten F. (2007). 'De pacificering van de Europese samenleving: repressie, gedragspatronen en verstedelijking in Brabant tijdens de lange zestiende eeuw' (Unpublished PhD Thesis: University of Antwerp).

Van Dixhoorn, Arjan (2014). 'The Values of Antwerp and the Prosperity of Belgica. Political Economy in Guicciardini's *Descrittione di tutti i Paesi Bassi* (1567)', in *Trading Values in Early Modern Antwerp*, ed. Christine Göttler, Bart Ramakers and Joanna Woodall (Leiden and Boston: Brill), 77-107.

Van Hofstraeten, Bram (2016). 'The Organization of Mercantile Capitalism in the Low Countries: Private Partnerships in Early Modern Antwerp (1480-1620)', *Tijdschrift voor Sociale en Economische Geschiedenis*, **13**, 1-24.

Van Houtte, Jan A. (1939). 'Ambernijverheid en paternostermakers te Brugge tijdens de XIVe en Xve eeuw', *Handelingen van het Genootschap Société d'Émulation te Brugge*, **82**, 149-84.

Van Houtte, Jan A. (1952). 'Handel en verkeer', in *Algemene Geschiedenis der Nederlanden*, Vol. IV: *1477-1567*, ed. Jan A. Van Houtte (Utrecht: De Haan), 154-201.

Van Houtte, Jan A. (1961). 'Anvers aux XVe et XVIe siècles. Expansion et apogée', *Annales. Économies. Sociétés. Civilisations*, **16**, 248-78.

Van Passen, Robert (1964). *Geschiedenis van Kontich* (Kontich: Gemeentebestuur).

Van Passen, Robert (1982). *Geschiedenis van Wilrijk* (Wilrijk: Gemeentebestuur).

Van Peteghem, Paul (1972). 'Lodewijk Van Schore, President van de Raad van State en van de Geheime Raad, 1540-1548' (Unpublished 'Licentiate' Thesis: Ghent University).

Van Uytven, Raymond (2001). 'De "Vieille Montagne" en het galmeimonopolie van de Schetsen', *Bijdragen tot de Geschiedenis*, **84**, 191-203.

Vanwelden, Martine (2006). *Productie van wandtapijten in de regio Oudenaarde. Een symbiose tussen stad en platteland, 15de tot 17de eeuw* (Leuven: Universitaire Pers).

Van Werveke, Hans (1944). *Bruges et Anvers: huit siècles de commerce flamand* (Brussels: Éditions de la Librairie encyclopédique).

Van Zanden, Jan Luiten (1993). *The Rise and Decline of Holland's Economy: Merchant Capitalism and the Labour Market* (Manchester and New York: Manchester University Press).

Vázquez de Ágredos Pascual, Luisa, et al. (2007). 'Kermes and Cochineal; Woad and Indigo. Repercussions of the Discovery of the New World in the Workshops of European Painters and Dyers in the Modern Age', *Arché. Publicación del Instituto universitario de Restauración del Patrimonio de la UPV*, **2**, 131-6.

Veeckman, Johan (2002). 'Production and Consumption of Glass in 16th and Early 17th Century Antwerp: The Archaeological Evidence', in *Majolica and Glass from Italy to Antwerp and Beyond: The Transfer of Technology in the 16th-Early 17th Century*, ed. Johan Veeckman (Antwerp: City of Antwerp), 79-93.

Veeckman, Johan et al. (2019). 'De zestiende-eeuwse omwalling van Antwerpen', in *Gilbert van Schoonbeke: Visionair ondernemer in Antwerpens Gouden Eeuw*, ed. Hugo Soly (Antwerp: Pandora), 174-209.

Venturini, Alain (2015). 'Le sel de Camargue au Moyen Âge: Étude des Pays d'Aigues-Mortes (Languedoc, royaume de France) et de Camargue proprement dite (comté de Provence, Empire) (IXe-XVe siècle)', in *Le Sel de la Baie. Histoire, archéologie, ethnologie des sels atlantiques*, ed. Jean-Claude Hocquet and Jean-Luc Sarrazin (Rennes: Presses Universitaires de Rennes), 365-92.

Veratelli, Federica (2013). *À la mode italienne. Commerce du luxe et diplomatie dans les Pays-Bas méridionaux, 1477-1530* (Villeneuve d'Ascq: Presses universitaires du Septentrion).

Verhofstad, Karel (1937). *De regering der Nederlanden in de jaren 1555-1559* (Nijmegen: J.J. Berkhout).

Verhuyck, Paul, and Corine Kisling (1987). *Het mandement van Bacchus, Antwerpse kroegentocht in 1580* (Antwerp and Amsterdam: C. De Vries-Brouwers).

Vermeylen, Filip (2001). 'The Commercialization of Art: Painting and Sculpture in Sixteenth-Century Antwerp', in *Early Netherlandish Painting at the Crossroads. A Critical Look at Current Methodologies*, ed. Maryan Ainsworth (New York: The Metropolitan Museum of Art), 46-61.

Vermeylen, Filip (2003). *Painting for the Market: Commercializaton of Art in Antwerp's Golden Age* (Turnhout: Brepols).

Vial, Eugène (1914). *L'Histoire et la légende de Jean Cléberger, dit 'Le Bon Allemand', 1485-1546* (Lyon: A. Rey).

Vieira, Alberto (1987). *O comércio inter-insular nos séculos XV e XVI: Madeira, Açores e Canarias* (Funchal: Centro de Estudos de História do Atlântico).

Vieira, Alberto (1996). 'Slaves With or Without Sugar: Madeira's Case', in *Slaves With or Without Su-gar*, ed. Alberto Vieira (Funchal: Centro de Estudos de História Atlântico), 9-25.

Vieira, Alberto (2002). 'A Madeira e o mercado do açúcar, seculos XV-XVI', in *História do açúcar: rotas e mercados*, ed. Alberto Vieira (Funchal: Centro de Estudos de História Atlântico), 55-89.

Vieira, Alberto (2004). 'Sugar Islands: The Sugar Economy of Madeira and the Canaries, 1450-1650', in Schwartz, *Tropical Babylons*, 42-84.

Vigneron, Sylvain (2007). *La pierre et la terre. Le marché financier et immobilier dans les dynamiques sociales du Nord de la France aux XVIIe et XVIIIe siècles* (Villeneuce d'Ascq: Presses Universitaires du Septentrion).

Viña Brito, Ana del Carmen (2012). 'Los flamencos en Canarias en el siglo XVI: Una comunidad extranjera? Especificidades en la isla de La Palma', *Revista de Historia Canaria*, **194**, 161-92.

Voet, Leon, et al. (1978). *De stad Antwerpen van de Romeinse tijd tot de 17de eeuw. Topografische studie rond het plan van Virgilius Bononiensis, 1565* (Brussels: Gemeentekrediet van België).

Vogt, John (1973). 'The Portuguese Gold Trade: An Account Ledger from Elmina, 1529-1531', *Transactions of the Historical Society of Ghana*, **14**, 93-103.

Vogt, John (1975). 'Notes on the Portuguese Cloth Trade in West-Africa, 1480-1540', *International Journal of African Hisorical Studies*, **8**, 623-51.

Voigt, August (1961). 'Bergbau und Hüttenwesen in der Geschichte des Dürener Landes', *Dürener Geschichtsblätter*, **25**, 489-528.

Von Stromer, Wolfgang (1963). *Die Nürnberger Handelsgesellschaft Gruber, Podmer, Stromer im 15. Jahrhundert* (Nuremberg: Verein für Geschichte der Stadt Nürnberg; *Nürnberger Forschungen*, 7).

Vries, Peer (2012). 'Europe and the Rest: Braudel on Capitalism', in *Aufbruch in die Weltwirtschaft. Braudel wiedergelesen*, ed. Guillaume Garner and Matthias Middell (Leipzig: Universitätsverlag), 81-144.

Vries, Peer (2013). *Escaping Poverty: The Origins of Modern Economic Growth* (Munich: V&R Unipress and Vienna University Press).

Wallerstein, Immanuel (1974). *The Modern World-System: Capitalist Agriculture and the Origins of the European World-Economy in the Sixteenth Century* (New York: Academic Press).

Wallerstein, Immanuel (1991). 'Braudel on Capitalism, or Everything Upside Down', *Journal of Modern History*, **63**, 354-61.

Weber, Benjamin (2013). 'L'alun de la croisade? Étapes et difficulté de la mise en place d'un monopole pontifical sur l'alun de Tolfa (1461-1471), *Cahiers de Recherches Médiévales et Humanistes*, **25**, 597-619.

Wegg, Jervis (1916). *Antwerp, 1477-1559. From the Battle of Nancy to the Treaty of Cateau Cambrésis* (London: Methuen).

Wells, Guy Edward (1982). 'Antwerp and the Government of Philip II, 1555-1567' (PhD Thesis: Cornell University; Ann Arbor, MI: University Microfilms International).

Westermann, Ekkehard (1971a). Das *Eislebener Garkupfer und seine Bedeutung für den europäischen Kupfermarkt, 1460-1560* (Cologne: Böhlau).

Westermann, Ekkehard (1971b). 'Das "Leipziger Monopolprojekt" als Symptom der mitteleuropäische Wirtschaftskrise um 1527/28', *Vierteljahrschrift für Sozial- und Wirtschaftsgeschichte*, **58**, 1-23.

Westermann, Ekkehard (1986). 'Zur Silber- und Kupferproduktion Mitteleuropas vom 15. bis zum frühen 17. Jahrhundert. Über Bedeutung und Rangfolge der Reviere von Schwaz, Mansfeld und Neusohl', *Der Anschnitt*, **38**, 187-211.

Weststrate, Job (2008). *In het kielzog van moderne markten: handel en scheepvaart op de Rijn, Waal en IJssel, ca. 1360-1560* (Hilversum: Verloren).

Wijnroks, Eric (2003). *Handel tussen Rusland en de Nederlanden, 1560-1640* (Hilversum: Verloren).

Williamson, Oliver (1993). 'Calculativeness, Trust, and Economic Organization', *The Journal of Law and Economics*, **36**, 453-86.

Wood, Ellen Meiksins (2017). *The Origins of Capitalism: A Longer View* (London and New York: Verso).

Wouters, Koen (2002). 'De invloed van verwantschap op de machtsstrijd binnen de Antwerpse politieke elite (1520-1555)', *Tijdschrift voor Sociale Geschiedenis*, **1**, 29-56.

Wouters, Koen (2004). 'Een open oligarchie? De machtsstructuur in de Antwerpse magistraat tijdens de periode 1520-1555', *Belgisch Tijdschrift voor Filologie en Geschiedenis*, **82**, 905-34.

Yans, Maurice (1938). *Histoire économique du duché de Limbourg sous la Maison de Bourgogne: les forêts et les mines* (Brussels: Palais des Académies).

Yante, Jean-Marie (1998). 'Entrepreneurs et transport terrestre. À propos des rouliers lorrains et luxembourgeois (XVe-XVIe siècles)', *Revue Belge de Philologie et d'Histoire*, **76**, 373-40.

Yazdani, Kaveh, and Dilip M. Menon, eds (2020). *Capitalism(s). Towards a Global History* (Oxford: Oxford University Press).

Index